371.260RG

PERFORMANCE STANDARDS IN EDUCATION

In Search of Quality

ORGANISATION FOR ECONOMIC CO-OPERATION AND DEVELOPMENT

ORGANISATION FOR ECONOMIC CO-OPERATION AND DEVELOPMENT

Pursuant to Article 1 of the Convention signed in Paris on 14th December 1960, and which came into force on 30th September 1961, the Organisation for Economic Co-operation and Development (OECD) shall promote policies designed:

— to achieve the highest sustainable economic growth and employment and a rising standard of living in Member countries, while maintaining financial stability, and thus to contribute to the development of the world economy;

— to contribute to sound economic expansion in Member as well as non-member countries in the process of economic development; and

— to contribute to the expansion of world trade on a multilateral, non-discriminatory basis in accordance with international obligations.

The original Member countries of the OECD are Austria, Belgium, Canada, Denmark, France, Germany, Greece, Iceland, Ireland, Italy, Luxembourg, the Netherlands, Norway, Portugal, Spain, Sweden, Switzerland, Turkey, the United Kingdom and the United States. The following countries became Members subsequently through accession at the dates indicated hereafter: Japan (28th April 1964), Finland (28th January 1969), Australia (7th June 1971), New Zealand (29th May 1973) and Mexico (18th May 1994). The Commission of the European Communities takes part in the work of the OECD (Article 13 of the OECD Convention).

Publié en français sous le titre :

LES NORMES DE RÉSULTATS DANS L'ENSEIGNEMENT

A LA RECHERCHE DE LA QUALITÉ

FOREWORD

Educational standards have been the subject of intense public scrutiny in several countries over the past decade. In some countries, especially those where local authorities and schools had traditionally enjoyed substantial autonomy in curricular and assessment matters, there have been moves towards greater centralised control over what is taught and how standards are set. By contrast, in those countries where central government has historically played the major role in defining curriculum content and assessment procedures the movement is in the opposite direction, towards granting more autonomy to local authorities, schools and teachers. The opportunity for educational authorities to learn from each others' experiences is therefore substantial.

This book is the outcome of a study undertaken by the OECD in 1994 at the request, and with the co-operation and financial support, of the Government of the United States. Other Member countries also expressed strong interest in a study of how student performance standards are set and monitored. A conference was held in Paris in December 1993 to launch the study. Carefully chosen experts from ten countries were commissioned to write country case-study reports, working to a set of guidelines produced by Professor John Lowe, an OECD consultant. The country reports were discussed at a seminar in Paris in October 1994, attended by the country experts and by representatives of seventeen OECD Member countries. These discussions took the study forward and a number of important cross-country issues were identified. These form the basis of the overview which precedes the studies and the synthetic analysis which concludes the study.

The study, carried out under the auspices of the Centre for Educational Research and Innovation (CERI) and the Education Committee, draws upon a substantial body of OECD work and publications in the field of curriculum and assessment, notably *Curriculum Reform. An Overview of Trends* (1990) and *Curriculum Reform. Assessment in Question* (1993). It will feed into ongoing work on school assessment, school effectiveness and combating failure as well as CERI's work on Teachers and Curriculum Reform in Basic Schooling.

The study would not have been possible without the active co-operation and financial support of the United States Department of Education. The work was also facilitated by the secondment of an official from the Office for Standards in Education in the United Kingdom.

This report is published on the responsibility of the Secretary-General of OECD.

ALSO AVAILABLE

Decision-Making Processes in the Education Systems of 14 OECD Countries
(96 95 03 1) ISBN 92-64-14421-8, October 1995
France: FF 120 Other countries: FF 155 US$ 30 DM 45

Education and Employment/Formation et emploi
(91 95 05 3) ISBN 92-64-04357-8, April 1995
France: FF 90 Other countries: FF 115 US$ 22 DM 34

Education at a Glance. OECD Indicators
(96 95 02 1) ISBN 92-64-14405-6, March 1995
France: FF 220 Other countries: FF 285 US$ 54 DM 83

Measuring the Quality of Schools/Mesurer la qualité des établissements scolaires
(91 95 02 3) ISBN 92-64-04355-1, April 1995
France: FF 120 Other countries: FF 155 US$ 29 DM 47

Measuring What Students Learn/Mesurer les résultats scolaires
(91 95 06 3) ISBN 92-64-04538-6, May 1995
France: FF 110 Other countries: FF 140 US$ 27 DM 40

OECD Education Statistics 1985-1992/Statistiques de l'enseignement de l'OCDE 1985-1992
(96 95 04 3) ISBN 92-64-04361-6, April 1995
France: FF 160 Other countries: FF 210 US$ 40 DM 60

Public Expectations of the Final Stage of Compulsory Education/Le dernier cycle de l'enseignement obligatoire : quelle attente ?
(91 95 04 3) ISBN 92-64-04356-X, April 1995
France: FF 100 Other countries: FF 130 US$ 25 DM 38

Schools under Scrutiny
(96 95 10 1) ISBN 92-64-14567-2, September 1995
France: FF 150 Other countries: FF 195 US$ 40 DM 55

TABLE OF CONTENTS

OVERVIEW

by

John Lowe
OECD consultant

An OECD concern

In OECD countries, since the early 1980s, policy-makers, practitioners and researchers have been showing unprecedented interest in the setting and evaluating of educational standards and improvement of assessment procedures. At their last meeting (1990), OECD Ministers of Education agreed that the evaluation and assessment of students, institutions and systems as a whole today constitute an integral component of educational policy making and practice. Effective education systems and schools are those which continually monitor progress, identify shortcomings and take immediate and appropriate action. Certification, which is the most public form of student assessment, should provide clear information about the positive accomplishments of each student that is useful to all those concerned, including employers, rather than simply grade success or failure by norm referencing.

Education authorities are asking such questions as: How can research findings on learning help in the setting of realistic goals for schools? What are the most effective ways and means of enabling each student to attain his or her full potential through all the levels of schooling and in each subject? How can high standards be established and sustained? How can assessment be used not only to improve learning in the classroom but to evaluate the outcomes and monitor the progress of educational systems and individual schools?

It has been against this background of concern, questioning and inquiry that the OECD has initiated a number of interrelated activities. The Education Committee's activity on "Educational Evaluation and Reform Strategies" focused on the creation or reorientation in Member countries of agencies and machinery whose purpose is to assess the quality of schooling. Currently, there is an activity on effective schooling. The bold CERI project on international indicators is concerned not only with the performance of schools and pupils, but also with contexts, resources and processes (see OECD, 1995*a-f*). CERI has just completed a specific study on assessment procedures and practices in selected Member countries. Every potential object of evaluation is under scrutiny. Thus, instruments have been designed for measuring the effectiveness of programmes aimed at target groups. The focus of a meeting in 1993 organised in Washington as part of a CERI activity was the evaluation of programmes for children and youth at risk; contributions covered the topics of evaluation and public policy, quasi-experimental designs in compensatory education and longitudinal case studies.

The interrelationship between subjects and standards has been studied both directly and indirectly under CERI's wide-ranging and long-term activity on curriculum reform and school effectiveness. A major conference was held in April 1993 on "The Curriculum Redefined: Schooling for the 21st Century". Focusing on priorities for the reform of curriculum, pedagogy and organisation, it considered all CERI's more recent work, notably the five in-depth areas of inquiry – Learning to Think to Learn; Science, Mathematics and Technology; Humanities, Arts and Values; Core Curriculum; Assessment – pursued since 1989. The report of this conference was published in 1994.

Issues and problems in setting standards and developing assessment procedures are extensively addressed in two up-to-date publications. *Curriculum reform: Assessment in Question* (1993) concludes that in today's schools assessment has become one of the main influences on how children learn and teachers teach. Its influence is pervasive, often distorting teaching and learning through testing, examining, and short-term memorising. Learning to cope with examinations is as important as the learning itself. Although some evaluation is necessary to make pupils aware of their weaknesses and strengths in order to channel efforts, evaluation practices in general should nevertheless be revised. Examples are cited of assessment in schools in seven OECD countries: France,

Germany, the Netherlands, Spain, Sweden, the United Kingdom and the United States of America. *Science and Mathematics Education in the United States: Eight Innovations* (1993) demonstrates how globally dependent science, mathematics and technology education have become.

The contextual imperative

The ten country case studies on standards and assessment synthesised herein were commissioned so as to be broadly representative of the twenty-five OECD Member countries. Four of them are federal and six are unitary States.

The model for the control, administration, financing and evaluation of their education systems extends from the highly centralised to the relatively decentralised. Their perceptions of, and policies towards, performance standards in education reflect a cross-section of the overall OECD experience as is evidenced by the fact that, although asked to adhere as far as possible to common guidelines, the case-study authors present a variety of national interpretations of key concepts and issues and show that education authorities differ considerably in their explicit or implicit definitions of educational standards and in their choice and ordering of priorities for school improvement. Thanks to this diversity each case study has some specific information or experiences to offer as exemplified by the **Irish** account of a large-scale exercise in public consultation by means of a National Education Convention or the **English** and **French** use of nation-wide diagnostic testing for formative purposes. This synthesis will cite such distinctive country experiences. It begins, however, by placing the national policies and strategies for performance standards described in the case studies within their historical and contemporary context.[1]

The studies demonstrate – the **Spanish** one in unequivocal terms – that "performance standards" cannot be considered in isolation from the total condition of schooling, not least from such factors as the expansion in recent times of participation rates at the upper secondary level, and often radical changes in school and class organisation, in pedagogical methods and in the relations between schools and parents as well as the wider community. To a greater or lesser degree, the analyses and descriptions of each case study are set within the overall systemic framework and within a secular perspective. The explanation for this is that – to borrow an image from the **Australian** case study – a marriage must be arranged between psychometric and curricular considerations. On the one hand, the design, application and evaluation of performance standards are a domain of technical expertise and the use of sophisticated procedures and instruments. On the other hand, policy-makers, administrators, teachers and all the other actors in education are obliged to take into account a wide range of contextual factors of a historic, social, economic, political, cultural, environmental and, above all, value-laden, order. Thus, all the studies stress the heterogeneity today of secondary school populations and its consequences for teaching methods and how students learn, and the contemporary societal desire to provide a good basic education for **all** and to strive as far as possible for equality of educational outcomes.

In addition, governments and the general public insist on an adequate return from the national investment in education, which means, realistically, that they desire greater equity but at less or no greater cost.

The studies all equally stress the pre-eminent weight of curricular goals and content. As the French study points out: "performance standards are not set independently of the procedures whereby curricula are defined (...)". According to the **German study**: "Good teacher training, the existence of compulsory curricula for all subjects and areas of study in all types of school and the provision of text books complying with the curriculum are the factors which have the greatest influence on school performance."

The studies confirm that, outside certain **Canadian provinces** and the **United States**, which has long had "a highly developed system for measuring student achievement (...) used extensively in school systems, at state levels, and at the national level for a variety of purposes", the interest in *setting* performance standards is very recent. For example, having asserted that "There is almost no tradition of standardised assessment of any kind (...)", the authors of the case study on **Ontario** then convey the impression that, since 1986-87, there has been a ferment of inventive activity in the setting and monitoring of standards, including no fewer than nine programme (curricular) reviews – grade 9 geography, senior chemistry, senior physics, grade 6 reading, grade 6 mathematics, grade 8 mathematics, grade 10 mathematics, grade 12 mathematics, and grade 12 writing.

The French study notes that the use of standardised tests in both primary and secondary education was developed only over the last three years. For many reasons, such tests do not fit in with the traditional French conception of education. One reason is that as much importance is attached to writing skills and methods of reasoning or argumentation as to final answers or results. Another is the principle of teacher autonomy. The teacher is judged to be competent to select the appropriate measurement tools for assessing students without the need for any external evaluation: in other words, the teacher is best placed to observe each student and assess his or her performance. There is also a fundamental assumption that educational performance cannot be measured in a purely objective way by empirical methods and that subjective appraisal is inevitable. As a consequence, standardised tests are often perceived as irrelevant.

The recent commitment of national and regional education authorities to standard setting is shown to be motivated by pro-active rather than reactive considerations. There is a genuine desire to set standards and use assessment primarily for formative rather than summative purposes. Countries wish to collect statistical and other information that will facilitate curricular reform and improve classroom practice throughout their education systems. The process model is that of determining political priorities and then defining clear educational goals, redesigning the curriculum accordingly, monitoring its application, ascertaining the extent to which the goals and intentions have been achieved, and identifying faults and omissions with a view to remedying them within the framework of a rolling reform. In Ontario: ''All of the large-scale assessments have been designed to include good instruction and assessment and to contribute to the process by providing teachers with models and examples that they can use in their classrooms. The reviews and the grade 9 reading/writing test include rich descriptive information about programme implementation (*e.g.*, resources, instruction, opportunity to learn) that can be used to change practice. The OAC (Ontario Academic Credit) examination review gives teachers direct feedback about how to improve their examinations to bring them into line with provincial expectations.''

In a similar vein, the author of the French study points out that the overriding purpose of the diagnostic assessments of all students, at three key stages of schooling (ages 8, 11, and 16), is to help teachers evaluate the strengths and weaknesses of their students at the beginning of the school year by providing them with more objective tools (expressing explicit or implicit national standards), and inform students themselves and their parents where they stand. In other words, assessment is mainly a pedagogical tool for improving teaching methods and practices and thereby enhancing the learning of students.

A final contextual point should be made. When addressing the issue of standards, policy-makers and administrators have largely in mind the secondary level and, more particularly, the upper secondary cycle. The primary level attracts very little of their attention. This notable difference in emphasis is no doubt largely explained by two facts: *i)* secondary education is viewed as subject-centred whereas primary education is not or, at least, not to the same degree; *ii)* formal assessment only takes place in most countries at the end of secondary education, usually to determine entrance to university. As a result, although national tests in England and France now focus on 7-year-olds as well as 11- and 14-year-olds and the Irish study, exceptionally, gives some weight to primary education, the great majority of the explicit references to standards in these studies is focused on secondary education. This does not reflect any personal prejudice on the part of the authors but the reality in their respective countries.

Reasons for public concern about standards

Historically, despite occasional spasms of alarm in a few countries, there has been public satisfaction with schools and teachers, who have been generally held in high esteem and seldom exposed to criticism. If some students did badly, it was their own fault or due to the rules of the game whereby in schools, as elsewhere in life, there are inevitably winners and losers. The exception has been the **United States** where: ''Almost since its inception, the public education system has been subjected to scrutiny and repeated calls for improvement and change'' and where ''(...) the area of education is less likely to be considered the province of expertise when compared with other (...) endeavours, for instance, the delivery of health care or the criminal justice system. On an absolute level, respect for educational pre-collegiate institutions is not high''. Today, however, in a number of OECD countries there is a deep concern about the outcomes of education. The **Ontario** case study refers to a crisis of confidence. Education systems in most countries have ceased to be sacrosanct territory.

In particular, both parents and public opinion have become aware of the gravity of the phenomenon of under-achievement and the unpalatable truth that many school leavers are virtually unemployable for lack of even minimal academic or vocational qualifications. The **Irish** case study reports that: ''Depending on definition, various studies have calculated that between 10 and 20 per cent of pupils are being failed in the system or failed by it.'' In several countries there is a conviction, at least in certain quarters, that standards have fallen even when there is no corroboratory evidence. In any case, it is increasingly argued by responsible people that even if standards have not fallen, they have failed to keep abreast of new social and labour-market expectations and are not high enough: in today's world of rapid change learning targets need to be ambitious and continually updated. Several countries have been shocked by the publication of international comparisons – IEA (International Association for the Evaluation of Educational Achievement) and IAEP (International Assessment of Educational Progress) – showing the performance of a critical mass of their students in a poor light *vis-à-vis* students in rival and successful trading countries. The **English** study makes the additional telling point that "perceptions that standards have fallen, or are not high enough, are important in themselves and can lead to changes in education systems whether or not they are well founded. Thus, the lack of convincing evidence of a fall in standard has been a strong factor in the development of a National Curriculum". In **Australia,** interest has shifted from the question of whether performance levels have been declining to whether, given substantially increased public expenditure per student in real terms, they are rising as much as they should. In 1984, the Federal Minister for Education appointed a committee "to advise on the priority of attaining higher basic skills standards in primary schools and the need to ensure that strongly rising participation in Years 11 and 12 is associated with the attainment of appropriate standards relevant to subsequent employment opportunities and improved preparation for tertiary education". The prevailing message is that all students, except for those mentally impaired, should be expected to attain high standards given adequate material support and a determined effort on their part.

The status of public education has also been affected by the ripple effect of the emergence in contemporary societies of a clamour for transparency in all sectors of government activity and at all levels – national, regional and local. Virtually all public services today are required to be fully accountable for their actions and to publish frequent and reliable information. In a few countries a "performance conscious culture" now exists. For their part, education authorities have discovered that it no longer suffices to provide more or less equal resources to schools and to ensure that the rules and regulations are obeyed. Rather they must formulate and make public clear operational goals and adopt appropriate instruments for evaluating their outcomes. In Australia, for example, "the attempts to specify curriculum content and scope in terms of sequenced curriculum outcomes have brought a new clarity to debate about the purposes of schooling and of particular curriculum areas. Disagreement and debate have not disappeared, but they have become more precise because specifications of intent are clearer".

Several case studies refer pointedly to the recent appearance of "the accountability movement", which has been conspicuous for many years in the United States. The **French** study makes the point that: "the introduction of new assessment tools and the emergence of a new culture of evaluation is a cumulative process. The new information is increasing the awareness and the concern of the public and of the professionals and calls for more information and objective evaluation in order to increase the quality of education for all".

Accountability entails monitoring learning outcomes and the efficiency and productivity of education systems and individual schools. All the case studies confirm the switch in public and governmental concern from input to output control and several refer to the differences in the performance of schools receiving similar resources, sometimes citing the now extensive literature on effective schooling. The contemporary preoccupation with educational standards is thus explained, on the one hand, by *a priori* considerations of social justice and the optimum exploitation of "human capital" and, on the other hand, by the *a posteriori* necessity of demonstrating what education has or has not achieved in practice, that is, of monitoring educational progress both nation-wide and at the school and classroom levels, and legitimising public action.

In conclusion, it is to be noted that the degree of disquiet about standards varies from one country to another. It is strong in Australia, England, France, Ontario, and the United States. In Ireland "Modes of assessment and performance standards have become a central issue in contemporary education debate and policy, both among the professionals and the general public". In **Sweden** disquiet has tended to fluctuate with the changing fortunes of the national economy. In **Germany**[2] and **Japan,** there is concern about standards but in a neutral static sense. In **Spain,** public concern is with the quality of education in general: "defining and measuring is not the focal point" nor is the concern "manifested through a debate on academic standards".

Governmental concerns

Governments have been forced to respond to public disenchantment or disquiet with the condition of education for obvious reasons of political expedience but, at the same time, alerted by their own advisers and officials and the recommendations of consultative bodies, working parties, commissions and pressure groups, they have compelling reasons of their own for wishing to enhance the "quality of education" and to ensure that satisfactory standards are set for, and achieved by, all students. For example, in **Ontario**, in 1988, the Premier's Council, an advisory group to the provincial Premier, reported that it "had serious concerns that the education system is not delivering value for the money it receives". They recommended, among other measures, regular province-wide testing, strengthening public accountability through the reporting of the performance of individual schools and the province, and participation in national and international testing. In the **United States**, in 1989, "(...) at an historic meeting on education attended by the governors and the federal administration, a set of National Education Goals was articulated, later endorsed by President Bush in 1990, and proposed as legislation in 1991. One element of this legislation created a Council jointly appointed by the governors, the administration,

and by Congress, to consider whether national standards and national assessments w
The deliberations of this Council resulted in recommendations supporting the devel
standards and assessments on a voluntary basis, and by setting up a process by wh
standards and assessments could be judged (National Council on Education Standards
bibliography at the end of the United States case study). Of particular concern during th
impact of such standards and assessments on disadvantaged students and the preservati
authority for educational matters''.

The studies identify four main aims of government in education and training that invoke
and achieving high standards in all subjects through a curriculum that is regularly updated:

a) to ensure that the national workforce is skilled and versatile against the backgrou   ng
structural adjustment of national economies and labour markets and of intensifying inter   al competitiveness in the global economy;

b) to improve the quality and efficiency of education and training provision while deploying the available
resources more effectively during a prolonged period of budgetary constraints. Value for money has
become a watch word with its implications for strict auditing of learning outcomes and quality control;

c) to monitor educational progress in a systematic fashion. The devolution in many countries of greater
responsibility for the control and management of education to local authorities reduces the powers and
functions of the central administration, but increases the necessity of ensuring equitable inputs and
outcomes across a country. As the **French** study points out, more sophisticated analyses of learning
outcomes have produced new evidence of geographical as well as other inequalities;

d) to put an end to school failure and, in particular the propensity of many socially disadvantaged young
people to leave school without qualifications. This implies closing the gap between what the curriculum
prescribes and what students actually learn – in other words, focusing on learning outcomes and on
improvement of student, teacher and school performance.

Defining standards

The case studies confirm just how difficult it is to define standards of performance in education to the
satisfaction of all those concerned, even when, as for the purposes of the present study, the dimension of content
is excluded. They can refer, for instance, to specific criteria of performance or to the attainment of individual
students. The authors of the **Ontario** study caution that the very word "standards" is often confusing because it
is given a number of different meanings. In their own study, they define standards as "indicators of quality that
specify expectations for students". Ontario is currently engaged in establishing criterion- or outcome-referenced
standards. Since there has been no long-standing testing programme, there are no empirical data to serve as
measures of average attainment or as baseline data for comparisons over time.

In the **United States**, "(...) the term performance standard has a loose definition, perhaps assigning different
content standards to age ranges, but stopping well before qualitative or quantitative standards of performance
have been articulated''.

In **Sweden**, the term standards is "difficult to translate in an idiomatic way". As curricula, syllabi and
criteria for marking students' work constitute the actual demands or standards, the term is used to mean the interrelationship among them.

Sweden has introduced "a goal-based curriculum for the compulsory school". And in Ontario, where the
emphasis is also on achieving goals or outcomes, the common curriculum includes the following ten "essential
learning outcomes" that are seen as cross-curricular and the responsibility of all teachers:

– be able to use language to think, learn, and communicate effectively;
– be able to use mathematical knowledge and skills effectively;
– be able to apply scientific methods and knowledge in understanding the world, solving problems, and
making responsible decisions;
– be able to use a wide variety of technologies effectively;
– be able to apply historical and geographical knowledge in analysing world events and understanding
different cultures;
– show a commitment to peace, social justice and the protection of the environment in their own community, Canada and the world;
– have the skills needed to get along well with other people, show respect for human rights and practise
responsible citizenship;

properly for entering the work force or continuing education;
ppreciate, enjoy and participate in the arts;
build healthy life-styles and relationships.

It is to be noted that these ten learning outcomes are broadly similar to those espoused in other countries. (*Cf.* for example, the ten national goals agreed in 1989 by the State, Territory and Federal Ministers of Education in **Australia**, appendix to the case study, and the nine goals cited in the Swedish case study).

The mathematics standards in Ontario for grades 3, 5 and 9 cover the following areas: problem solving, geometry and spatial sense, measurement, patterning and algebra, data management and probability and number sense and numeration. Each description includes a general description of what students can do in the mathematical area and a list of sample "performance indicators" providing specific examples of what students can do in the area. The middle two levels "adequate" and "proficient" define the expected range set for the grade. "Superior" performance is beyond expectations for the grade and "limited " is below expectations for the grade.

The Language Standards describe 6 levels of performance (dependent, limited, adequate, competent, proficient, superior) for grades 3, 6 and 9 in the following domains: reading, writing, speaking, listening, viewing and responding both in English and French.

In **France**, the increasing desire for equality of outcomes has spurred an intensive effort towards a more rigorous definition of performance standards and measurement of student achievement in both cognitive and non-cognitive fields. Performance standards are defined in terms of knowledge (facts, notions, concepts, rules, etc.) and competences (to understand information, to solve an equation, to structure an argument) which are more or less accurately defined in the national curriculum, according to the subjects. Usually, the statements of standards remain implicit and are not independent of the scoring procedures and criteria. It has been only recently through the use of national standardised tests that a systematic effort has been made to arrive at an explicit *a priori* definition of levels of competences. The process of definition requires a conceptual reflection on each subject, on the inter-relations between subjects and goals and on the objectives of the different grade levels. It is then necessary to define categories of competences, to set up a hierarchy among them according to their level of difficulty, and to design appropriate testing items. Finally, the findings of the conceptual and empirical research on assessment must be taken into account in order to determine the percentages of acceptable answers to the items. The DEP (Direction de l'Évaluation et de la Prospective) uses pilot studies to help determine the levels of difficulty of the selected items. In all cases, the previous performance of the students observed and the distribution of the scores are major factors. Thus, there is feedback from the results on the previous ones: standards are defined through a dialectic process.

In **England**, levels of attainment are determined empirically through reviews of subjects. Some standards reflect what subject (area) working parties considered pupils ought to be able to achieve, even where this conflicted with available evidence or best estimates of the difficulty of the task concerned. The reason for this approach was the desire to raise performance above existing levels by means of the National Curriculum. Other standards have been incorporated in order to encourage teachers to include specific content or activities in their instruction. National Curriculum standards are essentially descriptive.

In **Japan**, the national curriculum, designed by the Curriculum Council and prescribed by the Ministry of Education, Science and Culture, defines not only general guidelines but also the aims and content of each subject and every school level. This is seen as equivalent to defining standards. As in **Spain**, each school may organise its own programme on the basis of the guidelines, taking into account its distinctive needs and the special characteristics of the surrounding community.

In **Ireland**, a standard is assumed to be the performance of a student in a terminal and generally written test, and is a composite grade. Performance standards relate to the quality both of the courses in each subject and that of the examinations set to assess the achievement of students.

In Spain, certain minimum attainment targets are prescribed which must be distinctive to, and adapted by, each school so as to meet the real needs of its students. At classroom level, the teacher sets specific targets for his or her subject and group of pupils, on the basis of which the assessment mechanisms and instruments to be applied throughout the year will be selected.

The process of standard setting

The process of standard setting is at the heart of this study. It is also the most problematic topic and the most difficult to treat within a comparative perspective, as revealed by the lack of commonality in the scope and type of information supplied in the case studies. The very idea of standard setting is manifestly more familiar and sharply conceived in some countries than in others: certainly, administrators and researchers in a number of countries, notably in the **United States**, have paid more attention to it than in the majority of countries, notably in **Germany** and **Japan**. It is a process that can be transparent or covert, or simply taken for granted. Whereas a few case study authors are able to give detailed – even technical accounts – of procedures and methods, others offer more or less general descriptions that apply to curriculum development in general rather than setting standards *per se*. It is also noticeable that in some countries setting and assessment are not clearly distinguished for a reason that will be suggested below. Collectively, however, the set of ten studies – despite these reservations – provides far too much useful information and far too many thought-provoking insights to be comprehensively reflected within the confines of this particular synthesis. The intention here, therefore, is to present several key findings or conclusions and to pick out some of the more important points made in the separate studies.

The first finding is of overarching significance and highlighted in the **Australian** study: the *best standard setting occurs when curriculum and psychometric considerations are married*. Curriculum considerations alone produce *a priori* prescriptions of outcomes to be achieved which may be unrealistic in their level or their sequence. Psychometric considerations alone can yield a "dust-bowl empiricism" in which the data on student performance are sifted to find ways of imposing some structure on what is observed.

The case study points up the critical fact that in Australia, performance standards have been developed both *a priori* and *a posteriori*. The development of national profiles represents an *a priori* approach in which the statements of standards to be achieved were derived as a way of expressing desired learning outcomes. Some monitoring programmes, on the other hand, have developed definitions of performance standards *a posteriori* following examination of the measured outcomes that students actually achieve.

Most of the six states are using psychometric procedures, devised by the Australian Council for Educational Research, which map levels of performance on to scales representing levels of students' attainment. This approach contrasts with the introduction of national profiles designed to specify in advance a sequence of levels of performance to be attained by students at the end of the several stages of their schooling.

A second finding is a corollary of the *a priori-a posteriori* polarisation just described. In some countries – **Ireland** is a clear-cut example – national standards are mainly set according to the *a posteriori* mode. Standards have been established over a long period of time through the system of external examinations. Each year the results of examinations are minutely studied to identify lapses in quality, irregularities, inconsistencies, and examples of unfairness. Thereafter the findings are made known to the education authorities and to schools and, as a rule, fed into the curriculum development process. This is, essentially, an assessment-driven model for setting standards.

The third finding is that a paradoxical situation prevails in some countries. On the one hand, the "high-stakes" external examination for 17-18-year-olds, whose primary purpose is selection or rejection for university entrance, sets standards in a top-down, elitist fashion through its profound influence on the school curriculum. (Significantly, two of the studies write about *setting* standards almost entirely within the framework of the upper secondary level.) On the other hand, the same countries are all committed to the democratic ideal of high quality (*cf.* "high-stakes") education for all students at all levels and today show concern to develop national standards and equivalency. Is that ideal compatible with the examination model? There is, undoubtedly a fundamental problem of reconciling conflicting educational aims. Some countries, for example Spain, avoid the problem by not having any external examinations. And several of the case studies stress that, in practice, teachers are continually setting standards for their students at all grades or levels.

The fourth finding is that there is general recognition that standards must be set through a patient process of consensus building – the Irish study presents an eloquent case study – and that they should be seen to be demanding but fair and relevant to the real learning needs of young people. The Curriculum Council in Japan publishes draft recommendations for each of its revisions of the national curriculum and invites comments from a wide range of interest groups.

The fifth finding is that most of the case studies assume a necessary interaction between the setting and assessing of standards. Standards must be sufficiently specific to permit measurement of the results obtained and assessment should be used to validate them and, where appropriate, to lead to consequential modifications.

Most case-study authors who, unlike the Australian author, have little or nothing to say on psychometrics, stress that no regime of minimum standards is in force and that students are not prevented from passing from one grade to the next, grades being governed strictly by age and not by performance (see below "cut-offs"). In the following paragraphs key points in the separate studies will be mentioned.

In Ireland: "There is an obvious place for standardised tests in such a system to provide normative and diagnostic information as a basis for designing teaching programmes." Moreover, "Empirical methods are not used to determine levels of attainment, and no specification is published of what pupils are expected to achieve at each grade level. There are no minimum thresholds. Reliance is placed more on experience and precedent in determining the percentage achieving particular grades in a particular subject. This leads to a fairly consistent distribution across the grades within a subject from year to year, in line with a norm-referenced system.''

As for **Spain**: ''(...) the Spanish educational system does not set 'performance standards', strictly speaking, at national or regional level. Precise student performance standards – addressing the question in the guidelines for the case studies ''how good is good enough?'' – are only set at school level. Nevertheless, some bridges are built and the guidelines issued to schools by the authorities are comprehensive as can be seen from the following sequence of specifications:

a) An *overarching statement* or explanation of the intention, approach and general principles of the subject area, accompanied by suggestions for the way it should be taught, generally extending over six to ten pages.

b) *General targets* which a student should have attained by the end of a stage. Between 10 and 12 per cent of each subject area are expressed in terms of learning abilities and supported by an explicit reference to content.

c) The *most suitable content* to develop the abilities included in the stage goals and subject area objectives. This is not a list of subjects to be dealt with but rather a set of modules to be covered during the several cycles of the stage. The content not only includes more traditional and conceptual matter but also takes account of procedures, values and attitudes. The core curriculum distinguishes among three types of content.

d) *Attainment targets or criteria* so as to facilitate assessment congruent with the general goals of the stage and the subject area objectives. The number of these is larger than that for goals and objectives, ranging from twelve to thirty.

It is to be noted that very similar guidelines and curricular frameworks are described in other case studies.

The **English** and **United States** case studies offer detailed information on approaches to, and the process of, setting standards. In the United States, three major technical approaches have been taken in articulating educational performance standards. The first two assume a linear process starting from the formulation of goals or content standards. Performance standards which follow the formulation are often verbal descriptions of attributes of desired skills at a particular age or proficiency level. For example, the statement that proficient writing is elaborated with detail and develops a clear line of argument would be an example of descriptive performance standards. The content standards, together with descriptive standards, are intended to influence the design of the assessment tasks, the approaches used for their scoring and nature of the reporting categories. For example, descriptions of performance standards could conceivably serve to facilitate the development of a scoring rubric for open-ended assessment.

A second approach to performance standards also begins with goals or content standards but, foregoing verbal description, operationalises their meaning in a set of assessment tasks. Variations in the challenge of the tasks themselves serve to illustrate expectations for students, and model performances that exceed, satisfy, or fail to meet standards may be supplied. Another form of performance standard may emerge when there is a pre-existing item pool intended to measure the general goals articulated. With this approach, performance standards may take the form of identifying quantitative ''cut-scores'' or levels of attainment.

The English study cites detailed arrangements for setting standards in order that the progress of students can be judged and the performance of schools evaluated. The national curriculum specifies both the curriculum to be taught for each stage and levels of performance from 1 to 10. The average 7-year-old is expected to be at level 2 with subsequent progress anticipated at the rate of one level for every two years.

Each subject is divided into attainment targets by either content or process area or a combination of the two. Each level of each target is currently defined by a series of Statements of Attainment, ranging in scope from highly specific to relatively general. The number of defining statements varies from level to level both within and across targets. The model is essentially atomistic, small elements of performance being defined, and descriptive, particular levels being anticipated for students of average attainment at given ages. The attainment targets and statements of attainment cover both formally administered and externally set national tests and the continuing internal assessment made and recorded by teachers.

Standards are defined in the National Curriculum by the ten levels. In the current version the statements of attainment describe the performance associated with each level of each attainment target. Performance data on these need to be combined in such a way as to award a student a level or an attainment target. Levels for subjects are also derived either from aggregating attainment target levels for a subject or directly from items or statements of attainment.

In **Scotland**,[3] which has its own distinctive system of education, the authorities opted to cover the age range 5-14 rather than 5-16, as in England. Only five levels were designated, each referenced to age. This option avoids overlap with the public examination system and consequent problems of comparability by not setting performance standards for ages above fourteen. The notion of progression by one level in two years' schooling is present in both the English and Scottish systems, but is more explicit in the official description of the Scottish levels. Performance standards in Scotland are similar to those in England at the micro level. The term "attainment targets" is also common to both, but those for Scotland are organised in strands such as "Reading for Information", "Money", and "Multiply and Divide". These strands are defined at each of the five levels and are explicit. Similar strands exist in the English attainment targets but are implicit and not necessarily defined at each level.

Although the English study provides a wealth of detailed information it still finds it necessary to make the provision that "(...) the procedures for setting standards are relatively covert, with experiences not generally publicised. The standards themselves are widely disseminated, but their production is accomplished in private. The speed of introduction has been such that time for reflection and development of ideas during the construction process has been largely absent".

One question which is not addressed in the case studies is whether standards are conceived and set in significantly different ways according to the subject or subject area. The answer to this question will no doubt be sought in subsequent inquiries.

Standards setters

Standards setters are appointed from relatively similar groups across the ten countries – experienced teachers, school principals, university faculty, research specialists, professional educationists, inspectors, where they exist, and representatives of the world of work, especially where vocational and technological studies are concerned. The criteria for their selection are that they should represent a wide range of interest groups, and be both proven experts and objective. The **English** study specifically mentions the absence of psychometricians.

In **Sweden**, national responsibility is vested in the Riksdag and the Government, which have delegated, however, partial powers to the National Agency for Education for setting standards and thereby controlling results. In other countries, standards are set, as a rule, by working parties or expert groups. In **France**, most of the setting is done by the "Groupes techniques disciplinaires" (subject groups) or the CPC (for technical subjects) or other *ad hoc* groups, which are more concerned with assessment procedures. All the working parties are expected to take into account the general guidelines laid down by the Conseil national des programmes (National Curriculum Council), established by the Education Act of 1989.

In France, as in **England**, standards setters are appointed by the Minister of Education or his nominees. In **Ireland**, it is the inspectorate for secondary education, that is directly under the control of the Minister, which is charged with setting standards. Assisted by selected teachers, they design the annual examination papers, a process that continues throughout the year. The inspectors themselves are subject specialists.

In England, the process of appointment is confidential and setters are briefed rather than trained. Remuneration is designed to cover only the cost of a school replacing a seconded by a supply teacher. As a rule, appointments are for a specific task.

The **Australian** case study refers to interest groups that are disgruntled because they have been excluded from the standard-setting process – for example, mathematicians who criticised the mathematics profile and claimed they had had no opportunity to influence its form.

What stands out clearly from the case studies is the continuing preponderant role of teachers sustained by an implicit public faith in their professionalism. In **Spain**, they are exclusively responsible for setting standards for their students. In Sweden, following the devolution of power from the centre, their influence has become greater: "teachers much more than before (...) have the freedom to choose content and above all methods". The **German** case study implies that their role is fundamental. At the same time, some authors refer to the necessity of improving teachers' skills in evaluation and assessment in view of their critically important influence within schools and classrooms. The example of the Ontario Assessment Instrument Pool has already been cited. In **Ontario**, teachers play a widespread and powerful role in standard setting, determining policy and practice, developing test specifications, writing test items and performance tasks for curriculum reviews, marking test papers, piloting new materials and providing in-service training for colleagues. Although the Ministry of Education and Training has been responsible for assessment activities at the provincial level, the planning and development teams have all been composed of seconded teachers collaborating with internal technical support personnel. All the activities have included in-service training as a major component.

As for assessment in the classroom, teachers have played a central role in Ontario in curricular design and in the placement, promotion and certification of individual students. Sometimes several teachers having the same students in their charge co-operate together and with parents. Classroom assessment is seen as a critical element of school reform and teachers are being encouraged to improve their assessment procedures and align their instruction with the expected outcomes and standards.

In the setting of standards, inspectors play a major role in England and Ireland – though, in the latter, a posteriori rather than a priori – and a significant role in France. The nature of their role is less clear in other countries with inspectorates. Given their higher profile today in the assessment process, it would be useful to have more specific information about their roles in relation to a number of the topics featuring in this synthesis.

In Germany, it is believed that the individual school is in the best position to decide which educational goals, courses and methods are to be selected and put in practice so that teaching and learning can be effective in the light of the students' special characteristics and the resources available. It is a basic task of the teacher to relate the performance standards stated in the curriculum to the specific characteristics of a class of students and co-operate with other teachers in working out common programmes.

Centralised features exist only as regards the requirements of the *Abitur* examination. Teachers submit suggestions for examination questions in their subject to their school inspectorate. A committee then chooses suitable questions from those submitted. The school inspectorate has thus a good indication of the quality and level of the standards required in the *gymnasia*.

In Ireland, ''The Department of Education would wish to see a significant shift to more school-based assessment using a variety of techniques, administered and corrected by the students' own teachers''.

Assessing student performance

Everywhere written assignments continue to dominate. The **Irish** study refers to heavy reliance on written external assessments, although six other modes of assessment may be used in the examinations for national certification at the upper secondary level in written, practical, external oral, school-based oral, external course work and school-based courses.

In **England**, a written test or set of written tests is used each year for ages 11 and 14. At 7 the assessments are currently wider-ranging with individual assessments and some practical tests. The procedure is not directly criterion-referenced. The tests do not now cover those elements of the National Curriculum, only assessable over time by practical work or by extended tasks. Levels awarded by the current tests, now subject levels rather than attainment target levels, are derived from pencil and paper items.

Sweden has a long tradition of evaluating and assessing individual students but little experience of evaluating the school as a system. The term evaluation is associated with evaluating individual results and is linked in particular to the marking system.

In **France**, the evidence of attainment of performance standards is revealed through a variety of instruments and, increasingly, over the last 3 or 4 years, through standardised tests and profiles of student performances. But the evolution is rather slow, given the habits and a certain resistance on the part of teachers, who need encouragement to accept the new approaches and tools. This implies adopting a sensitive communications strategy and modifying teacher training courses so as to include preparation for assessment.

In **Spain**, assessment takes place entirely within schools. In contrast to nearly all other countries, there are no national or external examinations, either at the end of Primary or Secondary Education. Students are assessed by their own teachers throughout the period of compulsory schooling. The only external examination takes place after the Baccalaureate for those wishing to enter university. Although this is a prerequisite for university admission, it is not necessary for obtaining the Secondary Education Leaving Certificate or the Baccalaureate itself.

In **Japan** also there are no national examinations and assessment takes place within schools. Thus, in secondary schools paper tests are given by the subject teacher several times a year. A national assessment of the curriculum is conducted through nation-wide testing of student achievement in core subjects about every ten years. Its purpose is to determine the performance levels achieved by pupils and students in each subject and to ascertain the extent to which the content of each revised curriculum is understood, to clarify the problems involved in applying that curriculum and, eventually, to make use of any findings to improve the curriculum and teaching methods in the future.

The assessment takes two forms. One is an evaluation by paper test in subjects such as the Japanese language, social sciences, science, mathematics and foreign languages. 32 000 elementary school pupils of the 5th and 6th grades and 48 000 lower secondary school students (16 000 pupils or students for each grade) are tested. The second is an evaluation of practical activities in subjects that are difficult to measure by paper tests, such as music, drawing, art, gymnastics and environmental studies. The assessment is undertaken in five schools for each subject.

In the **United States**, testing and assessment needs have been met by commercial companies which develop – and sometimes administer – score, and report results to clients. Many of these services have been developed to assure economy of expenditure. Almost without regard to their purpose, most school tests have followed a multiple choice model and supported the goals of efficient measurement. Models of more constructed and open-ended assessments were provided through the early National Assessment of Educational Progress (NAEP). NAEP was originally conceived as a reporting mechanism to monitor national educational attainment and lead the nation's schools to consider new approaches to assessment. More open-ended assessments were applied in the 1980s, particularly for students' writing. Many States developed or contracted out the development of writing assessments. Although vocally opposed by members of the testing establishment, the imperative of enabling students to write satisfactorily overcame objections, and technical standards for the design and implementation of scoring rubrics became widespread. This experience in writing set the stage for considering more open-ended assessments to be used in large-scale or accountability situations.

Germany is a special case. "The system of delivering, introducing and controlling performance standards is not part of a procedure which is based on external evaluation, centralised tests or large scale assessments." It is rather a kind of "systematic network" in which different frameworks are combined in order to "guarantee", to implement and to control quality and standards of education, learning and teaching. The experience with external evaluation and assessment in normative areas has neither found general political or expert acceptance, nor stimulated any reconsideration of standards. As a result, external evaluation, centralised testing and large-scale assessments do not play a decisive role in the *Länder* when it comes to formulating, applying and verifying performance standards. Since qualitative differences between schools of the same kind or between types of school in different *Länder* are in fact quite small, it is not surprising that no great interest is shown in comparative surveys or inquiries. On the other hand, internal comparisons are considered important for individual schools. In subjects and subject areas with written examinations, the tradition is that classroom tests using identical exercises are set in parallel classes with a view to ascertaining whether conditions in a particular class encourage or impede performance. But comparisons are confined to each individual school and the assessment of performance falls within the framework of school organisation and teaching. The traditional methods of classroom tests and reports are criticised for having a selective rather than a learning support function. Questions such as which kinds of assessments can help to show whether pupils have really understood a problem are becoming increasingly important.

Assessment activities in **Ontario** have been closely linked historically with their inherent purposes. A clear distinction has been drawn between assessments that have, as a major purpose, curricular improvement and accountability to the public and those focused on individual students. The Ministry has supported the assessment role of teachers in the classroom by commissioning experienced teachers to develop the Ontario Assessment Instrument Pool, a series of banks of instruments and items for: Languages [Junior Language Arts, Basic English (secondary), French as a Second Language (grades 5, 6 and 10) and Intermediate English]; Mathematics (Junior Division); Science (OAC Biology, Senior Physics and Chemistry and Junior Division Science); Geography (Intermediate-Division); and History (Intermediate Division).

Teachers in general have played a key role in developing and extending assessment practices within schools and classrooms. The assessment of individual students has been a priority for over a decade. The policy paper governing grades 7-9 "Ontario Schools: Intermediate Senior" (1984) required varied and continuing student assessment to be a key ingredient of teaching and learning because of the desire to help students become independent and self-directed. The paper stated that "evaluation is not an end in itself; it is rather a part of the learning process for both the student and the teacher".

In **Australia**, all the new monitoring programmes in the State education systems, including those that test only samples of students or whole cohorts, have the capacity to monitor changes in performance levels over time for the system as a whole by calibrating instruments used on different occasions onto a common scale. This is being achieved by repetition of some items to provide the link necessary for the calibration or by special linking exercises in which items from both tests are used with a sample of comparable students in a different system.

In **Sweden**, The National Board of Education has launched a "National Evaluation" programme – a programme on the results of the last grade of the compulsory school, which was taken over and completed by the National Agency for Education. All subjects were tested extensively in a sample of 100 schools and

10 000 pupils. The tests were designed not only to cover the content of courses but also cognitive levels. In addition to subject-oriented tests, problem-solving tests were administered. The results of this survey became the basis of the report of the National Agency for Education on the state of Education in Sweden delivered in 1993. The results revealed that whereas there is a very good average attainment in reading, some students do not reach an acceptable level.

The English study describes the construction of instruments and scoring for assessment. Items for the National tests are developed by trialling review committees set up for the purpose, and closely scrutinised for validity so as to ensure that they are true assessments of particular statements of attainment. Particular attention is also given to ensuring that items support and guide good curriculum practice, and this sometimes conflicts with their psychometric and measurement properties. The difficulty of items is established by trialling, and items are included if this is appropriate for the level of the National Curriculum being assessed. There are, however, sizeable variations since not all of the statements of attainment which comprise a level are of equal difficulty.

The marking of National Curriculum tests is currently done by teachers according to detailed compulsory marking schemes for each item, which are developed during trialling and by systematic review. (In future the tests for 11- and 14-year-olds are to be marked centrally.) The relationship with overall standards is then embodied in the system.

Differences in student achievement or performance

Data on differences in student achievement or performance were not available in most countries until the 1980s. The **Irish** study reports that there were "few longitudinal studies". Already, however, within a surprisingly short period, education authorities have begun to produce plentiful relevant data and there is a general trend towards establishing baseline data for monitoring progress in educational attainment. **Sweden** has introduced a "National Evaluation" programme on a comprehensive scale that will certainly permit the comparison of standards of achievement over time.

Differences are deduced from:

- national diagnostic testing;
- large-scale national surveys;
- standardised testing;
- international surveys.

The focus is, as a rule, on the key subjects in the curriculum, notably mathematics and reading: in other words, numeracy and literacy. In **England**, "Reading standards among 11- and 15-year-olds have changed little since 1945, apart from slight rises around 1950 and the 1980s. Among 7-8-year-olds, however, standards fell slightly in the 1980s". In **France**, there has been a rise in the achievement level over time, particularly of the lowest achieving students, in French language and mathematics.

France has also greatly increased its stock of knowledge on regional differences thanks to a rapid methodological advance in defining national and regional indicators, especially outcome indicators constructed from the results of nation-wide tests. A *Géographie de l'École* (school map) was first published in 1993 and is to appear annually.

In England, much reliable evidence was gleaned from the enquiries of the Assessment of Performance Unit (APU), set up by the government in 1976 but now abolished. National surveys were carried out between 1978 and 1988 based on large-scale surveys of mathematics, science and technology and smaller-scale surveys of foreign languages, design and technology. Evidence is also available for performance by region, gender, age and other variables. Wide differences were found between high and low performers.

Empirical data show that **Spain** continues to suffer from inequalities in education, which have mainly to do with access but also with performance. The length of time spent in the classroom is notably shorter and the qualifications achieved inferior for pupils from disadvantaged socio-economic backgrounds. Differences are also shown to depend on where students live (they do better in urban areas) and gender (girls do slightly better than boys).

Most of the **German** *Länder* show little interest in central performance assessment methods designed to provide comparisons. External school comparisons have not found wide acceptance. Moreover, there is a critical attitude towards comparison as such, mainly evoked by the experiences of those *Länder* which have instituted procedures for assessment of performance. The main criticism is that the prevailing type of external assessment does not reflect true performance levels or provide realistic guidelines for improvement and innovation in schools. The suspicion exists that, with the traditional form of comparative assessment, "bad" tests unduly influence teaching and learning ("teach what you test").

In addition, there is a structural reason for scepticism. The school system has a regulatory framework which, on the whole, helps to guarantee good student as well as school performance standards. It is argued that there are no grounds, therefore, for extensive assessments and comparisons: the types of regulation applied so far are widely considered to be a sufficient guarantee of quality control. The framework, which is a kind of control mechanism for "self-stabilizing feedback", should nevertheless be critically reviewed.

Despite the general aversion in Germany to comparisons of achievement some evidence of a decline in standards and of gender differences does exist. Thus, studies have been conducted and published by trade associations, banks and industrial firms at regular intervals, showing that the literacy and numeracy skills of some young people are inadequate. As to gender, the introduction of new subjects in communications and information technology has given an unexpected boost to comparisons of the performance of girls and boys, respectively.

Four of the studies refer to ways and means of maintaining standards over time. In France there is constant feedback from the results of the regular evaluation of standards. Furthermore, in technical, technological and vocational subjects, the curriculum and standards are reviewed, on an average, every 5 years. It is much more irregular in other subjects.

In **Ireland**, a bank of test items and questions is being continually built up. In England, the papers completed by students awarded a particular grade in one year are checked against those produced by students awarded the same grade in previous years to ascertain whether the quality of understanding and demonstrated skills is comparable. The method is judgmental, involving examiners in a committee structure. There are also statistical mechanisms to check that the number of marks needed for the award of a grade in one year is in line with that required in previous years. At the same time, the public examination system is not well suited to monitoring change over time, particularly if any change is gradual or if the curriculum is modified.

North-Rhine/Westphalia is committed to comprehensive curriculum development in order to maintain and build on effective performance standards. The basic idea is to integrate teaching in the reform process as soon as possible. Through intensive feedback with schools, information is continually exchanged between those responsible for curriculum development and the schools. Accordingly, collaborative activities are becoming an important factor in bringing about qualitative change in schools and maintaining universally accepted performance standards.

Cut-offs and levels of achievement

Most of the case study authors do not address this topic probably because in their countries cut-offs are not applied, the idea of pass or fail having been repudiated as a selective, invidious device for grading or labelling students. In **England**, however, there is a subtle form of classification of achievement. Up to age 14 each student is awarded one of the ten National Curriculum levels. There is no pass/fail as such, but the expected relationship between level and age provides a way of classifying performance as average, above or below this, and by how much. The level of the National Curriculum achieved in an attainment target or subject is the performance standard in the system. Thus, the student is placed at a point on a scale rather than being given a simple pass/fail. Placing a student at level n should be interpreted as indicating that he or she has achieved the requirements of levels up to and including n, but not those for levels $n + 1$ or higher. With national tests now awarding levels on the basis of marks for ages 11 and 14, rather than by directly criterion-referenced methods such as achievement of statements of attainment, setting level boundaries in this system is now being explored. For ages 16 and 18 grades are awarded. At age 16, GCSE grades A to C are often regarded as "pass" since these match the pass grades of the previous O-Level examination, which catered for a more restricted and higher attaining entry than GCSE. At age 18, grades A, B or C are likely to be specified by universities in their entrance requirements.

At ages 16 and 18, examination papers are marked centrally according to prescribed marking schemes. Grade boundaries are set after the mark awarded to each pupil is known. Statistical information is therefore available to ensure that the distribution of grades awarded is similar from year to year unless there is evidence available to suggest that the entry for the examination concerned is of higher or lower overall attainment than previously. This is supplemented by reviewing current scripts expected to be awarded a given grade against those from previous year(s) which were awarded that grade. A judgement is then made on whether similar standards of performance are required to be awarded a given grade over time.

In at least two countries the pass/fail factor does operate but only at the very end of the upper secondary school cycle. In **Ireland**, the pass/fail is regarded popularly as the cut-off feature of the external examinations, with a Grade E or lower, that is, less than 40 per cent, corresponding to failing grades. Students are very aware of the importance of the grades and the more able pupils are usually well motivated to achieve at the highest possible grade. In **France**, there are different levels of acceptable proficiency, but in the external examinations there is a cut-off, pass/fail standard. Generally, it consists of obtaining a global (weighted) average mark of 10 out of 20.

Costs of setting, assessing and monitoring standards

Six of the case studies are silent on the subject of expenditures which would seem to indicate that no significant information is available. The four studies that do comment would further indicate that costs are not separated out from the general expenditure on such items as administration and the salaries of civil servants, teachers and inspectors.

In **France**, no rigorous estimate of costs is available. Only the direct costs of devising and administering the national tests and examinations are known. In **England**, no precise data are available on costs "as yet". However, the process of consulting about and developing proposals for standards certainly give rise to various costs, including sizeable printing bills for documents and questionnaires.

In **Ireland**, the cost of administering examinations for 1992/93 was calculated at £9.2 million out of a total current expenditure on upper secondary education of £572 million. This did not include the allocation of staff time since this is treated as part of normal civil service duties. Expenditure on research and development on performance standards is very low.

In **Australia**, the costs of monitoring standards are not available since they are usually covered under the overall expenditure of the head offices of the education authorities. Even where substantial components of the work are contracted out to external agencies, there are usually quite substantial internal departmental costs concerned with liaison and communications with schools.

Consistency and fairness

The consistency or constancy of standards over time was considered above. Not much information is forthcoming, however, on the concept of consistency in relation to fairness. In **England**, as already mentioned, national tests and standards are used up to age 14. The need for consistency is therefore most apparent in examinations for ages 16 to 18 where different boards set papers in most subjects. The history of test development in the **United States** has created expectations for technical standards of validity and reliability, usually achieved through testing models that depend upon wide sampling of content and normative comparisons of students and schools. The penchant for litigation has reinforced the emphasis on the technical defensibility of tests, particularly their fairness when applied to disparate populations.

Ontario appears to be confident that the standards provide high and consistent targets for students, teachers and parents. They are designed to provide a description of performance at each level so that the improvements required to move from one level to another are visible. The Ministry of Education and Training is currently attempting to ensure greater consistency and coherence by developing an Assessment Policy Framework that will outline assessment principles and roles and responsibilities at all levels. Consistency of application of the examination procedures and expectations for students are monitored at school leaving through the examination review process and the concomitant in-service training for teachers. This process includes preparation of a handbook describing examination design and marking procedures for the purposes of in-service training. The Ministry also monitors consistency through province-wide sampling of examinations and marked student papers and alerts teachers when their examination results are not acceptable and call for a plan of corrective action.

In **Germany**, various institutions, such as the Conference of Cultural Ministers and the Federal *Länder* Commission are responsible, among other functions, for maintaining comparable school leaving certificates, despite the different types of education systems, and for guaranteeing their recognition throughout the *Länder*. The aim of these and other bodies is to ensure a minimum degree of uniformity in educational developments across the individual *Länder*.

In countries with national external examinations, especially at the end of schooling, exceptional efforts are made to ensure fairness in marking students' work and the constancy of standards. Over time countries such as England and Ireland have developed highly sophisticated procedures and instruments for administering, controlling and monitoring national or regional examinations.

Reporting of student achievement

Public reporting of student achievement is of relatively recent origin and arises mainly from the emergence of the accountability movement described above. The contemporary credo is that parents and students have the right to know what an individual has achieved at the end of a given period of school life, usually at the end of each year. As a rule, the information disseminated is derived from sample surveys or examination results.

The performance of schools is only incidentally a concern of this synthesis. However, it is revealing that several case studies perceive it as intrinsically related to individual student achievement, especially with regard to reporting. They cite a general reluctance to publish results for individual schools or even individual school districts. Thus: "In the early announcements of the proposed new programme of cohort testing in **New South Wales**, the Minister declared that the test results would provide helpful public information on the quality of schools that might guide parents' choices about enrolments. In the face of claims that the data could not be used sensibly in this way because the student achievements would reflect home as well as school effects, the Minister banned public comparison of schools with the data and further declared that data on achievements of students in individual schools should not be provided to the Minister's office. Other States, now planning to introduce such population testing, have similarly ruled out the use of the data for comparison of schools."

In **Ontario** where, in the past, public reporting on student achievement had not been a feature: "School boards will be required to report publicly on their board results and to use the information for programme planning and implementation. Public comparisons of individual school or board results are not appropriate." At the same time, "The results of provincial reviews are reported publicly in several forms – an extensive full report, a 5-6 page provincial report card, press releases and board reports for participating boards."

In **Ireland**, "(...) teachers oppose making (...) results available to the Department of Education on an individual school basis because of the concern on the way accountability might be used". The Examination Branch of the Department of Education releases the results of individual students to the individual school managers, who, in turn, inform students and parents. General aggregate statistical data are made available to newspaper correspondents and are eventually published in the Department's Annual Statistical Report. The Department of Education does not make available to the public the results of individual schools or students or different regions. In recent years, research bodies have conducted analyses of the results, but, traditionally, the Department has been loathe to release to researchers examination documents and data or to publish research studies based on them. The senior inspectorate approves results before release.

In **Japan**, the results of the ten-yearly national assessments "(...) are utilised only for deliberations on the improvement of the new curriculum and teaching methods (...). Specific results of individuals, schools and regions are not published".

The traditional reporting of schools or teachers or both to parents continues. This usually takes the form of a report card, indicating the marks achieved in discrete subjects and containing written general comments not only about results but also behaviour. In **France**, the reporting of results differs according to the assessment instruments used. The results of class assignments are regularly given to students and every term to their parents. The results of external examinations are published at the national, regional and school levels. Recently, a set of indicators was designed in order to permit publication of net results, taking into account the special characteristics of the student population of each school. The results of national diagnostic tests are published at the national and regional levels, but not at school level. The main analyses of results concern national average scores (global and by item), regional differences, comparative performances of girls and boys, influence of home and socio-economic background, evolution over time, distribution of students according to different levels of proficiency and in-depth case studies of samples of schools or classes. The results of the national standardised tests are published by the DEP.

In **Sweden**, the National Agency for Education is required to furnish the *Riksdag* and government with a comprehensive report on the state of schooling at three-yearly intervals. These reports form the basis of a national development plan for schools. The Agency also regularly furnishes the municipalities with the results from a variety of evaluation projects and publishes statistics in order to create grounds for judgement at the local level through which comparisons between municipalities and individual schools can be made.

In **England**, the publication of National Curriculum levels for schools and Local Education Authorities, which has given rise to much controversy, has been a major factor in provoking a boycott of National tests. Publication, which is the considered government policy, is intended to keep parents and others well informed, while helping to create a market for choice of schools within the education system. The statistics produced have been simple, based on the percentage of the age cohort achieving specific levels. No adjustments are made to allow for differences in attainment between students on entry to the school where they are taught and their taking of national tests. As a consequence, the use of tables to compare the effectiveness of schools is widely viewed as unfair and had led to teachers either refusing to administer the tests or to report the results after they have been administered.

The **Scottish** experience is illuminating. The production of comparative tables of school performance requires consistent data on each pupil in each school. In England, the mandatory national tests taken simultaneously by all pupils of certain age cohorts, are intended to provide the necessary consistent data. In Scotland, nation-wide testing at fixed times was also introduced for 9- and 12-year-olds, but resistance was strong, so much that many parents withdrew their children from it and the system had to be modified. Teachers in Scotland now use tests selected from a published bank with a view to confirming their judgement that a pupil has achieved one of the five levels. The timing of testing is thus at the discretion of the teacher, tests being administered when a level is judged to have recently been attained by a student. A nation-wide snapshot at a fixed point in time is therefore not available in the same way as is still proposed for England.

Because public concern about standards in the great majority of the OECD Member countries is relatively recent and, in the past, information about student attainment was not systematically collected, let alone interpreted, it does not follow that useful evidence has never existed. Thus, in **Ireland**, ''The results of the national certificate examinations are available for well over a century, but up to recently, few statistical studies have been done on them. The *rich data bank* has not yet been sufficiently drawn upon.''

The Irish case study incidentally refers to a noteworthy proposal to provide *parents* with full information about their children's progress. A Pupil Report Card of performance and competence based on observation and the use of standardised tests should be available to parents. The cards should be designed to provide a comprehensive record of student achievement and be available for the transfer from one school level to another.

The international dimension

Given the purpose of this overall exercise, it is scarcely surprising that all the case studies are in favour of international comparisons and co-operation among countries in order to share information on experiences and research findings. According to the **English** case study, by comparing practices and the effectiveness or imperfections of their results, countries can pare down the list of desired benefits to a shorter list of realisable objectives. Setting standards *per se* will not improve a system. The process must be embedded in a long-term process of research, development and evaluation, taking into account the relevant international experience.

Like most other countries, **Sweden** has participated in the IEA reading study and in earlier IEA mathematics studies. It is also participating in the IEA TIMS project. The **French** case study also reports that the system has has benefited ''greatly'' from participating in IEA and ETS (Educational Testing Service) international surveys of students' achievement as well as in OECD activities. It adds that the international comparison of performances is important, even though time consuming and costly process. The results are significant only in terms of orders of magnitude and should not focus on the ranking of countries. What really matters is to know the relative weaknesses and strengths of a national education system. For this reason, analysis of the factors leading to the observed results is as important as the results themselves. The comparison of procedures for setting performance standards in OECD Member countries should be of significant value for all Member countries, given the conceptual and practical difficulties that bedevil them.

The **German** study points out that in OECD countries schools constrained by rigid regulations are becoming more liberal. As such concepts as autonomy and freedom take hold, school-based initiatives are becoming increasingly attractive. Simultaneously, education systems in which individual schools have enjoyed considerable freedom in the past are now tending towards more centralisation and the creation of national curricula in order to maintain comparative standards throughout the system. *Accordingly, the scene is set for exciting policy discussions in which countries can ''learn'' from one another when it comes to defining their own approaches to reform.*

Policies of restructuring and reform in the national or regional context also require the back-up of international experience. However, because of the distinctive social, cultural and political conditions prevailing in individual countries, comparative activities and studies are helpful only when concerned with common approaches and practices.

Ireland has engaged in studies on reading, mathematics and science with the IEA, and the International Assessment of Educational progress (IAEP). It sees scope for further development and more precision in international studies before they can make a significant impact on setting performance standards in individual countries. Nevertheless, these studies do act as a valuable stimulus and spur to those with local responsibilities, for instance, for science subjects in Irish schools. They provide useful, if general, benchmarks and alert countries that are falling badly behind in some subject areas. They can also inform internal government debates either by providing assurance that money spent on education is yielding results in line with international trends or by helping to justify increased public investment in policies targeted towards exposed weak areas. Given the continuing increase in occupational mobility across countries, it is also desirable that equivalence among national qualifications and certification be more energetically promoted.

Finally, the Irish case study points to the need for improved dissemination of relevant information from international studies to educational bodies and schools throughout the country. Sound future-oriented policy is best built on the informed awareness of all the individuals and groups concerned.

The **Australian** case study cites a specific example of the value of international comparisons. Data on the performance of students in the first and second international studies of science achievement conducted by the IEA were useful in revealing the maintenance of a steady level of performance at a time when performance levels in a number of other OECD countries were rising, thereby forestalling invidious comparisons by politicians or the media. Australia is now looking to the third international study for evidence of the position a decade further on.

There are, however, important problems and limitations with comparative studies of the type conducted by IEA, the greatest being the differential curriculum validity of the tests used. When large numbers of countries are involved in such surveys, development of the test instruments involves inevitable compromises about content and coverage. There is always then the risk that international differences in achievement will be compounded by international differences in the validity of tests.

If the focus of international work were to be on curriculum specification, particularly in terms of outcome statements such as those used in the Australian curriculum profiles, and if countries had sufficient common interest to yield usefully comparable specifications, then comparisons of student performance levels would be most valuable. The key point is that international collaboration and comparison are most likely to be of value if they begin with collaboration or, at least, agreement about curriculum development and proceed to assessment only where the comparability of curriculum is of genuine interest.

Conclusion

The case studies confirm that the process of improving procedures for setting, applying and monitoring standards requires both time and caution. It is a process which must inspire public trust and confidence by means of consensus-building and ample and reliable feedback. It usually necessitates a change in the attitudes of administrators, teachers, students, parents and communities as a whole and calls for a sensitive communications strategy on the part of education authorities and schools. It entails continuing in-depth conceptual enquiries into the definition of competences and levels of proficiency, especially in such subjects as philosophy, citizenship and social studies. It also means that standards setters should be fully aware of the limits to their own objectivity in defining *a priori* levels of proficiency and humble before the difficulty of assessing non-cognitive skills.

There is also agreement in the studies that a clear purpose for standards must be defined, with their level of generality and coverage closely matched to the intended assessment procedures and their manageability. An appropriate balance is needed between too many detailed and too few general standards since the effective transmission of standards and public understanding of them are hampered when they are too numerous or too specific. When general standards are defined, attention must be paid to how they are to be made operational in tests or formal assessments. When specific standards are defined, the method of aggregating them so as to produce broadly-based and better information should be taken into account from the start and reflected in their very construction.

Standards that seek to be multipurpose are to be viewed with extreme suspicion. Those intended to avoid narrowing the curriculum by including process and practical elements need to be evaluated for the manageability of the assessment arrangements if they are to be implemented on a wide scale. Standards for different subjects should be co-ordinated in order to ensure that they do not conflict and that there is adequate time for their synchronised application.

Time and effort should be devoted to research and the extensive piloting of performance standards at each stage or grade level. There must be a solid investment of resources in efficient standard setting, particularly the mastery of up-to-date techniques. Systematic training should be available for standards setters and training in assessment skills should be a component of initial and continuing teacher education. The **French** study states that although the new procedures for setting standards are already influencing teaching styles, they could make a still greater impact if teachers were properly trained to apply standards and testing items and to benefit from the information yielded by tests. The **Irish** study makes a similar point with particular reference to older teachers, who tend to have had little preparation for designing or implementing new forms of standard setting and to be reluctant to give up old forms. Where significant innovations occur, however, in-service training courses for updating skills are usually on offer. Pre-service training courses pay greater attention to assessment issues than heretofore. Any changes in standard setting introduced as a compulsory feature of the system of public examinations have direct and immediate effects on teachers and teaching styles since much teaching is oriented towards assessment. However, changes that are not compulsory tend to have little influence on practice.

The speed of applying new or modified standards should be carefully regulated so as to obviate the need for too frequent revision and to eliminate or reduce the effects of undesirable components. Too frequent revision can lead to instability which demotivates teachers and hampers the evaluation process. Whether standards are generally defined and relatively few or specific and relatively numerous, they should be constructed with the assessment of student performance very much in mind. The **English** experience highlights the difficulty of developing satisfactory methods of assessment *after* standards have already been applied.

The **Ontario** study is distinctive in referring not to "preconditions" but to "challenges" in the light of a precarious future. The authors state that: "(...) a number of forces are converging that are likely to make the work that is being done in establishing standards and assessing performance much more 'high stakes', especially for educators and potentially for students. This shift will put Ontario schools in the spotlight in a way that they have not experienced before. Already the editorial boards of many of the newspapers have established policies that support ranking schools in 'league tables'. We can see this period in the history of education in Ontario being rather rocky, indeed. We are faced with a number of imminent challenges".

One challenge will be how to nurture what is memorably termed "assessment literacy". Very few people either within education or the general public have any understanding of the principles or concepts that underlie assessment in schools. For the most part, scores, regardless of their quality, are likely to be interpreted very simply and viewed as absolute entities "rather like money in the bank". In Ontario, because, historically, there has been no emphasis on assessment there are only a few educators and academics with the kind of technical expertise or preparatory training calculated to influence policy choices or help other educators in extending their own knowledge.

A second challenge will be how to identify ways of analysing, interpreting and presenting the results of assessments in order to ensure fairness and take into account other factors likely to contribute to achievement, especially if school effectiveness is to be judged primarily on the basis of scores. Although there are many difficulties inherent in undertaking "value-added" analyses, Ontario is hampered by the lack of any of the data that would make them "remotely" possible.

The **German** study makes a crucial point on the alignment between the curriculum and the definition of standards. The curriculum should be streamlined and any "unnecessary educational ballast" and subject matter, often unquestioned for decades, should be swept away. A modern democratic society, having to take into account the interconnection of political, economic, cultural and ecological factors, must define accurately what students must learn for tomorrow if they are to cope with the challenges of an uncertain future.

The case studies present many considerations for policy-makers, in the main implicitly rather than explicitly. However, the French and Irish case studies do make an explicit reference to the connection between setting standards and policy formulation. The **French** case study states that findings about the experiences of standard setting are used to assist policy formulation and decision-making at the national, regional, school and classroom levels. They influence the revision of national objectives and curricula, policies at regional and school levels, and the aims and practices of teachers and students. On the other hand, there is not as yet a systematic link between standard-setting procedures and the development of the national curriculum, even though the two processes are increasingly interdependent. The General Inspectorate plays an important role in this respect, as some of its members participate in both processes.

In **Ireland,** reviews take place on evolving patterns of performance, relying on the accumulated experience of the inspectorate and those who assist in processing the national examinations. As the personnel involved are closely in touch with curricular innovations and developments in teachers' attitudes, new insights and perspectives are fed into the assessment process through the subject committees. However, it is neither a systematic nor a publicly discussed arrangement. The form of monitoring is informal rather than systematic but it does feed into future approaches. The inspectorate is linked to the National Council for Curriculum and Assessment – an advisory and not an executive body – and also gives key professional advice to the Minister on the Council's proposals. Thus, the advice of those with responsibility for performance standards is conveyed directly to the Minister, who ultimately determines national curriculum policy.

The **Japanese** study points out one serious problem with regard to assessing and monitoring standards. Some observers believe that the reason for the high academic scores of Japanese pupils and students as compared with those of other countries is not the quality of the curriculum and the pedagogy but the fierce competition to pass the university entrance examinations. It becomes necessary, therefore, for Japan to explore measures to assess the real effectiveness of schooling and review the attainment of performance standards as defined by the national curriculum.

The Japanese concern springs from a fear that concentration on academic achievement alone may stultify creativity and neglect the non-cognitive and affective development of students. Other countries share this fear, stress that performance standards should not be restricted to achievement that is readily quantifiable, and require that standards be assessed and interpreted in a broad, constructive and thoroughly reliable fashion.

Nevertheless, two overriding conclusions can be drawn from the ten case studies. The first is that raising standards in core subjects for all students and at all levels is today the main priority of national, regional and local education authorities. The second is that the public, parental and student interest requires that education systems provide sound information on how schools and individual students are performing. The vital question of how to improve education remains to be answered.

Notes

1. Much of the text that follows is directly extracted from, or closely follows, the specific national information provided by the separate authors but, wherever appropriate, an attempt is made to present a composite picture of trends, issues and problems or to point up comparisons and contrasts.

2. The German case study is concerned partly with the federal dimension but mainly with the jurisdiction of the North Rhine-Westphalia *Länder*. In this text a distinction will be made, as appropriate, between "Germany", as here, and NRW.

3. The author of the English case study was specially requested to refer to Scotland whenever a contrast or comparison appeared significant.

Bibliography

OECD (1995*a*), *Education and Employment/Formation et emploi*, Paris.

OECD (1995*b*), *Measuring the Quality of Schools/Mesurer la qualité des établissements scolaires*, Paris.

OECD (1995*c*), *OECD Education Statistics 1985-1992/Statistiques de l'enseignement de l'OCDE 1985-1992*, Paris.

OECD (1995*d*), *Public Expectations of the Final Stage of Compulsory Education/Le dernier cycle de l'enseignement obligatoire : quelle attente ?*, Paris.

OECD (1995*e*), *Measuring what Students Learn/Mesurer les résultats scolaires*, Paris.

OECD (1995*f*), *Education at a Glance – OECD Indicators*, Paris.

Case studies

AUSTRALIA

by

Barry McGaw
Australian Council for Educational Research

Summary

In Australia's federal system, where education is the responsibility of the states, control over standards up to the 1960s was exercised within states through centrally-determined curricula, school inspectors and external public examinations. After several decades of devolution of curriculum responsibility to schools, education authorities have introduced various monitoring programs to assess outcomes. Some assess samples of students to characterise system achievement, others assess whole cohorts of students to report their performance levels to them, their parents and their schools. Use of these data to rank schools has been prohibited.

Since the late 1980s, the Australian education systems have been co-operating on the development of national curriculum statements for eight key learning areas, with a significant component for each area being a profile of sequenced learning outcomes that students are expected to achieve during the first ten years of schooling. The learning outcomes in each profile are grouped into eight successive levels.

Some of the monitoring programs that predated the formulation of the curriculum profiles used bands or levels on the performance scales to generate a language with which to describe performances. These bands or levels were defined *a posteriori* after scale construction. In current work, the levels on the national curriculum profiles represent *a priori* definitions of desired standards of achievement to which performance scales are keyed. The best work marries curriculum and assessment perspectives by using the performance data as a basis for empirical investigation of the properties of the scales represented by the profiles.

Context

Current attempts to set performance standards for students in Australian schools (Appendix A describes the Australian Education System) have two origins. The longest standing and dominant one reflects debate about the adequacy of existing levels of performance and considerations of accountability. The second emerges from a growing willingness, in the context of Australia's federal system, to think nationally about curriculum in terms of learning outcomes that schools should seek to achieve.

Public debate about the adequacy of current performance levels has tended to be driven by claims that they are in decline. The evidence advanced is typically anecdotal and not systematic. The first national effort to document performance levels arose from concern for students at risk of leaving school without adequate literacy and numeracy skills for adult life. This survey of 10- and 14-year-olds, undertaken for a House of Representatives Select Committee on Specific Learning Difficulties, was designed to estimate the proportions of each age group performing below levels defined to represent minimum competence in literacy and numeracy. The committee itself concluded from the survey that significant numbers of children were failing to reach adequate levels but acknowledged that data on a single occasion could not reveal anything about changes in levels of performance. A major national weekly news magazine, however, interpreted the results as documenting "a massive failure of education in primary and secondary schools" and declared that the nation was "paying more and educating less" (Samuel, 1976).

The Council of State, Territory and Federal Ministers of Education commissioned a repeat survey in 1980 to obtain trend data and declared an intention to commission an ongoing series. The 1980 survey was completed and demonstrated no decline in performance levels since the 1975 survey but plans for further national surveys were abandoned in the face of substantial opposition from both teachers' organisations and education bureaucracies, on the grounds that such surveys were inevitably narrow in their scope and thus likely to distort the curriculum. The Directors-General of Education, having opposed the continuation of national assessment, established the Australian Co-operative Assessment Program as a collaborative program through which the states and territories might develop and share strategies and materials, and as a shield against further national initiatives. While very little was actually done through this project in the development of shared approaches to assessment it was the agency through which significant curriculum collaboration was subsequently commenced.

The focus of the debate shifted by the mid-1980s from the question of whether performance levels were declining to whether, with substantially increased expenditure per student in real terms, they were rising. In 1984, the Federal Minister for Education appointed the Quality of Education Review Committee to advise on the "priority of attaining higher basic skills standards" in primary schools and "the need to ensure that strongly rising participation in years 11 and 12 is associated with the attainment of appropriate standards relevant to subsequent employment opportunities and improved preparation for tertiary education". The committee noted that, in contrast with earlier committees of review which had focused on increasing educational inputs, its brief had caused it to be outcomes oriented. It reported, however, that its assessments of benefits of the increased expenditure were constrained by "the absence of unanimity about what students should achieve [and] the lack of effective measures of achievement across the spectrum of educational objectives".

In the late 1980s, pressure for more curriculum consistency across the state and territory systems was mounted by the Federal Minister for Education and gained support from the business community. The Directors-General of Education commissioned a succession of curriculum mapping exercises. Initially, the objective was little more than to seek to demonstrate that considerable consistency already existed and that initiatives for national consistency were unnecessary. The work, however, then moved beyond this to a collaborative effort to develop curriculum and assessment frameworks in English and mathematics. A key to the level of success achieved was the curriculum focus and the attempt to address directly issues of classroom instruction and assessment for the purpose of reporting to parents. Support for the initiative, particularly from teachers, was obtained because neither national nor system monitoring was among its purposes.

By the 1990s, these new curriculum and assessment initiatives and the earlier ones concerned primarily with assessment and accountability had come together. There was still some confidence that performance levels were not declining but continuing anxiety about whether the levels were high enough. A new Ministerial Review Committee concluded "that Australian schools are doing at least as well as they ever have and that our young people emerge from schooling with levels of literacy comparable to their peers in leading OECD countries" but argued that the "focus of effort must be on improving school outcomes" and proposed the development of a standards framework (Australian Education Council Review Committee, 1991, pp. 71-72). The House of Representatives Standing Committee on Employment, Education and Training (1993) similarly concluded that there had probably been no change in performance levels but suggested that "ten to twenty per cent of children finish primary school with literacy problems" (p. v). Four members, in a dissenting report, declared that they "were appalled that (...) education authorities were unable to tell the Committee (...) the extent of the problem [in literacy] as it exists in primary schools because most systems do not test basic skills on any systematic basis" (p. 63). They went on to suggest that the numbers of students with problems "could be as high as 25 per cent" a comment which, in the hands of Clare and Johnston (1993, p. 42) became a claim that the House of Representatives Standing Committee itself had reported that around 25 per cent of children beginning secondary schooling are not able to read and write properly.

Demands for clear curriculum frameworks, improvement in student performance levels and the development of monitoring systems are clear in various pronouncements from business and industry groups. The National Industry Education Forum (1991) nominated, as one goal for Australia's schools, the development "in all major curriculum areas of national curriculum statements and frameworks which will identify common learning tasks and agreed performance standards" and, as another goal, the development of "a comprehensive system of performance and accountability measures which will allow for valid and reliable assessment of student and teacher performance as a basis for national and international comparison". In pursuit of these goals, the Forum commissioned a paper on assessment and monitoring systems which analysed the inadequacies of available data and described strategies for implementing national monitoring procedures (Masters, 1991) and then itself elaborated strategies for achieving the goals (National Industry Education Forum, 1992). The Institute of Public Affairs, a think-tank with substantial business support, similarly promotes the introduction of national assessment "preferably in years 3, 6 and 9, to ensure that acceptable standards in English and Mathematics are being attained, and to identify strengths and weaknesses at the individual, school and systemic levels" (Kramer et al., 1992).

At an official level, the Council of Australian Governments, a Council of which the members are the national Prime Minister, the State Premiers and the Territory Chief Ministers, has commissioned the Industry Commission to examine strategies for benchmarking and performance monitoring in a range of services provided by state and territory governments, including education. Consideration is also being given to a National School Literacy Survey following a recommendation in the Federal government's May 1994 White Paper on Employment (Commonwealth of Australia, 1994). A key question being considered is, if agreement can be reached to derive national estimates, whether existing state and territory data could be used or whether separate national surveys would be required.

The absence of national assessment does not reflect a current rejection of assessment and monitoring programs. It reflects the constitutional allocation of responsibility for education to the states and territories. The nature and extent of system-level monitoring is in flux but Figure 1 represents the current actual or announced position.

Figure 1. **School years in which monitoring programmes are conducted**

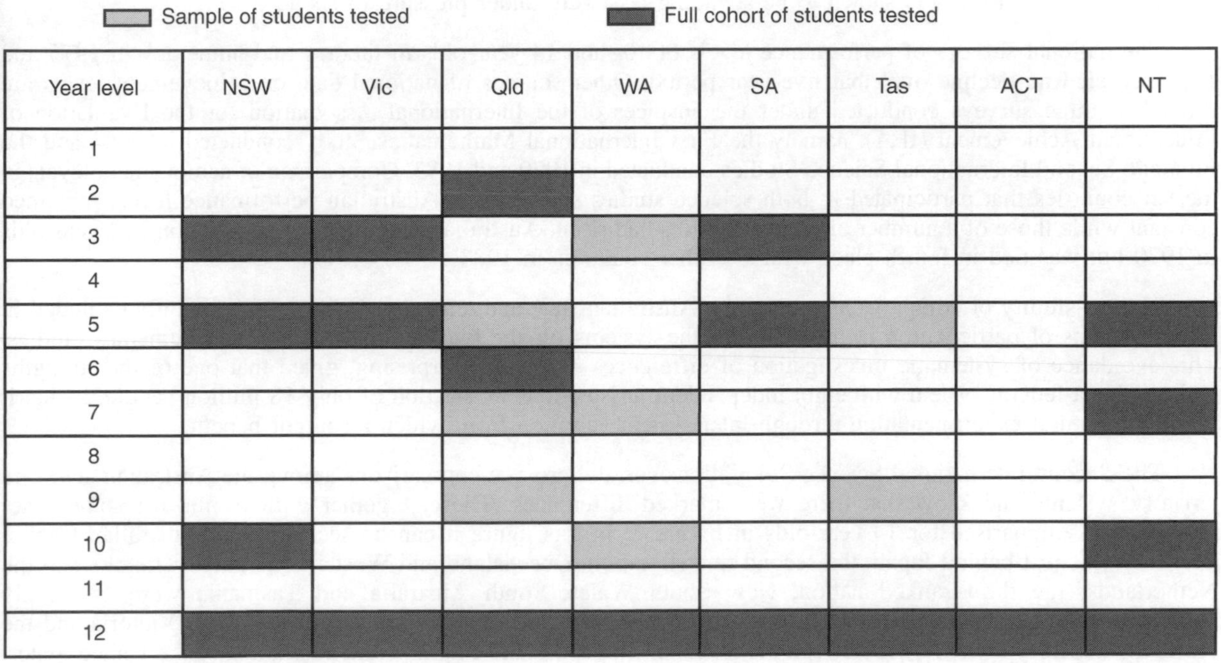

Legend: ▢ Sample of students tested   ▦ Full cohort of students tested

Year level	NSW	Vic	Qld	WA	SA	Tas	ACT	NT
1								
2			Full					
3	Full	Full		Sample	Full			
4								
5	Full	Full	Sample		Full	Sample		Full
6			Full					
7			Sample	Sample				Full
8								
9			Sample			Sample		
10	Full			Sample				Full
11								
12		Full	Full	Full	Full	Full	Full	Full

Source: Lokan and Ford (1994).

All systems in the past conducted syllabus-based external examinations at the end of primary school and in the middle and at the end of secondary school. Only those at the end of secondary school remain but these provide little evidence about performance levels since results are distributed normatively each year, in essentially predetermined ways over the group of students presenting. Participation rates to the end of secondary school have risen from around 30 per cent of the age group in 1980 to almost 80 per cent in the mid-1990s so that the cohort of students in Year 12 has changed dramatically. The normative allocation of scores or grades in the same fashion within the cohort of candidates from year to year provides no means for identifying or representing changes in performance levels over time. Some systems, particularly Queensland and Victoria have attempted to develop and use grade-related performance criteria for the allocation of grades within individual subjects but the dominance of the normative tertiary entrance score, constructed as a scaled aggregate of subject results for each student, means that more attention is generally given to this normative aggregate than to individual criterion-related subject results.

31

Tasmania and Queensland maintained periodic surveys of performance of students at lower levels with tests of random samples of students and Victoria introduced such surveys in 1988. In order to report on individual students' performances to parents and schools, full cohort testing was introduced in the Northern Territory at primary level in 1983 and mid-secondary in 1989. New South Wales introduced cohort testing in 1989 and South Australia has adopted the New South Wales tests from 1995. Victoria will introduce cohort testing at primary level in 1995 and Queensland, while maintaining sample surveys at three grade levels, will introduce cohort testing at two others from 1996. Apart from South Australia's adoption of New South Wales' tests, there is no direct comparability of assessments across the systems.

The primary justification claimed for the new monitoring programs at system level has been satisfaction of demands for accountability and there is one important reason for which some of the traditional opposition might now weaken. The absence of any extensive data over the last two decades has provided two grounds on which strong claims are currently made that resource levels for schooling can be reduced without detrimental effect. First, since there is no clear evidence that performance levels rose during the period of increased funding, it is being claimed that no improvement occurred. Secondly, since there are no data to detect differences in outcomes among the states and territories, it is being claimed that the marked interstate variations in levels of expenditure per student yield no differences. Both of these arguments are advanced to put pressure on state and territory Ministers spending more per student than others to spend less (*e.g.* Victorian Commission of Audit, 1993). Twenty years ago, Ministers shown to be spending less were under pressure to spend more.

The national surveys of performance levels of 10- and 14-year-olds in literacy and numeracy in 1975 and 1980 revealed no decline over that five-year period. Other sources of national data on achievement levels are limited to three surveys conducted under the auspices of the International Association for the Evaluation of Educational Achievement (IEA), namely the First International Mathematics Study conducted in 1964 and the First and Second International Science Studies conducted in 1970 and 1983. Comparison of achievement levels in the ten countries that participated in both science studies showed that Australian performance levels remained constant while those of a number of other countries had risen. Australia ranked a clear third among 14-year-olds in 1970 but was tied in fourth place with six other countries in 1983.

The possibility of comparisons among the Australian state and territory systems was explicitly excluded in the conditions of participation negotiated with the systems for the two national literacy and numeracy studies. This avoidance of systematic investigation of differences may seem surprising, given that one of the strengths claimed for a federal system with eight independent jurisdictions in a nation of only 18 million people, is that it permits a natural experimentation through inter-system variation from which all might benefit.

The Second International Science Study, however, did provide comparisons among the Australian state and territory systems and show that there were marked differences. These, together with results for some other nations, are summarised for 14-year-olds in Figure 2. In this figure it can be seen that the Australian Capital Territory was just behind Japan, the second ranked nation, Queensland and Western Australia were close to the Netherlands, the third ranked nation, New South Wales, South Australia and Tasmania were essentially equivalent to Australia as a whole and thus also to the set of nations tying at fourth rank, and Victoria and the Northern Territory lower down between the levels of Singapore and England and above that of the United States.

Some monitoring of performance levels over time within states is available. Tasmania established a survey cycle taking its data from the 1975 national survey as a benchmark. This series of surveys reveals, for Tasmania, no change in basic reading skills since 1975 and, until the appearance of a decline in the early 1990s, no change in basic numeracy skills. Surveys in Victoria, providing comparisons with its data from 1975 and 1980, concluded that there has been no decline in standards of performance.

Within individual systems, the new monitoring programs are beginning to yield comparisons of achievement levels for subgroups of students and also comparisons over time. For the New South Wales program, a full public report was published for the first year of testing in 1989 and showed females performing better than males in literacy and numeracy at Year 3 and in literacy and number at Year 6 but males performing better in measurement and space at Year 6 (Masters *et al.*, 1990). Students of non-English speaking background and students from the indigenous Aboriginal and Torres Strait Islander populations had lower performance levels than the overall student population. Similar analyses have been undertaken in subsequent years, with the addition of analyses of emerging trends over time, but these have not been formally published for wide distribution. There is some evidence of improvements in the performance levels of students of non-English speaking background but, in these early years, there has also been some adjustment to the language used in the tests to control better against any "disadvantage" suffered by students without an English-speaking background so that the effects are somewhat confounded.

Figure 2.   **Achievements of 14-year-olds by education system, 1983/84**

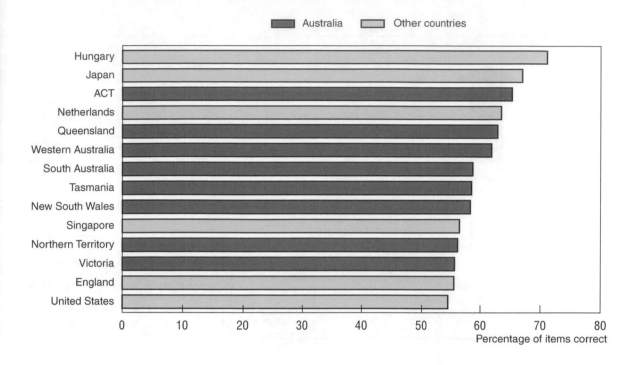

Source: Rosier and Banks (1990), p. 128 and Postlethwaite and Wiley (1991), p. 60.

The Western Australian monitoring program provides comparisons of achievement levels in writing and mathematics in 1990 and 1992 which show significant improvement in writing at both years 7 and 10 and in mathematics at Year 7 but with no change at Year 3 or 10. Some of these improvements were attributed to emphases in the curriculum. For example, improvement in the conventions of writing – punctuation, spelling and form of writing – were attributed to emphasis on process writing in the English curriculum (Titmanis *et al.*, 1993, pp. 16-17).

Queensland tested aspects of mathematics, reading and writing at years 5, 7 and 9 in 1990. Reading and writing were assessed again in 1992, revealing a slight but consistent upward shift at all three Year levels in reading and writing, with the most marked improvements being in writing at years 5 and 7 (Evaluation and Assessment Unit, 1993). Performance levels in mathematics were assessed again in 1993 and show a slight improvement at the lower range of the scale at Year 5, no change at Year 7 and a slight improvement over the full scale at Year 9 (Quality Assurance Directorate, 1994).

These state monitoring programs typically use some items common to tests at the different Year levels to permit calibration of the tests onto a single scale and thus to permit direct comparisons of performance across Year levels. These comparisons reveal substantial overlap of the distributions. The Queensland reading survey, for example, provides the diagram reproduced as Figure 3 which shows the top 25 per cent of Year 5 students to be above the mean of Year 7 students and the bottom 25 per cent of Year 9 students to be below the mean of Year 7 students. Similar substantial overlap of the distributions of Year 5 and Year 9 students is evident in Victoria in literacy and numeracy (McGaw *et al.*, 1989) and in science (Adams *et al.*, 1991).

The process of standard setting

The current debate about levels of student performance reflects the substantial shift in focus from inputs to outcomes over the last two decades in Australia, as elsewhere. More important in the long run will be the accompanying shift in questions asked about performance levels from the normative ones about whether they are falling or rising to ones about whether or not they are adequate. This shift has raised important technical

Figure 3. **Distribution of reading performance in Queensland**

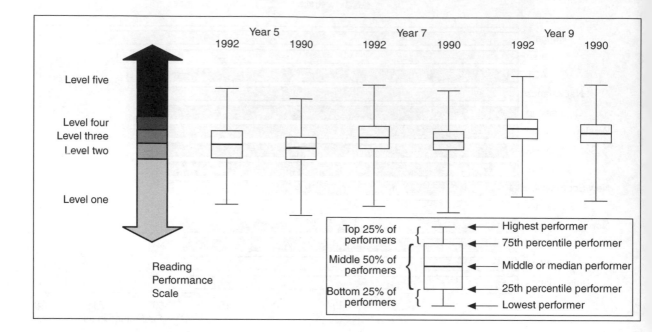

Source: Review and Evaluation Directorate (1993), p. 10.

questions about how adequate standards might be defined and about how performance levels might be assessed in relation to them. Two approaches have been adopted, one starting with measurement and the other with curriculum, though these are now coming together in mutually beneficial ways (see Figure 3).

Highly centralised education systems had developed in the separate colonial jurisdictions on the Australian continent before federation in 1901. Under the federal arrangements, responsibility for education remained with the states and territories which persisted with centralised prescription of the curriculum through detailed syllabuses for teachers to follow. Whether these simply prescribed content or actually set standards is a matter primarily of historic interest but some translation into "standards" was provided through itinerant school inspectors and state-wide public examinations at the end of primary schooling and in the middle and at the end of secondary schooling. By the 1970s, all but the end of secondary school examinations had been abolished, since the earlier ones had ceased to perform a selection function controlling progression to the next stage. By this time a strong move to school-based curriculum development had also reduced the dependence on central prescription and diversified the institutional offerings across schools. Less than two decades later, in the late 1980s, there were moves for new controls over the curriculum, not to the extent of the former centralised prescription, but through the establishment of frameworks designed to ensure certain key learnings for all students. This same trend is also evident in the establishment of new monitoring programs.

While these initiatives, particularly the new monitoring programs, were specific to the separate educational systems, there was increasing willingness in the systems to develop a shared national perspective and to eliminate unnecessary differences. Through the initiative of the Directors-General of Education, the states and territories were collaborating on the development of national frameworks in English and mathematics. In April 1989, at a meeting in Hobart, the State, Territory and Federal Ministers of Education declared themselves "conscious that the schooling of Australia's children is the foundation on which to build our future as a nation" and "willing to act jointly to assist Australian schools in meeting the challenges of our time". They defined ten agreed national goals of schooling, set out in what is sometimes referred to as the *Hobart Declaration on Schooling,* the text of which is included as Appendix B (Department of Employment, Education and Training, 1990). In 1990, the Ministers established the Curriculum Corporation, as a jointly owned company, through which collaborative work might be facilitated.

After the initial work on national English and mathematics profiles commissioned by the Directors-General of Education and managed by their Directors of Curriculum, development of the national curriculum statements and profiles for all eight learning areas was taken over by the Curriculum and Assessment (CURASS) Committee established by the Council of Ministers. This change and the assumption of the chair by the New South Wales Director-General of School Education reflected increased commitment to the enterprise. The Committee became increasingly broadly-based, finally including representatives of the federal, state and territory Departments of Education and their Boards of Studies, non-government schools, parents, teachers, the Curriculum Corporation, the Australian Council for Educational Research and New Zealand.

It was originally expected that individual state and territory Departments of Education would take the lead in organising the national effort in different learning areas. Reaching agreement about what each would do proved difficult so that the work was put out to tender. For one area, a university won the tender. For others various consortia were successful. For one, a teacher educator was seconded to work with a state-based project team. For another, no satisfactory tenderer was found so CURASS put together a development team. The full-time members of the teams were generally curriculum specialists. For each learning area special consultants were appointed with the task of ensuring that gender equity and Aboriginal and Torres Strait Islander perspectives were reflected in the materials.

An extensive consultation process was intended with a wide range of groups such as parents, teachers, teacher educators, professional associations, subject and discipline specialists, curriculum developers, employers and unions. This consultation was difficult to sustain, given the very tight timelines once the Ministerial Council had decided that it wanted all eight learning areas dealt with at the same time and quickly, but draft documents were circulated widely for comments. The mathematics materials, for example, were sent at five points to mathematics departments in universities as well as to education faculties and other groups outside universities. Some of the disaffection with final products, where it was articulated, may well have reflected a feeling that views expressed were not heeded rather than a lack of consultation. The very width of the consultation, of course, ensured that conflicting responses were likely to be received and the speed of the process reduced the likelihood that the conflicts would be resolved in a consultative way.

Training in standard setting was essentially developed on the job since the whole enterprise was new to Australia. In some learning areas there was a stronger research base than in others for developing the sequence of learning expressed in the profiles. One difficulty encountered arose because the new profiles had a different purpose from more traditional curriculum documents. Curriculum documents tend to outline all that might be attempted in a particular teaching program while the profiles were intended to set out what students would typically learn. The choice of eight levels with which to represent 10 to 12 years of schooling was a deliberate attempt to break away from notions of lock-step learning rates tied to years in school and to acknowledge the fact that students differ markedly in the extent and rate of learning. The new Victorian variation of the national profiles, however, ties the levels to school years.

Once developed the profiles require empirical validation and adjustment. As a first step towards validation, the Australian Council for Educational Research was commissioned to provide empirical validations of draft profiles using teacher judgement as the data. These revealed some disagreements between the judgements of the teachers and those of the developers and the materials were modified. More important than validation against teacher judgement, however, will be validation of the presumed progression of learning typically achieved by students against student achievement data.

The standards

From the ten national goals, the Council of Ministers identified eight broad learning areas – the arts, English, health and physical education, languages other than English, mathematics, science, studies of society and environment, and technology – as the overall structure of the curriculum. There is a certain convenience about dividing the total curriculum into a relatively small number of areas, particularly if these are then to be areas in which all students must study, but there is debate about the results. Traditional areas like English, mathematics and science can be reasonably dealt with as distinct learning areas but others are less coherent. According to Collins (1994, p. 10), the document on the Arts "is confined to making rather bland generalisations because what it says has to be valid across a range which covers music, crafts, all traditional and new visual arts and the performing arts", Society and the Environment deals with "socio-cultural questions [which] are fundamentally of a different epistemological order than questions about the physical/ecological environment" and Health and Physical Education wins "the prize for the least compatible components".

For each learning area, the Council of Ministers commissioned the development of a statement and a profile. Statements provide a framework for what will be taught. Profiles set out what students are expected to learn.

A statement defines a learning area in terms of strands that specify content and process and provides a curriculum framework by suggesting a sequence for developing knowledge and skills within each strand across four bands, which are broad stages across the school years. Table 1 gives the strands for the Studies of Society and Environment learning area and identifies the scope of the bands used for all learning areas. Of the six strands into which this learning area has been organised, the first deals with key processes used in all studies in the area and the other five identify key concepts to be learned. The statement provides some elaboration of each strand but does not provide a syllabus. It provides a structure for courses that schools or other agencies might develop.

Table 1. **Structure of statement for studies of society and environment**

Strands	Learning area: Studies of Society and Environment
1.	Investigation, communication and participation
2.	Time, continuity and change
3.	Place and space
4.	Culture
5.	Resources
6.	Natural and social systems
Bands	Broad, overlapping stages for all learning areas
A.	Roughly lower primary (years 1-4)
B.	Upper primary (years 4-7)
C.	Junior secondary (years 7-10)
D.	Post-compulsory (years 11-12)

Source: Curriculum Corporation (1994*c*).

A profile is a description of the progression in learning outcomes typically achieved by students during the years of schooling in a particular learning area. While statements are sequenced into four bands to correspond to successive but overlapping stages of schooling, profiles are sequenced into eight levels, which correspond roughly to the first ten years of schooling.

Details in the profiles are provided for subdivisions of the strands, referred to as strand organisers. Within each strand organiser, student learning outcomes are defined for each of the eight levels. For English, there are three strands: speaking and listening, reading and viewing, and writing, each of which is subdivided into the same four strand organisers: texts, contextual understanding, linguistic structures and features, and strategies (Curriculum Corporation, 1994*b*). The outcome statements for two of the four strand organisers in the Speaking and Listening Strand are shown in Table 2.

For each level there is a statement which gives a general description of student performance at that level. This is accompanied, for each outcome of the type shown in Table 2, by a set of pointers which are indicators of the achievement of an outcome. Unlike the outcomes, they are only examples. These elements of the profiles are illustrated in Table 3 for Level 5 in the Linguistic Structures and Features Strand Organiser and the Strategies Strand Organiser in the Speaking and Listening Strand the English profile. This material is further accompanied by annotated samples of student work which demonstrate achievement of one or more outcomes at the particular level.

National statements and profiles are now available for all eight learning areas but their status is somewhat ambiguous. Having adopted the Hobart Declaration in 1989, endorsed the development of national profiles in English and mathematics in 1990, and resolved in 1991 that the structure of statements and profiles should also be the basis for national work in the remaining six learning areas, the Ministerial Council in 1993 backed away to a substantial extent from this commitment to national collaboration. One explanation lies in a change in membership of the Council and, more significantly, in a change in the political balance of members following changes in some state governments at elections. The national initiative was seen in some circles as a Federal government initiative which carried risks for the autonomy of the state and territory systems so, with the Federal Minister in a political minority for the first time in a considerable period, there was a loss of consensus about co-operation. A more subtle variant of this explanation acknowledges the development of the statements and profiles as a

Table 2. English profile: outcome statements for two strand organisers in the speaking and listening strand

	Strand: Speaking and Listening	
Level	*Strand organiser:* Linguistic Structures and Features	*Strand organiser:* Strategies
1.	Draws on implicit knowledge of the linguistic structures and features of own variety of English when expressing ideas and information and interpreting spoken texts.	Monitors communication of self and others.
2.	Experiments with different linguistic structures and features for expressing and interpreting ideas and information.	Speaks and listens in ways that assist communication with others.
3.	Usually uses linguistic structures and features of spoken language appropriately for expressing and interpreting ideas and information.	Reflects on own approach to communication and the ways in which others interact.
4.	Controls most linguistic structures and features of spoken language for interpreting meaning and developing and presenting ideas and information in familiar situations.	Assists and monitors the communication patterns of self and others.
5.	Discusses and experiments with some linguistic structures and features that enable speakers to influence audiences.	Listens strategically and systematically records spoken information.
6.	Experiments with knowledge of linguistic structures and features, and draws on this knowledge to explain how speakers influence audiences.	Critically evaluates others' spoken texts and uses this knowledge to reflect on, and improve, one's own.
7.	Uses awareness of differences between spoken and written language to construct own spoken texts in structured, formal situations.	Uses a range of strategies to present spoken texts in formal situations.
8.	Analyses how linguistic structures and features affect interpretations of spoken texts, especially in the construction of tone, style and point of view.	Uses listening strategies which enable detailed critical valuation of texts with complex levels of meaning.

Source: Curriculum Corporation (1994a).

Table 3. English: Level 5 statement for two strand organisers in the speaking and listening strand

Level 5 statement: Speaking and Listening

Students who have achieved level 5 have command of a range of standard text types and features and experiment with writing longer texts that discuss challenging aspects of subjects and present justified views on them. They understand important elements of how texts are constructed and experiment with these elements in their own writing.

Students work well in formal groups where they take on roles, responsibilities and tasks, and they show progress in planning and delivering formal spoken presentations to their peers. They systematically listen to, and record, spoken information.

Students can give detailed accounts of texts in speech and writing, justifying them by referring to the text. They compare texts to examine their structures and ideas more closely, and show a sound understanding of the conventions of narrative texts.

Students use a variety of text types to write at length and with some sense of complexity. In writing longer pieces, they ensure clarity by checking layout, cause-and-effect sequences and grammar. They show a sense of the requirements of readers and experiment with manipulating prose for effect.

Strand organiser: Linguistic Structures and Features	*Strand organiser:* Strategies
Outcome:	**Outcome:**
Discusses and experiments with some linguistic structures and features that enable speakers to influence audiences.	Listens strategically and systematically records spoken information.
Evident when students for example:	**Evident when students for example:**
• Observe and discuss the way in which voice and body language affect audiences and can be used to enhance meaning and influence interpretation (the way gestures, posture, facial expression, tone of voice, pace of speaking may engage the audience's interest).	• Prepare for listening (take pen and notebook or laptop computer to the viewing of an information video or a talk by a guest speaker).
• Note aspects of language use, such as vocabulary, rhythm, similes, which enhance particular spoken texts.	• Note cues such as change of pace and particular words which indicate that a new or important point is about to be made.
• Discuss and experiment with the effect of intonation on meaning (say the same word, phrase or sentence in different ways to convey regret, anger, annoyance, humour).	• Develop and use a personal abbreviation system to record information quickly.

Source: Curriculum Corporation (1994a).

genuinely collaborative enterprise in which states and territories had carriage of the work, but attributes their withdrawal from full co-operation to proposals from the federal authorities to use the profiles as a basis for national monitoring and reporting. A third explanation lies in public criticisms of some of the statements and profiles. A group of university mathematicians, for example, had been publicly critical of the mathematics profile and had generated some loss of confidence in that product.

All of the state and territory education systems are now actually introducing the national statements and profiles or some variant of them. The smallest systems, South Australia, Tasmania, the Northern Territory and the Australian Capital Territory, for which the benefits of collaboration are greatest, are using the national materials. Queensland has adopted the mathematics statements and profiles and, with slight editing, the ones for English but published under the title ''Student Performance Standards''. Western Australia is using the title ''Outcome Statements'' and has adopted the national materials in some learning areas such as mathematics but has substantially reworked them in others such as health and physical education. In New South Wales, the Board of Studies is progressively building the outcome statements from the national profiles into its syllabus documents, adding some additional ones (for example, in hand writing in English), deleting a few, but preserving the national wording in all that it keeps. Victoria has dropped Level 8 and collapsed the statements and profiles into a single publication, *Curriculum and Standards Framework* (Board of Studies, 1994). It retains the eight key learning areas and a strand structure. In some learning areas the material is essentially the same as the national material while in others it is different. In English, for example, the strands are the same. In the case of the components of Speaking and Listening extracted from the national documents in Table 3, the Victorian materials differ only in deleting Level 8 and in defining Level 7 for Strategies as ''Draws on a range of strategies (...)'' rather than ''Uses a range of strategies (...)''. In others, such as mathematics and science, the Victorian materials are quite different from the national materials. The elaboration of the objectives is simpler and less extensive in the Victorian materials and there are no samples of student work to illustrate achievement of various levels.

In the first stages of the national development it was intended that the profiles have only six levels and cover the period of compulsory schooling, Years 1 to 10. The Ministerial Council requested the addition of Levels 7 and 8 to cover Years 11 and 12 but the diversification of the curriculum in Years 11 and 12 and the specialised nature of some of the courses made this task extremely difficult. The scope of the profiles was then limited again to Years 1 to 10 but Levels 7 and 8 were retained to capture some of the outcomes that might be achieved by advanced students in Year 10. Profiles are said to describe ''the progression of learning typically achieved by students during the compulsory years of schooling (Years 1-10)'' with the twofold purpose ''to help teaching and learning and to provide a framework for reporting student achievement'' (Curriculum Corporation, 1994c, p. 1).

Implementation, review and adjustment

Work on the national profiles, and subsequent work on state and territory variants, to cover the compulsory years of schooling from Years 1 to 10 was informed primarily by prior curriculum development experience and, where available, research evidence on the developmental sequence of skill acquisition. The statements and profiles express goals and aspirations for schooling, moderated by experience of some of the participants in actually teaching students at various levels of schooling in the relevant learning area. They represent a first attempt to develop a national perspective in Australia on the standards of performance to be achieved by Australian students.

Empirical validation and adjustment of standards

Empirical considerations of what students can achieve has been a secondary consideration in the development of the curriculum profiles but they have had a stronger role in some of the monitoring programs designed to establish benchmarks against which to judge student achievement and in terms of which to monitor changes in achievement levels. State-wide monitoring programs mostly predated the development of the profiles but they increasingly reference the profiles, in their national or local state or territory form, as a way of defining benchmarks against which to judge student performance.

Performance standards have been developed both *a priori* and *a posteriori*. The development of the national profiles represents an *a priori* approach in which the statements of standards to be achieved were derived as a way of expressing desired learning outcomes. Some monitoring programs, particularly those established before the development of the profiles, developed definitions of performance standards *a posteriori*, following examination of the measured outcomes that students actually achieve.

One example of *a posteriori* standard setting is provided by an evaluation of literacy and numeracy levels in Victorian schools commissioned by the Minister of Education to identify how many students were completing schooling with inadequate skills, as well as to provide comparison of current with past levels of achievement. The survey was based on samples of Year 5 and 9 students and used tests for each level, keyed to the curriculum but with sufficient common items for all items at both levels to be calibrated onto a common scale (McGaw *et al.*, 1989). The distributions of performances of Year 5 and 9 students on the mathematics scale are shown in Figure 4. The locations of common items are indicated with a bullet and the locations of items unique to each test with an arrowhead. The units of calibration on the scale, ranging from around 20 to around 60, were chosen arbitrarily in order not to use numbers of the type frequently used in educational testing in schools and related to number or percentage of correct items. Inspection of the specific content of items on the scale led to the location of the level of minimally acceptable performance for adults as 35. The percentages of Year 5 and 9 students below this level were then estimated and reported as an answer to the Minister's first question. Exposing the definition in this way permits others, on examination of the items on the scale, to nominate more or less generous definitions of minimum competence but necessitates that their definitions be explicit.

Figure 4. **Distribution of mathematics performance of grade 5 and 9 students**

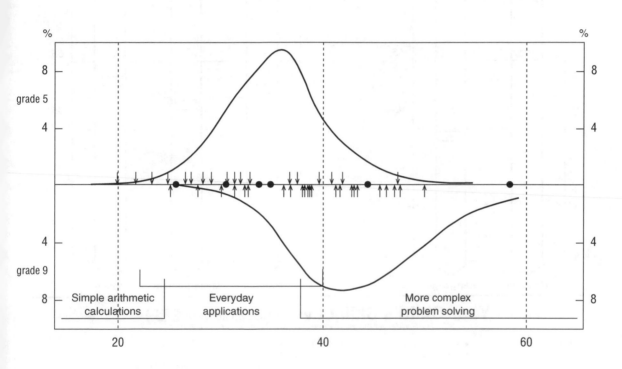

Source: MacGaw *et al.* (1989), p. 28.

In the New South Wales Basic Skills Testing program, a similar approach to scale calibration was taken but a new form of presentation of results was developed to permit a verbal description of the performance levels of all students for use in reports to parents. From a detailed examination of the content of items, descriptions were developed of performance bands on the scale (Masters *et al.*, 1990). Each student then received a personal report in the form shown in Figure 5 in which the student's performance was visually located on each of the five scales used. For each scale, the student was thus located within a performance band for which the description is printed at the foot of the report. Descriptions for all bands on all scales were printed on the back to indicate the range of performances represented on the scale.

The location of the bands was influenced to some extent by normative considerations since the bands were located in regions in which the performances of reasonable numbers of students at the year level lay. It is in precisely this sense that the setting of standards was *a posteriori* but that fitted the purpose, which was to establish a benchmark against which performances in subsequent years could be compared.

Figure 5. **Parents' report form from NSW Basic Skills Testing Programme**

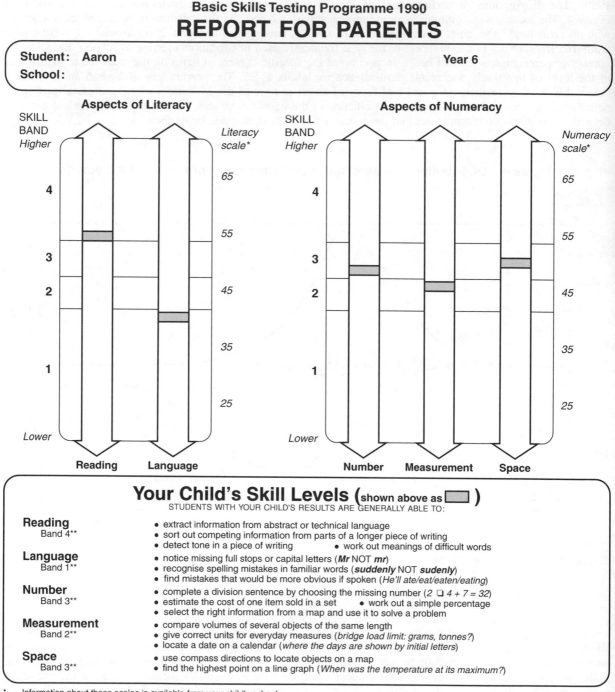

Basic Skills Testing Programme 1990
REPORT FOR PARENTS

Student: Aaron   Year 6
School:

Your Child's Skill Levels (shown above as ▭)
STUDENTS WITH YOUR CHILD'S RESULTS ARE GENERALLY ABLE TO:

Reading
Band 4**
- extract information from abstract or technical language
- sort out competing information from parts of a longer piece of writing
- detect tone in a piece of writing   • work out meanings of difficult words

Language
Band 1**
- notice missing full stops or capital letters (*Mr* NOT *mr*)
- recognise spelling mistakes in familiar words (*suddenly* NOT *sudenly*)
- find mistakes that would be more obvious if spoken (*He'll ate/eat/eaten/eating*)

Number
Band 3**
- complete a division sentence by choosing the missing number (2 ❑ 4 + 7 = 32)
- estimate the cost of one item sold in a set   • work out a simple percentage
- select the right information from a map and use it to solve a problem

Measurement
Band 2**
- compare volumes of several objects of the same length
- give correct units for everyday measures (*bridge load limit: grams, tonnes?*)
- locate a date on a calendar (*where the days are shown by initial letters*)

Space
Band 3**
- use compass directions to locate objects on a map
- find the highest point on a line graph (*When was the temperature at its maximum?*)

*   Information about these scales is available from your child's school.
**   Your child's skills also include those described for skills **up to** this band.

Prepared by the Australian Council for Educational Research
for the NSW Department of School Education

Source: Masters *et al.* (1990), p. 93.

An *a priori* approach to standard setting is feasible if statements of student learning outcomes provided in the profiles are taken as a starting point. When the Western Australian *Monitoring Standards in Education* project commenced the first national profiles, the Western Australian outcomes had been developed so that the monitoring program was keyed to the profiles, with particular test items designed to tap particular levels in the profiles (Titmanis *et al.*, 1993). The monitoring program then provides student achievement data for an empirical validation of the classification of outcomes to levels. The calibrations of some of the test items designed to assess outcomes at Levels 1 to 4 on the space strand of mathematics are shown in Figure 6.

Figure 6. **Some calibrated items from space strand in WA Monitoring Standards Project**

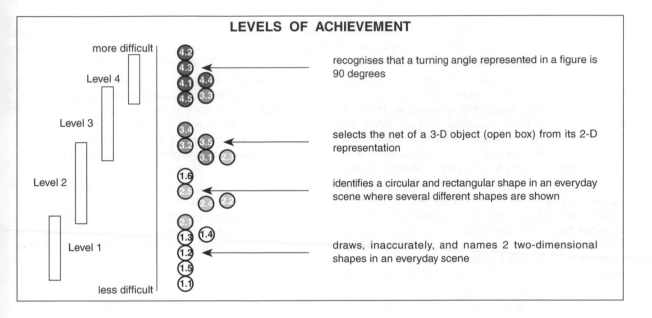

Source: Titmanis *et al.* (1993), p. 7.

The level of outcomes tapped by each item shown in Figure 6 is indicated by the first digit in the item number. From the calibrated location it is clear that item 1.6, designed as an item to tap a Level 1 outcome is more difficult than most of those shown as tapping Level 2 outcomes. Apparent anomalies such as this may reveal a fault in the item or a misallocation of the outcome to the particular level. As more items are developed and used, the testing process "will provide an enhanced definition of each level (...) which will most likely result in some adjustment to the boundaries" (Titmanis *et al.*, 1993, p. 8) and will probably also suggest adjustment to the locations of some specific outcomes.

The development of clear scales with calibrated item locations permits clear reporting to the profession and the general public. It also brings together curriculum and assessment considerations in a way that was not possible without the development of the item response theory that underpins the calibration of test items and tasks and the measurement of individual performance.

Empirical validation of sequenced outcome statements can lead to adjustments to standards other than the technical ones indicated by misfitting items. Normative considerations can also justify adjustments to standards. If only few students are able to achieve outcomes set as desirable for their stage of schooling, then one appropriate response would be to move these outcomes to a higher level where they could be achieved by students at that level. An alternative approach would be to hold the outcomes where they are as an expression of goals earnestly held and to seek better means of instruction to facilitate earlier learning. In a similar way, if almost all students at a particular stage can achieve certain outcomes actually set at a higher level than they have yet generally reached, there may be grounds for moving those outcomes to a lower level.

Careful development of assessment procedures can also clarify and refine a set of outcome statements in another significant way. The need to develop assessment tasks along a continuum of achievement can require more precise definition of the continuum than is provided in student learning outcomes of the type defined in the profiles, particularly in areas not so richly addressed in typical curriculum statements. "Speaking and Listening", as one of the strands in the English profile, is a case in point. Using tasks such as taking notes from a set of recorded instructions from "mother" and from an announcer at a parade, Forster *et al.* (1994) have developed a protocol for scoring responses that produces the continuum of skills shown in the listening scale of Figure 7. This continuum is much more detailed than that provided in the national profile for English (Curriculum Corporation, 1994*a*) on which it is based (*cf.* Table 2) and which it, therefore, elaborates.

Evidence of attainment of performance standards

Where state-wide testing of whole student cohorts is undertaken by agencies outside the school, the range of instruments used tends to be limited because of the amount of data to be processed and the need for speedy turnaround. These requirements typically necessitate the use of machine scoring of responses though that does not restrict the assessment to straightforward multiple-choice test items as Lokan and her colleagues demonstrated in developing the tests for the New South Wales Basic Skills Testing Program (Masters *et al.*, 1990).

Where only a sample of students is used to monitor performance levels in a system as a whole, then more innovative and extensive instruments can be used. In a survey of students' science achievement, Adams *et al.* (1991) used simple equipment to assess students' skill in the design and conduct of experiments and open-ended responses to cartoon sequences inviting interpretations of everyday phenomena to tap students' conceptual understanding of principles such as force and motion, the structure of matter and planetary motion. Doig *et al.* (1994) have extended this latter technique to an assessment of conceptual understanding in social education as the key strategy in a project to monitor student achievement in social studies.

A key benefit of full cohort testing is that reports on individual students are possible. A key benefit of sample testing to monitor performance levels in a system is that it is usually possible to use a richer set of assessment strategies that require more resources per student for data collection and analysis. As a compromise between these two approaches, there is an approach used in the Western Australian Monitoring Standards in Education program in which the more complex assessment instruments are used with only a state-level sample of students but in which parallel instruments, with clear scoring rules, are made available to teachers as an option to enable them to assess their own students on the same scale as that derived for the state-level monitoring.

An important point to be noted is that scoring of responses need not be restricted to a simple right/wrong dichotomy. With partial credit analysis (Masters, 1982; Adams and Khoo, 1993) it is possible to calibrate the boundaries between any successive pairs of scores on a multi-point scale just as it is possible to calibrate the single boundary on a two-point right/wrong scale.

The first task in assessing levels of student performance is item calibration and scale development. Item calibration for dichotomously scored items can be based on any probability of correct response that one might wish to choose. For a case where notions of "mastery" are involved, $p = 0.7$ or $p = 0.8$ could be used instead of the more traditional $p = 0.5$. In the reports for the New South Wales Basic Skills Testing Program, Masters *et al.* (1990, p. 121) used $p = 0.7$ for calibration of item difficulties except in the relatively detailed Individual Student Profile reports provided to teachers in which item difficulties were calibrated at $p = 0.5$ since that calibration is more familiar to the teachers who would be interpreting the profiles.

The number of bands that might be used to describe levels of performance on achievement scales is a matter of more or less arbitrary judgement. Where the outcomes anticipated in the curriculum have been expressed in terms of levels, then it is best and most consistent to use them. Where there is no such external referent, the creation of bands as in Figure 5 compared with preservation of the underlying scale as in Figure 4 has the advantage of providing a language in terms of which the performance of individual students can be described.

One difficulty with measurement and reporting in terms of bands is that the boundaries between bands are relatively unstable. Representations of population performance on successive occasions in terms of proportions of students scoring in each band can reveal differences which are more likely to be due to errors of measurement than to real changes.

Where multiple scales are used, and levels are defined in similar ways on each, it is possible to provide some empirical validation of the levels across scales. Figure 8 provides the five subscales of the Development Assessment Resource for Teachers (DART) English (Forster *et al.*, 1994) designed for teachers to assess student performance in terms of the national profile in English. In this case, some compromises have been reached in locating the separate subscales in terms of the Levels 2 to 5 which each is designed to tap. If all items were

Figure 7. **Location of items on Listening Scale in DART English**

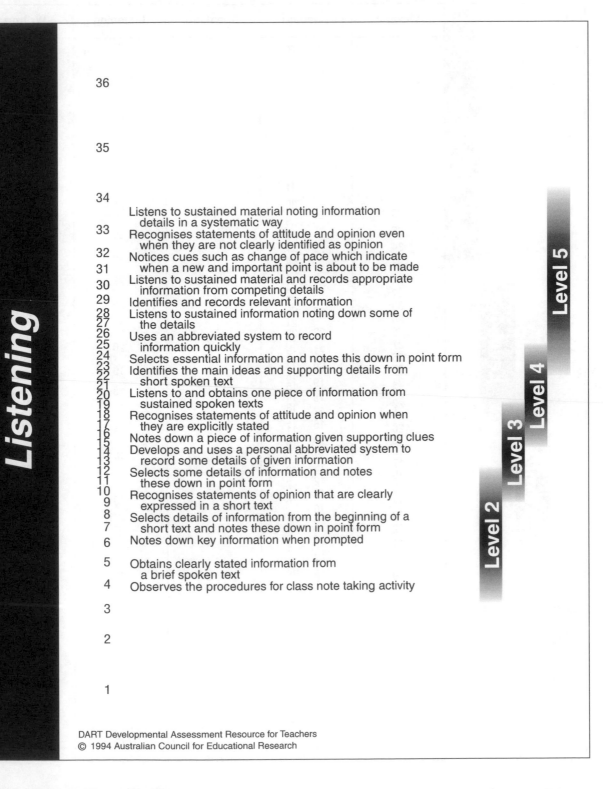

DART Developmental Assessment Resource for Teachers
© 1994 Australian Council for Educational Research

Source: Forster *et al.* (in press), p. 65.

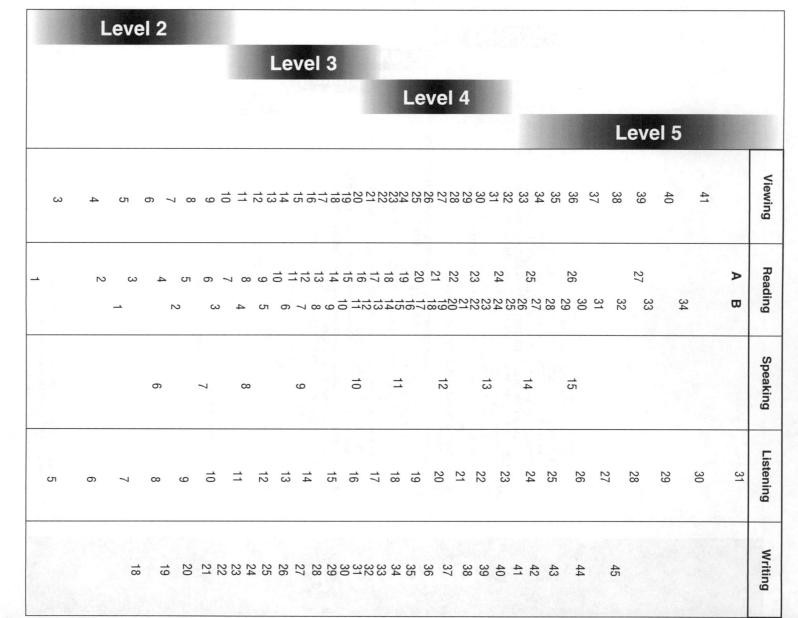

Figure 8. Subscales in DART English

Source: Forster et al. (in press), p. 153.

calibrated together as though on a single scale, provided the degree of fit of the data to such a single dimension were sufficiently good to justify the collapsing of scales for this purpose, the allocation of items to the four levels across all scales would be directly and empirically comparable. In the case in Figure 8, the fit of the items to a single dimension was sufficiently good to have permitted this approach. The actual resolution provided in Figure 8 is something of a compromise between this purely empirical approach and an outright acceptance of the *a priori* allocation to levels in the profile document.

Reporting results

Where samples of students are used to monitor a system, only reporting on the system as a whole is possible. This typically takes the form of a public document giving details of the testing and providing, where available, comparison with earlier occasions (*e.g.* McGaw *et al.,* 1989; Adams *et al.,* 1991; Review and Evaluation Directorate, 1991, 1993; Titmanis *et al.,* 1993; Quality Assurance Directorate, 1994).

All of the new monitoring programs in Australian education systems, including those that test only samples of students and those that test the whole cohort, have the capacity to monitor changes in performance levels over time for the system as a whole by calibrating instruments used on different occasions onto a common scale. This is being achieved by repetition of some items to provide the link necessary for the calibration or by special linking exercises in which items from both tests are used with a sample of comparable students in a different system. Various forms of reporting are being developed with one used in Queensland having been illustrated in Figure 3. This figure displays the reading scale and indicates the boundary locations for five levels. The distributions of performances of students in Years 5, 7 and 9 in 1990 and 1992 are displayed in a way that illustrates top and bottom scores for each group on each occasion as well as the locations of key points in the percentile rankings. This display makes clear the extent of differences, and the degree of overlap, in the distributions for students at different year levels and it also displays the extent of improvement for all year levels from 1990 to 1992.

Where all students in a cohort are tested, reports can be provided on individual students for the students themselves, their parents, teachers and schools. An example of a report to parents from the New South Wales Basic Skills Testing Program was given in Figure 5. Reports to teachers and schools in that program provide more technical details about patterns of performance so that teachers can identify unusual performances by individual students revealing, for example, surprising strengths or weaknesses, or unusual performances by a class group as a whole that might suggest particular strengths or weaknesses in teaching.

In the early announcements of the proposed new program of cohort testing in New South Wales, the Minister declared that the test results would provide helpful public information on the quality of schools that might guide parents' choices about enrolments. In the face of claims that the data could not be used sensibly in this way because the student achievements would reflect home as well as school effects, the Minister banned public comparison of schools with the data and further declared that data on achievements of students in individual schools should not be provided to the Minister's office. Other states now introducing such population testing have similarly ruled out the use of the data for comparison of schools.

Problems and critical issues

Widescale adoption of the national curriculum statements and profiles is in process. It is too early, therefore, to judge the impact of this approach to the specification of a curriculum framework in terms of intended student performance standards. It is also too early to judge how substantial the emerging benefits of a better link between curriculum and assessment might be. There are sceptics, some who doubt the technical feasibility of achieving the full benefits anticipated, others who doubt the motives of those seeking to define standards and monitor performance.

Purposes

Several purposes lie behind current attempts to set standards and monitor student performance. The restructuring of the curriculum framework can be seen as an attempt to specify the intentions of schooling in terms of what students are expected to learn. Linking of system-level, or even national, monitoring to the curriculum framework can be seen as an attempt to monitor the extent to which the desired standards are being achieved.

Where surveys of student performance levels are conducted using samples of students the purpose is plainly to monitor the system as a whole and, if appropriately large subsamples are included, its performance with identifiable subgroups of students, such as disadvantaged groups or groups differentiated by residence, such as rural and urban. Teachers' organisations and some parents' organisations often oppose formal monitoring of any sort on the grounds that any such system-level testing will be limited in scope and fail to reflect the full curriculum and that it usually fails to engage the professional judgement of the classroom teachers who know the students best.

Where full cohort testing is involved, one primary purpose is to report direct to parents and students themselves about the student's level of performance. Opposition to this form of monitoring from teacher and parent organisations has been based on claims that the information will be used to make unjustifiable comparisons among schools through the creation of simple league tables and on claims that the limited testing feasible in these circumstances will not match the rich information about individual student performance already accessible to teachers.

The opposition has not been effective in stopping any of the new initiatives to date. When the New South Wales Basic Skills Testing Program was introduced as the first of the full cohort testing programs in 1989, student attendance levels were higher than at any other day of the school year, despite calls from teacher and parent organisations for parents to keep their children at home. The cost of the opposition is not disruption to the assessment programs but rather a weakening of any effort at productive, shared commitment to the raising of standards and the monitoring of performance.

Marrying curriculum and assessment considerations

The Australian experience suggests that the best standard setting occurs when curriculum and psychometric considerations are married. Curriculum considerations alone produce *a priori* prescriptions of outcomes to be achieved which may be unrealistic in their level or their sequence. Psychometric considerations alone can yield a "dust-bowl empiricism" in which the data of student performance are sifted to find ways of imposing some structure on what is observed.

None of the Australian approaches was sufficiently extreme to constitute "dust-bowl empiricism" because even those which were primarily concerned with monitoring used instruments keyed to existing curricula. Those curricula, however, were not based on clear conceptions of student learning outcomes. The change in recent years to the specification of curriculum frameworks in terms of sequenced learning outcomes permits the development of assessment materials that reflect these desired outcomes.

The curriculum comes first and assessment second but assessment ought not to be entirely subservient in this marriage of the two. Specification of learning outcomes as a curriculum structure has brought a new clarity to debate about the purposes of schooling and of particular curriculum areas. Disagreement and debate have not disappeared but they have become more precise because specifications of intent are clearer. Some parts of the Victorian *Curriculum and Standards Framework* (Board of Studies, 1994), for example, can be read as an explicit rejection of aspects of the national profiles and promulgation of an alternative in an equally explicit form. When assessment materials are then developed to reflect the sequence of learning outcomes, the process can force both further clarification and elaboration on the curriculum specification. When the assessment materials are actually used, the student performance data provide the basis for an empirical validation of the structure of learning outcomes that may lead to confirmation or change. Temporally, curriculum comes first and assessment second but the relationship between the two needs to be reciprocal if the full benefit of a marriage of the two is to be gained.

Consistency of populations for comparisons

In programs monitoring system level performance, students in special schools are generally excluded. When system-level changes over time are being estimated, then changes in policy regarding integration of special education students into regular classrooms can affect changes in overall performance levels.

For the New South Wales Basic Skills Testing Program, special schools are excluded and teachers and parents are given the option of excluding special students integrated into regular classrooms. For visually impaired students, braille versions of the materials are provided and for non-English speaking background students, the material in numeracy at Year 3 is read out.

A problem can arise if serious attempts are made to shape tests so that particular groups will not be disadvantaged. It can, in the end, be unclear whether lack of differences in achievement levels reflects control of the instrument design to reduce the likelihood that they will reveal differences or the establishment of real educational equivalence of the different groups. Control of language so as not to disadvantage students from non-English speaking backgrounds can lead to systematic reduction in the complexity of the language used, the result of which is tests which have a somewhat denuded language content.

The international dimension

Just as it is useful for the Australian systems to have data on comparative performance levels of students in different systems, so it can be helpful to have data that permit comparisons with other similar countries. Data on the performance of Australian students in the first and second international studies of science achievement, conducted by the International Association for the Evaluation of Educational Achievement (IEA), were useful in revealing the maintenance of a steady level of performance in Australia at a time when performance levels in a number of other OECD countries were rising. Australia is now looking to the third international study for evidence of the position a decade further on.

There are, however, important problems and limitations with comparative studies of the type conducted by IEA, the greatest being one of differential curriculum validity of the tests used. When large numbers of countries are involved in such surveys, development of the test instruments involves inevitable compromises about content and coverage. There is always then the risk that international differences in achievement are simply compounded with international differences in test validity.

If the focus of international work were on curriculum specification, particularly in terms of outcome statements such as those used in the Australian curriculum profiles, and if countries had sufficient commonality of interest to yield usefully comparable specifications, then comparisons of student performance levels would be most useful. The key point is that international collaboration and comparison are most likely to be of value if they begin with collaboration, or at least agreement, about curriculum and proceeds to assessment only where comparability of curriculum is genuinely of interest.

Australian Education System

Schooling in Australia is compulsory from ages 6 to 15 (16 in Tasmania) and between these ages there is virtually 100 per cent enrolment. The structure of the formal education system in Australia is shown in Figure A1.

Most children start primary school at 5 and the majority of 4-year-olds attend kindergarten, normally part-time, before commencing primary school. Kindergarten programs, which are partly subsidised, are operated by local government and community groups. Generally, these programmes focus on structured play. A large number of 3-year-olds also attend a kindergarten or other pre-school centre. Programs for 3-year-olds are usually not subsidised and parents pay full fees.

Primary education lasts for either 6 or 7 years, depending on the state or territory concerned. In 1993, there were 1.8 million primary students, of whom 25 per cent were enrolled in private schools. The scattered rural population has necessitated a large number of very small primary schools, although this number is declining. All government primary schools and most private primary schools are co-educational. The primary school day normally lasts for about 5 hours of tuition and the school year for around 200 days.

Secondary education is available for 5 years in states and territories where there are 7 years of primary education and for 6 years where there are 6 years of primary education. One of the most marked changes during the 1980s was the increase in the proportion of students who remain beyond the minimum school-leaving age of 15 years. The proportion of commencing secondary students retained to the final year of school rose from 35 per cent in 1980 to 77 per cent in 1993. The secondary school completion rate is higher for girls than boys, largely because more boys than girls leave school to enter an apprenticeship. Almost all government secondary schools are co-educational, but the majority of private secondary schools are single sex. About 30 per cent of secondary students enrol in private schools, a proportion that has gradually risen since 1970. The secondary school year operates for approximately 200 days, with about 5.5 hours of tuition per day.

The tertiary sector comprises colleges of technical and further education (TAFE) and universities. TAFE colleges provide a wide variety of courses including pre-employment programs, apprenticeships, retraining and updating programs, and liberal adult education. TAFE is the most accessible part of the tertiary sector. In 1992 just over 1 million students were enrolled in award courses in TAFE. Just over 90 per cent of these enrolments were part-time and one-half of the students were aged 25 years or more. A further 0.7 million students enrolled part-time in recreation and leisure courses.

In principle, entry to many TAFE courses is possible after Year 10 but the combination of a tight labour market and rising school retention rates during the 1980s meant that many TAFE entrants have now completed Year 12 at secondary school. The nature of TAFE makes it difficult to calculate student-teacher ratios, but they would probably be comparable to those in secondary schools.

Prior to 1990 higher education comprised universities and colleges of advanced education (CAEs). Relative to universities the CAEs placed more emphasis on teaching than research. In 1988 there were about 20 universities and 50 CAEs in Australia. In 1990, the formal distinctions between universities and CAEs were removed and amalgamations stimulated by the federal government reduced the number of separate institutions to about 45. Since the late 1980s several privately funded universities have been established, but high tuition fees have limited enrolments.

In 1993, total higher education enrolments were just under 0.6 million, a rise of 70 per cent since 1980. Much of this increase was a flow-on from the substantial rise in secondary school completion rates noted earlier. About 50 per cent of Year 12 graduates enter higher education within a year or two of completing secondary school. Entry to higher education is normally based on academic results in either school or external examinations. Competition is fierce for entry to the more prestigious faculties and institutions. Provisions also exist for entry by people who lack a Year 12 qualification. In 1993, about one in seven commencing undergraduate students was admitted on the basis of prior informal study or work experience. About two-thirds of higher education enrolments are full-time and around 20 per cent of students are engaged in postgraduate study. Despite the rapid expansion in the system since the early 1980s, students are still drawn disproportionately from managerial and professional backgrounds.

Difficult economic conditions have focused attention on the provision of vocational, technical and business education. All governments have expressed a commitment to the development of more diverse and flexible vocational pathways for young people. These pathways are intended to allow the achievement of industry-recognised vocational qualifications through varying mixes of classroom instruction in schools, TAFE colleges and other providers, paid employment, and unpaid structured vocational placements. These new approaches to initial vocational education are intended to overcome limitations

Figure A1. **Structure of the Australian formal education system, 1990**

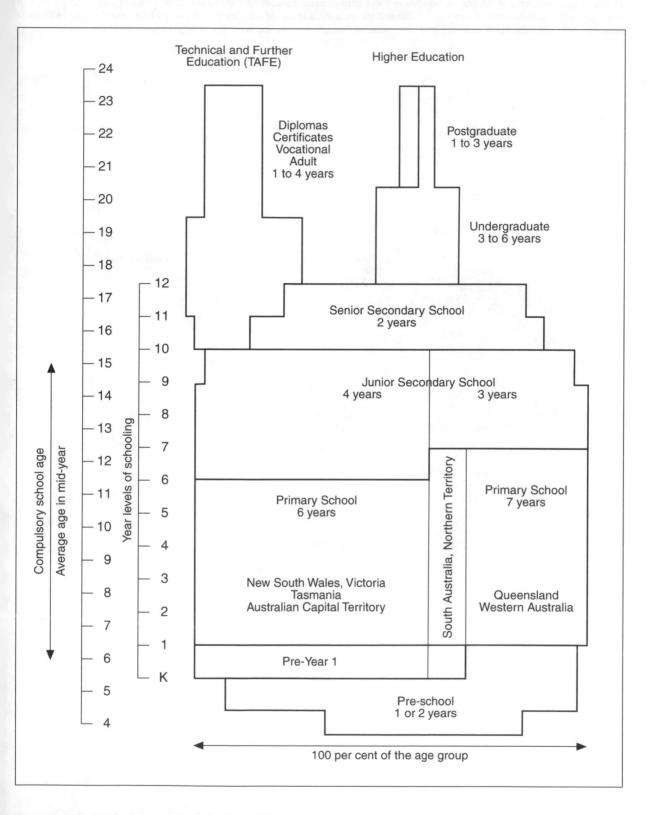

Source: Australian Council for Educational Research.

in the long-established apprenticeship system. The organisational framework for these initiatives is provided by the Australian Vocational Certificate Training System, which is intended to be fully implemented by 1996. It draws together a number of relatively new concepts in Australian education and training: generalisable employment-related competencies; recognition of prior learning; credit transfer; a national framework for the accreditation of training providers; and the development of flexible pathways between education, training and employment that people can use over the course of their working lives.

The Hobart Declaration on Schooling

The State, Territory and Commonwealth Ministers of Education met at the 60th Australian Education Council in Hobart, 14-16 April 1989, chaired by the Minister for Education in Tasmania, Hon. Peter Rae, MHA. Conscious that the schooling of Australia's children is the foundation on which to build our future as a nation, Council agreed to act jointly to assist Australian Schools in meeting the challenges of our times. In reaching agreement to address the following areas of common concern, the State, Territory and Commonwealth Ministers of Education made an historic commitment to improving Australian Schooling within a framework of national collaboration.

Common and agreed national goals for schooling in Australia

Ten national goals for schooling will, for the first time, provide a framework for co-operation between schools, States and Territories and the Commonwealth. The goals are intended to assist schools and systems to develop specific objectives and strategies, particularly in the areas of curriculum and assessment.

The agreed national goals for schooling include the following aims:

1. To provide an excellent education for all young people, being one which develops their talents and capacities to full potential, and is relevant to the social, cultural and economic needs of the nation.
2. To enable all students to achieve high standards of learning and to develop self-confidence, optimism, high self-esteem, respect for others, and achievement of personal excellence.
3. To promote equality of educational opportunities, and to provide for groups with special learning requirements.
4. To respond to the current and emerging economic and social needs of the nation, and to provide those skills which will allow students maximum flexibility and adaptability in their future employment and aspects of life.
5. To provide a foundation for further education and training, in terms of knowledge and skills, respect for learning and positive attitudes for long-life education.
6. To develop in students:
   - the skills of English literacy, including skills in listening, speaking, reading and writing;
   - skills of numeracy, and other mathematical skills;
   - skills of analysis and problem solving;
   - skills of information processing and computing;
   - an understanding of the role of science and technology in society, together with scientific and technological skills;
   - a knowledge and appreciation of Australia's historical and geographic context;
   - a knowledge of languages other than English;
   - an appreciation and understanding of, and confidence to participate in the creative arts;
   - an understanding of, and concern for, balanced development and the global environment; and
   - a capacity to exercise judgement in matters of morality, ethics and social justice.
7. To develop knowledge, skills, attitudes and values which will enable students to participate as active and informed citizens in our democratic Australian society within an international context.
8. To provide students with an understanding and respect for our cultural heritage, including the particular cultural background of Aboriginal and ethnic groups.
9. To provide for the physical development and personal health and fitness of students, and for the creative use of leisure time.
10. To provide appropriate career education and knowledge of the world of work, including an understanding of the nature and place of work in our society.

Bibliography

ADAMS, R.J. and S.T. KHOO (1993), *Quest: The Interactive Test Analysis System,* Australian Council for Educational Research, Hawthorn, Victoria.

ADAMS, R.J., B.A. DOIG and M. ROSIER (1991), *Science Learning in Victorian Schools: 1990,* Australian Council for Educational Research, Hawthorn, Victoria.

Australian Education Council Review Committee (1991), *Young People's Participation in Post-compulsory Education and Training,* Australian Government Publishing Service, Canberra.

Board of Studies (1994), *Curriculum and Standards Framework: Draft for Consultation,* Board of Studies, Carlton, Victoria.

CLARE, R. and K. JOHNSTON (1993), *Education and Training in the 1990s,* Background Paper No. 31, Economic Planning and Advisory Council, Australian Government Publishing Service, Canberra.

COLLINS, C. (1994), *Curriculum and Pseudo-science: Is the Australian National Curriculum Project Built on Credible Foundations?,* Occasional Paper No. 2, Australian Curriculum Studies Association, Canberra.

Commonwealth of Australia (1994), *Working Nation: The White Paper on Employment and Growth,* Australian Government Publishing Service, Canberra.

Curriculum Corporation (1994*a*), *English – a Curriculum Profile for Australian Schools,* Curriculum Corporation, Carlton.

Curriculum Corporation (1994*b*), *A Statement on English for Australian Schools,* Curriculum Corporation, Carlton.

Curriculum Corporation (1994*c*), *A Statement on Studies of Society and Environment for Australian Schools,* Curriculum Corporation, Carlton.

Department of Employment, Education and Training (1990), *Australian National Report on the Development of Education,* International Conference on Education, 42nd Session, Geneva, 1990, Australian Government Publishing Service, Canberra.

DOIG, B., K. PIPER, S. MELLOR and G. MASTERS (1994), *Conceptual Understanding in Social Education,* Australian Council for Educational Research, Melbourne.

Evaluation and Assessment Unit (1993), *1992 Survey of Basic Numeracy Skills of 10-year-old Tasmanian Students,* Department of Education and the Arts, Hobart.

FORSTER, M., J. MENDELOVITS and G. MASTERS (1994), *Developmental Assessment Resource for Teachers (DART): English,* Australian Council for Educational Research, Melbourne.

House of Representatives Standing Committee on Employment, Education and Training (1993), *The Literacy Challenge: Strategies for Early Intervention for Literacy and Learning for Australian Children,* Australian Government Publishing Service, Canberra.

KRAMER, L., S. MOORE and K. BAKER (1992), *Educating Australians,* Institute of Public Affairs, Canberra.

LOKAN, J. and P. FORD (1994), *Mapping State Testing Programs,* National Industry Education Forum, Melbourne.

MASTERS, G.N. (1982), "A Rasch model for partial credit scoring", *Psychometrika,* Vol. 47, pp. 149-174.

MASTERS, G.N. (1991), *Assessing Achievement in Australian Schools,* National Industry Education Forum, Melbourne.

MASTERS, G., J. LOKAN, B. DOIG, S.T. KHOO, J. LINDSEY, L. ROBINSON and S. ZAMMIT (1990), *Profiles of Learning: The Basic Skills Testing Program in New South Wales 1989,* Australian Council for Educational Research, Hawthorn.

McGAW, B., M.G. LONG, G. MORGAN and M.J. ROSIER (1989), *Literacy and Numeracy in Victorian schools: 1988,* ACER Research Monograph No. 34, Australian Council for Educational Research, Hawthorn.

National Industry Education Forum (1991), *Declaration of Goals for Australia's Schools,* National Industry Education Forum, Melbourne.

National Industry Education Forum (1992), *Improving Australia's Schools: Building a Foundation for a Better Australia,* National Industry Education Forum, Melbourne.

POSTLETHWAITE, T.N. and D.E. WILEY (eds) (1991), *The IEA Science Study II: Science Achievement in Twenty-three Countries,* Pergamon Press, Oxford.

Quality Assurance Directorate (1994), *Assessment of Student Performance 1993 – Aspects of Mathematics: Overall Results,* Department of Education, Brisbane.

Review and Evaluation Directorate (1991), *Assessment of Student Performance 1990 – Aspects of Reading and Writing: Overall Results,* Department of Education, Brisbane.

Review and Evaluation Directorate (1993), *Assessment of Student Performance 1992 – Aspects of Reading and Writing: Overall Results,* Department of Education, Brisbane.

ROSIER, M.J. and D.K. BANKS (1990), *The Scientific Literacy of Australian Students,* ACER Research Monograph No.39, Australian Council for Educational Research, Hawthorn, Victoria.

SAMUEL, P. (1976), ''Australia's education scandal: We're turning out millions of dunces'', *The Bulletin,* 15 May.

TITMANIS, P., F. MURPHY, J. COOK, K. BRADY and M. BROWN (1993), *Profiles of Student Achievement: English and Mathematics in Western Australian Government Schools 1992,* Ministry of Education, Perth.

Victorian Commission of Audit (1993), *Report of the Victorian Commission of Audit,* Melbourne.

CANADA (Ontario)

by

Lorna Earl
Research Director, Scarborough Board of Education

and

Neil Graham
Assessment and Evaluation consultant

Summary

In recent years, Ontario, like many other countries has been grappling with issues of assessment, perform-ance standards and accountability. Although Ontario does not have a long-standing history of standardized assessment or testing, there has been a ferment of activity in the setting and monitoring of standards since the mid-1980s. This activity has included a number of program reviews (assessments of achievement using sampling to evaluate the effectiveness of various curricular programs and provide information for focusing program improvement efforts), a literacy assessment for all students in grade 9, and examination reviews (routine checks on the adequacy of examinations and marking) in the final secondary year. At the same time, groups of educators are working to define outcomes and standards that are intended to serve as reference points from which the Ministry of Education, boards of education and individual teachers can develop a full range of assessment procedures for their own purposes. A key feature of the Ontario assessment landscape is the central role played by the assessment done by teachers in classrooms on a regular basis. Classroom assessment is seen as one of the critical elements of school reform.

The next few years will be important ones as Ontario tries to juggle the critical issues associated with changing social, economic and political conditions; with the role of teachers in assessment; with the complexity and difficulty of communicating with a broad-based audience; and with interpreting and using assessment results wisely.

The process of developing standards and ways of assessing performance in Ontario has been rather like a helix with a number of intertwined strands surfacing, having prominence and drifting to the back. Each one of the strands has influenced the other and taken together, they have had considerable impact on education in the province. At the time of writing, Ontario is at a crossroads. It remains to be seen whether Ontario will maintain the ''school improvement'' focus to developing standards or whether the intensifying public pressure will change the focus into a mechanism for controlling schools. Many countries appear to be arriving at a similar place from different vantage points. Hopefully, we can all learn from the experiences in other jurisdictions to capitalize on successes and avoid pitfalls.

Context

Education in Ontario

Ontario, like all other parts of the world, is in the midst of rapid political, social and economic change. Although Ontario is not unusual in this regard, it has its own unique history that has influenced the character and development of the educational system.

Ontario is not the largest Canadian province geographically but it is the most industrialized and has the largest population. It has traditionally also been one of the "have" provinces, with a relatively high standard of living.

Education in Canada is constitutionally a provincial responsibility. There is no federal department of education and the provinces have, for the most part, kept education very much within the provincial boundaries. This independence has been demonstrated by the involvement of participating provinces in international studies of education as separate "countries".

Funding for education comes largely from within each province through various kinds of taxation. In general, provincial funding is provided from a mix of general revenue and property taxes, and is delivered to school boards through formulas that take into account general as well as specific needs. There is variation across the provinces in spending per student, with Ontario among the highest (Economic Council of Canada, 1992).

Because there were a number of founding cultures in Ontario, there are several different publicly funded school systems (public school boards and Roman Catholic separate school boards, each of which includes a number of French language school boards), all operating under the jurisdiction of the Ministry of Education and Training. In total, these school systems serve approximately 1 300 000 elementary and 681 000 secondary students across the province in 170 school boards and approximately 5 200 schools (Ministry of Education and Training, 1993a). Local school boards are governed by elected trustees in each school district. The province is quite urban in the southern region with a number of large (50 000+ students) school boards in and around Metropolitan Toronto. In the north, the boards are quite small (under 1000) and scattered across great rural expanses.

Ontario is the only province in Canada that has a 13-year elementary and secondary school program (in addition to a possible two years of kindergarten). Elementary school extends from grades 1-8 and secondary is a four-year program, with three streams (tracks) after grade 9 to earn an Ontario Secondary School Diploma (30 credits). Because six credits must be Ontario Academic Credits (OAC) for entry to post-secondary institutions, most students who aspire to study at a university continue for an additional year.

Participation rates in upper secondary are relatively high in Ontario. In 1991, 91 per cent of 17-year-olds and 64 per cent of 18-year-olds were in school. This is a dramatic increase from earlier decades (e.g., comparable 1975 statistics are 73 per cent and 35 per cent) (Ministry of Education and Training, 1993a).

Teachers in Ontario are well-qualified (78 per cent of elementary and 93 per cent of secondary are university graduates), experienced (over half with more than 15 years experience) and relatively mature (1991-92 median age of 42 years) (Ministry of Education and Training, 1993a). All Ontario teachers are members of one or more teacher's federations. Collectively, these federations exert a strong voice on educational matters. Teaching is an attractive career in Ontario, with relatively high status as a quasi-profession. Unlike some other countries, there has not been any shortage of qualified teachers or of willing recruits for the teaching profession. In fact, entry to Faculties of Education is highly competitive, requiring high grades.

The history of assessment in Ontario

The Ontario context in relation to standardized assessment of student performance is unique. This is a critical starting point for understanding the ways in which the Ontario picture has developed. There is very little tradition of standardized assessment or testing of any kind in Ontario. Throughout the 1950s and 1960s there were standardized exit exams from grade 13 (departmental exams) in all subject areas and these formed the sole basis for entry to university. In the mid-1960s the results from these exams were coupled with teachers' marks for university entry. In the late 1960s the exams were discontinued and teacher marks became the basis for university entry and that practice has been in place ever since. Teachers had considerable autonomy to design their own exams and make judgments about the quality of student work. These exams were not moderated. For most of this time, teacher marks were an acceptable and adequate method of determining student placement, promotion and program (Russell et al., 1978).

In the 1970s and 1980s, some school boards chose to administer norm-referenced standardized tests at selected grade levels but the results were used only as additional information to assist teachers in making decisions about individual students placement or program and the tests were decidedly "low" stakes. On a provincial level, there was no testing program.

This history is quite different from the other provinces and from Canada's neighbour to the south – the United States. For example, Newfoundland has had a system of public examinations since 1893 with the range of courses and grade levels changing over time. In addition, Newfoundland has administered commercial norm-referenced tests since 1975 for accountability purposes (Fagan, 1994). Alberta has administered two provincial assessment programs: the achievement testing program, conducted with all students in grade 3, 6 and 9 in four subjects, since the early 1980s and a diploma examination program in 6 subject areas in the final secondary year, since 1984 (McEwen, 1994; United States GAO, 1993). British Columbia has had a provincial examination program for graduation (grade 12) that determined 40 per cent of the students final grade, since the 1920s (with a nine-year hiatus from 1974-83). They also introduced a provincial Learning Assessment Program in 1976 with a sample of students in grades 4, 7, and 10 to monitor student outcomes in the absence of provincial examinations (Hodgkinson, 1994). The United States, of course, has had a long-standing history of large-scale testing of many different kinds.

These examples draw attention to the fact that Ontario has been surrounded by neighbours who have been involved in large-scale assessment programs and in examinations at the end of secondary school. Particularly in the 1970s and early 1980s, when other provinces and many American states were expanding their assessment programs, Ontario had no central examination program and the provincial reviews that were begun in 1986 (described below) were typically done in just one subject area at one grade level, using a sample of students. Ontario, during this time, was leaving assessment in the hand of educators at the district level. Teachers were expected to develop evaluation procedures and examinations that measured the achievement of students in specified courses and programs based on provincial curriculum guidelines, as stated in this quote from a provincial policy document covering grades 7-12 (Ministry of Education, 1984):

> "For the most part, it is recognized that the most effective form of evaluation is the application of the teacher's professional judgement to a wide range of information gathered through observation and assessment. In order to help teachers evaluate student achievement, curriculum guidelines will describe appropriate evaluation techniques."

In the early 1980s, there was some evidence that the public in Ontario was beginning to lose confidence in the educational system. A semi-annual opinion poll found that about two-thirds of respondents felt that there should be province-wide testing (Livingstone, 1984). A provincial study in 1983-84 showed that there was considerable diversity across the province in OAC (Ontario Academic Credit) English examinations, a key element in university entrance (Ministry of Education, 1991). At the same time, the universities began asking for a return to province-wide examinations. These early indications of public concern prompted the Provincial Advisory Committee on Evaluation Policies and Practices and the Ministry of Education to begin exploring a variety of issues related to student evaluation, including a need to ensure consistency in the OACs. These deliberations resulted in several provincial assessment initiatives – program reviews and examination reviews.

The cry for accountability and standards

The late 1980s and early 1990s were times of tremendous change in Ontario. The demography of the province changed dramatically with an influx of immigrants from all corners of the globe; the province suffered a serious economic recession with unprecedented unemployment rates; and there were large political swings in both the province and the country. Educational institutions, which had long been held in high esteem, found themselves, along with other public institutions, facing a crisis of confidence. The pressure has taken the form of demands from both the general public who want to be assured about the quality of Ontario education and individual parents who want to be reassured that their children are going to succeed. A repeat of the semi-annual poll found that there were still ⅔ of respondents who wanted standardized testing (Livingstone and Hart, 1988). In 1988, the Premier's Council, an advisory group to the provincial Premier, reported that it "had serious concerns that the education system is not delivering value for the money it receives". They recommended, among other things, regular province-wide testing, strengthening public accountability through the reporting of the performance of individual schools and the province, and participation in national and international testing.

The concern about education was fuelled by Ontario's participation in several international assessments (*e.g.* SIMS, IAEP) and the recognition that the province's results were "middle of the road", generally scoring somewhere near the mean and below a number of the other provinces. These studies provided the impetus for a movement to raise standards and ensure a global position. The Economic Council of Canada spoke about all of the provinces when it stated, in its 1992 report *A Lot To Learn* that:

> "Canadians, as a society and as individuals must now give an urgent priority to improving the overall performance of their learning system (...) by setting targets and developing a series of indicators to help monitor progress towards these goals."

This period was also characterized by an increased concern about "equity" and that young people who were already disadvantaged were being further disadvantaged by their schooling and denied opportunities to learn (Radwanski, 1987). The Ontario system has historically reflected a commitment to equity of opportunity and recent policy initiatives have indicated a move towards "removing established barriers and biases in school policies, programs and practices so that the intended learning outcomes may be achieved by students of all societal groups, including those that have been traditionally disadvantaged'' (Ministry of Education and Training, 1993*b*).

At the same time, there was growing unease that many young people were leaving at the end of schooling without having adequately mastered basic skills and without proper preparation for entry to the work world (Premier's Council, 1990).

The increasing pressure of the accountability movement has had a dramatic effect on the educational community. This pressure was heightened when Ontario adopted ''observer status'' concerning the planned national test of 13- and 16-year-olds in mathematics and reading/writing being developed by the Council of Ministers of Education, Canada (CMEC). Public and media pressure, however, forced Ontario to become a full partner in the fall of 1990 and join a two-province consortium (Alberta and Quebec) developing these tests. To date the mathematics and language have been completed and science has been added. There are plans to administer these tests on a 3-year cycle.

In addition, it has forced the Ministry of Education and Training to modify its review process to accommodate a political desire to demonstrate accountability on a broader scale and signal the intent of the government to set high standards and ensure they are taken seriously. A planned grade 9 reading/writing review was modified to become a test to be taken by all 140 000 students in grade 9. A second grade 9 reading/writing test is planned for 1994-95, again for all students in the province.

At the same time, individual boards have begun or extended their local assessment programs. A number of boards have purchased tests from publishers. Other boards or consortia of boards have developed or are developing their own testing materials, in an attempt to match assessment with curriculum and to move beyond the traditional testing model that educators in the province have largely rejected in the past. Perhaps the most notable of these is the Toronto Benchmarks program, a very sophisticated combination of print and videotaped material that describes in rich detail what Toronto students were able to do at the time the Benchmarks were created and forms the basis for teacher training programs within the board and beyond (Larter, 1991).

The growing public concern about education generally and curriculum and assessment specifically, prompted the government, in 1993, to appoint a 5-member Royal Commission on Learning with a mandate to hold public hearings, undertake research and make recommendations for change before the end of 1994.

Because of the way the provincial assessment program has developed, it is somewhat fragmented. All of the various components have been ''under construction'' at the same time so there is no obvious temporal order. Nevertheless, there is some underlying coherence at the base of the different components. Throughout the past 10 years, this process has been moving, on a variety of fronts, towards the creation of a common set of standards and a system of related assessments and reporting activities, as key components of educational reform. The next three sections of this paper describe these different intertwined elements of the Ontario history. The Ministry of Education and Training is currently attempting to ensure greater consistency and coherence by developing an Assessment Policy Framework that will outline assessment principles and roles and responsibilities at all levels. The framework builds upon the premise that the various initiatives and assessment components that are created should utilize appropriate assessment instruments and procedures in order to ensure reliable and valid information on which to base decisions about policy and practice.

The process of standard setting

The word ''standards'' is often confusing in education because it has a number of different meanings. In this study, they are defined as ''indicators of quality that specify expectations for students''. If it is accepted that there are three different kinds of standards used in education as reference points (norm-referenced, criterion-referenced and self-referenced). Ontario is currently involved in establishing criterion or outcome-referenced standards. Since there has been no long-standing testing program, there are no empirical data to serve as measures of average attainment or as baseline data for comparisons over time. Instead, educators and others have been making informed decisions about the adequacy of student performance. Since the early 1980s this activity has been more formalized in the program review and examination review process.

- *Program Reviews:* In the mid-1980s the Ministry of Education embarked on a series of Program Reviews, using sampling, to evaluate the effectiveness of various programs and provide information for focusing program improvement efforts.
  These Reviews were presented as part of the Curriculum Review, Development and Implementation cycle (CRDI) that was being used as a model for curriculum renewal in the province (Ministry of Education, 1982).

The first few attempts at actually reviewing curriculum were focused on implementation of initiatives. A review would include observations in schools and self-report surveys of classroom practice, but there was no systematic collection of data about student achievement. Throughout the 1980s, the emphasis shifted from this focus on only the implementation process to an interest in attainment as well.

The review model that the Ministry of Education adopted was based on the Second International Mathematics study that included assessing *intended* curriculum (analysis of curriculum documents), *implemented* curriculum (teacher report of resources used, time use, instructional strategies, concepts covered, etc.) and *attained* curriculum (student performance on tests and performance tasks) as a basis for identifying weaknesses in program that can influence reforms in curriculum and instruction.

There have been 9 such reviews since 1986-87 (grade 9 geography, senior chemistry, senior physics, grade 6 reading, grade 6 mathematics, grade 8 mathematics, grade 10 mathematics, grade 12 mathematics, and grade 12 writing).

The tests used for reviews were designed to have high content validity and to match the Ontario curriculum. The early reviews that were undertaken included a large number of multiple-choice items to cover the curriculum and utilized a multi-matrix sampling procedure to distribute the items among the students. The grade 12 writing review took the form of a process-based assessment that reflected the normal classroom writing environment and permitted the use of available resources, including computers. Over 3-5 class periods, students were provided with a context and motivation for their writing, and they were able to work through the drafting and editing and revising stages and confer with classmates about their work in progress. In the assigned task, students were randomly assigned tasks in different modes (expressive, narrative, explanatory, persuasive) and were given a wide choice of the specific forms in which to write (*e.g.*, report, speech, letter, article). Students were also asked to select a ''best piece'' of writing from the writing they had done during the course. The papers were marked centrally, by specially trained teachers using a six-point holistic scale. The full scale is included in Appendix A. A sub-sample was marked analytically for specific features such as use of conventions of language.

– *Examination Reviews*: At the same time, the Ministry of Education began a program of examination reviews and teacher in service in the OAC (final secondary) year as a quality control device to ensure consistency across the province and to meet the need for greater accountability while providing assistance for the assessment and evaluation of student achievement and direction for guideline implementation (Ministry of Education, 1992). They are intended to provide a routine check on the adequacy of examinations and the marking that teachers use with graduating students.

All publicly supported secondary schools and inspected private schools that offer the particular OAC being reviewed participate in the examination review process. The process includes five stages, conducted over a 3- to 4-year period (Ministry of Education, 1992):

• *Research/data collection* – This stage involves an assessment of evaluation practices and the level of guideline implementation, through surveys and visits to a representative sample of schools.

• *Development* – A handbook on designing and marking the examination is developed based on the research findings for use in a series of in-service workshops for teachers responsible for the course.

• *Teacher Program* – A series of day-long workshops is held in locations around the province, for teacher representatives from each secondary school offering the course.

• *Review* – After a period of implementation, each school is required to submit a copy of their examination, along with three marked student responses, representing school consensus of ''high'', ''average'' and ''low'' achievement. An analysis is conducted by a provincial review team, of examinations and evaluation materials submitted by schools to determine the extent to which the examinations and marking are consistent with provincial expectations as outlined in the handbook.

• *Maintenance/follow-up* – Schools whose results confirm a high degree of implementation in the design and marking of the examinations are encouraged to maintain the high standards established. Schools whose results indicate areas requiring attention are expected to take steps to address these areas and information on the corrective action taken is to be filed with the Ministry of Education. In addition, local school boards are encouraged to establish their own OAC review process based on the Ministry model. To date, the OAC exam review has been conducted in 12 subject areas (English, visual arts, calculus, economics, accounting, French, physics, chemistry, geography, history, French as a second language and family studies).

Throughout the implementation of the program reviews and the OAC examination review, the focus and philosophy of the assessment agenda have been to gather and provide information that would inform program and lead to educational improvement. The assessments were *not* directed at evaluating individual schools or school boards and there was no intention of using the results to rank schools.

Teachers have been active participants throughout these assessment activities. They have been involved in the program reviews and the OAC examination reviews by developing assessment materials, conducting enabling in-service and assessing student performance. This is particularly true in the case of the OAC examination reviews. This process was initially conceived and developed by a teacher who was a head of English in a secondary school. He was concerned that the agitation from the universities might, indeed, prompt a return to provincial examinations and he felt strongly that the loss of flexibility in resources and instruction would narrow the curriculum and limit teachers' ability to adapt their programs to the students in their classes. At the same time, he was aware of the need for consistency. During a sabbatical leave from his board of education, he undertook at study of the OAC English examinations in the large urban school district where he worked and with a sample of schools elsewhere in the province. His study involved classroom observations, surveys, and an analysis of examinations from all of the English classes in the final year of secondary. This study confirmed the existence of diversity in marking and resulted in a document *A Resource Guide for Designing and Marking OAC Examinations in English.*

When the Ministry of Education was considering the ways in which they could improve evaluation in the province, they decided to adopt the OAC examination review model as one that was consistent with prior practice but would lead to more reliable results.

Teachers have also played a key role in developing and extending assessment practices within their own schools and classrooms. Student evaluation in classrooms has been a priority in the Province for over a decade. The policy document that governed grades 7, 8 and 9 – *Ontario Schools: Intermediate Senior* (1984) made varied and ongoing student evaluation a key ingredient of teaching and learning in these grades because of a recognition of the importance of learning how to articulate criteria as a crucial element in producing independent, self-directed learners. It stated "evaluation is not an end in itself; it is rather a part of the learning process for both the student and the teacher" (Ministry of Education, 1984).

The ministry has tried to support the assessment role of teachers in classrooms by commissioning teachers to develop the Ontario Assessment Instrument Pool – a series of banks of instruments and items that could be used in classrooms by teachers to assess their students. These Pools have been developed in the following areas: Language [Junior Language Arts, Basic English (secondary), French as a Second Language (grades 5, 6 and 10) and Intermediate English]; Mathematics (Junior Division); Science (OAC Biology, Senior Physics and Chemistry and Junior Division Science); Geography (Intermediate Division); and History (Intermediate Division).

The standards

Defining standards

In the early provincial reviews, standards were set by interpretation panels consisting of representatives of parents, teachers, school administrators, consultants, the business community and university professors. The first task of the interpretation panel was to decide what constituted "acceptable" and "desirable" performances on the test questions. The second task of the interpretation panel was to create overall ratings of student achievement by examining the standards they had set and the scores achieved by the students on each of the questions in the assessment booklets (Ministry of Education, 1990).

More recently, the Ministry of Education and Training has combined the need for appropriate curriculum and assessment and has embarked on a program of defining *a priori* outcomes for grades 3, 6 and 9 as part of the creation of a policy document that defines "The Common Curriculum" for grades 1-9 (Ministry of Education and Training, 1993*b*).

The Common Curriculum includes the following 10 "essential learning outcomes" (currently under revision) that are seen as cross-curricular and the responsibility of all teachers:

- communicate effectively for a variety of purposes and in a variety of contexts;
- solve problems and make responsible decisions using critical and creative thinking;
- use technology effectively;
- demonstrate a knowledge of the world and its system;
- get along well with other people;
- participate as responsible citizens;
- explore educational and career alternatives;
- apply aesthetic judgement in everyday life;
- make wise and safe choices for healthy living;
- manage their learning effectively.

In addition, the Common Curriculum defines 4 Program Areas (Language; Arts; Self and Society; and Mathematics, Science and Technology), with specific learning outcomes identified within each program area.

The Ministry of Education and Training has also begun the process of establishing standards of expected attainment for selected areas within these outcomes, beginning with mathematics and language (Ministry of Education and Training, 1993c and 1994a).

The Mathematics standards describe four levels of performance (limited, adequate, proficient and superior) for grades 3, 6 and 9 in the following strands of mathematics: problem solving, geometry and spatial sense, measurement, patterning and algebra, data management and probability and number sense and numeration. Each description includes a general description of what students can do in the mathematical area and a list of sample ''performance indicators'' providing specific examples of what students can do in the area. The middle two levels (adequate and proficient) define the expected range set for the grade. Superior performance is beyond expectations for the grade and limited is below expectations for the grade. A sample of the mathematics standards of performance is included in Appendix B.

The Language Standards describe 6 levels of performance (dependent, limited, adequate, competent, proficient, superior) for grades 3, 6 and 9 in the following domains: reading, writing, speaking, listening, viewing and responding in both English and French. A sample of the language standards of performance (in English) is included in Appendix C.

The Mathematics and Language Standards for grades 3, 6 and 9 have been developed by several committees representing teachers, consultants, speech pathologists, and school librarians, and in the case of the language standards, working in writing teams under the direction of provincial education officers. These standard setters were chosen to represent a broad-based group of educators with a vested interest in the standards. They spent considerable time reviewing materials and curricula and studying relevant theories to form the basis for creating appropriate standards. For example, the language standards committee drew on work already done in England, Scotland, some other Canadian provinces and some Ontario schools. The following table gives the principles for developing the standards identified by the writers of the language standards.

- The standards provide a high and consistent set of expectations for students, teachers and parents. They are designed to provide a description of performance at each level so that improvements required to move from level to level are visible.
- The language standards are based on the language outcomes (knowledge, skills, and values) for grades 3, 6, and 9 in the Common Curriculum. Standards for Viewing and Representing have been developed as an extension of the Common Curriculum.
- One set of language standards has been developed for all students, including students whose first language is not English and students who have been identified as exceptional.
- The standards accommodate Ontario's practice of age appropriate placement of students. The Ministry believes that the provincial standards should be used for describing student learning rather than for determining student placement.
- Although learning activities in reading, writing, listening, speaking, viewing and representing are integrated, provincial standards have been developed for each of these components.
- For the ends of grades 3, 6, and 9, a provincial language standard for each of these areas has been in terms of an expected range of performance. The scale describes six levels of performance, *with the standard (the expected range of performance for that grade being levels three, four, and five)*. Performance at levels one and two would be considered to be not yet at the standard, and level six performance to be beyond the expected performance for that grade.

These outcomes and standards are embedded in a curriculum policy that is based on the following principles (Ministry of Education and Training, 1993b):

- Learning involves developing values as well as knowledge and skills.
- Learning means asking questions and making connections.
- Learning requires effort and self-discipline.
- Learning builds on existing knowledge, skills, and values.
- People learn in different ways and at different rates.

The following box, from the standards document for mathematics (Ministry of Education and Training, 1993c), shows the purposes of, and relationships among, outcomes, standards, assessment and reporting.

Although the Common Curriculum and the Standards documents are considered to be policy in the Province, they have been released as working documents and have been distributed for use by educators and for consideration by other interested in education for validation and response. After a short while in the field, the Ministry of

Education and Training issues an invitation for response and the documents are revised based on the responses received in this process. The analogy to software development is current in Ontario to depict the response and revision process. Each version is seen as the current version with the expectation that feedback from users will form the basis for regular updates, much as software programs are routinely updated based on the needs of clients.

The outcomes and standards provide a reference point from which the Ministry, boards and individual teachers can develop a full range of assessment procedures to determine student performance, depending on the purpose. The outcomes and standards identified in the provincial policy documents are expected to form the basis for 1) large scale assessment and 2) classroom assessment conducted by teachers on a routine basis as part of instruction for both formative and summative purposes. Their primary purpose is to make expectations clear to teachers, parents and students (Ministry of Education and Training, 1993*c*).

At this stage, the outcomes have been designed to encompass a broad based common curriculum that serves as a starting point for teachers to develop their own plans for implementation in their classrooms that accommodate the diversity and the local needs of the students they serve.

The standards that have been developed so far are performance standards in areas of learning that are considered to be fundamental building blocks of subsequent learning in all areas. It is likely that other performance standards will follow in areas like science and social studies. There is no indication, as yet, that the Province will develop other kinds of standards like ''opportunity to learn standards'' or standards for evaluation practice, although they may be embedded in an upcoming provincial assessment policy framework.

The Ontario approach to the development of standards falls into the category that Lowe (1993) describes as ''setting targets into a broad framework of goals and content areas (while) leav(ing) schools with considerable latitude and not encourag(ing) active competition (among schools)''. The focus has clearly been on coordinating assessment with such things as in-service, curriculum reform, and changes in school organization, in order to raise quality across the board.

It is important to note that, up to now, this approach has been embedded in a broader model of improving schools that is undertaken by districts and teachers groups. Because student evaluation has been a major focus for learning for students and teachers, many districts and the teachers federations (unions) have produced extensive support documents, developed guiding principles of evaluation and provided many staff development opportunities. Some Ontario educators have also shown interest in the Principles for Fair Student Assessment Practices for Education in Canada as a useful tool for teachers in designing their classroom evaluation practices. A summary of this document is included in Appendix D.

Implementation

Assessing and monitoring performance

Provincial monitoring of student performance is a relatively recent activity in Ontario and has happened through the large scale program reviews, the OAC examination reviews and, more recently, the grade 9 reading/writing test.

Assessment activities in Ontario have historically been closely linked with the underlying purpose for the assessment. There has been a clear distinction drawn between assessments that have, as a major purpose, the improvement of program and accountability to the public and assessments that are designed to contribute to decisions about individual students. This distinction is embodied in two of the principles of assessment in the Common Curriculum (Ministry of Education and Training, 1993c):

- The evaluation and reporting of student achievement is the task of the teacher, who must consider the special requirements of individual students and work in consultation with them and their parents.
- The evaluation of school programs should effect improvement and should be based on school board and provincial standards.

These principles continue Ontario's tradition of honouring the classroom assessment that is done as a daily part of teaching and learning. This kind of assessment is still the one on which decisions are made about individual students, and, as such, is arguably the most important kind of assessment.

The accountability and program improvement purpose has been addressed through the program reviews and the OAC examination reviews. The stated purposes for reviews were: to determine how well students were performing and to provide data for program improvement (Ministry of Education, 1990). The purpose of the OAC examination reviews is: the achievement of consistency in the areas of assessment and evaluation (Ministry of Education, 1992).

Recently, the grade 9 test has extended the role of provincial assessment by moving beyond a sample to a census testing and by returning the judgments made by the central markers about student's level of performance to the students and their parents. This approach includes influencing decisions about individual students. The purpose is described as: to provide information to students and parents about the student's level of performance judged against provincial standards.The following are brief descriptions of the various assessment activities that exist in Ontario (some of which have been described earlier, in detail).

Program reviews

Levels of attainment are determined empirically through the program reviews based on a sample of 100 schools (respectively for English and French language schools). This process provides a report of the percentage of students who have reached the standards for a particular grade or program. The Ministry provided an option in this process for school boards to "buy in" and conduct a full board review. In this case, the Ministry provided the materials and scoring on a fee for service basis.

OAC Examination review

Consistency of application of the examination procedures and expectations for students are monitored at school leaving through the OAC examination review process and the concomitant teacher in-service (OAC-TIP). This process involves the development of a handbook that describes examination design and marking procedures for teachers, and details procedures for in-service of teachers. The Ministry also monitors consistency through province-wide sampling of examinations and marked student papers and alerts teachers when their examinations are not acceptable and requires a plan for corrective action.

Grade 9 Reading/Writing test

The grade 9 reading/writing test is a two-week integrated unit of work, including assessment activities that model good assessment practices. Teachers consider the students' work throughout the unit as part of their term mark and the writing portfolio and the reading test booklets are submitted to the Ministry for scoring against a set of consistent standards developed from the provincial standards. These scores are summarized in a provincial report, similar to the reports from prior reviews. In addition, the scored student submissions are returned to each student, their teachers and their parents, as a basis for discussion about the student's performance level in reading and writing and for further classroom follow-up. It is interesting to note that, although this test counted for 10-15 per cent of a student's term mark, the classroom teacher made the decisions about how they would use the material and the external marker's statements of performance levels were not to be used in this way, nor were they to be used for promotion purposes (Ministry of Education and Training, 1994*b*).

School Achievement Indicators Program

In the early 1990s, Ontario and 8 of the 9 other Provinces and 2 Territories agreed to participate in a national assessment being planned by the Council of Ministers of Education (CMEC), representing all of these provinces (the School Achievement Indicators Program). These assessments of 13- and 16-year-olds in mathematics, reading/writing and science, use a similar process to the Ontario reviews (*e.g.* developed by teachers, curriculum-based, sampling). Each of these national assessments is planned by a pan-Canadian team and identical assessments are conducted in both official languages. The mathematics assessment was completed in 1993, reading/writing in 1994, and science is under way in 1995. These tests are given in both official languages and are marked by teams of teachers drawn together in teams across Canada using specified criteria. There is particular attention to inter-language comparability. The results are reported for Canada as a whole and for each Province.

International assessments

Ontario participates in international assessments (IEA, IAEP, TIMSS) as a country.

Classroom assessment

Classroom assessment done by teachers has had a central role in Ontario in decision-making about program, placement, promotion and certification of individual children. It is the sole basis for these decisions and sometimes involves a number of teachers who are working with the same students, as well as parents. Classroom assessment is seen as one of the critical elements of school reform and teachers are being encouraged to improve their assessment procedures and align their instruction and their assessment with the outcomes and the standards. Over time, teachers are expected to internalize the expectations for student performance that are expressed in the outcomes and the standards and to use them as reference points for a wide variety of assessment tasks to determine individual student's learning and reporting to parents and others.

Reporting results

Although accountability has been a feature of most policy documents in the Province, public reporting about student achievement has not been a major part of Ontario's history. For the most part, the public seemed very satisfied with schools and education in general and there has not been, until recently, a perceived need to provide them with formal indicators of the quality of education. Since the emergence of the accountability movement, there has been more attention to reporting.

The results of Ministry reviews have been reported for the Province as a whole but there has clearly never been any intent to use the data from the reviews as an indicator of school quality or to rank schools. In fact, the sampling procedure that was used precluded disaggregating the data into smaller blocks and making any statements about boards and schools. The results of provincial reviews are reported publicly in several forms – an extensive full report, a 5-6 page provincial report card, press releases and board reports for participating boards.

The *Provincial Report Card* gives a "plain language" summary of the results that includes highlights, a description of the review process and questions, tables and/or graphs to show achievement in all of the areas assessed, description of student attitudes and of classroom practice and a statement about how the results will be used.

The OAC examination review is reported in two ways: a provincial summary report and individual reports to schools and boards. This is followed by a requirement that schools with non-conforming examinations or marking take corrective action.

Because the Ministry allowed school boards to use their materials and scoring service to do their own board-wide reviews, many boards received results for their district and for the schools within the district. This option made board level reporting more common. In fact, the Ministry required any boards that decided to participate in a full board review to report publicly. This reporting, however, was to be presented within a local context and not to be used for comparisons with others. The information was distributed to boards and to schools with the following policy proviso:

"School boards will be required to report publicly on their board results and to use the information for program planning and implementation. Public comparisons of individual school or board results are not appropriate."

This policy has been heartily supported by educators at all levels who were very aware of the many potential misuses of test results that had been discussed in American educational journals. They agreed that the results would be invaluable for teachers and administrators to use in their school planning and that they would focus improvement efforts but were somewhat nervous about the possibility of public reporting.

Both the Province and boards used a process whereby the interpretation was done in the context of the community by interpretation panels made up of groups of people who had a stake in that community. The provincial results of the early reviews received little attention from the media or the public. In 1990, however, when the results of the review of mathematics and reading in grade 6 were released, there was considerable media focus and since that time, there has been a mounting interest on the part of the public and the results of each subsequent review has been widely publicized in the media.

At the time of writing, only the provincial reports and board reports in the boards that participated in full board reviews have been publicly released. On several occasions, individuals from special interest groups hoping to influence education have requested more detailed information but it has not been widely disseminated. The conditions have changed, however, with the grade 9 reading/writing test. The results of this assessment will be reported in the same way that the prior reviews were reported but the census approach makes it possible to report for all school boards and schools in the Province. In addition, the results for each student have been returned to the school with the requirement that they be shared with the student and the parents.

This comprehensive data set is creating a dilemma for the provincial education officials. There is considerable pressure for school-by-school release of the information and for rankings of the schools. Although the Ministry of Education and Training has been operating with a policy that declares such comparisons inappropriate, the situation is complicated by another piece of provincial legislation. In 1991, the Province introduced a provincial Freedom of Information and Protection of Privacy Act. This Act specified that material produced by the provincial government that did not identify persons was open and accessible to the public. It remains to be seen how this dilemma will be reconciled.

Given Ontario's focus on classroom assessment, there is also another important kind of reporting – the reporting that teachers do to parents and students. Traditionally this has been accomplished through a periodic report card that included marks (in percentages or percentage ranges) and or anecdotal comments, depending on the grade level. In the early grades, this has been augmented by regular parent-teacher interviews or conferences but this practice has been less evident in the higher elementary and secondary grades although the policy document for grades 7-12 strongly suggests parent conferences as well as written results (Ministry of Education, 1984). The advent of the statements of outcomes and standards is prompting many school boards to revise their reporting procedures.

Problems and critical issues

Implications for school improvement

Although the effective schools research has improved the understanding in Ontario of what is important in "improving" schools, the focus in the Province has been on utilizing the results of such studies, not on determining the effectiveness of individual schools. The driving force for changing schools has been the Curriculum Review, Development and Implementation (CRDI) model put forth by the Ministry of Education (Ministry of Education, 1988a), with an emphasis on implementation and planned change. Studies done by researchers like Michael Fullan, Ken Leithwood and Andy Hargreaves (as well as others), who are based in Ontario, have been part of an ongoing research agenda in the Province. These researchers have worked in and studied many Ontario schools with a view to understanding the complex nature of the change process, particularly as it relates to schools. These studies have not had as their purpose to identify and publicize good or bad schools but rather have focused on broader principles of school improvement.

All of the assessment activities that have occurred so far in Ontario are consistent with this approach. The intent of the large scale assessments, the OAC examination review and the emphasis on classroom assessment is to provide educators with the kind of procedures, data and resources that they need to change their curriculum and their practices. All of the large scale assessments have been designed to include good instruction and assessment and to contribute to the CRDI process by providing teachers with models and examples that they can use in their classrooms. The reviews and the grade 9 reading/writing test include rich descriptive information about program implementation (*e.g.* resources, instruction, opportunity to learn) that can be used to change practice. The OAC examination review gives teachers direct feedback about how to improve their examinations to bring them into line with provincial expectations and the grade 9 test models good integrated assessment practices. The focus on classroom assessment and teacher training in this area is a clear statement that educational change happens when teachers are able to understand and implement real change in their classroom practice.

Critical issues: present and future

Standards and assessment are important issues in educational reform in Ontario today. They are the central elements in the reform agenda of the current Minister of Education and Training and they are also key areas for discussion (along with such things as teacher training, curriculum, and governance) by the Ontario Royal Commission on Learning that will make recommendations to the government in December. There have certainly been many changes in the last decade and it is likely that many more are to come. The following sections draw attention to some of the features of the Ontario experience that the authors believe are critical issues that may provide lessons that are useful from an international perspective.

Social, economic and political conditions

Ontario, like many other countries is a rapidly changing society. Because Canada is a large receiver of new immigrants from many countries, the demographics of the urban areas have changed a great deal in recent years. These newcomers enter an educational system that is already structurally complex, in that there are three distinct provincial school systems that are publicly funded – public schools (jk-OAC), Catholic separate schools (jk-OAC) and, where numbers allow, Francophone schools (jk-OAC). In addition, Ontario serves many special education students in regular classrooms with support from specialist teachers. This diversity highlights equity as an important assessment issue for policy-makers and practitioners alike and raises large questions of validity in assessment. Providing appropriate curriculum and assessment for these diverse groups is a difficult task.

The planning teams for the various assessment activities have had long discussions about guidelines for accommodating the needs of students with special needs. If the assessment is going to provide useful information about the amount of diversity in programs and students that exist in classrooms in Ontario, as a basis for planning, it is essential that all students participate. Teachers worry, however, that for some of their students, the assessments can be a very negative experience. There is also concern that teachers and schools where there are significant numbers of students with special needs will be unduly punished if there is public reporting of results. At this point, the guiding principle is that there will be full participation and that teachers may make accommodations for students who are still acquiring English. In a few instances, a student may be exempted from the assessment. Although the guidelines have been set for now, this issue is still one that is causing considerable consternation and one that we believe is likely to become more confrontational in the future.

Ontario has also experienced an extended recession that has led to dramatic cutbacks and downsizing in education (as well as all other public services). The department within the Ministry of Education and Training that has responsibility for assessment has been reduced drastically. Not only does this result in more work for fewer people, but there is also significant loss of continuity and shared understanding of purpose and rationale for the policies and procedures that are in place. We have been involved in much of the activity both inside and outside the Ministry of Education and Training and have seen programs falter because key individuals have left the Ministry of Education and Training. It has been very difficult, in recent months, for the assessment team to function with a tiny core of people and a number of "drop in" educators who are either recently retired or seconded from the field for short periods to complete particular assignments. This haphazard arrangement increases the likelihood of errors and also increases the stress level of the people involved. We hope that the recent signs of an economic recovery, albeit slow, will make it possible to establish a structure with more stability. Nevertheless, it seems to us that there is an interesting paradox here. When there is economic uncertainty, there is also increased public pressure for accountability and more attention on standards and assessment as solutions. Since these activities are relatively expensive, the government must find additional funds to support these efforts. Attempts to do this as efficiently as possible may lead to cost cutting with the risk of jeopardizing the adequacy of the assessment itself. At the same time, the funds that are funnelled into the assessment many have to be withdrawn from other school improvement efforts. When governments are faced with difficult resource allocation decisions, it seems particularly important that they plan carefully and identify all of the implications of policy decisions that they make.

On the political side, it has been difficult to establish and maintain an assessment agenda over time in Ontario. Since education is so deeply ensconced as a provincial responsibility, the federal government has very little influence on educational policy. Consequently, policy decisions and directions are closely tied to particular provincial governments and their platforms. It is very difficult to establish long range plans that will withstand the next election, even for parties that remain in power. Over time, this has resulted in a lack of coherence and continuity in assessment policies and no clear directions for the future. Instead, the decisions are more likely to be reactive and motivated by political and financial expediency. The current government (a socialist one) is trying to pull things together but the prognosis for their success in the next election is uncertain. Consequently, many teachers and even whole school boards routinely adopt a "wait and see" attitude while others jump into new initiatives enthusiastically and are disillusioned when they are superseded.

The role of teachers

One of the distinguishing features of the Ontario case is the widespread involvement and leadership of teachers in assessment and standard-setting activities. Educators have been involved in determining policy and practice, developing test specifications, writing test items and performance tasks for the program reviews, marking test papers, pilot materials and providing in-service to colleagues. Although the Ministry of Education and Training has been responsible for the provincial assessment activities, the planning and development teams have all been made up of educators seconded from the field, working with internal technical support personnel. All of the assessment activities have included teacher in-service as a major component. For example, in the grade 9 reading/writing test, every participating teacher received a one half day on conducting the testing process. In some cases, like the development of the OAC examination review process, a teacher or teachers have taken the initiative to create a process and convince the provincial officials of its value and utility. This ongoing involvement of teachers has increased teachers' knowledge of curricula and instruction and led to the direct application of the standards to classroom practice. This was exemplified by a Director of Education (CEO) in a school board who remarked that when teachers from his district took part in the grade 12 writing review in their classes and participated in the central marking process, they were so impressed with how much they learned about writing that they had volunteered to teach grade 9 for the grade 9 reading/writing test and requested a chance to be involved in the marking for it as well.

Teacher involvement has also aided in the development of tests that are compatible with good classroom practice. Although the tests are sometimes relatively complicated and take up considerable class time, many teachers are inclined to see them as good instruction and assessment activities that are worthy, in and of themselves. The tests have also had the endorsement of the teachers' federations who are all represented on a provincial Assessment Advisory Committee.

All of this teacher involvement has happened in a "low stakes" environment where they supported the provincial assessment directions because they could see the benefits for enhancing program, without hurting either students or teachers. They believe that good assessment is good teaching and view the testing activities as learning opportunities for their students and themselves.

One concern that is looming on the horizon is a mass exodus of experienced teachers who have been the recipients of the training and been involved in the development of Ontario's process. This will put a heavy burden for teacher training on faculties of education and boards of education in the near future.

Communication, interpretation and utilization

Perhaps the most interesting and unpredictable facet of assessment in Ontario in the next few months and years will be associated with reporting and using results. Good communication is more than just sharing what is known; it is the essence of accountability not only with the public but with the parents of individual students as well. Accountability implies trust, shared understanding and mutual support – conditions that cannot happen without open, responsive and regular vehicles for sharing information and a genuine exchange of ideas. Creating a forum for such an exchange is a massive task.

This task, in relation to large-scale assessments in Ontario, is both complicated and aided by the fact that there has not been a history of public reporting about education in Ontario. Educators are unaccustomed to sharing information with the public or with the media and are wary about it. At the same time, the media and the public has received very little information as a result of any provincial assessment until very recently and consequently, have not experienced repercussions, either positive or negative.

Because other countries, states and provinces have had long standing experience with public reporting, Ontario may be in the enviable position of being able to learn from these experiences. On the other hand, we may suffer from a naivete that will leave us unprepared for the reality of the political process that surrounds public reporting of any kind.

Ontario is in a transitional period where things are changing very quickly – some educators steadfastly maintain that public reporting, especially about individual schools is inherently bad; others are naively prepared to provide uninterpreted raw data to whomever wants it for whatever purposes; and, others, aware of the difficulties associated with public reporting and the likelihood of misinterpretation and misuse of simplistic reporting strategies, are looking for ways to enhance public understanding and guard against abuse.

So far, there has been no reporting at a provincial level that relates to individual schools or school boards. The Ministry of Education and Training has only reported about the Province, as a whole, and has left the rest to the boards themselves. Because only some schools boards used the option to conduct a full board review using the Ministry's process, local reporting has been very low profile. The grade 9 reading/writing test that is currently underway is the first time that the Province has actually had data for each school and school board. They now have to decide how these results will be reported and who will be responsible for the reporting process.

Moving from "low" to "high" stakes

It is probably obvious that a number of forces are converging in Ontario that are likely to make the work that is being done in establishing standards and assessing performance much more "high stakes", especially for educators and potentially for students. This shift will put Ontario schools in the spotlight, in a way that they have not experienced before. Already the editorial boards of many of the newspapers have established policies that support ranking schools in "league tables". We can see this period in the history of education in Ontario being rather rocky, indeed. We are faced with a number of imminent challenges.

One challenge will be to very quickly develop what Stiggins (1991) calls "assessment literacy". Very few people either within education or in the general public have any understanding of the principles or concepts that underlie assessment in schools. For the most part, scores on assessments (regardless of quality) are likely to be interpreted very simplistically and viewed as absolute entities (like money in the bank). Unfortunately, because there has not been an emphasis on assessment in the Province, there are only a few educators and academics with the kind of technical expertise or training that would allow them to influence policy directions or help other educators extend their own knowledge.

A second challenge will be to find ways to analyze, interpret and present the results of assessments in ways that are fair and take into account other factors that are likely to contribute to achievement, especially if school effectiveness is going to be judged based on scores from assessments. Although there are any difficulties inherent in doing "value-added" analyses (Goldstein, 1993), Ontario is hampered from the very beginning by the lack of any of the data that would make such analyses even remotely possible.

Utilization is the next big challenge. It is difficult to predict how the results will be used. The original purposes for the assessment activity were quite closely tied to finding ways to improve education, not by wielding a "big stick" but rather by identifying areas where change was called for. If assessment becomes a mechanism for controlling schools, it is likely that Ontario educators will react in much the same ways that educators have in other jurisdictions. They will find ways to improve the scores, not necessarily the learning.

All of these conditions, taken together, have the potential to contribute to polarization and a power struggle between educators as professionals and other forces over control of education. Educators are beginning to feel abused and unfairly attacked while some members of the public are feeling that they are being misled and denied access to important information and decisions about educating the children of Ontario.

Grade 12 Writing Review Holistic Scale

Level 6

The overall impression of writing at this level is that it demonstrates mastery as well as artistry. All elements of writing work together to create a seamless whole.

Typical Characteristics:

The controlling idea and its development demonstrate insight and maturity and a creative command of the mode. Organization is clear and forceful. The writer's voice is distinctive and the sense of audience secure. The syntax, use of rhetorical devices, and the conventions of language all reinforce the meaning. The overall style adds an element of artistry to the effect.

Level 5

The overall impression of writing at this level is that it demonstrates a secure command of the elements of writing. Generally the writing is integrated and the elements reinforce each other to create a meaningful whole.

Typical Characteristics:

The controlling idea and its development demonstrate maturity and forcefulness. The writer has a clear sense of the conventions of the mode and of audience, and anticipates the reader's need for sufficient detail and a clear and focused organization. The writer is sincere, but may not be fully engaged in the topic. A firm grasp of the conventions of written language is evident. Any occasional slips in control or form are not enough to distract the reader.

Level 4

The overall impression of writing at this level is that it demonstrates a grasp of the elements of writing, but that integration of these elements is lacking. Generally the writing exhibits solid communication but does not come together as a secure whole.

Typical Characteristics:

A controlling idea is evident and the piece has a sense of direction. The writer has a general grasp of the conventions of the mode as well as organization and structure. The writer is aware of audience and provides some direction for the reader. Expression, though reasonably clear, may be mundane. Occasional problems with the elements of writing, particularly the conventions of language may occur, but they do not unduly interfere with meaning or distract the reader.

Level 3

The overall impression of writing at this level is that it demonstrates both strengths and weaknesses in the fundamental elements of writing. However, the strengths outweigh the weaknesses and the writer's meaning is generally clear.

Typical Characteristics:

A controlling idea is evident. The writing displays the fundamental principle of organization; that is, the reader is able to discern a beginning, middle, and end. The sense of audience may be weak or lacking. The inconsistent application of the conventions of the mode and/or the conventions of written language may at times interfere with the reader's understanding of the ideas.

Level 2

The overall impression of the writing at this level is that it demonstrates a weak command of the fundamental elements of writing. Generally, communication occurs, but lack of command of one or more of these elements is foremost in the reader's mind.

Typical Characteristics:

There is a controlling idea which does convey meaning, but the piece may not continually be governed or shaped by it. Adherence to the conventions of mode is not secure and organization is flawed. The writer's voice may not be apparent or may be inconsistent, resulting writing that is uneven or unclear. Consistent and frequent misapplication of the conventions of language interfere with the reader's understanding of the ideas, but do not prevent it.

Level 1

The overall impression of writing at this level is that it demonstrates little or no grasp of the fundamental elements of writing. Due to this, communication is either fragmented or prevented.

Typical Characteristics:

The piece lacks a controlling idea or purpose. This results in writing that has little or no meaning. There is scant evidence of organization; instead the writer makes a series of random points that may or may not be related. The writer is indifferent to the mode of writing and to the needs of the reader. The writing shows little or no control of the conventions of language and numerous errors in usage or syntax make the text difficult or impossible to read.

Grade 6 Geometry and Spatial Sense: Standards of Performance

Limited performance

The student uses the language of geometry loosely to describe the world. The student is beginning to make discriminations among members of classes of figures and objects but is not able to articulate the comparisons clearly. The student demonstrates an emerging spatial understanding of the effect of motion in geometry.

Sample performance indicators

The student:

– selects a protractor when asked to measure or construct angles;
– estimates angle size within a reasonable range;
– recognizes and names two-dimensional figures and three-dimensional objects in a variety of contexts;
– describes the properties of two-dimensional figures and three dimensional objects using appropriate language;
– constructs a three-dimensional object from a drawing using appropriate materials;
– recognizes similarities and differences among two-dimensional figures;
– recognizes similarities and differences among three-dimensional objects;
– recognizes mirror symmetry in two-dimensional figures and three-dimensional objects;
– identifies congruent figures by matching;
– identifies lines of symmetry in two-dimensional figures;
– applies slides, flips, and turns to concrete materials to make designs;
– given a shape and its image under a single motion, identifies the motion.

Adequate performance

The student uses the language of geometry appropriately to describe the world and makes distinctions in classifying figures and objects. The student demonstrates an understanding of the effect of motion in geometry.

Sample performance indicators

The student:

– uses a protractor to measure and construct angles with reasonable accuracy;
– classifies angles;
– classifies two-dimensional figures according to angle and side properties;
– classifies three-dimensional objects according to face, edge, and vertex properties;
– constructs three-dimensional objects from given descriptions;
– proves that a two-dimensional figure has mirror symmetry by identifying the mirror line;
– creates a two-dimensional figure or three-dimensional object that has mirror symmetry;
– identifies congruent figures by measuring side length and angle size;
– recognizes slides, flips, and turns in patterns and designs in the environment;
– solves problems in geometric contexts that involve the direct application of learned concepts and skills.

Proficient performance

The student uses the language of geometry effectively to describe shapes in the environment and to discuss geometric ideas. The student understands the effects of motion geometry and creates related patterns and designs.

Sample performance indicators

The student:

- uses slides, flips, and turns to generate patterns and designs;
- visualizes and describes the effects of slides, flips, and turns, singly and in combinations;
- uses computer programs such as Logo to explore and apply slides, flips, and turns;
- solves problems in geometric contexts that involve seeing relationships between or among concepts and/or skills;
- generates alternative solutions to problems in geometric contexts;
- recognizes and describes the occurrence or application of geometric properties and principles in the real world and in other subjects.

Superior performance

The student has internalized the language of geometry and independently generates novel applications of learned geometric concepts.

Sample performance indicators

The student:

- poses and solves a wide variety of geometry problems that involve relating geometry to other strands of mathematics and to other subjects;
- draws inferences and makes logical deductions in solving geometry problems.

Grade 3 Reading: Standards of Performance

Level 1 – Grade 3 Dependent Reading

The reading performance demonstrates minimal control of reading. The student is able to read simple, predictable, familiar texts with support. The student listens to stories read aloud and responds when encouraged. The reading demonstrates a limited use of strategies to construct meaning independently.

Forms/Purposes
- requires support to identify variety of purposes for reading;
- identifies and uses familiar environmental print including names, signs and logos;
- reads simple predictable text in favourite caption books or enlarged texts, with some support.

Process of Comprehension
- uses pictures to retell a story or relate past experiences;
- engages in slow, deliberate word-by-word reading;
- recognizes a small number of words on sight;
- follows a text page by page, attempting to match his/her memory of the selection with the actual words on the page;
- requires teacher support in using simple cues from the text (semantic, syntactic, and graphophonic cues) to construct meaning;
- requires teacher support in using strategies (predicting, confirming, gaining information from illustrations) to construct meaning.

Response
- responds to stories ideas that contain humour;
- makes comments or asks questions about favourite texts or selections.

Features of Text
- understands the meaning cues provided by print features such as most letters of the alphabet, bold face print, enlarged print, and special arrangements on the page;
- understands directionality of print (left-to-right, top-to-bottom and the concept of a word as a unit);
- needs reminders to recognize and use punctuation.

Level 2 – Grade 3 Limited Reading

The reading performance demonstrates some control of reading. The student shows an interest in reading and is able to read a selection of simple texts independently. The reading demonstrates an ability to construct concrete meaning.

Forms/Purposes
- demonstrates an awareness of the purposes for which people read;
- reads to gain information, relying on teacher support to access library resources;
- ''reads'' picture books, and self-created material as a means of sharing experiences;
- reads an increasing variety and number of simple texts.

Process of Comprehension
- relies on familiar patterns in predictable texts to obtain concrete meaning;
- recalls characters and/or sequences of events from a story;
- uses simple cues from the text (semantic, syntactic, and graphophonic) to construct meaning;
- requires teacher reminders in using strategies (predicting, confirming, gaining information from illustrations) to construct meaning.

Response
- responds to a range of simple texts by joining in on predictable and familiar texts during shared reading, commenting and/or questioning during discussions;
- responds to texts by engaging in writing, talking, re-reading, drama or visual arts;

Features of Text
- demonstrates an increased awareness of upper and lower case letters, bold face print, enlarged print, and special print arrangements;
- demonstrates understanding of the sentence as a unit of text;
- demonstrates an increased awareness of the meaning and functions of punctuation (*e.g.* periods, exclamation marks, question marks).

Level 3 – Grade 3 Adequate Reading

The reading performance demonstrates control of the reading process. The student reads with understanding texts which are within the student's actual or imagined experience. The student willingly shares responses with others. The reading demonstrates an ability to construct concrete meaning and some abstract meaning.

Forms/Purposes
- reads material to gain information which is relevant and meaningful, making use of school library resources with assistance;
- reads favourite stories and poems and other materials with assistance;
- recognizes the main purposes for which people read.

Process of Comprehension
- constructs concrete meaning in a range of simple texts and makes some inferences and predictions based upon information from the text;
- uses background knowledge of the topic, sound/letter correspondences, and language structures to gain meaning from text and self-corrects when there is an obvious disruption of meaning.

Response
- reflects upon reading and records ideas or expresses understanding (*e.g.* diary, journal, picture-making, drama) about the main element of a story.

Features of Text
- uses titles, headings and other features of the text (*e.g.* illustrations, size of print) to identify key ideas.
- demonstrates awareness of the paragraph as a unit of text;
- demonstrates awareness of simple plot structures;
- demonstrates awareness of punctuation as a cue to meaning but may not always respond appropriately to punctuation when reading orally.

Level 4 – Grade 3 Competent Reading

The reading performance demonstrates a firm control of reading. The student reads with understanding and fluency when text is sufficiently matched to personal experience in a variety of classroom situations for a range of purposes. The reading demonstrates an ability to construct both concrete and abstract meaning.

Forms/Purposes
- reads a variety of informational material, making use of school library resources independently;
- reads a wider variety of literature for entertainment;
- demonstrates understanding of the main purposes for which people read.

Process of Comprehension
- understands concrete meaning in more complex texts and can make inferences and predictions based on information in the text;
- uses background experience, knowledge of language and sound/letter correspondences to identify new words, with increasing fluency and adopts appropriate corrective strategies (*e.g.* rereads, asks for help) when inaccuracies disrupt the flow of meaning.

Response
- relates elements of a work of literature to personal feelings, attitudes and experiences (*e.g.* identifying favourite character, word or passages).

Features of Text
- uses a table of contents and simple graphs and charts to find information.
- recognizes some specific aspects of an author's type (*e.g.* plot structure, repetition, characterization);
- demonstrates understanding of the purpose of punctuation and usually pauses, alters tone and inflection appropriately during rehearsed oral readings.

Level 5 – Grade 3 Proficient Reading

The reading performance demonstrates a fluent and flexible control of reading. The student reads independently, taking risks with unfamiliar material. The reading demonstrates an ability to construct both concrete and abstract meaning and a growing understanding of reading as a means of extending personal experiences.

Forms/Purposes
- demonstrates understanding of the range of purposes for which people read;
- reads more complex informational material;
- reads more complex literature that reflects many cultural perspectives (*e.g.* chapter books).

Process of Comprehension
- identifies main ideas, significant details, sequence of events and interprets the actions of characters in relationship to self and can distinguish fact and opinion;
- uses all the strategies of a fluent, capable reader and monitors own comprehension (*e.g.* predicting, confirming, self-correcting, adjusting reading rate).

Response
- responds to reading, reflecting on the main elements of a story, using various forms of creative expression to communicate feelings and experiences.

Features of Text
- uses maps, charts and other graphic displays to gain information.
- recognizes aspects of style (*e.g.* story structure, sentence length, the importance of dialogue in bringing characters to life);
- responds appropriately to punctuation cues.

Level 6 – Grade 3 Superior Reading

The reading performance demonstrates a fluent and independent command of reading. The student demonstrates an appreciation that reading is a means of learning about other people's ideas, experiences and feelings. The reading demonstrates an ability to construct meaning from the simple and concrete to some complex and abstract.

Forms/Purposes	• selects reading material for a variety of personal and academic purposes;
	• reads a wider range of more complex informational material;
	• reads and understands a wider range of more complex literature that reflects many cultural perspectives.
Process of Comprehension	• uses all the strategies of a fluent reader, adjusting the rate depending upon the purposes and nature of the material, persisting with a text that goes beyond immediate knowledge and skill.
Response	• makes comparisons and judgements about ideas, characters and events in more complex texts in terms of personal experiences;
	• uses reading as a stimulus for personal writing, discussion, drama and other forms of expression.
Features of Text	• recognizes techniques used by the author to deepen and extend meaning for their readers (*e.g.* use of metaphor, use of illustrations and graphics);
	• uses experience with reading to add new words and phrases to vocabulary.

Principles for Fair Student Assessment Practices for Education in Canada

Assessment, broadly defined, is the process of collecting and interpreting information that is used *i)* to inform students, and their parent/guardians where applicable, about the progress they are making toward attaining the knowledge, skills, attitudes and behaviours to be learned or acquired, and *ii)* to inform various personnel who make educational decisions.

Assessments depend on professional judgement. The principles summarize important factors to consider in exercising this judgement and in striving for the fair and equitable assessment of all students.

- Assessment methods should be appropriate for, and compatible with, the purpose and context of the assessment.
- Students should be provided with a sufficient opportunity to demonstrate the knowledge, skills, attitudes, or behaviours being assessed.
- Procedures for judging or scoring student performances should be appropriate for the assessment method used and be consistently applied.
- Procedures for summarizing and interpreting assessment results should yield accurate and informative representations of a student's performance in relation to the goals and objectives for the reporting period.
- Assessment reports should be clear, accurate, and of practical value to the audiences for whom they are intended.

The full set of principles and their related guidelines are contained in *Principles for Fair Student Assessment Practices for Education in Canada,* copies of which are available in your school or jurisdiction office, or which can be obtained from.

Joint Advisory Committee
Principles for Fair Student Assessment Practices for Education in Canada
Centre for Research in Applied Measurement and Evaluation
3-104 Education Building North, University of Alberta Edmonton, Alberta T6G 2G5

Bibliography

Economic Council of Canada (1992), *A Lot To Learn: Education and Training in Canada*, Minister of Supply and Services, Canada.

FAGAN, L. (1994), *Accountability in K-12 Education: The Newfoundland Experience*, Presented at the Canadian Society for Studies in Education, University of Calgary.

GOLDSTEIN, H. (1993), *Assessment and Accountability*, Parliamentary Brief, United Kingdom.

HODGKINSON, D. (1994), *Accountability in Education: The British Columbia Experience*, Presented at the Canadian Society for Studies in Education, University of Calgary.

LARTER, S. (1991), *Benchmarks: The Development of a New Approach to Student Evaluation*, Toronto Board of Education.

LIVINGSTONE, D. and HART, D. (1984), *Public Attitudes Toward Education in Ontario*, OISE Press.

LIVINGSTONE, D. and HART, D. (1988), *Public Attitudes Toward Education in Ontario*, OISE Press.

LOWE, J. (1993), *Quality, Curriculum, Standards, Assessment*, Paper prepared for US/OECD Study on Performance Standards in Education.

McEWEN, N. (1994), *Educational Accountability in Alberta*, Presented at the Canadian Society for Studies in Education, University of Calgary.

Ministry of Education (1982), *Curriculum Policy: Review Development, Implementation*, Discussion Paper.

Ministry of Education (1984), *Ontario Schools: Intermediate and Senior*, Queen's Printer for Ontario, Toronto.

Ministry of Education (1988*a*), *Curriculum Management*, Queen's Printer for Ontario, Toronto.

Ministry of Education (1988*b*), *Provincial Report: Examination Review – OAC English*, Queen's Printer for Ontario, Toronto.

Ministry of Education (1990), *Mathematics – Grade 6: A Report to Educators*, Queen's Printer for Ontario, Toronto.

Ministry of Education (1991), *OAC Examination Handbook – English: Language and Literature*, Queen's Printer for Ontario, Toronto.

Ministry of Education (1992), *Geography OAC-TIP*, Queen's Printer for Ontario, Toronto.

Ministry of Education and Training (1993*a*), *Key Statistics: Elementary and Secondary Education in Ontario*, Queen's Printer for Ontario, Toronto.

Ministry of Education and Training (1993*b*), *The Common Curriculum: grades 1-9*, Queen's Printer for Ontario, Toronto.

Ministry of Education and Training (1993*c*), *Provincial Standards: Mathematics – grades 3, 6 and 9*, Queen's Printer for Ontario, Toronto.

Ministry of Education and Training (1994*a*), *Provincial Standards: Language – grades 3, 6 and 9* (validation draft), Queen's Printer for Ontario, Toronto.

Ministry of Education and Training (1994*b*), *Grade 9 Reading/Writing Test: Detailed Administration Guide*, Mimeograph.

Premier's Council of Ontario (1990), *People and Skills in the New Global Economy*, Queen's Printer for Ontario, Toronto.

RADWANSKI, G. (1987), *Ontario Study of the Relevance of Education and the Issue of Dropouts*, Ontario Ministry of Education, Toronto.

RUSSELL, H., WOLFE., C. and TRAUB, R. (1978), *Interface: Some Cold Facts in a Hot Argument*, E + M Newsletter, Ontario Institute for Studies in Education, Toronto.

STIGGINS, R. (1991), "Assessment literacy", *Phi Delta Kappan*, March, pp. 534-539.

United States General Accounting Office (1993), *Educational Testing: The Canadian Experience With Standards, Examinations and Assessments*, General Accounting Office, Washington, DC.

ENGLAND AND WALES

by

Graham Ruddock
National Foundation for Educational Research

Summary

Performance standards developed for the English National Curriculum define eight (formerly ten) levels of performance. These levels are used to summarise the attainment of pupils up to age 14 in all the main school subjects. Specified levels have been constructed to describe the average performance expected of pupils at particular ages, a form of norm referencing in an otherwise criterion referenced system. The standards for each subject exist separately for discrete areas of that subject, such as reading or writing.

These standards were set by subject working groups, appointed by government, representing relevant groups such as teachers, employers and educationalists. Simultaneously these groups also defined the curriculum for their subject. The groups produced proposals to create or modify the standards and curriculum by a consensus model. There were no formalised or statutory procedures for the internal mechanisms of their operation. Proposals were offered to government, and were then subject to a statutory public consultation process and, after modification, passed into law.

The initial set of standards, and the accompanying curriculum, proved to be too complex and detailed, and not manageable in schools. Revisions have been made to reduce the number of criteria specified in the performance standards and to reduce the amount of classroom time required to teach the curriculum.

The descriptive standards were not constructed to a firm model for deciding precisely what degree of success on the specified criteria was required for the achievement of each level. Considerable work on aggregating performance across criteria has therefore been required, particularly in formal assessments.

The experience in England suggests that clarity of purpose and an appropriate balance between generality and specificity of criteria are essential. Manageability, particularly of assessment arrangements, needs to be a prime consideration when performance standards are defined and implemented. A system consisting of both performance standards and new curricula was developed. Rushed implementation and lack of opportunity to pilot such a system have been shown to be unhelpful, and to contribute to the need for repeated revision. The creation of multi-purpose performance standards has been shown to be a hazardous venture, with a very real danger of failing to meet any of the various purposes satisfactorily.

Context

This study outlines the procedures for setting standards in England, illustrates their nature and provides background on the education system. Comparisons are made with Scottish practice and that elsewhere in the United Kingdom where the differences are illuminating. Practice in Wales is identical to that in England unless stated otherwise.

The paper focuses on standard setting in school subjects such as mathematics and English. Extensive work is also being undertaken in the United Kingdom to set and implement national standards for vocational qualifications at various levels. These important developments are beyond the remit of this paper and are not discussed.

The education system

In England all pupils start formal schooling by age 5, but there are local variations in the age when pupils are admitted to school. Some are closer to 4 years old than to 5. Many pupils change school at age 7, while nearly all change school at 11. This phase, up to age 11, is usually referred to as primary education. Variations are due to differing local practices in the age groups taught by particular schools. Compulsory education ends at age 16, while those who stay on at school mostly leave at age 18. Education for the 11 to 18 age range is usually described as secondary education. The titles primary and secondary education are not always used when transfer takes place other than at age 11 or for institutions teaching only 16- to 18-year-olds.

All of these ages when substantial numbers of pupils change or leave school (7, 11, 16 and 18), are the subject of formal assessment. The formal assessments at ages 16 and 18 are well established and are often referred to as public examinations. Traditionally the courses taken at the end of compulsory schooling, age 16, are selected at age 14. This point is also one where formal assessment takes place. The formal assessments coincide with the ends of the key stages in the National Curriculum (see Table 1).

Table 1. **Formal assessment in the English school system**

Age	Year	End of key stage	Assessment
7	Y2	1	National tests
11	Y6	2	National tests
14	Y9	3	National tests
16	Y11	4	General Certificate of Secondary Education (GCSE)
18	Y13	Post 16	A-Level (Advanced level)

Source: National Foundation for Educational Research.

Assessment up to age 14 is made on the basis of awarding levels of the National Curriculum. For ages 16 and 18 the existing public examination system, where lettered grades are awarded, is being retained. Current developments include extensive work to make vocationally oriented courses more widely available as alternatives to the academically oriented A-Level courses.

Most schools are maintained, controlled and funded by Local Education Authorities. The majority of the funding still, however, comes from central government to the Local Education Authorities rather than accruing from local taxes. A growing number of schools are now "Grant Maintained" directly by central government, having opted out of local control. This is a recent development. There are also Independent Schools (including "Public Schools") which are privately funded and are free to ignore the National Curriculum if they wish to do so. In practice most pay some adherence to the National Curriculum.

It should be noted that there has been no tradition in the British systems of pupils needing to achieve particular standards before progressing from one grade to the next. Pupils progress by age, with the term grade not used and classes identified as part of the year group of which they are a part. Between them, the classes in a year group therefore cover the full range of attainment to be expected at that age.

Within each year group pupils are often grouped into classes by attainment level either for all subjects ("streaming"), or, more commonly, for particular subjects ("setting"). These practices grow in frequency as pupils progress through secondary school, and setting is very common for the 14 to 16 age group. Where setting or streaming are not carried out pupils often work in groups selected by ability within each class, particularly up to age 11.

As a consequence of this age related progression from class to class, differences in attainment between pupils, whether formally assessed against national criteria or not, are dealt with by the setting, streaming or within-class grouping methods outlined above. All of these methods are intended to match the curriculum offered to the attainment level of pupils, but by grouping together pupils of the same age and attainment level rather than grouping pupils by attainment irrespective of age.

Grouping pupils by age rather than grade is the norm for United Kingdom education systems in general, but ages of transfer vary. In Scotland, for example, primary education lasts 7 years (P1 to P7) with four years in secondary education (S1 to S4) as opposed to six years in primary and five years in secondary in England.

Reasons for concern

The development of a National Curriculum for England can be traced back to the events which culminated in the 1988 Education Reform Act. Several factors can be identified as contributing to the introduction of a National Curriculum which included performance standards.

Accountability of publicly funded institutions in general, and therefore of the education system, has been a more prominent political issue in recent years. The development of national standards against which the performance of individual schools, and schools in particular areas, can be measured has been a natural result of such concerns. There had previously been no consistent data on which to evaluate the performance of pupils below age 16 by school and local area.

A distinctive feature of the education system also contributed to the introduction of the National Curriculum. Before the introduction of the National Curriculum there had been no national syllabus in England for pupils of any age. The headteacher of a school could, in theory at least, decide the curriculum for that school. In practice, however, there were pressures and constraints in the system which led to a great deal of conformity, although not to the extent now present in publicly funded schools since the advent of the National Curriculum.

For pupils in the 14-16 age range the chief constraint was the public examination system at age 16. Different syllabuses and associated examinations were offered by the examining authorities for the two-year course for each subject. There are currently four different examining authorities in England. They are independent bodies, and although they have regional identities schools can and do select which authority to use for their public examinations. Wales, Scotland and Northern Ireland, in contrast, each have only one examining authority. In practice the examinations on offer for a particular subject had much in common and led to a fairly consistent curriculum for a particular subject for this age range. Thus in mathematics and English, where most pupils sat public examinations, there was reasonable consistency between pupils in what was studied.

The curriculum outside mathematics and English tended to vary more, since there was a considerable choice of subjects and pupils could, and did, chose whether or not to take examinations in subjects such as the sciences, modern foreign languages, history and geography. There were, therefore, considerable differences between pupils in the curriculum they studied, since the general pattern was that if a subject was not to be taken in a public examination by a pupil, then that pupil would not be taught that subject between the ages of 14 and 16.

Below age 14 the public examinations influenced the curriculum to a lesser extent. Most pupils between the ages of 11 and 14 were already in the secondary schools where they would take these examinations at age 16. The curriculum for this age group was therefore usually designed to prepare pupils so that they could go on to take the subjects of their choice from an appropriate starting point of skills, concepts and knowledge at age 14. There was, however, considerable scope for variation between schools and schools took advantage of this freedom.

The examinations at age 16 exerted minimal influence, and more freedom was available to primary schools to vary the curriculum. One pressure for conformity arose from Local Education Authorities, which usually offered guidelines as to what should be taught to pupils in the most commonly taught subjects, such as mathematics. These guidelines were recommendations and could not be enforced.

There were also pressures from secondary schools to standardise the curriculum in the local primary schools feeding them pupils at age 11. Again such standardisation could not be enforced and transfer arrangements were sometimes haphazard. The documentation on what pupils had studied and achieved in their former school varied in both quality and quantity.

A third factor leading to similarities in curriculum was the availability of published textbooks. Different books were available for all subjects, none being compulsory. There was often much in common between different series of books, but there were always differences in curriculum coverage, emphasis and approach.

The theoretical freedom to vary the curriculum at will was therefore constrained, and increasingly so for older pupils by the public examinations at age 16. There remained a considerable amount of freedom for schools, particularly with regard to which subjects a pupil should study.

Concern over standards of performance in schools has been expressed for many years. Two views have recurred, that standards of performance have fallen or that they have not risen sufficiently to met the current needs of the nation. These views have seldom been supported by firm, objective evidence, and that which is available is discussed below (see "Differences in Achievement"). It should, however, be noted that perceptions that standards have fallen, or are not high enough, are important in themselves and can lead to changes in education systems whether or not they are well founded.

In recent years a further factor has been concern over the performance of lower attaining pupils. This has been strengthened by the findings of international surveys in which England has participated.

Three issues, concerns over standards and accountability and the lack of a uniform curriculum for all, can thus be seen as central in leading to the introduction of a compulsory curriculum including performance standards. The purposes for its introduction can be summarised as attempting to meet the concerns outlined above:

- To define a statutory curriculum common to all pupils in government funded schools.
- To define performance standards against which the progress of pupils can be judged and the performance of schools therefore evaluated.
- To develop and administer compulsory national tests for selected ages to provide the data needed for this evaluation.
- To raise standards of performance, and to be able to measure the extent to which this is being achieved.

A brief history of the introduction of the National Curriculum

As part of the process which included the passing into law of the Education Reform Act in 1988, the ideas behind the National Curriculum were formalised and then put into operation.

Prior to the passing of the Act, a committee, the Task Group on Assessment and Testing, was set up. This reported to the government in December 1987 and outlined a structure for the curriculum and its performance standards which was largely accepted.

Following this, working parties were set up for each National Curriculum subject. These working parties then defined the curriculum for their subject and the accompanying performance standards. After consultation and revision these new curricula and standards were given legal status and implemented in phases. As part of this implementation process compulsory national tests were developed. The first phase consisted of mathematics, English and science for the five to seven age range.

The introduction highlighted problems with the system and the mathematics and science curricula were revised in order to reduce their complexity. New versions of the curricula and standards for these subjects were introduced in 1991. Further experience of the system, with more subjects implemented and more age groups involved, demonstrated the need for further simplification and revision.

Consultation on the consequent proposals for a revised version of both curriculum and performance standards for all National Curriculum subjects was carried out in 1994. Proof copies of the revised version were available in November 1994, with final publication and distribution to schools scheduled for January 1995. For 5-14-year-olds the revised version was to be implemented in August 1995; implementation for 14-16-year-olds will follow one year later.

Differences in achievement

Given that concern over standards of performance has been a continuing feature of the system, it seems surprising that there is comparatively little sound evidence on changes in performance in England. The best evidence was that produced by the Assessment of Performance Unit (APU), set up by the central government. National surveys were carried out between 1978 and 1988. These were on a large scale in mathematics, science and English. Smaller scale work was also undertaken on modern foreign languages and design and technology.

Light sampling was used by the APU, with the names of the participating schools and pupils not published. It was thus possible to use the same items over time and to monitor standards of performance over time by this means.

The approach also allowed considerable curriculum coverage to be obtained, since each pupil took only a small proportion of the items used at any one time. Because of this it was also possible to assess those areas of the curriculum where one-to-one or other time consuming or expensive assessment methods were required. Assessments of oracy, practical mathematics, experimental science, investigations and problem solving were therefore able to be included.

The APU data played a part in the establishment of the National Curriculum, usually via the inclusion of an educational researcher in each subject working party. The input was not always, however, as large as those who had developed the APU assessments felt would have been desirable.

A wealth of evidence is available on performance by region, gender, age, and other variables. Most pertinent here are the data on trends in performance over time.

This evidence, and that available from other sources, were summarised in a briefing paper prepared by staff at the National Foundation for Educational research in England and Wales. This is reprinted in the appendix. The focus is on literacy and numeracy, and since standards of performance in these basics are central to policy interests, the findings on changes in performance are reproduced below. These were:

- Reading standards among 11- and 15-year-olds have changed little since 1945, apart from slight rises around 1950 and in the 1980s. Among 7-8-year-olds, however, standards fell slightly in the late 1980s. In writing performance, there was no overall change during the 1980s.
- British school students are above average in geometry and statistics, but below average in number skills, compared with other industrialised countries. Britain also has a wider spread of mathematics attainment, mainly due to the weaker performance of lower attaining pupils.
- Nationally, there was a fall in attainment among 11- and 15-year-olds in number skills between 1982 and 1987, and a rise in geometry, statistics and measures.

The results of public examinations at ages 16 and 18 are published each year, and any changes in the distributions of grades awarded are the subject of public debate. The difficulty levels of papers from year to year are scrutinised by a government agency, as are the procedures for awarding grades.

The questions set are different every year, and the maintenance of difficulty levels is approached in two main ways. Traditionally these methods have not been publicly documented, but the government has now developed and implemented a mandatory code of practice, which summarises the procedures used.

The papers completed by students awarded a particular grade in one year are checked against those produced by students awarded the same grade in previous years to ascertain whether the quality of understanding and skills demonstrated is comparable. The method is judgmental, involving examiners in a committee structure. There are also statistical mechanisms to check that the number of marks needed for the award of a grade in one year is in line with that required in previous years. This cannot be constant, however, since papers are not trialled and often differ in difficulty from one year to the next. The public examination system is not well suited to monitoring change in performance over time, particularly if any change is gradual or if the curriculum is changing.

It should be noted that systems for statistically calibrating items so that they are on the same scale of difficulty, and thus those of equivalent difficulty can be identified, have not won complete acceptance in England and are not used in the public examination system. Similarly, statistical equating methods are not routinely applied.

Concern over standards of performance has, in spite of the lack of convincing evidence of a fall in standards, been a strong factor in the development of a National Curriculum. The international comparative evidence has fuelled concerns about whether standards of performance are high enough, irrespective of whether they are changing. Taken together the pressure for a nationally prescribed curriculum designed to raise standards has been strong enough to lead to its introduction.

The standards

A brief history of the introduction of the National Curriculum was given in the previous section, together with a summary of evidence on differences in achievement. The nature of the curriculum and its standards is outlined before the process of constructing both is analysed below.

The subjects covered by the National Curriculum are mathematics, English, science, design and technology, information technology, geography, history, modern foreign languages, art, music and physical education. In Wales the Welsh language, as both a first and second language, also forms part of the National Curriculum. (Religious education was compulsory before the introduction of the National Curriculum and continues to be so.) The most common school subjects are therefore included.

For each subject the National Curriculum specifies both the curriculum which must be taught for each key stage and levels of performance, currently 1 to 10, with an expected relationship with age suggested. The average seven-year-old is expected to be at level 2, with progress expected to be an average of one level every two years. Figure 1 shows the expected distributions of National Curriculum levels by age posited by the Task Group on Assessment and Testing (TGAT) which made the initial proposals for the assessment system.

Figure 1. **Expected distribution of national curriculum levels by age**

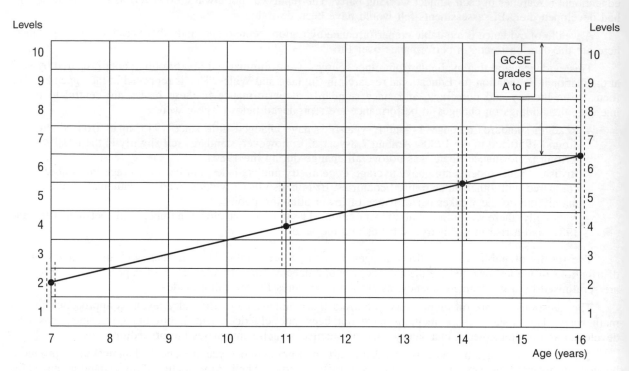

Source: Task Group on Assessment and Testing (TGAT).

Each subject is divided into *attainment targets* by either content area (such as Handling Data), process area (such as Using and Applying Mathematics) or a combination of the two. Each level of each attainment target is currently defined by a series of *statements of attainment*. These vary in scope, ranging from highly specific to relatively general. The number of statements defining a level varies from level to level both within and across attainment targets. This model is essentially atomistic, with small elements of performance defined, and descriptive, with particular levels being the expectation for average attainers at given ages.

In mathematics, for example, level 5 of Number is currently defined by four statements of attainment:

Number: Level 5

a) Use an appropriate non-calculator method to multiply or divide two numbers.
b) Find fractions or percentages of quantities.
c) Refine estimations by "trial and improvement" methods.
d) Use units in context.

The mathematics statements are amplified in an accompanying ***programme of study,*** and examples of tasks matching the statements are also provided. For statement *d)* at level 5 these three elements of the system are:

– Using Imperial units still in daily use and knowing their rough metric equivalents.
  Use in estimating, that 1kg is about 2lb, 8km is approximately 5 miles, 1 litre is about 1.75 pints.
– Converting one metric unit to another.
  Work out that 2.4kg is equivalent to 2 400g.
– Using negative numbers in context, including ordering, addition, subtraction and simple multiplication and division.
  Calculate the increase in temperature from –4°C (4 degrees of frost) to +10°C.

It should be noted that the statements of attainment and programmes of study are statutory, part of the law under the Education Reform Act of 1988, while the examples (in italics) are non-statutory and for guidance only.

The statements shown illustrate the range of assessment modes required for fully valid and reliable assessment. At level 5 statement *c)* is difficult to test in a short item format, and statement *d)* could best be assessed using real objects. Statements at other levels require mental computation, calculation with or without a calculator, conducting surveys, use of computers or making models.

The same subject also demonstrates the variation in the number of statements defining a level; level 9 of Number currently has two statements and level 10 only one:

Number: Level 9

a) Distinguish between rational and irrational numbers.
b) Understand the significance of approximations.

Number: Level 10

a) Determine the possible effects of errors on calculations.

The statements for English also require a range of assessment modes. The current level 5 statements for reading and writing are shown below.

Reading: Level 5

a) Demonstrate, in talking and writing about a range of stories and poems which they have read, an ability to explain preferences.
   Make simple comparisons between stories or poems; offer justification for personal preference.
b) Demonstrate, in talking or writing about fiction, poetry, non-fiction and other texts that they are developing their own views and can support them by reference to some details in the text.
   Discuss character, action, fact and opinion, relating them to personal experience.
c) Show in discussion that they can recognise whether subject matter in non-literary and media texts is presented as fact or opinion.
   Look for indications which suggest the difference; whether evidence is offered or whether persuasion is used in the absence of facts.
d) Select reference books and other information materials and use organisational devices to find answers to their own questions and those of others.
   Decide what information is required for a project on a topic of their own choice and locate it by reference to chapter titles, subheadings, typefaces, symbol keys, etc.
e) Show through discussion an awareness of a writer's choice of particular words and phrases and the effect on the reader.
   Recognise puns, word play, unconventional spellings and the placing together of pictures and text.

Writing: Level 5

a) Write in a variety of forms for a range of purposes and audiences, in ways which attempt to engage the interest of the reader.
   Write notes, letters, instructions, stories and poems in order to plan, inform, explain, entertain and express attitudes or emotions.
b) Produce, independently, pieces of writing in which the meaning is made clear to the reader and in which organisational devices and sentence punctuation, including commas and the setting out of direct speech, are generally accurately used.
   Make use of layout, headings, paragraphs and verse structure; make use of the comma.
c) Demonstrate increased effectiveness in the use of Standard English (except in contexts where non-standard forms are needed for literary purposes) and show an increased differentiation between speech and writing.
   Understand that non-standard forms for literary purposes might be required in dialogue, in a story or playscript; use constructions which reduce repetition.
d) Assemble ideas on paper or on a VDU, individually or in discussion with others, and show evidence of an ability to produce a draft from them and then to revise and redraft as necessary.
   Draft a story, a script, a poem, a description or a report.
e) Show in discussion the ability to recognise variations in vocabulary according to purpose, topic and audience and whether language is spoken or written, and use them appropriately in their writing.
   Discuss the use of slang in dialogue and narrative in a published text and in their own writing, and comment on its appropriateness.

In reading the requirements include having read a range of types of text and both talking and writing about aspects of what has been read. Similarly, in writing there is again stress on variety – for different purposes and audiences for example. In English the programmes of study are related to key stages rather than to levels as in mathematics.

The attainment targets and statements of attainment cover both formally administered and externally set *National tests* and the ongoing internal assessment to be made and recorded by teachers – *teacher assessment.* An important consideration in the construction of this version of the National Curriculum was that good classroom practice in the subject concerned should be encouraged. The statements of attainment are thus wide-ranging and include many aspects which cannot be assessed easily or economically, particularly with timed pencil and paper tests – they are more suited to ongoing teacher assessment. The fear of "what you test is what you get" in the classroom was strong, and the attainment targets and statements were designed to avoid narrowing the curriculum.

The National Curriculum has just been revised, and the new versions of level 5 for number, reading and writing, implemented in August 1995, are shown below. The individual statements of attainment have been replaced by level descriptions, as shown below. The former levels 9 and 10 have been removed as part of the revision. In mathematics the previously separate attainment targets for Number and Algebra have been combined in the new version of the National Curriculum as part of the process of reducing the number of separate criteria.

New level description for Number/Algebra, level 5

Pupils use their understanding of place value to multiply and divide whole numbers and decimals by 10, 100 and 1 000. They order, add and subtract negative numbers in context. They use all four operations with decimals to two places. They calculate fractional or percentage parts of quantities and measurements, using a calculator where appropriate. Pupils understand and use an appropriate non-calculator method for solving problems that involve multiplying and dividing any three-digit by any two-digit number. They check their solutions by applying inverse operations or estimating using approximations. They construct, express in symbolic form, and use simple formulae involving one or two operations.

New level description for Reading, level 5

Pupils show understanding of a range of texts, selecting essential points and using inference and deduction where appropriate. In their responses, they identify key features, themes and characters, and select sentences, phrases and relevant information to support their views. They retrieve and collate information from a range of sources.

New level description for Writing, level 5

Pupils' writing is varied and interesting, conveying meaning clearly in a range of forms for different readers, using a more formal style when appropriate. Vocabulary choices are imaginative and words are used precisely. Simple and complex sentences are organised into paragraphs. Words with complex, regular patterns are usually spelled correctly. A range of punctuation, including commas, apostrophes and inverted commas, is usually used accurately. Handwriting is joined, clear and fluent and, where appropriate, is adapted to a range of tasks.

The revision of the National Curriculum has been undertaken to reduce the quantity of recording and assessment required. The individual statements of attainment have been dropped, but can still be noted in the new level descriptions. The revision of English is more radical, and the new versions are simpler and more amenable to pencil and paper-timed tests.

The new level descriptions are intended to describe the types and range of performance that pupils working at a level should characteristically demonstrate. The new system is less atomistic than the current one, most noticeably here in level 5 for Reading. Nevertheless the description of a level often still encompasses a range of discrete, or relatively discrete, elements.

Since performance is specified atomistically in the current version of the National Curriculum, via statements of attainment, performance data on these statements need to be combined in some way to award a pupil a level of an attainment target. Even with the new version of the National Curriculum similar aggregation from the results of assessments of different discrete elements of the level descriptions will usually be needed.

Levels for subjects are also obtained, either by aggregating attainment target levels for the subject or directly from item or, currently, statement of attainment data. Item data are currently aggregated to produce subject levels in the tests for 11- and 14-year-olds, and this is likely to continue when the new version of the curriculum is implemented in the 1996 tests for these age groups.

Standards at ages 16 and 18 continue to be described by the grade achieved in the relevant examination, GCSE and A-Level respectively. These grades are not based directly on National Curriculum levels, and plans to modify the examination at age 16 to produce levels rather than grades have been dropped.

The definition of the examination grades is essentially normative, the statistical methods used to check that the distribution of levels awarded in one year is consistent whith previous years work on this basis, but grade criteria are in use to specify the difficulty level of the questions set.

Scottish developments contrast with England in this respect, since the performance standards for Scotland were developed only for ages 5 to 14, leaving the 14-16 age range to be catered for by the existing Scottish public examination system for age 16, which had just been totally revised. The public examinations for age 16 in England had, in fact, also been recently radically changed, but a second change to the system, to National Curriculum levels rather than grades, was planned but then abandoned.

The decision to opt to cover the 5-14 age range in Scotland, rather than 5-16 as in England, also impacted on the number of levels defined. Only five were produced for Scotland, again referenced to age. They are:

Level A should be attainable in the course of P1 - P3 (ages 5 to 8) by almost all pupils.
Level B should be attainable by some pupils in P3 or even earlier, but certainly by most in P4 (age 9).
Level C should be attainable in the course of P4 - P6 (ages 9 to 11) by most pupils.
Level D should be attainable by some pupils in P5 - P6 or even earlier, but certainly by most in P7 (age 12).
Level E should be attainable by some pupils in P7 - S1 but certainly by most in S2 (age 14).

The Scottish system thus avoids overlap with the public examination system, and consequent problems of comparability, by not setting performance standards for ages above 14. It should be noted that the notion of progression by one level in two year's schooling is present in both the English and Scottish systems, but is more explicit in the way the Scottish levels are officially described.

The performance standards in Scotland are similar in nature to those in England at the micro level. The term "attainment target" is common to both systems, but those for Scotland are organised in strands. Examples of strands are "Reading for Information", "Money", and "Multiply and Divide". These strands are defined at each of the five levels and are explicit. Similar strands do exist in the English attainment targets but they are implicit and not necessarily defined at each level.

The process of standard setting

The nature of the performance standards in the National Curriculum has been outlined, both for the current version and the new one. In this section the process of construction is described together with some aspects of their operation.

The standards setters

The National Curriculum and the standards built into it are set by government appointed working parties. Earlier working parties had fairly wide membership, including industrialists, educators in the subject, teachers and headteachers. Psychometricians have not been represented on these working parties. Government inspectors of schools have provided subject input in each case via specialists serving on or assisting the working parties. In the original working parties a balance was sought between different views on the nature of the subject concerned and hence what was most valuable within that subject. Thus in history those seeing knowledge of facts as highly important were balanced by those valuing interpretation highly. More recent working parties, convened to revise the National Curriculum, have contained more teachers.

The process of appointment is carried out in private, as is traditional for government committees and working parties in the United Kingdom. Often members are described as nominees of the government Minister responsible for education. An announcement of the membership is made, but there are no public consultations prior to this announcement. Any such consultations are carried out privately.

Members are briefed on the tasks required rather than formally trained. There is no system of payment to those involved other than expenses, but in recent years it has become the practice for the schools of teachers serving on working parties to receive payment for a temporary replacement teacher to be employed.

A typical pattern of work would be one-day meetings every few weeks for a period of months supplemented by weekend meetings where required. Beyond this members would also carry out work by themselves between meetings, usually in the evening or at weekends. This work takes place in private with no draft proposals publicly circulated. There have, however, been instances of selective leaking of parts of drafts in order to try to gain media and public support for particular points of view.

Appointments are normally made for a specific job – to create or revise a part of the National Curriculum – and there are not usually ongoing roles beyond this. Continuity in the process of construction and revision is therefore provided more by the professional officers of the government agencies involved rather than long term service by working party members.

Development of performance standards by working groups with teachers represented is typical of United Kingdom practice, although the composition of the groups and the degree of teacher involvement varies from country to country.

Controlling and financing the process

The actual process has been managed by government agencies, initially the National Curriculum Council (NCC) but now the School Curriculum and Assessment Authority (SCAA). The change was caused by the setting up of a new body to replace the former bodies responsible for curriculum (NCC) and assessment, the School Examination and Assessment Council (SEAC). This division of responsibilities between the two previous bodies had caused problems in a system where the curriculum, its performance standards and assessment arrangements were being developed simultaneously, and was one reason for the change. In all these bodies the views of Council, or now Authority, members, have been extremely influential, even leading to changes in matters of detail such as individual questions in tests.

The proposals of each working party are presented to the government Ministers by the government agency responsible, and Ministers can and do ask for changes to proposals to be made at this stage. Ministers and their advisers in the Department for Education will also have seen draft proposals at an earlier stage.

The whole process is governed by the Education Reform Act of 1988 and later legislation and the government bodies involved are statutory. Included in this legislation is the requirement for a public consultation on proposals for setting up or changing the National Curriculum. The law requires certain bodies to be consulted, but the process has traditionally been wider than this, with individual persons and schools participating. These consultations take the form of proposals from Ministers which are those of the working parties concerned after changes requested by Ministers have been negotiated. It is at this stage that proposals officially become public knowledge and are circulated outside government agencies or Ministries.

The consultation process requires interested organisations or individuals to answer a questionnaire on the proposals, and the opportunity to make points not directly covered by the questionnaire is provided. Replies are coded and a statistical analysis of responses is made. The proposals are then revised and pass into law.

The costs of the actual development of the proposals consist of the expenses incurred by the working parties plus the time of the professional officers of the government bodies concerned. The consultation process incurs sizeable printing costs for the documents and questionnaires and also involves the staff time and expenses of the contractor who codes and analyses the responses under contract. There are also parliamentary expenses incurred while amending legislation or preparing the proposals in the form required by law.

By this mechanism standards are set nationally for pupils in England and Wales up to age 14. For ages 16 and 18 independent (of government) examination boards set the papers and devise examination syllabuses. The latter have to be approved by the same government agency, SCAA, which is responsible for tests up to age 14 and in general for the curriculum up to age 18. SCAA also scrutinises the examination papers.

Consistency and fairness

Since national tests and standards are used up to age 14 in England and Wales, the need for consistency is most apparent in examinations for ages 16 and 18 where different examination authorities set papers in most subjects. Syllabuses have to be approved by SCAA, which has also developed codes of practice for awarding grades, marking examination papers and general conduct of these examinations. Comparability between examination authorities remains a cause for debate, and the consistency of the awarding of grades from year to year is open to discussion.

The education systems in Scotland, in particular, and Northern Ireland differ substantially from that in England and Wales and operate under separate legislation. Northern Ireland has a National Curriculum with standards broadly similar to those in England and Wales but with significant differences in some topics and in matters of detail. Scotland has a rather different set of standards. There are no formal mechanisms to harmonise standards between England and Wales on the one hand and Scotland and Northern Ireland on the other.

Factors influencing standards and the level at which they are set

Some data on performance levels were available to working parties, but not enough to cover the whole range of content included even in those subjects where APU surveys were administered. Where data were not available the members of the working parties used their judgement to ascribe a level to knowledge or skills they wished to include. For the higher levels of the system comparability of demand with public examinations at age 16 was required and was sought. Knowledge of performance in these examinations – what candidates awarded particular grades would be expected to be able to do – therefore influenced construction of the National Curriculum. In judging at what level to place the knowledge and skills selected for inclusion, the working parties had to use the data and experience at their command to construct a system which would have the expected distribution of levels at given ages, as illustrated in the previous section.

Within this framework some of the current statements of attainment reflected what the working parties considered pupils ought to be able to do, even where this conflicted with available evidence or best estimates of the difficulty level of the task concerned. The reason for such an approach was the desire to raise performance from existing levels via the National Curriculum. Other statements have been placed in the National Curriculum primarily to encourage teachers to include particular content or activities in their teaching rather than as measures of performance.

The mechanism can be summarised as the identification of desirable objectives followed by their being ascribed to a level using performance data, the relationship with the existing public examinations and/or judgement as appropriate. Thus the process is largely one of committees reaching a consensus, but without overt formal mechanisms for this.

Since the current performance standards are atomistic, their specification does not totally fix how difficult it is to achieve a particular level. This process is completed by the development of methods, statistical or judgmental, of making overall decisions about where a pupil should be placed on the 10 level scale. The developers of the national tests, and the professional officers of the government agencies they work with and for, have to conclude the process. In the tests this has to be done by statistical means as discussed below (see "Cutoffs – Levels of Achievement"). The same processes are likely to be needed after the new version of the National Curriculum implemented in August 1995.

In many education systems the construction of performance standards is linked to admission to a later phase of the system, to the next grade or to university for example. In such systems the implications of performance standards for transfer procedures would be of great importance. This is not so with the National Curriculum performance standards.

It has already been noted above that classes are age-related in the system rather than grade-related. Admission to university is also unaffected, since places are awarded by each university using its own criteria, which usually relate to performance in the Advanced Level examinations taken at age 18.

Typically a university will accept those students with the best results above its own minimum requirements for a particular degree course. These vary from university to university, and between subjects within a university. There is no right to a university place if a particular level of performance is achieved. The government now attempts to match degree courses available to labour market needs by differential funding for different subjects.

The mechanics of the standard-setting process

The process is similar for all subjects in the National Curriculum. The National Curriculum is constructed by working parties as outlined earlier. The way of working is not a mechanistic step by step procedure. The original working parties provided descriptive standards for each of the ten levels of the National Curriculum in their subject in parallel with defining the curriculum itself. A central influence was the need to produce the expected relationship between National Curriculum level and age illustrated above. For the highest levels the relationship with the existing GCSE syllabuses and performance levels was a strong consideration.

The National Curriculum covers all the commonly occurring Unided Kingdom school subjects, and each was developed in a similar way. However, some working parties, such as that for English, adopted a process model with the same processes in reading and writing followed up through the levels with increasing difficulty, range of texts or writing, or sophistication built in. Others, for example mathematics and science, chose a content-based model for most areas within their subject but a process-based area was also defined. These differences are still present in the new National Curriculum.

The original procedure of development by subject working parties led to a system which was wide-ranging for each subject but overwhelming in its complexity and requirements when the subjects were considered together. This problem has been addressed in the current revision of the National Curriculum by having working groups to oversee each key stage as a whole, with particular reference to checking that the system as a whole is more manageable when the various subjects are considered together rather than in isolation.

There are no interdisciplinary standards *per se,* but the information technology attainment target has elements of this.

Performance standards

National Curriculum standards are essentially descriptive as demonstrated in the section on standards above, and achievements of atomistic standards – statements of attainment in the current version – have to be combined (aggregated) to decide on achievement of levels of attainment targets or subject levels. The level of the National Curriculum achieved in an attainment target or subject is the performance standard in the system. Thus the pupil is placed on a point on a scale rather than being given a simple pass/fail. Placing a pupil at level n should be interpreted as indicating that the pupil has achieved the requirements of levels up to including n, but not those for levels $n + 1$ or higher.

Various systems of aggregating performance on statements of attainment into performance on levels have been tried. In tests, counting statements of attainment achieved has been used, and continues to be for 7-year-olds. In the current tests for this age group a pupil must achieve all but one of the statements of attainment at a level if three or more are addressed in the tests, but must achieve all of the statements if only one or two are defined or included in the tests. This method will no longer be used after the new version of the National Curriculum is implemented.

At ages 11 and 14 the tests now use marks awarded across levels and attainment targets to award subject levels. This system is not directly criterion referenced, but allows for reliability to be achieved by aggregating across all available score points. Further details of the procedures used to decide on the levels pupils are awarded from marks obtained are given below.

It should be noted that these methods of awarding levels were developed after the current National Curriculum was devised and did not form a part of the task of the working parties. This has led to problems in operationalising the award of levels, and it seems likely that the system would have developed differently had the working groups been instructed to produce a system incorporating a defined method of awarding levels.

Test developers, reviewers, including government inspectors and the professional officers of the relevant government agency, are all intimately involved in ensuring that the tests, and the methods of allocating pupils to National Curriculum levels they incorporate, reflect the desired standards. This is again a judgmental process.

The tests do not now cover those elements of the National Curriculum only assessable over time, by practical work or by extended tasks. Levels awarded by the current tests for 11- and 14-year-olds, now subject levels rather than attainment target levels, are derived from pencil and paper items.

Teacher assessment continues to involve a wider range of assessment modes, and the approach to guidance has been to provide samples of pupils' work with a commentary showing those elements of the National Curriculum of which evidence of achievement has been shown.

At ages 16 and 18 performance standards are essentially the grades awarded in examinations.

Implementation, review and adjustment

Implementing performance standards

New versions of the National Curriculum and the standards defined in them are not formally piloted. However it takes time to amend the law, and there is a period, late 1994 to mid 1995 being an example, when teachers and others have the new version of the curriculum but do not yet have to work to it. The national tests are piloted, but this takes place in parallel with the introduction or revision of the National Curriculum, and the ability to pilot them is impaired by lack of pupils who have been taught the new or revised curriculum over a number of years.

Dissemination of the National Curriculum to schools is by free distribution. Teachers are thus provided with the curriculum they must teach and with the attainment targets they must assess their pupils against. The documentation is extensive, to the point where reactions to simple reading time have been adverse. Copies of the same documents are also sent to Local Education Authorities and some other bodies.

These documents are too detailed for parents, and leaflets outlining the National Curriculum have been prepared and distributed to this audience. They summarise the expected relationship between National Curriculum level and age, and outline the nature of the National Curriculum. Employers continue to be more familiar with the grades awarded in the public examinations taken at ages 16 and 18.

Review and adjustment of standards

The National Curriculum has been revised to make it more manageable. This is a result of dissatisfaction with the existing version, rather than being a scheduled review. Teachers found the workload deriving from the curriculum too great and the amount of classroom time needed to teach the curriculum excessive. There were particular problems in primary schools where teachers teach all or most subjects rather than being specialists.

The amount of assessment and recording needed for teachers to make judgements on levels reached by their pupils in their own ongoing teacher assessment was found to be too great and attracted consistent criticism. Other features of the system leading to discontent include dislike of formal, compulsory tests, and, even more forcibly, disapproval and distrust of the purposes the test data were to be used for and the manner of their presentation.

The mathematics and science curricula have now been revised twice to make them more manageable. The 1994 revision was intended to:

a) Reduce the size of the compulsory curriculum in each subject.

b) Reduce the number of attainment targets and separately described criteria in each subject.

c) Make assessment and recording less time consuming by making the definition of standards less atomistic.

From inspection of the revised versions the reductions desired in a) and b) have been achieved. The way standards are described has changed, in the new version there are fewer, but broader, descriptions as illustrated in the section on standards above. It will only be possible to evaluate the degree to which c) has been achieved, and whether the reductions in a) and b) are sufficient, when the new National curriculum has been implemented.

As part of this process attention has been given to those statements of attainment which have proved to be more difficult or easier than the remainder at a particular level. The main reason for revision, however, is manageability rather than the desire or need to adjust standards up or down.

Evidence of attainment of performance standards

Two methods of assessment apply to the National Curriculum, ongoing teacher assessment and the national tests. The national tests are taken yearly by pupils aged 7, 11 and 14. Currently they are provided in mathematics and English for all three age groups, but in science only for 11- and 14-year-olds.

A written test or set of written tests, is used each year for ages 11 and 14. At age seven the assessments are currently wider-ranging with individual assessments and some practical tasks, but the trend is for these assessments to concentrate on those aspects of the curriculum that are most easily and quickly assessed, particularly with pupils in groups rather than individually.

The complete range of possible assessment modes can contribute to teacher assessment. Individual schools and teachers are free to choose the methods of making their assessments. Some assessments for use in teacher assessment have been distributed to schools, but their use is optional.

At ages 16 and 18 examinations are set by several different examination boards, giving more than one set of examinations in use each year. All include formal examinations, but some also include a coursework element.

Cutoffs – Levels of achievement

Up to age 14 each pupil is awarded one of the 10 current National Curriculum levels. There is no pass/fail, but the expected relationship between level and age provides a way of classifying performance as average, above or below this, and by how much. The system does not go beyond this and classify certain levels as acceptable or unacceptable for particular age groups. Commentators and politicians, however, have done so, regarding levels lower than expected for particular ages as indications of failure.

The national tests now award subject levels on the basis of marks for ages 11 and 14, rather than by directly criterion referenced methods such as achievement of statements of attainment. Pupils take a paper or papers containing items addressing selected attainment targets covering several adjacent levels of the National Curriculum – a tier. The tier a pupil is to take is decided by the teacher. Tiers overlap, and at age 14 in mathematics currently cover levels 3-5, 4-6, etc. A subject level is then awarded on the basis of the total number of marks obtained. The technical challenge is to set the cut-off scores so that the tests are of comparable difficulty from year to year, and so that it is equally difficult to obtain level n in any tier containing level n. Methods of doing this are currently being explored. Angoff's method, with experts rating the difficulty of items for minimally competent achievers at particular levels, was tried out for the 1994 mathematics tests for 14-year-olds. Further methods, including calibrating new tests against those from the previous year using a common sample of pupils are also being tried out.

It should be noted that the system has not yet achieved stability, due to changes in the National Curriculum and in the specifications for the national tests. Technical evaluation of these changes is being severely hampered by a continuing boycott of the tests by many teachers and schools.

For ages 16 and 18 grades are awarded. At age 16 GCSE grades A to C are often regarded as "pass" since these match the pass grades of the previous O-Level examination, which catered for a more restricted and higher attaining entry than GCSE. At age 18 grades A, B or C are most likely to be specified by universities in their entrance requirements.

At ages 16 and 18 examination papers are marked centrally to prescribed marking schemes. Grade boundaries are set after the mark awarded to each pupil is known. Statistical information is therefore available to ensure that the distribution of grades awarded is similar from year to year unless there is evidence available to suggest the entry for the examination concerned is of higher or lower overall attainment than previously. This is supplemented by reviewing current scripts expected to be awarded a given grade against those from previous year(s) which were awarded that grade. A judgement is then made on whether similar standards of performance are required to be awarded a given grade over time.

Construction of instruments and scoring

Items for the national tests are developed by trialling and are the subject of review by committees set up for the purpose. At the review stage items are closely scrutinised for validity; currently this is to ensure that they are true assessments of particular statements of attainment. Particular attention is also given to ensuring that items support and guide good curriculum practice, and this sometimes conflicts with their psychometric and measurement properties.

Actual difficulty of items is established by trialling, and items are included if this is appropriate for the level of the National Curriculum being assessed. There are, however, sizeable variations since not all of the statements of attainment which currently comprise a level are of equal difficulty. When the new level descriptions are in use, such variation may be reduced, but discrete elements of the new level descriptions are likely to pose similar problems.

Marking of National Curriculum tests is currently done by teachers according to detailed compulsory marking schemes for each item. These are developed during trialling and are reviewed in the same way as items. From 1995 the tests for 11- and 14-year-olds are to be marked externally using similar marking schemes. The relationship with overall standards is then embodied by the system for awarding levels.

A sample marking scheme for a mathematics item is shown below. Using a calculator pupils have to work out, from information supplied, that going to Milltown Funfair and having 8 rides will cost £7. The calculation involved is £2.20 + (8 × 60p).

For 2 marks states amount of money correctly in pounds or pence:
- states £7
- states £7-00
- states £7-00p
- states 700p

For only 1 mark indicates correct substitution into the formula for Milltown Funfair:

- states 700
- states 7
- ...

Addition guidance that units are required for 2 marks and that substitution in only part of the formula should not be accepted for one mark is also provided. The item assesses a current level 4 statement in Number requiring pupils to "Solve number problems with the aid of a calculator, interpreting the display". Marking schemes for items addressing statements at the higher levels are sometimes more complex, particularly where algebraic manipulation is involved or a variety of methods may be used.

The combination of results from different assessments is now accomplished by combining the marks awarded rather than by combining pass/fail results for particular standards or criteria except in the tests for 7-year-olds. Marking is checked, on a sampling basis for both tests and examinations.

Reporting results

Overall results for each subject are published for examinations at ages 16 and 18. These are compiled by the examination boards. Central government also produces performance tables of examination results for schools at age 16. The results of individual pupils are not published but are reported to the school and the pupil.

The publication of National Curriculum levels for schools and Local Education Authorities has been the subject of great controversy, and has been a central factor leading to the boycott of national tests. Such publication is part of government policy and is intended to inform parents and others, while helping to create a market in the education system. The statistics that have been produced have been very simple, based on the percentage of the age cohort achieving particular levels. No adjustments are made to allow for differences in attainment between pupils on entry to the school where they are taught and then take the national tests. The use of the tables to compare the effectiveness of schools is therefore widely seen as unfair. This has contributed to teachers either refusing to administer the tests or refusing to report the results when they have been administered.

Scottish experience is again illuminating here. The production of comparative tables of school performance requires consistent data on each pupil in each school. The national tests, taken by all pupils of certain ages at the same time, are intended to provide the necessary consistent data. This nation-wide testing at fixed times was also introduced in Scotland for 9- and 12-year-olds, but resistance was strong. Crucially, many parents withdrew their children from the testing and the system has now been changed. Teachers in Scotland now use tests selected from a published bank to confirm their judgement that a pupil has achieved one of the five levels in the system. The timing of testing is thus at the discretion of the teacher, tests being administered when a level is judged to have recently been attained by a pupil. A nation-wide snapshot at a fixed point in time is therefore not available in the same way in the revised Scottish system as is still proposed for that in England.

A further aspect of reporting results is checking on their accuracy before publication. The current system of quality control in England is that the marking carried out by a school is checked on a sampling basis, and if this is approved the results are then submitted for collation and publication. This has generally been done by contractors working to government contracts.

Provisions for children with special needs

Fair treatment of pupils with special educational needs is clearly important when performance standards are constructed or assessed. Provision varies at different ages. National Curriculum tests are available in English and Welsh, but not, by policy, in other languages. Presentation of items may be modified locally to allow for visual and other impairment, and versions are produced in Braille. Great emphasis has been placed on making the National Curriculum tests accessible to the widest possible range of pupils with special needs, and the current regulations allow more flexibility in this respect than those for the public examinations at ages 16 and 18.

The tests for pupils aged seven are designed so as not to depend on reading ability unless the Reading attainment target is being assessed. Outside reading, teachers may read out questions when asked to do so or if they so desire. For older pupils accessibility is addressed in various ways. At age 14, for example, levels 1 and 2 of the National Curriculum in mathematics and science are assessed by means of practical tasks, individually administered if necessary, rather than pencil and paper tests. The system of tiers, covering ranges of adjacent levels, also assists accessibility since the teacher should be able to select an appropriate tier for each pupil to allow the highest level of performance to be demonstrated without facing too many dauntingly difficult questions or too many extremely simple ones.

Extra time in particular circumstances is allowable for those with impairment, but not for those whose first language is not English. No special allowances are made for socio-economic background. Differential scoring is not a feature of the United Kingdom system.

Problems and critical issues

Lessons from the United Kingdom experience

The United Kingdom experience in general, and that in England and Wales in particular, highlights a number of areas where development has not met the original aims and where modifications to practice should produce improvement. It also points up areas where the problems are likely to prove to be difficult to solve.

The following summarises what can be learnt.

A clear purpose is needed for the standards, and from this their specificity or generality should be decided. The original version of the National Curriculum provided more detail than was useful and its manageability was impaired as a result. The relationship between purpose and form needs to be clearer than was the case in the National Curriculum. The manageability of the system needs to be evaluated from the start. An appropriate balance between too many detailed standards and too few over-general ones is needed.

Whether the standards are general, and relatively few in number, or specific, and relatively large in number, they need to be constructed to a model for deciding whether or not they have been achieved. The United Kingdom experience highlights the difficulty of developing satisfactory methods of deciding whether standards have been achieved after they have been developed.

Whatever level of generality of standards is adopted, their operationalisation in assessments needs to be considered throughout the construction process, with extra guidance on intended complexity, context and similar matters provided, if necessary in separate documentation.

The modes of assessment, and the administration time and arrangements they require, need to be considered throughout the construction process. The scale on which they will need to be carried out also needs to be considered. Many of the problems experienced in England and Wales derive from this source.

Public understanding, and even effective transmission, of the standards, is difficult to obtain if they are too numerous and specific and form part of a complex structure. These problems are exacerbated if the system has to be constantly revised.

Standards which attempt to be multi-purpose should be viewed with extreme scepticism. Those which are intended to avoid narrowing the curriculum by including process and practical elements need to be evaluated for the manageability of the assessment arrangements if they are to be implemented on a wide scale.

Standards for different subjects need to be co-ordinated to ensure they do not conflict and that, taken together, the assessment time and arrangements are reasonable.

Extensive piloting is desirable in order to assess manageability and to identify aspects of the system which are not of the desired level of difficulty. If the standards are to be accompanied by a new curriculum, rather than superimposed on an existing one, this needs to be allowed for when plans for piloting are drawn up.

The speed of implementation needs to be controlled to avoid the need for frequent revision to eliminate or reduce the effect of undesirable characteristics. This has led to virtually constant change which has demotivated teachers and hampered evaluation.

Policy formulation and decision making

The procedures for setting standards in the United Kingdom are accomplished in private, with experiences not generally publicised. The standards themselves are widely disseminated, but the production of them is accomplished in private. The speed of introduction has been such that time for reflection and development of ideas during the construction process has been largely absent.

The compulsory National Curriculum is wide-ranging, both specifying the curriculum to be taught and performance standards. This simultaneous introduction makes it difficult for one to inform the development of the other, particularly when both are being revised simultaneously.

Teachers have not been prepared to devote the amount of time to assessment and recording required by the current version of the United Kingdom National Curriculum. It is also seen as leaving too little time for other curriculum activities. The latest revision of the National Curriculum has been designed to address these problems, but the existing version has produced benefits, particularly in the teaching of 5- to 7-year-olds. The curriculum and its assessment arrangements have been in place longest with this age range, and the first national tests incorporated assessments of the process elements of mathematics and science and an analytical procedure for testing reading. These aspects of the assessments were time consuming but school inspectors welcomed them and identified improvements in classroom practice as a result.

The international dimension

The chief significance of comparing standard-setting procedures, as in the current exercise must be to learn from the experience of others. This is likely to be particularly helpful for countries about to set standards but also of interest to those seeking to modify or improve existing procedures.

The problems involved, generality or specificity of standards, wide ranging or narrow standards, and making criterion referencing manageable and informative, for example, are well known. The assessment issues which accompany standard setting are also being explored. By comparing practices, and the effectiveness or otherwise of the results, the list of hoped for benefits can be pared to a shorter list of realisable objectives based on relevant experience. Setting standards *per se* will not improve a system. The process must be embedded in a long term process of development and evaluation which the experiences in other countries can inform.

Appendix

Summary of Evidence of Change in Performance Levels in England

Paul Hamlyn Foundation

National Commission on Education

December 1992

Standards in Literacy and Numeracy

by Derek Foxman, Tom Gorman and Greg Brooks

National Foundation for Educational Research (NFER)

Summary

Reading standards among 11- and 15-year-olds have changed little since 1945, apart from slight rises around 1950 and in the 1980s. Among 7-8 year-olds, however, standards fell slightly in the late 1980s. In writing performance, there was no overall change during the 1980s.

Less than one per cent of school-leavers and adults can be described as illiterate. Basic literacy skills are however insufficient to meet the demands of many occupations.

British school students are above average in geometry and statistics, but below average in number skills, compared with other industrialised countries. Britain also has a wider spread of mathematics attainment, mainly due to the weaker performance of lower attaining pupils.

Nationally, there was a fall in attainment among 11- and 15-year-olds in number skills between 1982 and 1987, and a rise in geometry, statistics and measures.

Attainment both in literacy and numeracy may need to rise considerably to meet the requirements of the next century.

We do not have an effective system of monitoring educational standards throughout the UK. Arguments about standards will continue until such a system is in place. National Curriculum assessment is not best suited to monitor national performance: for this purpose, specially-designed, regular surveys are needed, using representative samples of pupils.

In addition to national monitoring, we need to compare ourselves with competitor nations, some of which are setting ambitious targets for the 21st century. The debate about standards of attainment must continue, but against a background of sound evidence.

1. Introduction

Public concern about educational standards is not new: criticism of standards has appeared regularly since the last century and is probably due to tensions between society's changing values and requirements, and the response made by the education service. Skills in literacy and numeracy are prerequisites for full participation in our society; it is not therefore surprising that public controversy about standards often focuses on them. This summary asks what we mean by educational standards, and considers how they are measured and monitored. What is happening to standards in literacy and numeracy, and what will be the best way to monitor performance in future?

2. What are educational standards?

A "standard" is a fixed measure against which performance is judged. A physical standard, such as a metre length, is objectively defined and is fixed over time, but educational standards in this sense, such as the letters denoting the grades attained in GCSE or the statements of attainment in the National Curriculum, are less easily pinned down. Furthermore, the term ''standards'' in educational discussion often refers not to particular criteria of performance but to the actual attainment of pupils, *i.e.* a mean score in a test or the proportion getting a question correct.

3. Methods of monitoring standards

Monitoring implies attempting to determine changes over time in attainment. Five types of assessment have provided fuel for the debate on standards.

Public examinations, such as GCSE and A level, and Scottish Standard Grade and Highers, consist of different questions each year. Nevertheless, the letter grades awarded are intended to be comparable in standard from year to year and between examination boards. But the yardsticks that the grades represent are implicit; they are carried around in examiners' heads, and there are therefore no simple methods of determining whether the grade standards remain constant. Public examinations have other limitations as devices for monitoring standards: they are taken by candidates from more than one age group, and not all of the predominant age group are entered for the examination in any one subject.

National Curriculum Assessment (which applies to England and Wales) was carried out officially for the first time with 7-year-olds in 1991. Assessment of 14-year-olds will begin in 1993 and that of 11-year-olds in 1994. At these three ages, the assessments will be confined to strictly defined age groups, and all pupils in the age group will be assessed. Also from 1994, the GCSE in various groups of subjects will progressively change to become National Curriculum assessment for all 16-year-olds except those at National Curriculum levels 1-3.

At all four ages, the assessments will consist of teacher assessments and externally set tests. The teacher assessments will vary inherently in content from school to school, and it is likely that the external tests will use different questions each year, although each question has to exemplify one of the statements of attainment which relate to a particular level in a particular subject. Since the statements of attainment are explicit, there would seem to be a lesser problem of comparability from year to year than in the present GCSE. However, as the system develops, points to watch in this regard will be the comparability of different questions supposedly exemplifying the same statements of attainment, methods of deciding when a statement of attainment has been achieved, and ways of aggregating statements achieved to attainment target level.

It is likely to be some years before the suitability of National Curriculum assessment for monitoring can be fully evaluated, but it is already clear that only limited aspects of the National Curriculum can be assessed in the external tests on each occasion.

There are also national assessment programmes in Scotland and in Northern Ireland, but these are more limited in scope than those in England and Wales.

Standardised tests consist of a fixed set of items relating to a particular area such as reading or mathematics. A test is initially given to a representative sample of the population whose attainment is to be measured. The results provide scores or ''norms'' for particular ages of children against which the attainment of individuals can be measured. Attainment can then be monitored by repeating the test on representative samples at intervals. However, views on the nature of the content being tested may change and so the overall format of the test becomes outdated. In English, some items become outdated as language itself becomes outdated. Scores could fall as a result of these factors and be falsely interpreted as a fall in standards.

The surveys by the Assessment of Performance Unit (APU) represent the most extensive attempt to measure and to monitor performance nationally before the emergence of National Curriculum assessment. The APU (see Foxman *et al.,* 1990*a*), a unit at the DES, commissioned surveys in five subjects from independent agencies between 1977 and 1990, but only those in mathematics and (English) language will be mentioned in this summary. These were conducted by the NFER on representative samples of pupils in England, Wales and Northern Ireland.

The APU surveys were very large-scale, each subject including written, practical and oral modes of assessment and assessing a wide range of knowledge, skills and processes. They gave a much more detailed picture of performance than had previously been obtained either by standardised tests or public examinations. A number of different methods were used to monitor change in performance over the period of the surveys: the principal one was comparing the results of the same questions used in different years. The APU programme was terminated by the government in 1990 when the National Curriculum was introduced. The parallel programme in Scotland, the Assessment of Achievement Programme (AAP), began in 1983 and still continues.

International surveys. The rising importance of the global economy has produced increasing interest in comparative standards in different countries. International studies conducted over the past thirty years have compared attainment levels in some subjects in relation to the curricula in various countries and other factors in their schools and the home backgrounds of their pupils. There are obvious problems in attempting these comparisons: the test questions are likely to suit some countries more than others, translation can effect the levels of difficulty posed by specific questions, and comparable samples of pupils are difficult if not impossible to achieve because of the different features of education in the participating countries. These studies are also intermittent and the same countries do not always take part, so that monitoring changes in comparative differences is not easy. Despite these drawbacks there have been some very interesting results, especially in mathematics, as described below in Section 5.

Trends in performance. In the following analysis of trends in literacy and numeracy, National Curriculum assessment and public examination statistics will not be used as evidence for trends: the former because no data over time were available at the time of writing, even for 7-year-olds, and the latter because although public examination statistics suggest a long-term rise in success rates, there are difficulties in interpretation.

4. Trends in literacy

International studies of performance in literacy which included Britain have taken place (reading comprehension in 1967, written composition in 1983), but few conclusions can be drawn from these surveys about our performance relative to other countries. Consequently, this section focuses on data from national surveys and standardised tests.

Literacy at age 7/8

For pupils in Year 3, national data are available only for England. They are available only for reading, and only for the years 1987 and 1991. In 1987, the NFER standardised a new series of reading tests, one of which was intended for pupils in Year 3. In 1991, the standardisation exercise of this test was repeated. The main finding was that average reading scores of pupils in Year 3 fell by 2½ standardised points between 1987 and 1991 (see Gorman and Fernandes, 1992). This result corroborated on a national scale more localised findings, which showed a fall in particular LEAs of about one standardised score point in the average reading attainment of 7-year-olds (Year 2) between 1985 and 1988, and again between 1988 and 1990.

Literacy at ages 11 and 15

For 11- and 15-year-olds, national data on *reading* performance are available from several surveys using standardised pre-APU tests between 1948 and 1979, mostly conducted by NFER. APU surveys of the *reading and writing* performance of 11- and 15-year-olds were conducted annually from 1979 to 1983 and again in 1988.

There was an apparent abrupt decline in average reading scores in the 1970/71 surveys, following apparently steady rises since 1948. This caused great concern about "illiteracy" among pupils. But the decline was perceived only by overlooking the fact that most of the differences between the mean scores reported were statistically non-significant. When normal statistical criteria are applied, the proper conclusion appears to be that the aspects of reading of pupils in Year 6 and Year 11 measured by the tests then in use rose slightly between 1948 and 1952, then remained essentially unchanged until 1979.

The APU tests from 1979 were repeated in 1983, as were tests from 1983 in 1988 (see Gorman *et al.,* 1991). The findings are summarised in Table A1.

Table A1

		Year 6	Year 11
Reading	1979-83	Slight rise	Slight rise
	1983-88	Slight rise	No overall change
Writing	1979-83	Slight rise	No overall change
	1983-88	Slight fall	No overall change

Some findings for spelling were obtained in 1991/92 from samples of APU writing tasks undertaken by Year 6 pupils in 1979 and 1988, and by Year 11 pupils in 1980 and 1983. For the tasks examined (not a comprehensive set) an improvement in the performance of Year 6 pupils occurred and the performance of those in Year 11 remained the same. For all aspects of literacy the absolute size of the changes was small: the size of the APU samples ensured that even fairly small changes were statistically significant.

In Scotland the AAP (see Scottish Education Department, 1989) has conducted three surveys in 1984, 1989 and 1992. The results for 1992 are not yet available, but there was no change in the reading scores of Year 4 and Year 7 pupils from 1984 to 1989 and a small rise for Year 9 pupils. The same pattern was obtained for writing scores.

Literacy of adults

There have been two national performance surveys of the literacy attainments of young adults in Britain, in 1972 and 1992. The results of the 1992 survey, organised by City University, London, on behalf of the Basic Skills Unit (ALBSU), were not yet published at the time of writing. Since the tests used on this occasion were different from those used in 1972, they will provide no basis for an estimate of change over the intervening 20 years.

The 1972 survey used a version of the Watts-Vernon reading test. It was carried out as part of the continuing National Survey of Health and Development, the 1946 British birth cohort study which covered England, Wales and Scotland: the people involved were thus aged 26 at the time of the 1972 survey. This cohort had also taken the same reading test in 1961 when they were aged 16. The results (see Rodgers, 1986) showed a general increase in reading scores, and an illiteracy rate "as low as one per cent".

Illiteracy

The best available information from the APU surveys indicates that less than 1 per cent of those leaving school (excluding pupils from special schools) are unable to read in the sense of being unable to answer correctly simple comprehension questions about a passage. This accords well with the adult illiteracy rate just mentioned. The APU surveys also indicate that up to 3 per cent of school leavers would be unable or unwilling to communicate in writing in the sense of being unable to compose a short paragraph that is intelligible on first reading.

Given these figures, it may be wondered where media reports of large numbers, usually millions, of illiterate adults in the population come from. Most such estimates between the 1950s and 1980s were based on extrapolation from the number of 15-year-olds found to have a reading level at or below that of the average 7-year-olds or 11-year-olds. More recently, estimates of adult illiteracy have been based on self-report data from young adults on problems with reading and writing since leaving school. Neither form of extrapolation estimate basic literacy in the sense given in the previous paragraph.

Basic literacy is not, however, adequate for responsible involvement in the social, economic and political life of the present day, nor to meet the specialised demands of many occupations. Research in the United States has consistently found that the relationship between "job literacy" and school-based attainment is poor. There are two main reasons for this. The first is that people with literacy difficulties usually find methods of coping with their difficulties, with assistance. Secondly, specific jobs require job-specific literacy or numeracy skills, some of which can be developed on task. Teachers cannot be expected to prepare students for specialised literacy and numeracy requirements of particular occupations. However, there is a need for literacy teaching in schools to include a higher proportion of non-literary texts, for example those addressing science topics and social studies issues.

5. Trends in numeracy

"Numeracy" is the term invented to parallel "literacy" and, like it, has been interpreted in various ways. One narrow way is to assume that it relates only to the ability to perform basic arithmetic operations. Here we shall take the broader approach, meaning not only an "at homeness" with numbers, but also the ability to make use of mathematical skills which enable individuals to cope with the practical demands of everyday life. These skills must include some knowledge of spatial representation and data handling, as well as computational ability. In school, such skills may be used to a greater or lesser extent in a number of subjects in the curriculum. Given this broad definition of numeracy it is reasonable to consider the evidence on standards in Britain from APU national surveys of mathematics, supported by data from international studies.

National surveys of mathematics

APU surveys of the mathematics performance of 11- and 15-year-olds took place annually from 1978 to 1982, and again in 1987. Between 1978 and 1982, performance in items common to the two occasions resulted in a small overall increase of 1.5 percentage points at both age levels. In the interval between the surveys of 1982 and 1987 there was a very general pattern of performance changes at both 11 and 15 years, with improvements in the APU categories of geometry, probability and statistics, and measures, and a decline in number and in algebra (there were some variations in the detail of this general pattern) (see Foxman *et al.*, 1990*b*). These changes were thought to have been influenced by changes in curriculum emphases since the publication of the Cockcroft Report (Department of Education and Science, 1982) on Mathematics education in 1982. Cockcroft, however, did not sanction a decline in number skills, but placed more emphasis on mental computation, estimation, and appropriate use of different methods of calculation than had been apparent in the curriculum.

In Scotland the AAP conducted surveys of the mathematics performance of Years 4, 7 and 9 (secondary 2) in 1983, 1988 and 1991. There was a significant decline in all three year groups between 1983 and 1988 (see Scottish Education Department, 1989), but it differed in extent and in different areas of mathematics between age groups. There was no further change in 1991.

International surveys of mathematics

The International Association for the Evaluation of Educational Achievement (IEA) undertook surveys of 13- and 18-year-olds in 1964 and 1981. Another organisation, the International Assessment of Educational Progress (IEAP), carried out two later studies in 1988 and 1991 (IAEP 1 and IAEP 2). England (or England and Wales) has participated in all four of these international surveys. Scotland has usually been represented as a separate system, but was part of the "United Kingdom" sample in IAEP 1.

The results have demonstrated two main features of England's (or England and Wales's) comparative performance (Scotland's pattern of performance is fairly similar to England's):

- A profile of performance across topics among 13-year-olds which shows England to be below average in number and above average in geometry and statistics. This profile is consistent with the changes found by APU for 11- and 15-year-olds during the 1980s.
- Our top-ability students at 17+ are among the highest scorers in mathematics, while our below-average younger students do less well than those in many other developed countries.

The results for 13-year-olds are discussed first, since this age group is regarded as the basic one in international studies and so has been most frequently surveyed.

Mathematics at age 13

In the two IEA surveys, separated by an interval of 17 years, over 30 questions were common to both occasions in the tests for this age group. Comparison of the results reveals a general decline among the 10 education systems participating on both occasions in all but one of the categories tested: number, measurement, geometry, statistics and algebra. The exception was algebra, in which all countries except England and Wales improved their success rates. The relative position of England and Wales slipped in all categories between 1964 and 1981 (see Robitaille and Garden, 1989).

Many changes occurred between 1964 and 1981 in the organisation of education in Britain and the content and breadth of the curriculum, which could account for a general decline in respect of the questions common to the two occasions. Nevertheless, few of these seemed inappropriate for pupils in the later study.

In the international studies carried out since 1981, the same or similar cross-topic mathematics profile has been evident. For example, comparing the surveys carried out in 1981 and 1991 (IAEP 2; see Foxman, 1992), England's position relative to the five other countries participating in both years remains the same: first in statistics/data handling and sixth in arithmetic/number and operations. Apart from the data handling area, Hungary and France were the highest scoring countries of the six in both years.

Mathematics at age 9

The 1991 IAEP 2 survey included 9-year-olds – the first international study of that age group – and the results indicate that the same cross-topic profile is evident at this age as at 13 years. The participation rate of schools was low in IAEP 2, indicating the possibility of some bias in the results. If they are valid, we should question when the lower emphasis on number begins, especially as the survey of teachers' perceptions of their emphasis on calculations conflicted with the results obtained.

Mathematics at age 17+

One of the older populations surveyed in the two IEA studies consisted of students in the Upper Sixth who were studying mathematics as a substantial part of their academic programme. Our students (who were about to take A levels) came third or fourth out of 15 countries in 1981, in each of the three topics in the test. Japan and Hong Kong were the leading nations. Eight countries participated at this level in both 1964 and 1981, and the rank of England and Wales was just slightly worse in 1981 than in 1964.

Innumeracy

Culturally it has always been more acceptable to be innumerate than illiterate. There are no definitions of "innumeracy" as such, but APU and other mathematics surveys have shown that there is a very wide range of performance by age 11, and that the bottom 20 per cent of 15-year-olds still have a very limited grasp of even the most basic mathematical ideas. Mathematics in some form has been reaching more areas of daily life and more individuals at home and at work in recent decades and is now regarded as a subject for all to learn in school, although what aspects and in what depth remain matters for argument.

6. How can future changes be monitored effectively?

There are two main reasons why there has been so much controversy recently about whether or not standards are changing: irregular monitoring and the use of unsuitable monitoring instruments. At present, no effective monitoring of educational standards is occurring in England, Wales and Northern Ireland.

To be effective, monitoring needs to:

- provide an accurate picture of performance;
- give early notice of rises or falls in curriculum areas;

- detect whether changes are "blips" or becoming trends;
- be sufficiently wide-ranging in each curriculum area to detect whether performance in different aspects of a subject is changing in different directions, at different rates;
- be able to detect, for each age group monitored, whether changes are taking place in a particular attainment band, or operating throughout the range of attainment.

In order to achieve these aims, monitoring must be reliable, and should include nationally representative samples of pupils, tackling appropriate tasks repeated at regular intervals. Unlike National Curriculum assessment, monitoring does not require data from every child in the age groups concerned, only from a small sample, and each pupil involved would take only a fraction of the total assessments in a survey. The total picture would be obtained by aggregating across the sample. For this purpose, it is essential that externally set tests and not teacher assessments be used, since standardisation of conditions for all pupils taking the tests is a basic requirement for the reliability of the results. In this fashion, monitoring surveys on the one hand, and National Curriculum assessment on the other, could complement each other: the latter by providing detailed information on individual pupils, and the former an in-depth picture of the knowledge and skills of the nation's children. A future effective monitoring system could be designed not only to detect trends over time in overall attainment in various curriculum areas, but also to help check that the levels of National Curriculum assessment (including the new-style GCSE) are being held consistent across years – this could be done by targeting some monitoring tests at particular parts of the National Curriculum.

There needs to be a continuing debate on the standards of attainment we should aim for as we move towards the 21st century. Some countries are setting ambitious targets. For instance, in the United States the National Governors' Association has adopted the following goal: "By the year 2000, every adult American will be literate and will possess the skills necessary to compete in a global economy and exercise the rights and responsibilities of citizenship".

In these circumstances it may not be sufficient to say that standards are not falling, or are rising slowly; it may be necessary in certain areas to progress more quickly as requirements become clearer. However, this debate must take place against a background of assured knowledge not only about how our competitors are developing their pupils' educational achievements, but also, and more importantly, about how our school pupils are performing nationally. Such knowledge can only come from a system of regular and effective monitoring.

Bibliography to the appendix

Department of Education and Science (1982), *Mathematics Counts (Cockcroft Report)*, HMSO, London.

FOXMAN, D. (1992), *Learning Mathematics and Science: The Second International Assessment of Educational Progress in England*, NFER.

FOXMAN, D., HUTCHISON, D. and BLOOMFIELD, B. (1990*a*), *The APU Experience*, SEAC. (Lists all works published under the aegis of APU.)

FOXMAN, D., RUDDOCK, G. and McCALLUM, I. (1990*b*), *APU Mathematics Monitoring 1984/88 (Phase 2)*, SEAC. pp. 6 and 7.

GORMAN, T.P. and FERNANDES, C. (1992), *Reading in Recession*, NFER.

GORMAN, T.P., WHITE, J., BROOKS, G. and ENGLISH, F. (1991), *Language for Learning: A Summary Report on the 1988 APU Surveys of Language Performance*, SEAC.

ROBITAILLE, D.F. and GARDEN, R.A. (1989), *The IEA Study of Mathematics II: Contexts and Outcomes of School Mathematics*, Pergamon Press, Oxford.

RODGERS, B. (1986), "Change in the reading attainment of adults: a longitudinal study", *British Journal of Developmental Psychology*, Vol. 4, pp. 1-17.

Scottish Education Department (1989), *Assessment of Achievement Programme. Reports on Mathematics* and *English Language* (1990), HMSO.

The Commission bases its thinking on the best available statistics and research findings, national and international. The purpose of the Briefings is to enable authoritative writers to analyse and discuss key education and training issues. They are thus intended to inform the Commission's work and contribute to public debate. The text may be reproduced without permission and may be quoted provided that its source is acknowledged. Enquiries to John Hillman (Series Editor) or Louise Priestley, National Commission on Education, Suite 24, 10-18 Manor Gardens, London N7 6JY. Tel: 171 272 4411; Fax: 171 281 6778.

Bibliography

The procedures for setting standards in the English system are not usually publicly documented, while the standards themselves are. This bibliography lists publications helpful to a reader wishing to find out more about the standards and other issues discussed here. Entries are listed under the sections into which this paper is divided.

A brief history of the introduction of the National Curriculum

Task group on Assessment and Testing (1987), ''National Curriculum, Task Group on Assessment and Testing, A Report'', Department of Education and Science, London.

Differences in achievement

The reference below summarises the work of the Assessment of Performance Unit and gives further references if more detail is desired:

FOXMAN, D., HUTCHISON, H. and BLOOMFIELD, B. (1991), *The APU Experience 1977-1990*, School Examination and Assessment Council, London.

The code of practice for public examinations is:

School Curriculum and Assessment Authority (1994), *Mandatory Code of Practice for the GCSE*, School Curriculum and Assessment Authority, London.

The standards

The current National Curriculum is documented in a series of documents entitled ''Mathematics in the National Curriculum'', ''Science in the National Curriculum'', etc. These give the performance standards and accompanying information. They were published in London by the Department of Education and Science and the Welsh Office.

The proof proposals for the revised National Curriculum are presented in a document entitled ''The National Curriculum Orders''. This was published in London by the School Curriculum and Assessment Authority in 1994. It has been replaced in January 1995 by the final version.

The current performance standards in Scotland are documented in the series ''Curriculum and Assessment in Scotland, National Guidelines, Mathematics 5-14'', ''Curriculum and Assessment in Scotland, National Guidelines, English Language 5-14'', etc. These were published by the Scottish Office Education Department.

FRANCE

by

Alain Michel
Inspecteur général, ministère de l'Éducation nationale

Summary

There has been growing concern in France over the last ten years about schools' and students' performance standards. This concern has been translated into substantial reforms of the educational system and to the introduction of national diagnostic tests at three key stages of schooling. The traditional *baccalauréat* has also undergone considerable reorganisation and diversification. Standards are set in France by adjustments to the National Curriculum and its associated attainment targets. The process is complex, involving wide-spread consultation. The national inspectorate plays a key role. Analysis of the results of the national diagnostic tests has brought empirical evidence to bear on a process which was until recently only criterion-referenced and based on professional knowledge and experience. However, external examinations, especially, the various forms of the *baccalauréat* are still carried out by traditional methods.

Context

Introduction

Some preliminary remarks are necessary in order to clarify the use of the key words of this study: performance standards, quality, curriculum, standards and assessment. As a matter of fact, these words are not standardized at an international level and have different meanings among the different countries. Moreover, their meaning can vary with the context or the conceptual framework within which they are used.

In current American context, performance standards specify "how good is good enough". They raise issues of assessment to gauge the degree to which content standards have been attained. They are not the skills, the modes of reasoning or understanding that assessments attempt to measure. Instead, they are "the indices of quality that specify how adept or competent a student demonstration must be". A performance standard indicates both the nature of the evidence required to demonstrate that the content standard has been met and the quality of student performance that will be deemed acceptable.

Thus, the present study should focus on the issue of defining levels of proficiency and criteria for gauging them, including the assessment tools for doing so. This means a specific approach to the issue of defining standards in education: it is only a particular aspect of a more general issue. In this sense "performance standards" could be translated into French as *normes d'exigence* or *normes de performance*.

However, this particular issue is intimately related to the broader issues of curriculum content standards, attainment targets, quality of education, assessment processes and their interrelations. Thus, it cannot be treated separately. For instance, the indices of quality of students' attainment depend on expectations in terms of targets and content of the school process; the latter depend on the performance which has been previously observed, and thus on the assessment tools which are currently being used (and on the way they are being used, which is related to the attitudes of the different actors involved). In other words, the issue of performance standards should be considered within a systemic approach showing the main interactions among the different aspects of the search towards more standardization of the educational processes and between the different actors involved.

This report on the French approach to performance standards will attempt to be systemic, without trying to formalize by a model all these interactions.

But, first, it is necessary to make a few comments about the vocabulary used in the French context.

The word "curriculum" is not used in France in the field of education. It is used only within the expression "curriculum vitae", which is used mainly for professional purposes. Thus, school curriculum is usually translated by "programmes d'enseignement", which is not exactly equivalent. The *programmes d'enseignement* include general goals of the different subjects, programmes of study, attainment targets (*objectifs de référence*), some teaching and assessment instructions. One major feature is that in France these "programmes" are published for each grade and each subject and constitute an implementation of the "general objectives" of primary and secondary education, as stated by the Education Act of 1989 and subsequent statutory provisions (*décrets* et *circulaires*). So, there does exist de facto a French national curriculum, which includes both the legal and statutory provisions about the general goals of education in their diachronic and synchronic dimensions, and the *programmes d'enseignement* concerning the different grades and subjects.

Reasons for concern

In France, there has been, over the last 10 years or so, growing concern among the general public and education professionals about students' and schools' performance standards. Particular attention is given to targeted groups considered to be at risk of school failure, but there is concern about the total school population.

The main reasons for this growing concern are:

- The increasing public spending on education (at the end of the 1980s, the education budget became the most important chapter of the State's budget), mainly due to increasing participation rates in upper secondary and higher education, within a context of economic slowdown. This implied more concern about the effectiveness of the education processes (value for money).
- The necessity of improving the quality of education in order to meet the needs of more qualified labour required by the growing international economic competition and to overcome new social issues, very much linked with growing unemployment, particularly of young people.
- The will of the government to establish a new monitoring of the education system, based more and more upon objectives and evaluation of outputs, to replace previous monitoring based upon the control of the respect of regulations (control of conformity). This requires setting up operational objectives (*i.e.* which can be assessed), standards and measurement tools. Such an evolution has been related to the process (starting in 1985) of more decentralization (new responsabilities given to the local authorities and increasing autonomy of schools).
- The social demand for more transparency of the education system and of its performance. More objective evaluation of education is regarded as favoring more democracy, more effectiveness and more equity. This is related to the accountability movement.
- The increasing heterogeneity of students in secondary education related to mass education and the challenge of conciliating mass education, and the objective of quality for all students.
- The educational research findings on effective schools but also on effective teaching methods and practices, as well as on geographic and social inequalities in students' achievement and attainment of qualifications.

Last but not least, the introduction of new assessment tools and the emergence of a new "culture of evaluation" is a cumulative process. The new information produced increases the awareness and the concern of the public and of professionals. More information and objective evaluation is then called for to increase the quality of education and to reduce the number of drop-outs.

Main structural features of the French education system

There are three main levels of education (see appendix):

- Primary education, pre-elementary (from age 2 or 3 to 6) and elementary (from age 6 to 11): ISCED O and 1 levels;
- Secondary education, lower secondary (from age 11 to 15) and upper secondary, which includes 3 tracks: general or technological (from age 15 to 18) or vocational (from age 15 to 17 or 19): ISCED 2 and 3 levels;
- Tertiary education, after the *baccalauréat*: either technological or professional (2 or 3 years) – ISCED 5 – or university and *grandes écoles* (4 to 9 years according to the subjects and degrees achieved) – ISCED 6 and 7.

Some specific features of the French education system are:

- The principle of education as a public utility and the principle of secularity, which underpin the importance of the state's role and the emphasis on equal opportunity.
- Widespread early schooling: 35 per cent of each generation are enrolled at the age of 2 and about 100 per cent at the age of 3.
- The existence of comprehensive lower secondary education and the ban on streaming before the end of the 4th grade of *collège* (*classe de troisième*): all students are enrolled in the same type of school, called *collège*.
- The relatively small number of apprenticeships, though more training based on alternate classroom and workplace instruction is being introduced in the vocational tracks.
- The distinction at upper secondary level between 3 streams: general, technological and vocational.
- The importance given to the *baccalauréat* which qualifies holders for higher education, with the consequence that university admissions are non-selective, while other existing higher education streams are selective.
- The dual higher education system of universities and *grandes écoles* on one hand and short-cycle (2 year-) higher education degrees on the other hand.

Administration

Even though the system has been "decentralized" to a certain extent over the last decade, the State has retained important powers: recruitment and payment of teachers, the definition of a national curriculum, the attribution of nationally recognized degrees, in particular the upper secondary diploma of *baccalauréat*.

The French education territory is divided into 28 *académies*. Each academy is run by a "Recteur" (usually a university professor) who represents the Minister of Education and is the interlocutor of the local authorities (regional and local), who are mainly responsible for the building and maintenance of schools and teaching facilities.

According to a recent OECD study, within the INES project, about one third of decisions are made at central, intermediate and school levels. The schools' autonomy concerns mainly teaching organization, methods and practices. The schools and teachers are inspected or audited by the central and regional Inspectorates. Also, new national school indicators have been build up at the national level to contribute to the steering of the schools.

Major assessments of students' performances are of two types:
- "Summative" assessments in the form of national examinations.
  - *Brevet des Collèges* at the end of lower secondary education (4th year of the French *collège*).
  - *Baccalauréat général* or *technologique,* at the end of upper secondary education (3rd year of *lycée*) for students in the general or technological track.
  - Vocational degrees for students in vocational tracks, at the end of the 2nd year of *lycée professionnel* – *Certificat d'Aptitude Professionnelle* (CAP) or *Brevet d'Études Professionnelles* (BEP), and for an increasing proportion of students, at the end of two more years in *lycée professionnel,* the *Baccalauréat Professionnel*.
  - Higher education degrees: at the end of two years (*brevet de technicien supérieur* or BTS and *diplôme universitaire de technologie* or DUT), three years (*licence*), four years (*maîtrise*) or beyond (DEA and DESS, which are equivalent to a master's degree, or doctorate).
- National "diagnostic assessments" of all students, at three key stages of schooling: beginning of the 3rd year of elementary education (*classe de CE2* at the age of eight), beginning of the 1st year of lower secondary (*classe de 6ᵉ* at the age of eleven) and beginning of the 1st year of upper secondary (*classe de seconde* at the age of sixteen).

The main purpose of these assessments is not only to help the teachers evaluate the strengths and weaknesses of their students at the beginning of the school year by providing them with more objective instruments (expressing explicit or implicit national standards), but also to provide feedback to the students themselves and their parents. Thus, these assessments are primarily a pedagogical tool aimed at improving teaching methods and practices and the learning process for students.

The issue of equality of educational opportunities remains a central concept of the French education policy. It is explicitly stated in the Education Act of July 1989 and widely supported by public opinion, as two recent polls have confirmed. One basic goal stated by the Act of 1989 is that, by the year 2000, 100 per cent of an age cohort should be obtaining qualification recognized by the labour market, *i.e.* at least a CAP or a BEP (certificate of vocational competence). Another objective of the Act is to increase the proportion of students completing secondary education and taking the *baccalauréat* to 80 per cent of a generation (figures were about 60 per cent in 1993 as against 25 per cent in 1970). The emphasis is more and more on equal access and equal outcomes and less and less on equal resources, as it had been until recently.

This evolution stems first from the awareness that "formal" equality of opportunities does not mean "real" equality and that more resources must be provided to those who need more in view of specific handicaps. The creation of the *Zones d'éducation prioritaires* (priority education areas) in 1982 was an important landmark in this respect. However, a balance must be found between the necessity of providing more resources to the schools in areas with special difficulties and the basic principle of the equality of all citizens with respect to the supply of public utilities.

The focus on equality of outcomes was sharpened too by progress in the analysis of assessment outcomes, which provided new information about geographical and social inequalities. This increasing concern about equality of outcomes spurred intensive effort towards more rigourous definition of performance standards and measurement of students' achievement in cognitive and non cognitive areas.

Differences in achievement

Two kinds of instruments are used to evaluate the spread of students' achievement at a given time and over time:

– tests on student samples drawn from different grades, implemented on an average of every 5 years;
– diagnostic tests of all students, as described above: reduced samples are analyzed although the main purpose of these tests is not to establish cross-section or longitudinal comparisons.

Evidence about geographic differences and over time

The knowledge of regional differences in achievement has been greatly improved in the last three years, thanks to methodological progress in defining national and regional indicators, particularly outcome indicators based on the results of the formal diagnostic tests described above. The *Géographie de l'École*, published by the Ministry of Education for the first time in 1993 and again in 1994, represents this important progress. The ensuing phase, started recently, calls for better analysis of differences at a variety of local levels and among schools.

The evolution over time of students' achievement and of interstudent differences is less well identified, since the national tests are recent (1989 for *CE2* and *6ᵉ*; 1992 for *classe de seconde*). However, a few longterm data sources are available: tests organized by the Ministry of Defense, regular sample surveys organized by the Ministry of Education in certain subjects and some specific studies by educational researchers.

Evidence of differences among students, grade levels and classes

The differences among students are analyzed on the basis of national diagnostic test results, period national surveys (usually at the end of the school-year for a sample of grades, every five years) and international surveys like IAEP2 (ETS) or IEA's "Reading literacy". Some surveys' sample design permitted some comparison of classes, but it is conceptually difficult to clearly distinguish between "class effect" and "teacher effect". With the same sources, comparisons are made between grades (for cognitive and, more recently, for non cognitive aspects), usually for various cohorts of students. The new data base *scolarité* and regular national testing will permit longitudinal studies of students' cohorts. In particular, it is now possible to track the individual path of each student. A new study is now being designed to compare outcomes at the beginning and at the end of a chosen grade with the participation of teachers on a voluntary basis. Data do exist on the comparative performance of girls and boys, as well as on differences due to home and socio-economic background. These differences have been decreasing over time, like regional differences. The issue of the effects of different curricula on learning outcomes is not relevant in France under a sole national curriculum. However, new research will analyze which teaching methods are the most effective in given contexts.

A significant effort has been accomplished over the last years to develop school indicators. They are of two main types:

– a core of common indicators which permit both schools' self-evaluation and a better understanding of the "school effect", in that otherwise comparable schools may be analyzed in terms of added outcome values;
– a set of non-compulsory indicators, which are available to the schools and can be adapted and used for self-evaluation, according to each school's program of objectives.

The process of standard setting

With respect to the basic issue of setting performance standards, the approach in France remains mostly pragmatic (based on the experience of teachers and inspectors). But, there have been important changes over the last years toward more systematic and scientific approaches in this field. The development of national standardized tests contributed to this evolution and the results of these tests are used, to a certain extent, to check the relevancy of the current standards and to set new standards. However, this is not entirely new, in that the results of examinations and other assessments have in the past always influenced (albeit in a more subjective way) teachers' and examiners' expectations and assessment criteria.

The analysis of the national tests results made by the *Direction de l'Évaluation et de la Prospective* (DEP) of the Ministry of Education and by educational researchers show improvement of students' achievement over time, particularly in the worst performing students, in two basic subjects: French language and mathematics.

Formally, in all types of public sector schools, every student is expected to achieve minimum thresholds of knowledge and skills (and only more recently attainment targets). Until the Education Act of 1989, such a threshold existed at each grade level, which explained the high proportion of students repeating a grade. Many studies showed that repetition was not systematically effective. The new education policy prompted a decrease in repetition and established a more flexible system of pluri-annual cycles making room for different speeds of learning according to students' abilities. The implementation of such a system implied use of more sophisticated assessment tools and standards, enabling definition of student profiles and the formation of sub-groups with which different educational approaches can be used. But, within the new system, there are still minimum thresholds to be attained at the end of the different cycles: *i.e.* end of the 2nd year of elementary school (or *CE1*), end of the 5th year (or *CM2*), end of the 2nd and the 4th years of *collège* (or *5e* and *3e*), end of 1st (general and technological track) or 2nd (vocational track) year of *lycée*. These thresholds are assessed by the teachers themselves through ''continuous monitoring'' of students' achievement, including written or oral assignments at school.

The first external examinations are the *Brevet des collèges,* the *baccalauréat* (general, technological and vocational) and the vocational degrees (CAP and BEP) which require an average mark of 10 out of 20 (a weighted average with differing subject coefficients). Passing one's exam and obtaining qualification is particularly important in France for finding a job or going into higher education.

In all cases the minimum threshold is primarily defined in terms of ''sufficient'' student performance in the consideration of teachers or boards of examiners. The definition of such acceptable performance takes reference in the national curriculum and is mainly based upon the teachers' perceptions. It is not quite independent of the distribution of the scores attained by a class or a cohort of students (or candidates in the case of an exam). An expected level of performance reached by only a very low proportion of students would be revised as inappropriate.

However, there has been, for many years in the vocational tracks, and in the last years in the general and technological tracks, an increasing effort to define more objective criteria in terms of competences to be achieved at different grades. This is related to the emergence of a new education paradigm: the move from a curriculum expressed mainly in terms of content and knowledge toward a curriculum expressed mainly in terms of competences, skills and attainment targets.

''Implicit performance standards'' are set for all subjects. More explicit or systematic standards have been defined, first in vocational subjects, and, more recently, in technological subjects, in physical education and, to a lesser extent, in foreign languages, in French language literacy and in mathematics. Implicit standards are those which are the result of history, of the accumulated experience of teachers, inspectors and examiners. They do not rely upon a systematic analysis of identified, required competences defining *a priori* levels of proficiency, justified by rational and rigorous argumentation. They have instead a significant subjective dimension, which is bounded by the national curriculum, exchange of experience between teachers, inspections carried on by the Inspectorate and national examinations or assessments. Performance standards have become more and more explicit in relationship with the fact that the national curriculum became expressed more and more in terms of attainment targets, and with the experience of creating items for standardized tests. Thus, the setting of performance standards is tightly linked to the procedures and methods of setting the content standards of the national curriculum on one hand, and to the process of building standardized tests on the other.

Procedures and methods for setting up content standards

In defining the national curriculum, the standard setters are mainly inspectors, university professors, teachers and members of the central administration, who are all civil servants employed by the Ministry of Education or the Ministry of Higher Education and Research. For the technological and vocational tracks, representatives of the trades and professions also participate in definition.

As an example, we will describe the current procedure for revising the national curriculum for secondary education. It is a rather complex procedure gradually implemented over the past years, according to the general provisions of the 1989 Education Act, which notably created the *Conseil National des Programmes* or CNP (National Curriculum Council). The procedure concerning primary education is slightly different. The Directorate for Secondary Schools (*Direction des Lycées et Collèges*) of the central administration of the Ministry of Education coordinates the procedure. The Director for Secondary Schools is commited to implementing the education policy decided by the Minister: after having consulted the chairman of the CNP, he puts in an order for designing new programmes of study to specific working groups, which are named:

- for the academic subjects of the *collège* and the *lycée, Groupes techniques disciplinaires* or GTD (Technical groups by subject);
- for technological and vocational lycée subjects, *Commissions professionnelles consultatives* or CPC (vocational advisory boards).

The role of the CNP, an advisory body composed of members selected *intuitu personae* for their competence, is to formulate general recommendations for adapting the curriculum to the evolution of knowledge and of society. Its approach should be global (general goals of the primary school, of the *collège* and of the *lycée*) and should encourage consistency between subjects, cross-curricular competences and articulation between grades. For example, in a 1991 report concerning the *collège* (junior high school), the CNP stressed that the objectives of the *collège* should relate to three domains: competences within each subject (which should be defined in terms of "situations that the students should be able to understand and to deal with"), methodological capacities (some of them transversal across subjects), and fundamental values and attitudes identified as prerequisites for a democratic society. The CNP also issues an opinion on the conclusions of the GTD and CPC.

Most of the work concerning the conception of the new programmes of study is done within the GTD or the CPC (for technical subjects). All working groups are supposed to take into account the general orientations set by the CNP. The members of these groups are appointed by the Minister of Education. They are not permanent and they do not undergo any specific training. They are all chosen for their competence in the subjects concerned.

Each GTD is chaired by both a General Inspector and a University Professor. The other members are professors, teachers and regional inspectors. *Ad hoc* consultants on particular issues may be invited to join the group. Each GTD is mandated to consider a specific subject but has to take into consideration the links between this subject and the other subjects. In 1994, 13 GTDs exist: arts, chemistry, civics education, physical and sports education, French language and literature and ancient languages (greek and latin), history and geography, foreign languages, mathematics, physics, economics and social sciences, life and earth sciences (biology and geology), technology at *collège,* technology at *lycée.*

Each GTD must respect rules stated in a *Charte des Programmes* published in 1992. This Charter stipulates in particular that the programmes must formulate attainment targets and define content in terms of knowledge and competences. The draft programmes prepared by the GTD are submitted to General and Regional Inspectors, to the associations of teachers of the subjects concerned and to groups of teachers. Their comments are summed up by the Directorate for Secondary Schools (DLC) and transmitted to the GTD. A revised version of the programme is then transmitted to the DLC, charged with preparing the statutory text. This is then submitted to the CNP and to the *Conseil supérieur de l'Éducation,* the highest advisory body of the Ministry of Education.

For the Technological and vocational tracks of upper secondary education, the CPCs perform the same work as the GTDs in the academic subjects. Within these CPCs, there is actually a real partnership between the Ministry of Education and the industry and trade professions. According to legal provisions, any vocational degree or qualification can be modified without consulting the CPCs.

The CPCs were created in 1948 and renovated in 1972 and 1983. The domains of competence of the CPCs are distributed according to 20 sectors of economic activity, such as: building and public works, chemistry, food industry, metallurgical industry, tourism, finance, health and social sectors, communication. Each CPC has around 35 members: 10 employers' representatives, 10 trade union representatives, 6 representatives of the Ministries and other public bodies involved in the economic sector of the CPC, 11 persons of suitable standing (teachers' unions, parents' associations, Chambers of Trade and Industry, etc.).

A wide variety of qualifications covering more than 600 vocational and technological diplomas are proposed. Among them are:

- 115 BTS and 39 DUT;
- 48 vocational *baccalauréats*;
- 50 BEP and 240 CAP.

All these diplomas and their programmes of study are regularly updated (every five years on average) by the CPCs.

The process of creating or upgrading a vocational or technological diploma takes about one year and includes four phases:

a) Assessment of whether it is appropriate to create or overhaul a diploma or a cluster of diplomas, taking into consideration the kind of link to be established between training and employment. Education representatives tend to emphasise adaptability and tranversal abilities. The aim is to reach a suitable compromise between students' and economic sectors' real "absorption" capacities, and the need to train young people not just for a first job but for an entire working life, and hence for the likelihood of subsequent retraining. Therefore, it is necessary to analyse recruitment patterns in the sectors concerned, to assess the extent of future employment opportunities and to identify precisely the nature of vocational demand.

b) Definition of a "frame of reference for vocational activities" (*référentiel des activités professionnelles*) in the shape of a 5- to 10-year prospective analysis of the activities covered by the jobs likely to be filled by future holders of the qualification. This phase is crucial because it implies choosing and weighting different possible functions. The contribution of representatives of the trades and professions is vital to ensuring proper fit.

c) Definition of a "frame of reference for certification" (*référentiel de certification*), which involves translating the analysis of vocational activities into knowledge, skills and know-how to be acquired. The contribution of teachers and educationalists is central to this phase.

d) Definition of the conditions of validation. This phase, under the responsability of the Ministry of Education, involves defining regulatory aspects (*e.g.* entry conditions, timetables, etc.) and conditions for the validation of learning, generally in the shape of overall validation of students and of credits for adults in continuing education. The draft diploma and programme of study is submitted to the full vocational advisory board for approval and then to the Higher Council for Education. It is then made official by ministerial order published in the Official Bulletin of the National Education Service.

The process of regular curriculum revision has certainly been improved over the last years. In particular, this is true for the technological and vocational tracks. However, its main weakness remains the dominance of a subject-oriented approach, which prevents an overall curricular approach taking into enough consideration cross-curricular competences and subject complementarity. Moreover, it is rather difficult for subject specialists to give a simple definition of "core knowledge and competences" in their own field, as nearly everything seems to them to be important. Reducing the encyclopedic aspect of the programmes and concentrating more on essential concepts, facts and competences remains a challenge.

In such a context, performance standards are set at the national level (curricula, general objectives and guidelines) and at the local level (teachers in the classroom, school level, regional board of examiners) for actual implementation. The *Direction des Écoles,* the *Direction des Lycées et Collèges,* the *Conseil National des Programmes,* the General Inspectorate and the *Direction de l'Évaluation et de la Prospective* (DEP) play the major role in managing the process at the national level, under the authority of the Minister of Education.

No rigourous estimation of the cost of this process is available. Only the direct costs of national standardized tests and examinations have been estimated.

The national curriculum and educational objectives, and the role of the Central Inspectorate, are a factor of homogeneity across the country. However, in the absence of accurate national performance standards in most of the subjects, uniformity of expectations and of evaluations across the country cannot be guaranteed. For external examinations there are special regional procedures aimed at harmonizing expectations, scoring grids and marks.

There are many factors influencing standards and the level at which they are set. The main factor is the empirical experience of previous exams and tests. Historical experience certainly plays a major role. Concerning the standardized tests organized by the DEP, pilot studies help establish the levels of difficulty of the selected items. In all cases, the previously observed performance of the students and score distributions are major factors. Thus, there is feedback of observed results on the previous standards: standards are defined through a dialectic process.

More fundamental factors are the expectations of employers and parents, and more generally of the public, in a changing technological, economic and social environment. Current public debates or controversies about education call for new demands on schools and students and more rigourous analysis of required competences and abilities.

The normative choice of increasing the general educational attainment, by the year 2000 – 100 per cent of an age cohort gaining a minimum qualification (*i.e.* a CAP or BEP) and 80 per cent attaining the *baccalauréat* level – also had an effect on the definition of standards required at different grades, in terms of programmes of study, of expected competences and of assessment procedures. In particular, the "100 per cent objective" required defining a core of basic competences necessary to be able to reach a minimum level of qualification expected by employers. On the other hand, the "80 per cent objective" called for a new definition of the different types of *baccalauréat* (general, technological and vocational) and thus a reform of the programmes of study in the lycées. This reform started to be implemented in 1992/93 and was completed in 1994/95.

The ongoing reform of the lycée aims at:

– reducing the number of *baccalauréats* of the general and technological streams and thus simplifying a system which had become too complex;
– reequilibrating the prestige of the different general *baccalauréats,* as the section C (major in mathematics) was considered as the only prestigious one;
– making more flexible the choices of the student through the creation of a "decision" cycle and more freedom for the choice of electives;
– taking more into account the heterogeneity of the students, by a systematic assessment of every student at the beginning of the first year of *lycée* through national standardized tests and the introduction of a "modular" system of teaching. The "modules" are special teaching sessions to sub-groups of students with the same weaknesses, which have been revealed through the diagnostic test at the beginning of the school year. Provision is made for three hours of modular teaching a week in four subjects: French, mathematics, first foreign language and history/geography.

There are now three sections (*séries*) of the general *baccalauréat* – economic and social sciences (ES), liberal arts (L) and sciences (S) – and four sections of the technological *baccalauréat* – health and social welfare, industrial science and technology, laboratory science and technology and tertiary science and technology. The students took this new *baccalauréat* for the first time in June 1995.

The reform of the *lycée* and the *baccalauréat* will be followed by a new curriculum in primary education, currently prepared, and then by a new curriculum of lower secondary education. The approach of the working groups is influenced by the general move towards defining the curriculum in terms of attainment targets and competences.

Thus, there is more and more systematic analysis of the different levels of competences in all subjects and of transversal or interdisciplinary abilities and concepts and about the way to measure to what extent they are mastered.

This evolution is more advanced in technical subjects (particularly in the vocational track), mainly because of the fact that the demands of employers are more concrete and easier to define in terms of observable and measurable skills.

This is also the case in the subject of physical education, in which levels of performance are easier to define, to observe and to assess in an objective way, even though there are still some difficulties. But important conceptual work is now also being done in the field of foreign languages (definition of standards of competences, like communication skills), in reading and mathematics [from the experience of the tests at the beginning of the first year of *collège* (junior high school)] and in economic and social sciences (first year of *lycée*).

Performance standards

Performance standards are defined in terms of knowledge (facts, notions, concepts, rules, etc.) and competences (to understand some kind of information, to solve an equation, to structure an argument, etc.) which are more or less accurately defined in the national curriculum (*programmes des enseignements* and *instructions*) according to the subjects. They are assessed through the accomplishment of different tasks: written assignments, oral exercices or practical work, in school or at home, in all grades, and external examinations in certain grades.

The use of standardized tests was developed only over the last five years in primary and secondary education. Such tests do not fit with the French traditional conception of education, for many reasons. One is the importance given, in most subjects, to writing abilities and to methods of reasoning or argument as much as to the final answer or result. Another one is the principle of the autonomy of the teacher, who is supposed to be able to select personally the measurement tools for assessing students. In other words, the teacher is considered to be in the best situation to observe the student and assess his or her performance.

Basically, there is also the assumption that education performance cannot be measured in an objective way, *i.e.* with scientific methods, and that subjective evaluation is inevitable. Thus, standardized tests are often perceived as irrelevant. Moreover, the use of "external" tools of assessment can be felt as a threat to the power of the teacher (the *magister*), who is supposed to be the expert who knows and who therefore has the power to evaluate. Finally, it is very difficult to reach a consensus about what competences can be effectively assessed and about the indices which can be considered relevant.

The traditional standards of curriculum contents and performance were sometimes tested before being generalized to the national level, but this was rather rare. The new approach, partly related to the increasing use of standardized tests, for diagnostic, formative or summative purposes, integrates experimentation or a pilot phase as a normal stage of the process. Moreover, the analysis of the results of previous tests contributes to defining expected levels of performance. This was particularly the case in defining three main levels of competence in reading literacy and in mathematics at grades *CE2* and *6ᵉ*.

The new standards are disseminated by instructions and other written material, as well as through the Regional Inspectors, for all schools. The performance standards are not set independently of the procedures whereby curricula are defined, either because they are part of the curricula (for example in the *référentiels* of the technical subjects) or because some General Inspectors of the subjects concerned participate in both procedures.

In technical (technological and vocational) subjects, curricula and standards are reviewed, on average, every five years. Review is much more irregular in the other subjects. The main reason for review is to take into account new knowledge and new social and economic demands. Another reason can be the goal of improving the effectiveness of the education processes, in order to allow for more students to reach certain levels of competences (for instance by cancelling some parts of the curricula and insisting more on basic tranversal competences). But, in principle, the proportion of students attaining the previous standards should not be an important determinant of the new standards: the goal of 80 per cent of an age cohort at the *baccalauréat* level should not lead to lowering the standards in the way they are defined. However, this does not mean that this will not actually happen or that the "value" of the *baccalauréat* will remain constant in its value for entry into certain advanced programmes or into the labour market.

The evidence of attainment of performance standards is revealed through all the instruments mentioned and, more and more over the last three or four years, from standardized tests and profiles of student performances. But the evolution has to be rather slow, given the habits and some reluctance of the teachers. The new approach and tools have to be accepted by the teachers. This implies an adapted communication strategy and training of the teachers.There are different levels of acceptable proficiency, but in the external exams there is a cut-off standard: pass/fail. Generally, it is situated at an overall (weighted) average mark of 10 out of 20.

In most cases, the statements of standards remain implicit and are not independent of scoring procedures and criteria. Only recently with the use of national standardized tests has a systematic effort of explicit *a priori* definition of levels of competences been developed.

Such an *a priori* definition implies a conceptual reflexion about each subject, interrelations between subjects and the goals and objectives of education at different grades. Then, it requires defining different categories of competences and setting up a hierarchy among them according to their level of difficulty. Then, test items associated with the different categories of competences must be created. Finally, the results of conceptual and empirical research on assessment must be taken into account in order to define the percentages of correct answers that will equate to the defined levels of proficiency. Thus, it is a complex dialectic process which is never perfectly terminated. Such a procedure is being implemented in building diagnostic tests for the beginning of the *CE2* and *6th* grades.

Three main principles of such an approach should be emphasised:
- only a few levels of competences are defined;
- these levels are defined in absolute terms;
- the assessment tools must be relevant and therefore designed in relation with the procedure of defining proficiency levels.

The protocol of these evaluations includes very precise instructions and scoring grids. On the one hand, the tests must be stable enough over time to make it possible to compare performances of different cohorts of students. On the other hand, they must be adaptable to the evolution of the world, new education policy goals and the results of educational research.

However, such a systematic approach is carried out only for diagnostic assessment. It is not adopted yet for summative assessment, notably for external examinations.

The reporting of results differs according to assessment instruments. The results of class assignments are regularly given to the students and every term to their parents. The results of the external examinations are published at national, regional and school levels. Recently, some indicators were designed in order to publish net results for schools, instead of gross results, *i.e.* results taking into account some basic characteristics of the student population of each school.

The results of national diagnostic tests are published at national and regional levels, but not at school level. The main analyses of results of these tests are: national average scores (global and by item), regional differences, comparative performances of girls and boys, influence of home and socio-economic background, over time evolution, distribution of students according to different levels of proficiency, in-depth case studies on samples of schools or classes, etc. The results of the national standardized tests are published by the DEP.

There are special provisions for children with special needs, mostly in terms of educational resources and teaching methods, not so much in terms of assessment procedures.

Preconditions and problems

The process of improving standard-setting procedures requires time and caution. It implies an evolution of mentalities of teachers and students, and thus a communication strategy. It also requires more conceptual work for defining competences and levels of proficiency, especially in subjects like philosophy, social sciences, experimental sciences, civics education. One should be particularly careful about the limits of objectivity in defining *a priori* levels of proficiency and be aware of the difficulty of assessing non-cognitive competences (which are essential). In other words, one must be aware of the limits of a scientific approach to assessing proficiency, but still try to improve the rationality of the present procedures, which remain far too subjective.

Policy formulation and decision making

Findings about standard-setting experiences are used to assist policy formulation and decision making at national, regional, school and class levels.

They influence the revision of curricula and national objectives, the policy at regional and school levels, and the objectives and practices of teachers and students. There is not yet a systematic link between the development of standardized tests, of the performance standard-setting procedures and of the national curriculum, but these processes are more and more interdependent. The General Inspectorate plays an important role in this respect, as some of its members partipate in all three processes.

The relationship between the notion of a core curriculum and the reality of teacher and students' performance cannot be revealed mechanically through applying standardized achievement tests. It is sensitive to the limits of objectivity in assessment procedures and teaching and learning practices. The education process is a complex process which cannot be totally modelled and the goals of education cannot be entirely expressed in terms of measurable objectives.

The new standard-setting procedures are influencing teaching styles. This influence will be stronger if the teachers are properly trained for participating in the design of standards and testing items and making the best use of the information provided by the tests. As yet, despite some progress, there is still a lot to be done in training teachers in this area. Here too, the Inspectorate has a major role to play. The new institutes for the initial training of teachers (the *Instituts Universitaires de Formation des Maîtres*) should also integrate this ''assessment culture'' into their syllabus.

The international dimension

France has very much benefitted from participating in IEA and ETS international surveys of students' achievement as well as in the OECD activities. The international comparison of performances is very important, even though it is a time-consuming and costly process. The results are significant only in terms of orders of magnitude and must not focus on the ranking of countries. What really matters is to know the relative weaknesses and strengths of the national education system, and, of course, the main causes of such a state. That is why the analysis of the factors explaining the observed results is as important as the results themselves. This implies relevant questionnaires to the students, teachers, headteachers and parents.

The comparison of procedures for setting performance standards in OECD Member countries should be of significant value for each of them, given the conceptual and practical difficulties encountered in this field.

Appendix
The French education system

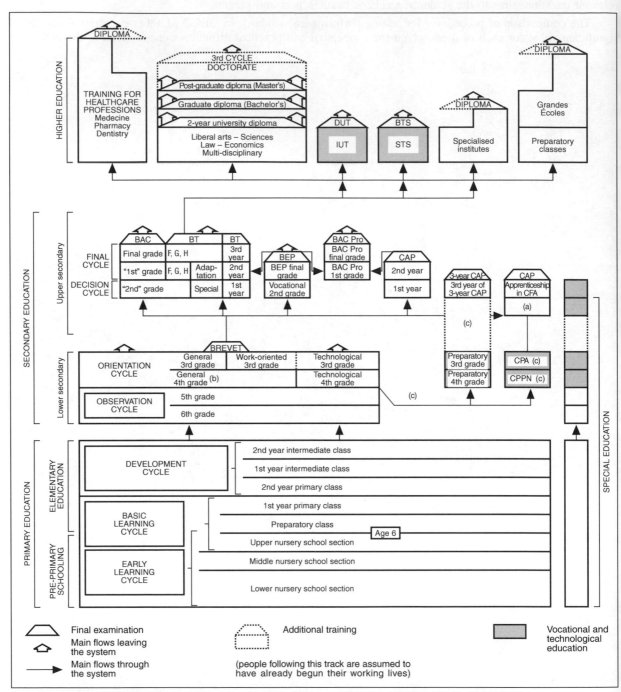

BAC: Baccalauréat. BAC pro: Vocational baccalauréat. BEP: Diploma of Vocational Studies. BT: Technician's Diploma.
BTS: Advanced Technician's Diploma. CAP: Certificate of Vocational Competence. CFA: Apprentice Training Centre.
CPA: Preparatory Apprenticeship Class. CPPN: Streamed Pre-vocational Class. DUT: University Diploma of Technology.
F, G, H: Technological Baccalauréat series F, G, H. IUT: University Institute of Technology. STS: Advanced Technician Section.
Each box represents 1 year's study, except for pre-primary schooling (from 2 to 5 years of age) and for higher education.
a)   Mainly CAP and BEP, but also other diplomas.
b)   Introduction of a "remedial 4th grade" in September 1993.
c)   Gradually being phased out.
Source: Repères et références statistiques, 1993.

GERMANY (North Rhine-Westphalia)

by

Heinz Schirp
Head of the Departments of Curriculum Development & Education and School Research
Landesinstitut für Schule und Weiterbildung

Summary

Fixing performance standards in a curriculum is directly connected with the intention of controlling educational processes and comparing results. Unlike other European countries or, for instance, the United States, most of the German *Bundesländer* show little interest in central performance assessment. External school performance comparisons have not found wide acceptance in education policy fields. As a matter of fact, there is a critical attitude to the need for centralised comparisons. This limited interest derives mainly from three different sources of educational awareness:

- *Experience with central performance methods* that provide comparison nurture the suspicion that the currently prevailing type of external school performance assessment does not reflect true performance levels, and that it provides neither help nor support for school improvement and innovative developments towards school quality.
- *The existing parameters of the educational system* in *the Bundesländer* is an added problem for effective and reliable assessment methods. Performance standards are not defined and explicitly stated in detail; as such they cannot simply be used as a firm basis for assessment. The system, by which performance standards are to be safeguarded, rather has the character of a more regulatory framework. It forms a kind of a "self-stabilizing feedback system".
- *Fostering the educational autonomy of schools* – a current main focus of school development policy – is a third perspective from which central assessment approaches are regarded as counter-productive. Internal and school-based school evaluation methods have got a higher priority in the field of evaluation and educational control.

Context

The education system in North Rhine-Westphalia

The following report concerns the education system in North Rhine-Westphalia, the most populated *Land* in Germany. Since the unification of the FRG with the former GDR, Germany has had 16 *Länder*. Every *Land* has its "cultural sovereignty", meaning that it can decide how its education system is to be organised and structured.

Various institutional bodies such as the Conference of Cultural Ministers and the Federal *Länder* Commission are responsible, for example, for maintaining comparable school leaving certificates despite the different types of education systems and for guaranteeing recognition of these certificates in all the German *Länder*. The aim of these (and other) bodies is to ensure a minimum degree of similarity in educational developments in the individual *Länder*.

The basic structure of education in North Rhine-Westphalia (NRW) is as follows (see appendix):

- Primary education starts at age 6 and lasts four years. After primary school the choice is between four different types of Level I secondary schools.

- the *Hauptschule* (general school)
- the *Realschule* (intermediate school)
- the *Gymnasium* (high school/grammar school)
- the *Gesamtschule* (comprehensive school)
- Special schools of various types for children and young people with specific handicaps.

The *Hauptschule* and *Realschule* go up to grade 10 and, after successfully completing the course, their pupils can go on to Level II secondary schools or various vocational schools. In addition, the high school and comprehensive school also have senior classes which, like the Level II secondary stream, comprise grades 11-13 and lead to the *Abitur* (higher leaving certificate). The *Abitur* is, among other things, the qualification for university entrance.

After the general school or intermediate school course, the many branches of an extremely wide range of vocational schools give possibilities of obtaining occupational qualifications and/or higher qualifications such as the *Fachabitur* (technical higher leaving certificate) and university matriculation. Unlike other *Länder,* NRW has a type of school (*Kollegschule*), in which pupils can enroll for a dual course of study, *i.e.* they obtain an occupational qualification in addition to the *Abitur.*

Despite all the differences in the education systems of the 16 *Länder,* there are still some similar basic structures. These concern mainly:

- the requirements and educational qualifications for the teaching profession;
- the function and importance of directives and curricula;
- the school inspection system;
- legal provisions concerning schools.

To that extent the main points raised in this report can be seen as applicable to the entire German education system.

The present interest in performance standard and assessment issues

The education policy discussion

At present three main points are raised when performance standards, possible changes to them and the related ideas for the structural reform of schools are being discussed.

Reducing school attendance from 13 to 12 years

First, there is the central issue of whether the current period spent in the types of school leading to the *Abitur* can be shortened from 13 to 12 years. Now that Germany has more *Länder,* this debate has been amplified since in some of the new *Länder* (of the former GDR), the university entrance qualification (*Abitur*) was awarded after only 12 years, as compared with 13 in the "old" *Länder.* A related issue is what educational subject matter, goals and methods are essential if the present qualitative level of the *Abitur* and its matriculation entitlement are to be maintained.

Streamlining of curricula

Independently of the initiative for fewer years at school, demands are made at regular intervals in the educational policy debate that curricula should be streamlined, and that unnecessary "educational ballast" and subject matter which has been handed down unsolicited for decades should be removed from curricula in order to bring them up to date. The underlying argument is that a modern industrial nation and a democratic form of society with its interconnected political, economic, cultural and ecological factors must today define more accurately what schoolchildren must learn for tomorrow if they are to cope with the "modern" challenges of professional and working life.

School autonomy

An educational policy debate is now under way on whether and how schools should be given more freedom in their approach to teaching. The argument is that the individual school is in the best position to decide which educational methods, courses and goals are to be developed, defined and organised so that teaching and learning can be effective.

Only the individual school, it is claimed, can take such decisions about teaching and learning since in every case these involve the children's specific characteristics, the basic socio-economic conditions, the resources available for learning and the available support system.

At present the following questions are being asked in connection with all three of these points: "What do our school-children achieve?", "What must absolutely be learnt by schoolchildren today in view of the new social, technological and economic challenges?", "What structural, organisational and educational changes are needed for this purpose?"

Performance differences and comparisons

As already said, external evaluation, centralised testing and large-scale assessments play no decisive role in the German *Länder* when it comes to formulating, introducing and checking on performance standards. The traditional structures and regulatory provisions in the feedback control system which have been described have so far ensured a relatively high level of education. The qualitative differences between schools of the same kind or between types of schools in different *Länder* are in fact quite small. It is thus not surprising that no great interest is shown in studies comparing the performance standards of schools, types of schools and *Länder*.

The available studies comparing schools can be divided into four groups:

a) After the first comprehensives were founded in NRW – 25 years ago – there were educational policy controversies as to whether comprehensives performed just as well as the types of school in the traditional three-tier secondary system. This became a particularly important question since the answer was also the pointer to whether and how far the *Abitur* (higher leaving certificate) obtained in comprehensives was on a par with the high-school *Abitur*. The comparative studies carried out for this purpose did not produce conclusive results. However it became clear, for example, that the differences between schools of one type could be greater than between schools of different types. The decisive variable therefore did not seem to be the type of school, but how well its teaching was organised and the range of activities providing support and incentive the school could offer its pupils. It was also perceived that wherever comprehensives were in a position owing to their location – for instance in rural districts – to take the full complement of an individual age group, the school's results could stand comparison with those of the traditional high school. The structural conditions and variables contributing to the quality of a school could thus also be perceived. On the whole it became clear that these studies comparing school performance standards could not provide a definite basis for an educational and school policy consensus.

b) Performance comparison studies in NRW have also become important with regard to learning conditions specific to the sexes and the improvement of these conditions. The introduction of new subjects in the communication and information technology fields has given an unexpected boost in this respect. One question which has become important is whether, for example, mixed classes do not obstruct personal, active forms of access and assimilation particularly for girls, and whether it is therefore not more effective to teach information technology in groups in which both boys and girls receive specific kinds of teaching.

c) A kind of performance comparison is also provided by the studies which have been conducted and published by trade associations, banks and industrial firms. These studies which appear at regular intervals show, for example, that the literacy and numeracy of the pupils tested are continually declining. The criticism of these studies mainly concerns their methodological weaknesses and accordingly the lack of reliable, valid results.

It should be noted that there has been a marked reduction in such performance studies in the last few years. Although previously, for example, the deficiencies in school leavers' specialist and practical knowledge were deplored and remedial efforts were demanded, industrial firms are now urging schools to attach more importance to the "work ethic" and "structural qualifications", such as the ability to co-operate, decide and act, a sense of responsibility and social skills.

d) Lastly internal performance comparisons are important for the individual school itself. In subjects and areas of study with written examinations, there is a tradition whereby classroom tests with identical exercises are set in parallel classes. It can thus be seen whether conditions in a particular class encourage or impede performance. But the performance comparisons are limited to the particular school.

Centralised features exist only with regard to examination requirements for the *Abitur*. For this purpose teachers submit their suggestions for *Abitur* questions in their subject to their school inspectorate. A committee then chooses suitable questions from those submitted and rejects the others. In this way the school inspectorate has a good overview of the quality and level of the performance requirements in the high school course.

This debate has not yet been settled. There are, however, two distinct schools of thought. One basic position is that change should come through external structural reform of the school system. Here one idea, for instance, is to do away with the traditional system of four types of school (general, intermediate, high and comprehensive schools) and switch to two new types of school at secondary levels I and II (two-pillar concept).

In this case one type of school would concentrate on the activities and goals which so far have been the *Gymnasium*'s main concern. Accordingly the emphasis would be on preparing pupils for the *Abitur* and higher education. The second type of school would focus more on vocational and practical courses. In addition to professional qualifications, the senior level (Level II secondary) of this type of school would also provide qualifications giving access to specialised higher education establishments and university.

By contrast, the second basic position is that more will be achieved by the internal reform of schools. For this purpose, however, it is argued, schools must be given more scope to develop their own approach to teaching, more freedom and greater teaching autonomy. The main point in the internal reform approach is that the individual school is finally the medium and engine for change. Accordingly the concepts of enhanced organisation and support systems within the school have an especially important place in this basic position.

The present debate on possible changes to the education system is not influenced so much by the existence of empirical studies and comparisons between schools and performance, as by the fact that the attractiveness of individual types of schools has changed in the past few years. Owing to different attitudes to education, the school population streams have in fact changed, thereby confronting all types of Level I secondary schools with new challenges.

Changes in the school scene

While primary schools – not least because of the directives and curricula of 1984 – have focussed on teaching methods and developed clear approaches for a pupil-oriented organisation of school life and teaching (new forms of free work, independent and co-operative learning, cross-subject, project-oriented work, etc.), the changes in Level I secondary schools (general, intermediate, high and comprehensive schools) have mainly concerned their respective school populations.

- The trend towards higher forms of education triggered a wave of closures among general schools *(Hauptschulen)* in the 1980s ("the demise of general schools"). Although in 1970 there were still 1 478 general schools with about 630 000 pupils, their number has now shrunk to 837. In the meantime these schools have lost about half their pupils.
- The three other types of school have benefitted in quantitative terms. This has led, however, to an internal change in such schools. Intermediate and high schools *(Realschule and Gymnasium)* have had to recognise that their pupil intakes have become much more heterogeneous. This has necessarily affected performance requirements and teaching and learning methods.
- As the fourth type of Level I secondary school, the comprehensive schools *(Gesamtschulen)* in the 25 years of their existence in NRW have on the whole proved to be a credible alternative to the traditional three-tier school system.

There are now about 200 comprehensives in NRW. Their main problem is competition with the intermediate and high schools. Where for instance – as in rural districts – a comprehensive school can take almost the full complement of age groups, it can easily compete with the standards and requirements of the intermediate and high schools. In highly industrialised areas, however, in which the various kinds of school are competing, about 30 to 40 per cent of an age group opt for the high school and 25 to 35 per cent for the intermediate school. A comprehensive school therefore attracts only that proportion of the school population who, on the basis of their school record, do not seem to be qualified for high or intermediate schools. Such a distribution of aptitude and learning potential naturally leads to conditions that determine the profile of comprehensive schools. The comprehensives have therefore developed their own particular internal and external characteristics in order to stimulate various types of aptitude; for the same reason they have incorporated incentive and support systems in their work. Lastly, unlike most other types of school, most comprehensives are full-day schools, so that homework supervision, back-up courses, study groups and school societies as well as free time activities become possible.

The process of standard setting

How the system guarantees standards

Unlike other European countries or, for instance, the United States, most of the German *Länder* show little interest in central performance assessment methods that provide comparisons. External school performance comparisons have not found wide acceptance in the school and education policy field. In addition, there is a critical attitude to the need for comparisons; it is mainly based on experience in the *Länder* which carry out or have carried out such procedures for central performance assessment and comparisons. The criticism is that the currently prevailing type of external school performance assessment does not reflect true performance levels, and that it provides no help for improvements and innovative developments. The suspicion rather exists that, with the traditional form of comparative performance assessment, "bad" schools rather tend to become even worse and that the expected performance tests greatly influence teaching and learning ("Teach what you test!").

In addition to this limited interest in performance comparisons – for instance between schools and different types of school – there is a second structural reason for the sceptical attitude to performance comparisons. The present school system has a regulatory framework which on the whole helps to guarantee a relatively high level of education, high attainment standards and also good school performance standards. It is argued that there are no grounds for extensive performance assessments and comparisons. Accordingly the types of regulation used so far are to a large extent considered sufficient to guarantee performance standards. This framework, which can be described as a kind of self-stabilizing feedback control system should, however, be critically reviewed. The eight components in Figure 1 must be seen from two angles. On the one hand, they undoubtedly help to guarantee academic standards; on the other, they may also interfere with further internal development in teaching and learning reform.

Figure 1.   **The process of standard setting**

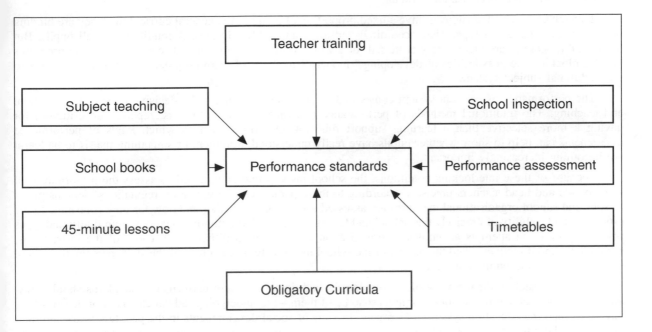

Source: OECD, based on national submission.

Teacher training is mainly concerned with the structures of the reference academic subjects and the way they are to be treated. The professional know-how of future teachers is still largely a matter of knowledge of their subject; knowledge of learning and teaching techniques, which many teachers consider more important and decisive, is given rather short shrift in the initial phase of our teacher training – a critical finding which is to be taken seriously in view of the difficulties and challenges with which teachers now have to cope. Similarly, criticism is directed at the second phase of teacher training which takes place in study or district seminars. In this second training phase, future teachers are familiarised with practical aspects of education. They plan and organise teaching under the supervision of experienced colleagues. At the same time, they are introduced to teaching, methodology and learning theory concepts by means of advanced and specialist seminars.

Subject teaching: the subject matter, goals and procedures involved in learning are to a large extent concerned with the academic aspects of the discipline concerned (''structure of the discipline''). Along with a still predominantly conventional form of teaching (particularly in the high school), a teaching (mono) culture is consolidated, in which an attempt is made to reproduce in the minds of pupils what is handed down as a scientific standard and structured on that basis. Accordingly specialised knowledge and skills are imparted – at least in the short term (Figure 1).

The text books used as specialised material are consistent with subject teaching. In most types of school, they are still the decisive instruments in planning. They are also used by many teachers as a secret curriculum; the particular text books in use frequently have a greater influence than the appropriate curricula on the standards and breakdown of subject matter and on the sequence planning of the course contents. In addition, school text books, their exercises and the steps they mark in the teaching process also influence the microstructures of this process.

Lessons at 45-minute intervals are necessarily the approach which complies with these types of teaching requirements. They create breaks in continuity and finally make it difficult for pupils to retain what they have learnt. Taking innovating methods into account (independent activities, projects, etc.), many teachers think that such rigid learning rhythms are increasingly counterproductive.

The educational principles behind traditional curricula, directives and regulations on the running of schools do point to innovative types of planning and organisation in teaching. Because of the other parameters, however, many teachers frequently consider that precisely the innovative parts of curricula are ''out of touch with the reality of schools and teaching''. The cohesion of these other parameters is frequently stronger. Moreover, the traditional curricula still reflect the old type of subject-oriented school. Along with a teaching know-how directed at a particular subject, conditions therefore arise which, for example, make interdisciplinary approaches to teaching, learning and organisation difficult.

Timetables ensure that subjects have a fixed proportion of hours in the general curriculum. They are binding on all schools of a given type. They accordingly ensure comparable educational conditions for all pupils. But traditional timetables are increasingly criticised for giving too little scope for interdisciplinary learning processes and for blocking the possibilities of developing ''modern'' methods of learning precisely because they stick to the traditional subject system.

The performance assessment system comes under – in a double sense – the decisive parameters of school and teaching. The traditional methods of performance assessment (classroom tests, reports) are criticised for having a more selective than a learning support function. Questions such as which kinds of performance assessments can help to show whether pupils have really understood a problem or something that is to be learnt are becoming increasingly important.

Because of these interlocking conditions, the school inspectorate is expected to assess the performance of staff, pupils and head teachers precisely according to these parameters. Examination regulations, demonstration lessons and school organisational measures are assessed according to whether and how far they contribute to the efficiency and stability of precisely this school and teaching culture. Even minor deviations from traditional types of organisation and attempts at innovative organisation are beset with difficulties because of the instructions, regulations, and directives – and the picture of the school they create in the minds of the staff, parents, the school inspectorate and the public concerned.

The deliberately critical review of the regulations laid down to ensure performance standards should draw attention to the fact that regulations – or at least some of them – are undergoing radical change. For decades they have governed the education system in Germany. In view of social developments in the past few years and their effects on the life of children and young people, there is an increasing demand for justification of these regulations. In addition to technical aspects, ideas such as ''experience-oriented, action-oriented and future-oriented teaching'' are coming into the educational picture. In such an educational context, individual regulations also necessarily undergo change.

The development of performance standards

Good teacher training, the existence of compulsory curricula for all subjects and areas of study in all types of school and the provision of text books complying with the curriculum are the factors which have the greatest influence on school performance. While teacher training provides the necessary qualifications for staff and text books are based on curricula, directives and curricula are the norms which determine the performance requirements for subjects and types of school. Their importance and function are therefore discussed below.

Directives and curricula binding on schools

Directives, curricula and timetables that must be observed exist for all subjects and areas of study in all types of school in NRW – and this also applies to all 16 *Länder*.

– The directives mainly refer to the type of school. They define the main educational ideas to which a kind of school is committed, what is included in its educational programme, and the teaching and learning principles governing its profile. The directives also provide statements on the organisation of education and teaching in the school. They also cover performance assessment, homework, the use of staff and, where necessary, the main aspects of work in the individual grades. They also refer to the requirements for an organisation system designed for the pupils (school life, co-operation between schools and their environment, the need for projects, etc.). Lastly, they state the certificates which can be obtained in the respective types of school and on possible transfers between schools. The corresponding school organisation and legal rules are based on the ''Educational and Examination Regulations''.

– In each case the curricula make statements on the individual subjects and areas of study. They basically cover:
  • the tasks and goals involved in the suject or the area of study, *e.g.* the qualifications to be acquired and basic aptitudes, skills and reflexes;
  • the teaching concept for a subject or area of study, *e.g.* in the form of information on elementary teaching and learning methods, the field covered by the subject and its main contents;
  • the main subject matter, topics and related goals; in some cases the curricula are supplemented by advice on teaching, with suggestions for schedules and methods as well as for the practical and organisational aspects of particular teaching sequences. In most curricula these instructions concerning subject matter are structured according to the particular grades (*e.g.* grades 5/6, 7/8, 9/10);
  • checks on learning goals, and encouragement and assessment of work. Here, for example, statements are made on the importance of oral or written work in the system, and on the assessment of individual or group work or other forms of work relating to a subject;
  • advice on work with curricula. This is mainly intended to encourage varying planning approaches. In addition some curricula give advice on documentation and aids for staff and pupils.

Directives, curricula and timetables along with the legal and organisation rules are binding on all schools in NRW. All 16 *Länder* have theoretically and structurally comparable directives, curricula, and timetables, as well as comparable legal regulations for their schools. Schools in the private sector (*e.g.* Rudolph Steiner schools) thus have greater organisational scope within their school programme.

The directives and curricula are not only binding on teachers and on the school timetables worked out by them, but are also important reference points for school books. Publishing houses which produce text books must base themselves on the existing directive and curriculum norms. The School Book Committee within the Ministry of Culture decides whether a new text book complies with the directives and curricula and whether it is to be included in the approved list. The school staff select the books from the wide range of approved titles for use in their schools.

Aids are frequently provided to explain curriculum instructions to teachers. Especially when curricula refer to teaching innovations (new planning methods), special methodological approaches (interdisciplinary project work), new subjects (religious instruction for Moslem pupils) and new courses (information technology), such aids provide back-up for the practical implementation of curriculum innovations. In keeping with their function, aids are simply intended as an incentive.

In-school curricula

Curricula provide instructions for planning and practical work by teachers. They can be seen as a system of instructions on the goals, subject matter and methods involved in learning. It is the teachers' job to implement these instructions in the teaching and learning process, *i.e.* in the planning approach designed for their pupils and in teaching practice. They are thus urged to take into account the actual characteristics of their pupils. Only the local teacher can therefore justifiably decide how the curriculum instructions can be implemented for his or her group of pupils.

An elementary task for the teacher is to relate the performance demands stated in the curriculum to the specific characteristics of a class of pupils. It is therefore their duty to co-operate with the teachers of other subjects and work out common programmes for a class or year. Such ''in-school'' curricula relate the general curriculum instructions to the specific conditions applicable to each school. In addition to the characteristics of the pupils, a school's local conditions also play a decisive role. In the same way, important points in a school's programme and profile are defined by particular types of co-operation with outside partners, the school's traditions, extra teaching, study groups, full-day schooling, parent inputs, project days, etc. It is the job of the entire staff and the teachers of different subjects to make these internal arrangements. The teachers of particular subjects decide, for example, which approved text books are to be used. Teachers of the same subject working with parallel classes co-operate, for example, in the planning of tuition and the preparation of classroom tests. Teachers working on different subjects with the same class will be involved in planning interdisciplinary teaching units and carrying out projects and similar activities.

It is assumed that the instructions in most curricula account for only about 70 per cent of available school time; the remainder of the time is therefore available for the school's own planning work.

From the teachers' viewpoint, however, the situation is frequently different. Teachers often have the impression that they are over-stretched by the amount of subject matter and demands in curricula and consider that the latitude provided for them is much smaller than the proportion of 70 to 30 per cent.

On the whole the system of interconnected directives, curricula, internal programmes and back-up material guarantees that demands on schools are very similar.

Organisation and methods for the development of curriculum standards and curricula

The Minister of Culture is responsible for the development of curricula. He instructs the State Institute for School and Adult Education to monitor curricula development work from the technical and educational viewpoints.

Curricula are usually worked out by curriculum committees. These committees comprise:

– six to eight teachers of the particular subject and from the type of school concerned;
– a representative of the school inspectorate, who is frequently the chairman of the curriculum committee;
– a member of the Institute as a supervisor.

The teachers on these curriculum committees are given four hours per week off from teaching for these activities. The committee members are appointed by the Minister of Culture. They are usually selected at the proposal of or in agreement with the Institute. In most cases such teachers are staff with thorough practical experience and with skills in teaching-activity planning and the organisation of schools and lessons. Accordingly many of these teachers are head teachers, have experience of teacher training or work as experts on study and district seminars (Phase 2 of teacher training).

Members do not usually receive any intensive, specific training for their curriculum committee activities. Their most important task is to incorporate the specific, practical conditions of schools, their wishes and their concern for certain necessary provisions in the curriculum development process – by providing guidance and proposing adjustments.

The curriculum committees usually meet once a month. It takes a total of three to four years to develop the curricula for all subjects for a type of school. Once they are completed, the curricula are submitted to schools for testing before they are introduced by the Minister of Culture.

Curricula are usually developed in parallel for all subjects in a particular type of school.

The process of preparing the general teaching directives for a type of school takes place while the curricula are being developed. Responsibility for this process is frequently delegated to a separate committee which also consists of teachers, representatives of the school inspectorate and academic advisers.

The necessary legal and organisational changes concerning schools are made by the Minister of Culture; such changes (e.g. the number of classroom tests, timetables and hours per subject, etc.) are included as new provisions in the Education and Examination Regulations (APO), or alternatively orders concerning them are given to schools.

Content and performance standards

Curriculum development standards

The organisation of curriculum work and supervision of its theoretical side are legally the responsibility of the Curriculum Development Department of the State Institute for School and Adult Education.

The Department consists of a main section which is responsible for education and teaching, educational research and school counselling. Six specialised sections (German, foreign languages, mathematics/science, social sciences/history/religion, art/music, sport) cover the subjects taught in schools; in addition, three co-ordination sections (primary, secondary and Level II secondary schools) are responsible for the schools in the corresponding category. One section – special teaching – deals with curricula for special schools, and one is exclusively concerned with vocational training.

Depending on the type of school and the volume of curriculum development work, the sections participate in all phases of development and revision work.

Since its creation in 1978, the Institute has become the central agency for curriculum development activities and further teacher training.

Trends in curriculum standards

Theoretical justifications for practical decisions on teaching played no role whatsoever in the curricula of the 1950s and 1960s. On the contrary, they were limited to presenting a catalogue of subject matter in addition to a "teaching preface". Accordingly the criticism about the lack of formulae, the volume of subject matter and the limited guidance for pupils was justified.

Apart from decisive and still valid information on the restructuring of directives and curricula, the "curriculum guidance" initiated in the curriculum revision process has also – unintentionally – produced negative side effects. Owing to vague concepts of learning-goal hierarchies with their "learning goal apparatus", a system of rough and finally-attuned goals and goals of the first and second order, many teachers developed a marked aversion to learning-goal theories and concepts. This very understandable attitude has, in some areas, generally impeded and prevented the acceptance of practical curriculum concepts.

Similarly, the concepts banking on the effectiveness of complete "curriculum packages" have not given extensive progress. These packages provided the teacher with a series of teaching briefs, in which the decisions concerning goals, contents and methods had already been taken, while their practical application to the classroom appeared to be guaranteed by the use of pre-prepared material. The curriculum packages too again showed the limited contribution to educational planning of curriculum development work when it is far removed from the pupils' specific characteristics.

In view of the difficulties described, what can be expected of a centrally prepared curriculum? It must establish the action to be taken by the school or in connection with the subject taught and how this can be done. For this purpose a precise description is required of the relationship between teaching goals, subject matter, organisation and working methods and, if possible, appropriate forms of quality control.

Curricula which meet these theoretical requirements:

- are the outcome of reflection on a systematic approach to the decisions concerning teaching goals, subject matter and processes (validation of the curriculum as a system);
- show the possibilities of how goals/subject matter can be established and distributed over the different school years (the curriculum's horizontal structure);
- explain how teachers can do justice to the curriculum by thinking in practical terms about planning (the curriculum's vertical structure) and thereby convert system decisions into process decisions.

Curriculum theory

A curriculum is planned so that its basic theoretical ideas and decisions are apparent to teachers.

This "curriculum theory trend" has made inroads in the last few years.

Curriculum standards comprise learning-goal guidance.

A connection is established between the tasks involved in the subject, the long-term goals and the teaching goals relating to the subject matter. The goals identified as central (*e.g.* qualifications, basic intentions):

- show which abilities and reflexes are to be acquired;
- also call for adjustments to teaching aims since they are always based on the central goals and must be validated by them.

Sequencing pattern

Since goals cannot be taught, the subject matter must be validated and clearly broken down among the individual school years. Here it must be made clear:

- on which principles the structure of the subject matter or topic lists is based;
- how the relationship between compulsory and freely selected subject matter and topics is to be defined;
- how the connection with actual teaching topics can be established in accordance with the curriculum.

Correlation

By correlation is meant the connection between the important messages of a subject and the related experience of pupils. Such a connection must be established if a learning process is to create involvement, individual interest and readiness to grapple with problems in the minds of children. At all curriculum levels it must therefore be apparent:

- how relationships between the messages given by subjects and the actual lives of pupils can be structurally ensured;
- how these relationships are connected with the curriculum goals;
- what aids are provided for the planning of a learning process which will back up this correlation at the teaching level.

Phases in curriculum development work

There are six phases in curriculum development work:

- statement of needs concerning new norms;
- planning and development of concepts and guidelines;
- production of curricula;
- assessment and participation by associations;
- introduction and testing;
- support and counselling for school teachers.

Statement of needs

Curriculum development work begins when it becomes clear there is a need for new or revised basic norms. This may come about, for example, when associations, teachers and parents turn to the public with relevant demands. But a need can also be expressed by education specialists. Thus, for example new approaches to teaching, new learning concepts and new aspects of a subject provide material for revisions. But the need can also become apparent when teachers themselves develop ''new'' possibilities. Here school teachers themselves send out the signals which are received by those responsible for curricula and are processed by them. Lastly, empirical studies may also lead to the development or revision of curricula.

Planning

In this phase the requirements for successful development work are laid down. First the facts of importance to development work are determined and assessed in order to define the extent of needs for curriculum development or revision. The results of this assessment which have a bearing on decisions and action are then submitted to those concerned with curricula (the Minister of Culture, the school inspectorate, academic world, teachers). This process is extremely important for the commitment of those working on the project, the thoroughness of treatment, the quality of results and their acceptance by schools and the public.

In particular the following activities are involved:

- examining and assessing criticism (*e.g.* reports, comments, surveys) of existing directives and curricula;
- assessing findings at the teaching, subject and educational research levels;
- producing or requiring and assessing expert opinion on technical and broader aspects;
- comparing the directives and curricula of individual types of schools and grades (if necessary also in other *Länder*);
- organising discussions, meetings and/or symposia with the participation of teachers, academics and association representatives so that all the interested parties are included in the curriculum development process at the earliest possible stage;
- working out and finalising subject matter and organisational norms for curriculum development work.

The procedure for the development of curriculum norms also remains "open" and "geared to practical concerns" in the curriculum production phase. Partial drafts are submitted to specialist groups, subject teachers and subject specialists so that it can be decided as soon as possible whether they will contribute to improvements in teaching or not. The respective contact schools and teachers are also to be included in the first "trials". The following activities in particular are important in this phase:

- advising the development group on educational, curriculum theory, organisational, teaching and subject-related issues;
- co-ordinating the development work relating to the subject/area of study with other subjects/areas with regard to content and form;
- substantiating intermediate findings, giving examples of contributions to development work where necessary and making suggestions for revision work;
- setting up information and feedback systems between development groups, and the parties and public concerned (integrating contact schools in the operation, organising surveys and meetings);
- integrating further teacher training in the development/revision process;
- supporting the development group by providing services.

Implementation, review and adjustment

Expert appraisal

In this phase it is considered whether and how far the product is up to the basic educational, curriculum theory, teaching and subject standards and whether the norms for the development/revision work have been respected. The participation procedure laid down in Section 2.4 and Section 16 of the Schools Co-operation Act is also used in this phase. Under this procedure, parent organisations, trade unions, the Union of Chambers of Commerce and Industry, the leading local associations and churches are requested to express their views.

The main activities in this phase are as follows:

- preparing the relevant criteria and questions for the expert appraisal and assessing the curriculum (or having it assessed) on the basis of these criteria;
- requesting and reviewing expert appraisals;
- seeking comments from the parties and the public concerned and assessing them (*e.g.* by means of symposia);
- in conjunction with the development group, revising the curriculum on the basis of all the comments and appraisals and forwarding it in draft form to the Minister of Culture for a decision;
- where necessary, reviewing the draft with the development committee according to the instructions given by the Ministry of Culture.

Introduction and testing

A new curriculum is introduced by subject and curriculum development experts working with school inspectors and teacher training bodies. Since directives in the curricula cannot be successfully introduced simply by sending them to all the schools and teachers concerned, special back-up measures are used to implement the directives and curricula.

In this phase it is also asked whether the new norms actually improve teaching. Compiling data on the practical experience of staff teaching the same subject and analyses concerning this subject are helpful in this respect, as is the feedback obtained from further teacher training. It is precisely in this phase that it becomes clear how closely curriculum development and further teacher training are interconnected.

The following activities in particular can be emphasized:

- along with the school inspectorate, organising meetings on the introduction of curricula;
- working out curriculum testing procedures and, along with the school inspectorate, carrying them out (*e.g.* surveys, discussions, interviews);

– reviewing testing experience, arranging for assistance for the implementation of directives and curricula and where necessary making suggestions for adjustments to them;
– support for teachers through ongoing counselling.

The curriculum development process itself does not come to an end when the approved curricula are introduced. The directives and curricula setting teaching norms assume their true value in actual teaching only if teachers are able to relate them to their particular teaching context and shape them for this purpose.

Teachers receive support for the implementation of new norms in the form of assistance with teaching planning and organisation activities. Such back-up is geared to the new curricula. It stimulates school-oriented work, provides the staff with teaching material, settles teaching method problems or ensures practical, organisational aid. Further training bodies also provide assistance with the curriculum.

Both these measures are intended to let teachers emphasize and improve their own practical teaching methods and help them to implement the new performance requirements in the classroom.

NRW is banking on a comprehensive curriculum development process in order to maintain, and build on, creditable and effective performance standards. The basic idea is to integrate actual teaching as soon as possible in the reform and revision process. Through intensive feedback with schools, information is continually exchanged between the curriculum development side and schools themselves. Accordingly the joint development process is becoming an important factor in qualitative changes in schools and in maintaining universally binding performance standards.

New approaches

New curriculum work concepts to maintain school and teaching standards are now being discussed. They are mainly intended to give schools more freedom to develop their own curricula, age group plans, programmes and profiles.

This would necessarily mean that:

– the so far extremely detailed curricula would have to be reduced to core or basic plans;
– the demands such as the qualifications provided by a type of school would have to be defined;
– schools receive help to produce their own age group plans and are able to use their freedom to set goals and subject matter for age groups, draw up interdisciplinary projects, etc.;
– help and facilities are increasingly provided for the internal assessment of schools.

Various *Länder* are discussing and working on such concepts. In NRW, the current procedure for developing new directives and curricula makes it possible to assemble information on experience with a curriculum model which is intended to strengthen the individual school's teaching autonomy.

Problems and critical issues

Education policy problems and conditions

Schools are constantly under pressure to produce results meeting the demands of different social groups. In addition to this external pressure, conditions in schools are changing as a result of the children's modified living conditions, the new socialising influences of the media, for example, media technologies, mediatization and the related opportunities and risks in the assimilation of knowledge.

Setting national standards

Since 1979 the joint conference of Ministers of Education (KMK) has issued national guidelines for the *Abitur* which all *Länder* follow when developing their curricula and assessment systems. The national guidelines for the *Abitur* were revised in 1989. The KMK has recently focused also on standards in lower secondary and primary, especially in German language. There is general recognition of the need for common standards, but concern also to preserve the autonomy of the *Länder* in educational matters. In the past, the issue of common standards has been forced onto the agenda by the need for mutual recognition of qualifications, especially of the *Abitur* (for university entrance) and the *Staatsexamen* (for acceptance into teaching). Acknowledgement that *Abitur* standards do in practice vary between *Länder* is shown by the acceptance of a bonus/malus system for the *Lander*'s *Abitur* when a *numerus clausus* exists – for example, for entry to medical schools. Students from

Länder where the *Abitur* was considered particularly rigorous – Bavaria is one example – received a *bonus,* and those from *Länder* where the *Abitur* was rated easier received a *malus.* One issue for debate, especially now that the five Eastern *Länder* have joined the KMK, is whether this co-operative approach can continue to provide the necessary minimum of national agreements or whether the federal government will be brought to intervene more closely in educational matters in order to safeguard standards.

New subject matter and fields as the starting point for new demands

In the past few years the value of subject matter as a teaching reference has changed. In addition to the traditional contents of school subjects and their reference know-how, new kinds of subject matter and topics have appeared as a result of social developments and education policy needs. Subject matter such as "drugs", "force", "Europe", "ecology", "media", "intercultural factors", "technological progress", "human rights", etc., have become key issues in education.

This new subject matter is invariably interdisciplinary; it does not fit in with the system of norms specific to a subject. It requires learning processes based on the goals of independent, interdisciplinary and problem-oriented work. Schools, curriculum norms and the entire regulatory system are therefore confronted with new demands, which will also lead to new performance standards.

New demands from the labour market

The labour market's new expectations are also increasingly exerting pressure with regard to what schoolchildren should learn. On the grounds that "nowadays knowledge becomes obsolete all too quickly", and that today's schoolchildren must "learn to learn, acquire more practical experience with real work and learning situations and be ready to learn something else", the major professional and industrial associations are placing greater emphasis on "structural skills", by which is meant:

- social behaviour: ability to face up to conflicts, team spirit, tolerance;
- learning behaviour: thinking things through, independent work, technical and functional thinking;
- occupational skills: understanding work instructions, work ethics, thoroughness;
- cognitive personality characteristics: ability to judge, flexibility, ability to improvise;
- affective personality characteristics: pleasure in work, sense of duty, determination.

Schools, where the concept of performance is greatly influenced by cognitive factors, (still) have no suitable methods of developing and assessing these and similar attainments. These new types of requirement also necessarily have implications for a discriminating definition of educational goals and pupil attainments.

New requirements as a result of changes in schools

The main criticism of norms which are centrally developed for all schools is that such norms – necessarily – to a large extent disregard the specific conditions in the individual school. In the dilemma between "compliance with the curriculum" and "pupil guidance", schools have taken the children's characteristics as the starting point for their work. The goals, subject matter and methods involved in learning are accordingly based on the prior experience, prior knowledge and learning potential of children and young people. From this viewpoint, central curricula are frequently seen as "overloaded", too "demanding" and too "far removed from reality".

Schools themselves have thus clarified the curriculum norms and adjusted them to their pupil's characteristics, the conditions in their own schools and the schools' resources in terms of staff and funds.

Such experience with in-house development and its positive effects on the quality of schools, performance results, the climate of the school and teacher satisfaction is a third approach to thinking more about the "more open" curriculum structures and performance requirements which are defined by the individual school and for which it assumes responsibility. Such ideas on greater teaching autonomy on an institutional basis are supported by the results of organisation and innovation research. It clearly emerges from the relevant school studies that the individual school must be the force behind innovations if ideas on the development of schools are to be effective.

With the increase in teaching freedom in the individual school, however, there is also a greater need for more internal assessment by schools. Practical and effective facilities for this purpose would also have to be provided.

Basic economic conditions

The basic economic conditions of the school and education system have been the subject of particularly intensive discussion in NRW in the last few years. The basic approach whereby schools and education are considered in business terms, so to speak, from the cost/benefit viewpoint is not uncontested in this debate. The various analyses, however, have led to some interesting aspects that have effects on learning profiles and performance requirements. A few findings will be briefly discussed in order to mark the trends in the current debate.

- A multi-component, segmented school system is seen as economically and socially disadvantageous. The division between courses leading to university (Level II secondary, high school) and vocational education (Level II secondary, vocational schools) is a disruptive factor in modern vocational training. It affects the competitiveness of the economy.
- Possibilities of choosing between university entrance and vocational training must be maintained up to the end of Level I secondary education so as to avoid any discrimination against vocational streams.
- A segmented school system affects the optimum use of human capital and prevents the development of interests and aptitudes.
- A segmented and multi-component structure encourages the exclusion of problem groups and creates "second-class schools". By contrast, efficient production systems are marked rather by a limited division of labour and a highly integrated organisation structure.
- A highly differentiated school system is uneconomic from the organisational viewpoint, since its control system and hierarchies are inflexible and interfere with the speedy and efficient use of resources.
- Co-operative school structures strike a balance between a united and segmented school system. Through co-operation, different capacities can be put to better use by the education system.
- The concentration of subjects is necessary if a broad, general education is to be provided. The traditional subject-oriented schools have to be restructured for this purpose.
- The hierarchies governing the school system have to be dismantled and formal regulations kept to a minimum. School authorities and schools must themselves attend more to planning, decision and control functions than in the past.
- In addition to and along with less pronounced hierarchies, school authorities and schools must also be able to take their own decisions on the use of available resources (budgeting). This is more cost effective than resource allocation "from above".
- Schools must become more flexible in their teaching and make greater use than previously of available learning and education resources.
- Through a new system of multi-purpose basic and further training for teachers and increased co-operation among staff, a different type of teaching and learning culture and a new vocational ethos must be developed so that teachers can be released from their role as individual performers.
- Instead of a large number of unconnected subjects, teaching must be provided in module form. A limited number of interconnected teaching units must form the core of what the school has to offer.

These critical comments on the economics of education in NRW show that some of the approaches to reform now under discussion would have to be taken into account in connection with the modernisation of schools and education.

The international dimension

If the existing concepts, examples and prospects concerning school development are compared in the various European countries and the United States, a trend towards an equilibrium can be seen.

Schools with a system of set regulations which, as binding norms, govern the subject contents, goals, methods and organisation of teaching, are now becoming more liberal. Such concepts as autonomy and freedom for schools, school programmes and school profiles are therefore becoming attractive. Systems which have traditionally given the individual school considerable freedom are now tending to rely more on centralisation and obligations (national curricula) in order to maintain comparative standards in all schools.

Accordingly the scene is set for exciting policy discussions in which countries can "learn" from one another when it comes to defining their own approaches to reform.

Attempts at restructuring, reform and conversion in the national or regional context also require the back-up of international experience. But because of the specific social, cultural and education policy conditions prevailing in the individual countries, comparative studies are helpful only when they concern transposable approaches.

From the viewpoint of the current debate on schools in NRW, such studies would have to cover:

– Forms of "open" learning. The cognitive, social and practical results obtained by co-operative, independent and project-oriented types of learning.
– The optimisation of learning performance by co-operation with bodies and partners outside schools.
– The effectiveness of school educational programmes for the integrated and co-operative teaching of subjects.
– The effectiveness of the self-assessment facilities and methods used by schools.

Such an exchange of experience could as a whole help to improve the acceptance and implementation of the necessary changes to the school and education system.

Appendix
The education system in North Rhine-Westphalia
(*not including* special schools, evening schools and correspondence courses)

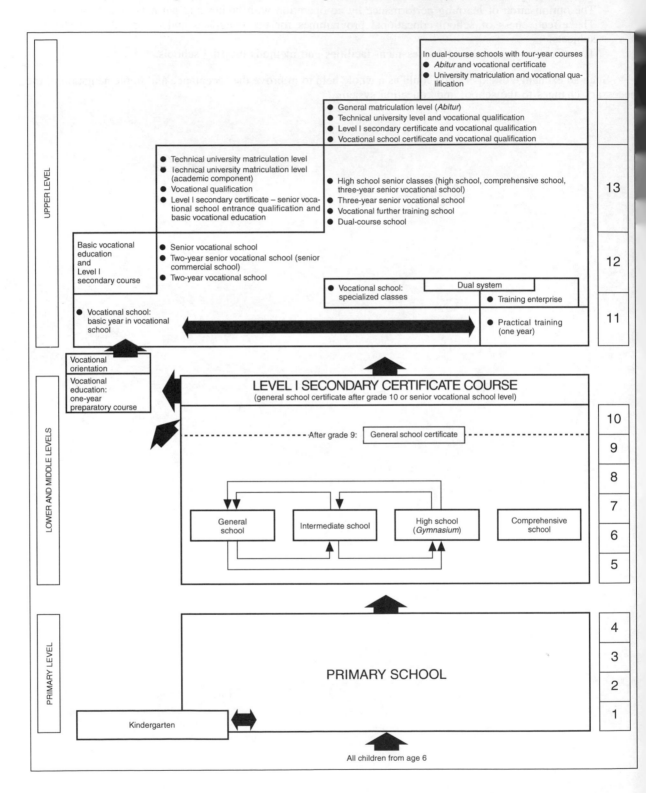

In dual-course schools with four-year courses
- *Abitur* and vocational certificate
- University matriculation and vocational qualification

- General matriculation level (*Abitur*)
- Technical university level and vocational qualification
- Level I secondary certificate and vocational qualification
- Vocational school certificate and vocational qualification

UPPER LEVEL

- Technical university matriculation level
- Technical university matriculation level (academic component)
- Vocational qualification
- Level I secondary certificate – senior vocational school entrance qualification and basic vocational education

- High school senior classes (high school, comprehensive school, three-year senior vocational school)
- Three-year senior vocational school
- Vocational further training school
- Dual-course school

13

Basic vocational education and Level I secondary course

- Senior vocational school
- Two-year senior vocational school (senior commercial school)
- Two-year vocational school

12

- Vocational school: specialized classes

Dual system
- Training enterprise

- Vocational school: basic year in vocational school

- Practical training (one year)

11

Vocational orientation

Vocational education: one-year preparatory course

LEVEL I SECONDARY CERTIFICATE COURSE
(general school certificate after grade 10 or senior vocational school level)

10

After grade 9: General school certificate

9

8

LOWER AND MIDDLE LEVELS

7

| General school | Intermediate school | High school (*Gymnasium*) | Comprehensive school |

6

5

4

3

PRIMARY SCHOOL

PRIMARY LEVEL

2

1

Kindergarten

All children from age 6

Source : OECD, based on national submission.

Bibliography

Akademie für Bildungsreform (Hrsg) (1984), "Leistungs in der Schule – Perspektiven eines pädagogischen Leistungsbegriffs", Tübingen.

BUER van J. (1990), *Pädagogische Freiheit des Lehrers im unterrichtlichen Alltag. Realität oder Illusion?*, Frankfurt/Bern.

Bundesminister für Bildung und Wissenschaft (Hrsg.) (1992), "Mädchen und Computer. Ergebnisse und Modelle zur Mädchenförderung in Computerkursen. Studien zu Bildung und Wissenschaft", H. 100, Bonn.

DALIN P. and ROLFF, H.G. (1990), "Institutionelles Schulentwicklungsprogramm", Soest (Landesinstitut).

HAENISCH, H., LUKESCH, H., KLAGHOFER, R. and KRÜGER-HAENISCH, E.M. (1979), "Gesamtschule und dreigliedriges Schulsystem in NRW. Schulleistungsvergleiche in Deutsch, Mathematik, English und Physik", Paderborn, München.

HELLER, K.A. (Hrsg) (1984), "Leistungsdiagnostik", Bern.

HOPMANN, S. (Hrsg) (1988), "Zugänge zur Geschichte staatlicher Lehrplanarbeit", Kiel.

INGENKAMP, K. (1989a), "Diagnostik in der Schule. Beiträge zu Schlüsselfragen der Schülerbeurteilung", Weinheim.

INGENKAMP, K. and SCHREIBER, W.H. (Hrsg) (1989b), "Was wissen unsere Schüler? Überregionale Lernerfolgsmessung aus internationaler Sicht", Weinheim.

KRAPP, A. (1989), "Der zweifelhafte Beitrag der empirischen Pädagogik zur rechtlichen Kontrolle der schulischen Leistungbeurteilung", in *Pädagogik*, Vol. 4, pp. 549-564.

KÜHN, R. (1989), "Untersuchungen zur Aufklärung von Schulnotenvarianz durch Angst und häusliche Anregungsbedingungen", in *Zeitschrift für internationale erziehungs und sozialwissenschaftliche Forschung*, Vol. 2, pp. 361-375.

Landesamt für Datenverarbeitung und Statistik (Hrsg.) (1994), "Allgemeinbildende Schulen in Nordrhein-Westfalen 1992", Düsseldorf, Heft 714.

Landesinstitut für Schule und Weiterbildung (Hrsg) (1993), "Aufgaben und Struktur des Landesinstituts", Soest.

ders. (Hrsg) (1994), "Ergebnisse und Perspektiven der Lehrplanarbeit", Soest.

LEHNER, F. and WIDMAIER, U. (1992), "Eine Schule für eine moderne Industriegesellschaft. Strukturwandel und Entwicklung der Schullandschaft in Nordrhein-Westfalen", Essen (nds).

LIKET, Th.M.E. (1993), "Freiheit und Verantwortung. Das niederländische Modell des Bildungswesens", Gütersloh.

Niedersächsiches Landesinstitut für Lehrerfortbildung, Lehrerweiterbildung und Unterrichtsforschung (Hrsg) (1991), "Mündliche Leistungen und ihre Bewertung in der Realschule", NLI-Bericht 43, Hildesheim.

OLECHOWSKI, R. and PERSY, E. (Hrsg.) (1987), "Fördernde Leistungsbeurteilung", Wien.

ROLFF, H.G. (1993), "Wandel durch Selbstorganisation. Theoretische Grundlagen und praktische Beispiele für eine bessere Schule", Weinheim, München.

RUEP, M. (1992), "Leistung und ihre Beurteilung", in *Lehren und Lernen*, Vol. 4, pp. 21-31.

SCHIRP, H. (1987), "Hauptschule und Lehrplanarbeit. Ansätze und Anregungen zur inneren Schulreform", Soest (Landesinstitut).

ders. (1993), "Brauchen wir eine neue Lehrplangeneration?", in *Päd. Führung*, Vol. 1, pp. 21-25.

STRAZNY, H. (1993), "Leistung und Leistungsbewertung in der Schule: Bemerkungen zu einem Dilemma", in *Päd. Führung*, Vol. 1, pp. 4-11.

IRELAND

by

John Coolahan
Department of Education, St. Patrick's College, Maynooth
National University of Ireland

Summary

The issue of performance standards and assessment policy is one of central importance in contemporary Irish education. A great deal of attention is focussed on the matter by professional educationalists and the general public. Public examinations, as key criteria for evaluating educational standards, have deep roots in Irish educational history. With the massive expansion in secondary education over recent decades whereby over 80 per cent of the age cohort now complete the secondary education cycle, many new pressures are in evidence which seek wide-ranging reforms in curricular and assessment policy. A fundamental concern is the reform of the traditional curricular content, pedagogic styles and modes of pupil assessment so as to cater in a more satisfactory manner for the needs of the greatly expanded and more heterogeneous pupil clientele now in the schools. Equality of access and greater pupil retention patterns are still a policy concern, but the greater emphasis has shifted towards educational outcomes. There is a particular concern about the under achievers.

New curricular policies are being planned, or being partly implemented, at present for primary school, junior cycle secondary and senior secondary schooling. There is a desire to ensure that curricular objectives are matched by much more active forms of pedagogy and more varied forms of pupil assessment. Well-devised performance standards are seen as integral to promoting higher quality education.

The Ministry of Education has placed a high priority on consensus building as a way of achieving the wide ranging agenda for change set forth in the Government's Green Paper on Education, issued in 1992. A notable instance of this was the holding of a National Education Convention in October 1993, and an account of this consensus building process is given in the paper.

In Ireland the state school inspectorate, with the assistance of some skilled, experienced teachers, is responsible for performance standards. Long experience and precedent play a major part in the process. Preparatory work on the national public examinations goes on throughout the previous school year. Proposed questions are devised at an early stage and a long process of analysing, refining, and appraising takes place until the inspectorate makes the final decisions in highly confidential circumstances. Examinations are devised using a combination of normed and criterion-referenced procedures in such a way that a passing grade in a subject represents the achievement of what would be regarded as a minimum level of competence in a subject. Empirical methods are not used to determine levels of attainment and no specification is published of what pupils are expected to achieve at each grade level. Marking schemes are made available to examiners which give detailed guidelines as to the level of award to be given to different standards of answering. The marking schemes are confidential to those correcting and are not published. There is pressure to make explicit publicly the criterion-referenced aspects of pupil performance standards, and it is likely that reforms in this direction will be implemented.

Machinery does not exist for the regular monitoring of standards in a systematic way which would indicate clearly whether standards were improving or deteriorating. However, with the aid of annual published reviews of the Leaving Certificate Examinations, in recent years, much greater analysis now takes place. The computerisation of examinations and a move towards greater transparency now facilitate research on the performance of pupils in the examinations. Concern exists on the variation of grades of success as between individual subjects, and a more coordinated approach to overall performance patterns is now in evidence.

The inspectorate reviews the levels of success and failure in each subject annually. The outcome of such reviews feeds into the planning for the following year by the inspectorate and the advising examiners. The personnel involved in the setting of performance standards are closely in touch with curricular developments and classroom experience. A circularity of influence occurs between those with responsibility for performance standards and those with responsibility for national curricular policy.

The paper concludes with an analysis of the strengths of the existing system and an itemisation of weaknesses which affect it. Suggestions are made on new orientations towards desired reforms. Much greater priority and investment needs to be given to the whole area of performance standards and assessment policies and processes. It is also proposed that Ireland should strengthen its involvement in international comparative studies on pupil performance levels.

Context

Background and structure

Ireland has had a state-aided primary school system since 1831 and a state-aided secondary school system since 1878. The state has exercised a significant influence on the operation and development of these systems and examinations have formed a central means through which the state monitored the quality of the education system and the performance standards of pupils (Coolahan, 1981). The public external examination for primary school pupils was dropped in 1967 but, linked to a long tradition and high valuation of public, external examinations at secondary level, the Junior Certificate, taken at about 15 years of age, and the Leaving Certificate Examination, taken at age 17 or 18, form central benchmarks of performance standards within the contemporary education system.

This education system has expanded and diversified greatly over recent decades. A significant era of educational reform was initiated in the sixties, which, when combined with changing social and economic circumstances, led to a transformation of the system. Figures 1 and 2 illustrate the changes in participation at

Figure 1. **Participation rates in full-time education for various age groups**

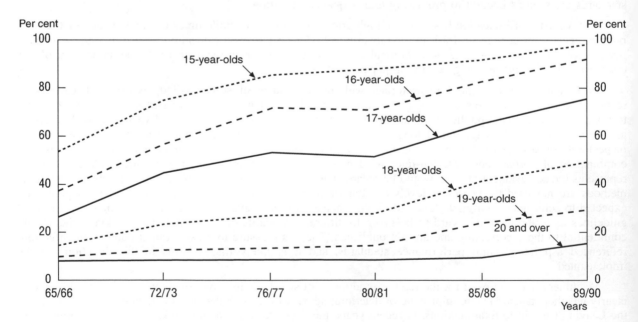

Note: The participation rate for 20-year-olds and over is estimated on the basis of the 20-24 age cohort of total population.
Source: Department of Education.

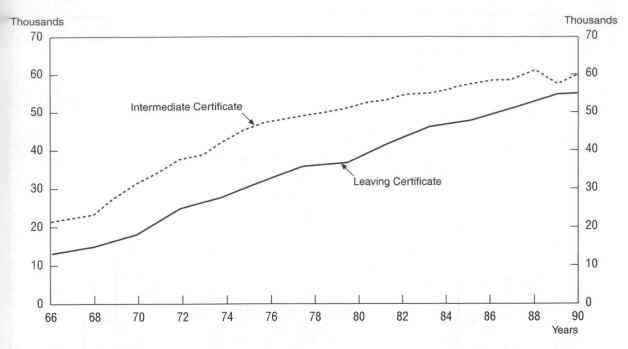

Source: Department of Education.

post-primary level which have taken place and the increased numbers which sat for the public examinations from 1966 to 1990. All pupils entering post-primary schooling now may avail of a six-year span, with three years in junior and three years in senior cycle. In 1993, 81 per cent of pupils completed the post-primary school course and 46 per cent entered higher education. The policy target is that 90 per cent of the age group would complete the senior cycle by the year 2000, with 50 per cent proceeding to higher education (Department of Education, 1992). Figure 3 sets out the overall structure of the system.

In general, the Irish education system is quite centralised in the sense that curricula, syllabi and examinations are all controlled by the Department of Education. The great majority of the schools relate directly with the Department, in the absence of a general local educational authority structure, although new Ministerial proposals (March 1994) plan to establish Regional Education Councils to which powers and functions would be devolved from the central Department. Significantly, control over examinations is not one of these.

The public examinations are devised, administered and corrected under the authority of the Department of Education. The professional aspects of the work are accomplished by the inspectorate, while the Examinations Branch in the Department of Education deals with administrative aspects. There is much tradition and experience accumulated with regard to the examinations procedures and they are operated with a high degree of efficiency. The results are disseminated by the Department of Education to the individual school authorities, who, in turn communicate results to pupils. The public examinations have tended to rely heavily on written, terminal examination papers.

In the early eighties there were moves to establish an agency, independent of the Department of Education to take responsibility for the examinations. A Curriculum and Examinations Board (CEB) was set up in 1984 and it was intended to give it statutory authority with regard to the examinations. This did not happen, and a change of government led to its replacement by a representative, advisory body in 1987, the National Council for Curriculum and Assessment (NCCA). Both the CEB and its successor the NCCA have issued many reports on curriculum and assessment issues which have helped to foster a more informed and participative debate on such issues. The government's Green Paper proposed subsuming the NCCA into an executive agency, the Curriculum and Assessment Agency which, among other things, would be responsible for "the administration of the certificate examinations". It is not clear what the final outcome will be. In the past, the inspectorate has been

Figure 3. **Structure of the education system and patterns of participation**

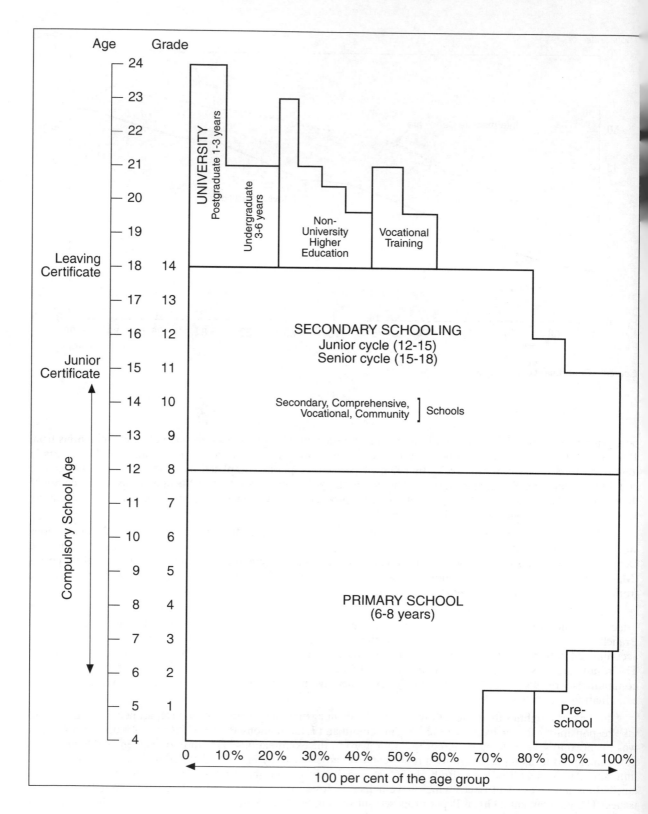

Source: Department of Education.

reluctant to agree to the examinations being removed from its control. Furthermore, as a great deal depends on the probity and efficiency of the examination process and administration, with the final accountability resting on the Minister for Education, there is a residual reluctance to remove the responsibility for examinations from the Department of Education.

Reasons for concern about performance standards

Because of the significance of pupil performances in the examinations for job opportunities and for access to higher education, a great deal of public attention is focussed on the examinations, particularly at the end of the senior cycle. Modes of assessment and performance standards have become a central issue in contemporary educational debate and policy, both among the professionals and the general public. A fundamental concern is the need to reform the traditional curricular content and modes of pupil assessment so as to cater more appropriately for the needs of the greatly expanded and more heterogeneous pupil clientele, four out of five of whom complete second-level education. The expanding participation has been a pressure for change which seeks to ensure that the system and its mode of testing performance standards are in line with the variance in achievements, aptitudes, interests and needs of the pupils. There is particular concern for pupils who achieve at low levels and who tend to drop out of the system.

Depending on definition, various studies have calculated that between 10 per cent and 20 per cent of pupils are failing in the system, or being failed by it. There is concern that these under achievers require remedial action on a number of fronts to improve their educational outcomes. These measures involve early diagnosis of learning problems, remediation of learning difficulties, attention to socio-economic factors inhibiting school achievement, reform of curricula, providing more varied curricular options, teaching styles and assessment processes.

Equal access and retention are still a policy concern, but the greater emphasis has shifted towards educational outcomes. There is serious concern about the under achievers, and this is focussed right down through primary school. The Department's proposal in the Green Paper to introduce national standardised tests at ages 7 and 11 has not been supported by teachers because of their fear that the results could be used for crude accountability purposes.

The NCCA, which includes teacher representatives, has made a series of recommendations in its publication *Curriculum and Assessment Policy – Towards the New Century* (1993), which would have a significant impact on primary schooling if adopted. It urged that the provision of a range of standardised tests (norm-referenced and criterion-referenced), should be available for all age levels. It recommended that a Pupil Report Card of performance and competence based on observation and the use of standardised tests should be available to parents. Pupil Profile Cards should be designed which would provide a comprehensive record of pupil achievement and be available for transfer to second-level schools. While access to assessment data should be available to designated persons such as the teacher, principal, parent and inspector, results of standardised or other form of assessment should not be published for school, class or individual.

The issue of assessment of primary pupils was discussed at the National Education Convention held in October 1993. The *Report on the National Education Convention* (Coolahan, 1994, p. 72) stated:

"Agreement exists on the assessment of individual pupils and on monitoring the performance of the education system as a whole, while there is disagreement on the provision of information on the performance of schools to outside bodies. There is general agreement that all schools should have, as part of their school plan, a system for the evaluation of the progress of individual pupils. The system should specify procedures for assessment and for reporting assessment results for individual pupils to parents. The assessment results should also be considered on a whole school basis. There is an obvious place for standardised tests in such a system to provide normative and diagnostic information as a basis for devising teaching programmes. The use of such tests is not opposed by teachers. Many already use them."

The key disagreement between the Department and the teachers focuses on the implementation of standardised tests at ages 7 and 11, and the use to which the results of such tests would be put regarding individual schools. The publication of such results is a very disputed issue. In other aspects of the tightening up of performance standards and assessment procedures in primary schools, much progress has been made, as is reflected in the NCCA policy, outlined above. The government may be in a good position to set out satisfactory lines of policy on performance standards in primary schools in its White Paper, which was expected in spring 1995.

The accountability movement has been having a significant influence, and while not adopting the "league table" approach to the publication of examination results as in the United Kingdom, there is pressure for greater transparency and more open access to information for parents. The key reason for the sensitivity of primary teachers towards publishing the results of standardised tests is the concern that the interpretation of results would be crude, have a distorting influence on the work of schools and ignore much of the educational activity of the school. As stated, teachers are not opposed to making results available on individual pupils to their parents.

The performance standards achieved by pupils in the secondary school public examinations play a part in the decisions of many parents as to enrolling their children in particular schools. The results are not published for individual schools, but informal patterns of communication form part of the sub-cultures associated with schools. Admission to post-primary schools takes place at the age of twelve, as a general rule, and it is not based on the results of any terminal examination at primary level, nor on selective entry tests at post-primary level, in the great majority of cases. The Minister is keen that all selection tests be dropped.

At post-primary level a significant factor in the contemporary concern is the lack of congruence which can exist between the mode of assessment and the curricular objectives. The heavy emphasis on terminal, external, written examinations is seen as having a distorting "backwash" effect on the styles of pedagogy employed in the schools. This is particularly so in the context of the new Junior Certificate, introduced in 1989, with the intention of promoting a comprehensive style curriculum with varied pedagogy promoting active learning methods. The modes of assessment are still largely based on the assessment processes of the older programmes. The Department of Education would wish to see a significant shift to more school-based assessment using a variety of techniques, administered and corrected by the pupils' own teachers. However, the largest post-primary teachers' union is opposed to this, considering that it would cut across the relationship of pupils and teachers if the teacher had responsibility for public certification of their pupils' performance. The other teachers' union is not opposed to the principle of school-based assessment, but agrees with the general body of teachers on the need for in-service training in assessment, external moderation of standards and increased remuneration of teachers for the work involved.

The NCCA is frustrated that its curricular plans for the Junior Certificate Course are being stymied by an assessment process which is not in alignment with them. It stated:

"The NCCA recognises that the introduction of a wider range of assessment modes and techniques is essential to the full implementation of the Junior Certificate programme (NCCA, 1993, p. 34)."

It has urged action because of the danger that teachers will teach to the assessment mode, largely external written examinations, rather than to the recommended methods. The *Report on the National Education Convention* (Coolahan, 1994, p. 74) endorsed this viewpoint stating:

"It is the view of the Secretariat that the present system of assessment at Junior Cycle is inadequate and unless reforms are introduced the objectives of the Junior Certificate programme will not be realised."

In an effort to work out a solution, the Minister for Education appointed a Working Group on Assessment for the Junior Certificate in March 1991 which reported in October 1992. It put forward a compromise solution which would involve an external written examination, supplemented by school-based oral, aural, practical, project work and assignments to be undertaken by the class teacher or, where the class teacher was unwilling, by a teacher from the same or another school (Report of the Working Group on Assessment, 1992). However, this proposal was not acceptable to the members of the largest teachers' union and the matter has remained deadlocked. The 1995 White Paper, is likely to set out Governmental policy in relation to assessment.

It should be noted that success in the Junior Certificate Examination is not linked to pupil access to senior cycle programmes, but standards of achievement do influence the level at which courses may be taken in senior cycle. While some progress could be expected in the Junior Certificate Examination, the problem of school-based assessment by teachers of their own pupils for public certification purposes at Leaving Certificate level is more difficult. With many small schools serving local, intimate communities, teachers fear that they would come under undesirable pressures from some parents, when, as in the Leaving Certificate Examination, the career chances of pupils are heavily dependent on their performances in the examinations. The cultural rootedness of long established educational practice is very pertinent in this context. As John Nisbet states in the OECD's *Curriculum Reform: Assessment in Question*:

"The main obstacles to a wider acceptance of alternative assessment are connected with public attitudes and expectation. In countries where grades from tests or examinations have become accepted currency for judging individuals, and where school-based assessments and teachers' judgements are not part of the 'assessment culture', doubts about the credibility of alternative assessment and suspicions of bias have still to be overcome (OECD, 1993, p. 143)."

A key "reason for concern" about the Leaving Certificate Examination is the heavy burden it carries, serving certification of achievement purposes as well as a selection mechanism for occupations, and particularly for entry to university.

With such a high proportion of pupils now staying on in school up to the end of senior cycle it is considered that the traditional Leaving Certificate courses are too academic for many students. Yet there is concern that providing alleviating measures for the weaker achievers should not lead to a dilution of general standards. Many subject syllabi have been remodelled, and three levels or grades of difficulty have been provided for Irish and Mathematics to help ensure a form of certification in line with the achievements of pupils in different subjects and course levels. The NCCA and the Department of Education have devised three orientations for the Leaving Certificate Programme to be operational from 1995 – the Leaving Certificate, a restructured Leaving Certificate Vocational Programme (LCVP) and the Leaving Certificate Applied Programme (LCAP). The Leaving Certificate will be the course followed by the majority of pupils. The use of a variety of assessment techniques is being promoted and these are discussed later. Despite establishing a more differentiated pattern of senior cycle curricular provision, the aim is to maintain a unified structure at this level, incorporating a number of course options, rather than opt for a dual track system.

One can conclude this section by stating that a variety of factors give rise to reasons for concern with regard to performance standards and pupil assessment reform. The planning for such reforms is still in process regarding the three levels – Primary, Junior Certificate and Leaving Certificate levels. The hope is that over the next few years the planned reforms can be put in place, responsive to the needs of the pupils and the system and attuned to, but not moulded by, the assessment culture which exists in Ireland.

Differences in achievement

The results of the national certificate examinations are available for well over a century, but up to recently, few statistical studies have been done on them. The rich data bank has not yet been sufficiently drawn upon. In recent years, the NCCA has commissioned analyses of the results which include cross comparisons between subject areas.

A significant study took place on the reliability and validity of the Leaving Certificate Examination in 1970, which led to improvements in the examining processes (Madaus and McNamara, 1970). A detailed appraisal of the form and function of the Intermediate Certificate Examination, as it was then known, was published in 1975, but its extensive proposals for reform involving much more school-based assessment were not adopted (Report on ICE, 1975). Neither were the findings of a follow-on study in 1980, the *Public Examinations Evaluation Project* (Heywood *et al.*, 1980).

Few longitudinal studies exist on specific areas, although periodic studies of reading performance of 11-year-old children were conducted over a twenty-year period, the outcomes of which indicated progress. The Educational Research Centre has conducted a number of studies on the public examinations and attitudes towards them. It has also devised a range of standardised tests for primary schools which are used extensively by teachers and inspectors, but which have not been employed in the public arena as national measures of achievement, over time.

Little substantial evidence has been established regarding such issues as varying performance between grade award levels, or on the effects of different curricula on learning outcomes. Limited research exists on the relative performance of boys and girls in the public examinations. In the context of a national policy promoting co-education, this is an issue attracting more public attention. The Economic and Social Research Institute has recently initiated a major study on co-education on behalf of the Department of Education which will include analysis of the performances of boys and girls in the public examinations. This is a comprehensive study which should yield significant outcomes. No detailed studies have been conducted on the effects of the socio-economic background of pupils or the performance standards attained by them, although some studies by the Economic and Social Research Institute indicate links between poor socio-economic circumstances and weak performance in the examinations.

Building consensus for change

Improving performance standards and assessment techniques forms but one item of a comprehensive agenda for educational change being processed currently by the Department of Education. As the strategy adopted by the government for building a consensus for educational reform is distinctive in international experience, it is considered useful to describe the process in some detail in this section.

While there has been impressive expansion of the education system in recent decades, the administrative, organisational and legislative aspects inherited from an earlier era remain largely intact. In the 1980s many reports proposed significant reforms. These gathered momentum in the early nineties with reports on the primary school system (1990), the primary curriculum (1990) and, notably, an OECD *Review of Irish Education* (1991). A comprehensive *Green Paper: Education for A Changing World* was issued by the government in June 1992.

This reviewed the full spectrum of educational activity and made many proposals affecting all areas of the system. When issuing the paper, the Minister for Education called for "a wide national debate". This was certainly forthcoming and many meetings, conferences and seminars took place on the Green paper throughout the country. Up to 1 000 formal written submissions were made in response to the paper. Furthermore, the Minister organised a series of regional seminars at which the Minister and senior departmental officials attended to make presentations, hear submissions and answer questions. Furthermore, evidence existed that heed was being taken of the debate, and the Minister displayed a flexible approach to issues raised.

The debate was very rich in terms of inputs but it was also very wide-ranging and diverse. An important issue arose as to how best to co-ordinate it and put a pattern to it which might give a more cohesive framework to assist policy making. It was in this context that the National Education Convention was conceived.

There was no precedent for such an event. The Secretary General and Secretariat had the right to produce an independent report on the Convention which would be published, and to which the Minister undertook to give careful consideration in preparing a White Paper. The Minister also broke new ground in agreeing to allow her senior departmental officials to make a presentation to the Convention and to be questioned in open forum by the Secretariat.

The Minister issued invitations to 42 organisations to participate including the major educational interests but also the social partners, such as the trade unions, employer bodies, farmers' organisations, the unemployed, the Council for the Status of Women.

The Convention took place from 11 to 21 October, 1993. The main structural features of the Convention were that invited organisations made formal presentations to the plenary sessions and were questioned on these by members of the Secretariat. In the second week participants were broken up into three concurrent "Analysis of Issues" groups which focussed on fifteen key themes, with the assistance of a Chairperson and a Rapporteur at each of the fifteen sessions. Eventually, on the last day, the Secretariat presented its reports from these groups to the plenary session.

The aims of the Convention were to promote concise communication and clarification of organisations' viewpoints, to foster multi-lateral dialogue and understanding between organisations, to analyse proposals and various reactions to them, to establish areas of agreement and disagreement, to explore possibilities of consensus where disagreements existed and to establish a framework for a coherent overview of the viewpoints. The various procedures and processes employed were designed with these objectives in mind.

In line with the general spirit of the consultative process, the Secretariat sought to extend awareness of, and interest in, the proceedings as widely as possible to the interested public. Over 800 "observers" were accommodated over the nine-day period, while national newspapers, radio and television were utilised effectively in covering the proceedings. Another striking feature of the process was the sustained presence of the Minister and her senior officials throughout the plenary sessions. Again, it emphasised the note of a listening attitude and a partnership approach to policy issues. The interest of other government personnel was demonstrated by the Prime Minister meeting with participants on the Friday evening of the first week, and by visits of at least seven government ministers to observe the proceedings. It would seem that an intersectoral interest was being demonstrated towards educational policy issues.

Following the Convention, it was the responsibility of the Secretariat to assimilate, interpret and evaluate the very extended debate which had taken place. The Secretariat's Report was made available to the public on the 19th January 1994 and national television provided a programme to disseminate to the general public the reactions of key participants to the Report.

Within the wider parameters of this consultative process the specific issues of assessment and performance standards have been addressed. It would seem that both the consultative process and the content of the dialogue have created a greater understanding of the issues involved, have fostered greater cohesion on the issues and helped to create a climate of expectation for educational change. The National Council for Curriculum and Assessment (NCCA) can also be regarded as a significant element in the consultative process, and has a crucial role in helping to promote consensus on curricular and assessment policies. The twenty-two members of the Council represent teachers, school managers, parents, industry and trade unions. Other members include Department of Education representatives and nominees of the Minister, with a Chairperson appointed by the Minister. The Council's tasks can be summarised under four main aspects: to advise the Minister on the curriculum in primary and second-level schools; on how pupils' progress in school should be assessed; on the standards reached by pupils in public examinations; on the in-service education of teachers. While acting as an advisory body, its committees engage in curriculum and assessment review and proposals for change, seeking to achieve consensus between the involved organisations. The Council also consults widely through discussion papers. The Minister and her Department are the decision-makers and carry the responsibility for financing new developments. Occasional tensions exist between Departmental personnel and the NCCA, but, overall, relationships are good and a cooperative tradition has been built up between the two agencies. The Green Paper envisaged giving significant new powers for examinations to a re-constituted NCCA, but it remains to be seen if this becomes a reality. It is not likely that the inspectorate would wish to lose their decision making and administrative roles in curriculum and assessment to an NCCA, however constituted, at least as far as the Leaving Certificate is concerned.

The process of standard setting

The standard setters

Performance standards are set by the state school inspectorate who are permanent public employees, with the assistance of some skilled, experienced teachers in the subject areas. The inspectors, who are given responsibility for the overall standard of the examinations, are subject specialists, and of senior standing. They "grow into" the job by experience and guidance, rather than through specialist training. Their competence is judged by the Inspectorate Management Group, including the Chief Inspector and, indirectly, through the responses and feedback from teachers and school managers to the examination papers which are devised. Significant and unexpected departures in the standards or style of setting the examinations tend to draw adverse reactions from the teachers. A good deal of public debate takes place on the difficulty or otherwise of these national examinations in the various subjects, and the media pay attention to the immediate feedback of teachers and pupils.

The inspectors' work on the examinations is regarded as part of their general work. The teachers who give assistance are remunerated for their work at set rates. The duration of the work of the standard setters is indefinite, and subject only to the decisions of the Chief Inspectors. Inspectors sometimes change around their areas of responsibility. Teachers who assist with the examinations have more discretion as to the duration of their involvement, but many of those who build up experience tend to continue for many years.

The universities have representatives on the course committees and on the examination panels for the Leaving Certificate courses. The universities now adopt performance on the Leaving Certificate as satisfying matriculation requirements for university entry, and, accordingly, the universities appoint subject specialists who liaise with the inspectorate on performance standards.

Devising the examinations

The process of the compilation of questions and test items goes on throughout the year. Normally, the expert, experienced teachers are invited to submit proposed examination papers at the beginning of the school year to the Chief Examiner, who is usually a senior inspector in the subject area. Such questions are appraised, analysed, and discussed over the school year with a gradual refining and selection being made, which is highly confidential within the inspectorate. Marking schemes are devised which allocate proportions of marks to various aspects of the questions being posed. There has been a long tradition behind this process, and experience and precedent have a big bearing on the process, although adaptations are made in the light of new curricular content or pedagogic approaches.

Standards are set in much the same way for each subject area and very few interdisciplinary elements are included. Examination standards are designed within a subject area without specific articulation of the criteria involved but related to the normal grade distribution. Marking schemes are devised and made available to examiners. During the marking process, monitoring takes place on emerging trends, and adjustments on the marking schemes may then be made to bring the results into line with normal and expected distribution patterns.

Examinations are designed using a combination of normed and criterion-referenced procedures in such a way that a passing grade in a subject represents the achievement of what would be regarded as a minimum level of competence within a subject. Quality of expected pupil responses is related to the grading system, descending from Grade A1 to "No Grade". The standards are set for each subject area of the Junior Certificate examination taken at age 15, and of the Leaving Certificate, taken at age 17/18.

Evidence of attainment

There are seven modes of assessment which may be used for examinations for national certification at senior cycle in written, practical, external oral, school-based oral, aural, external coursework, school-based coursework. Written, practical, aural and most oral assessments are currently administered externally, *i.e.* they are conducted by examiners from outside the school attended by the pupil. Six of the seven modes identified above are in use for assessment of pupils in the Leaving Certificate examination overall. No school-based oral assessment is used. Written assignments are used in the examination of all subjects. Eleven subjects, *e.g.* Agriculture, Art, also have non-written assessment components. The provision of school-based teacher assessment exists for only three subjects, Construction Studies, Agricultural Science and Agricultural Economics, and is focussed on practical work in these subjects. Overall in the examinations, the most heavy emphasis is placed on terminal written assessments, externally set and corrected. The Department of Education would like to see a wider use of school-based assessment with pupils' own teachers more responsible for the evaluation of performance. But, as stated earlier, there is teacher opposition to this. Certificates with grades achieved are given to all candidates. However, the pass/fail is regarded popularly as the cut-off feature of the external examinations, with a Grade E or lower, that is, less than 40 per cent, corresponding to failing grades. Students are very aware of the importance of the grades and the more able pupils are usually well motivated to achieve at the highest possible grade.

Controlling and financing the process

Performance standards are set at national level. The inspectorate manages the process, under the authority of the Minister for Education. The process takes up a great deal of the inspectorate's time at the expense of time spent in schools, guiding or evaluating teaching.

The cost of the examinations for 1992-93 was calculated at £9.2 million out of a total current expenditure on post-primary education of £572 million. This does not include costs of staff time as part of their normal civil service duties. In 1994, 60 000 candidates sat for the Junior Certificate Examination, and 63 000 sat for the Leaving Certificate. Expenditure on research and development on performance standards is very low.

Consistency and fairness

As national examinations, the performance standards are the same for all regions, and a uniformity exists nationwide. The examinations enjoy a high reputation for the fairness of the procedures.

Factors influencing standards

Empirical methods are not used to determine levels of attainment, and no specification is published of what pupils are expected to achieve at each grade level. Reliance is placed more on experience and precedent in determining the percentage achieving particular grades in a particular subject. This leads to a fairly consistent distribution across the grades within a subject from year to year, in line with a norm-referenced system.

A very high level of public interest exists in the upper secondary examinations. With a declining job market and limitations on entry to most university faculties the competition is intense. The universities employ a "points system", based on performance on the final school examination as the main criterion for selection. It is generally accepted that the "back-wash" effects of the points system significantly influence curricular content covered and styles of pedagogy used in schools (Coolahan, 1979). School life is also affected by the provision of "mock" examinations. These are "dry-run" or practice examinations provided by firms specialising in such examination materials and are usually taken by pupils in February or March prior to the public external examinations taken in June. To help enhance chances of greater success in the public examinations pupils from better-off backgrounds increasingly avail of extra tuition in "grind" schools in urban areas. Political influence plays no part in the examinations or standard setting. The issues are left to the professionals involved.

The standards

A standard is judged by the performance of a pupil on a terminal test, generally of a written mode and is a composite grade. The standards are set in relation to the objectives set out for the subjects. The performance standards relate both to the quality of the courses in each subject and that of the examinations set to assess the achievement of students.

Minimum thresholds of knowledge and skills which pupils are expected to achieve are not defined for grade levels. The award of a grade D is generally accepted as implying a mastery of the basics in a particular subject. The examinations have a strong dependence on a norm-base, with roughly the same proportions in a subject gaining particular grades each year. Accordingly, a proportion of candidates fail each year, *i.e.* do not achieve a minimum grade D (Williams, 1992).

There is a general understanding of the levels of achievement which merit the award of a particular grade. There is a heavy reliance on experience and precedent in this understanding. Marking schemes are devised and made available to those correcting. At examiners' conferences guidelines are provided as to the level of award to be given to different types of answers, in relation to the marking schemes. The marking schemes, however, are confidential to those correcting and are not made generally available to all teachers. Teachers acquire their knowledge of standards through their work on correcting the public examinations and the knowledge is normally transmitted to some other teachers at meetings of subject associations, following the results being made available.

The NCCA, in a recent publication, has made a strong plea that the criterion-referenced aspects of pupil performances should be made more explicit. The Council urged that course committees should be required to advise on the nature and preparation of such criteria for key threshold points in the grading system. In the interest of greater transparency, the Council has also sought the publication of an annual report from a chief examiner for each subject. It stated that schools should have ready access to the information relating to the organisation and administration of the examinations as well as the assessment techniques employed (NCCA, 1993). It would seem that reforms in this direction are unlikely to be long delayed.

The same national examinations and tests are set for all pupils in all types of second-level schools. At Junior Certificate, Irish, English and Mathematics are set at three levels of difficulty, with other subjects having two levels. At Leaving Certificate all subjects have Higher and Ordinary levels, except Mathematics which has a third, "Alternative" Ordinary level. Standards are set by the inspectorate for all subjects, and not just the core subjects.

It should be noted that outside the mainstream, second-level system, there has been a growth of many courses of an applied vocational training and technical character in recent years. They do not come within the ambit of the Junior or Leaving Certificate programmes. In 1991, a new body, the National Council for Vocational Awards (NCVA) was set up, part of whose remit is to set standards for certification for the many vocational courses outside the formal, second-level system.

Machinery does not exist for the regular monitoring of standards in a systematic way which would indicate clearly whether standards were improving or deteriorating. However, in recent years, the inspectorate, and, increasingly, the NCCA, with the assistance of the Educational Research Centre, is keeping a more careful overview of standards at Leaving Certificate level. The Educational Research Centre produces an annual review of results on the Leaving Certificate examination for the NCCA.

Student performance in the public examinations is graded in the following categories:

Grade	Percentage range
A1	90-100
A2	85-89
B1	80-84
B2	75-79
B3	70-74
C1	65-69
C2	60-64
C3	55-59
D1	50-54
D2	45-49
D3	40-44
E	25-39
F	10-24
No grade	0-9

The Review of the 1992 Leaving Certificate indicated that while a total of 32 subjects was available, the ten most popular subjects accounted for 82 per cent of all the examinations taken by the regular candidates. Significant gender differences in subject choice were seen to exist.

Concerning the spread of grades awarded, most fell in the B, C, and D categories. Grades at the extremes, *i.e.* A, E, F and "No Grade", were much less common. The percentage of grades awarded in each subject vary considerably from subject to subject. Most of the subjects with the highest percentages of A and B grades were taken by small numbers of students. Among popular subjects, English, Geography and Art all had relatively few A and B grades, compared to the overall pattern. Significant differences also occurred in the distribution of E and lower grades across subjects. Other statistical breakdowns illustrate "cohort performance" of "basic" and "high" levels in each subject. From the point of view of "candidate performance", 12 per cent of candidates were shown to have achieved less than five D grades and 26 per cent achieved the level of five Ds, popularly regarded as a "pass". More than half of the candidates were awarded less than two C3 grades on Higher Level examinations (Hickey and Martin, 1993 and 1994).

Unease exists about differences in the proportion of A and B grades which pertain to different subjects. Table 1 is based on the Leaving Certificate Examination Results for 1992.

Table 1. **Ten subjects with highest and lowest % of As and Bs**

Ten subjects with highest % of As and Bs		
Subject (H)	% As and Bs	Deviation above average
Applied maths	55	+28
Latin	49	+22
Music B	45	+18
Construction	42	+14
Spanish	38	+10
Chemistry	38	+10
German	37	+9
Economic history	36	+8
Biology	35	+8
Engineering	34	+6
Ten subjects with lowest % of As and Bs		
Subject (H)	% As and Bs	Deviation above average
Music A	10	−18
Agricultural science	16	−11
Art	17	−10
Geography	18	−9
English	21	−6
Business organisation	23	−5
Physics and chemistry	25	−3
Economics	25	−3
Home economics (gen.)	26	−2
French	27	0

Source: Leaving Certificate Examination results for 1992.

As far as failing is concerned, there are wide variations, also. Scoring an E, F or No Grade is generally regarded as "failing" the particular subject. Failure rates in the Leaving Certificate Higher Level papers vary from only 1 per cent in Construction, Engineering, Music and 2 per cent in English, to 15 per cent in Agricultural Economics, 10 per cent in Physics and Chemistry, 7 per cent in Economics and 6 per cent each in Accounting, Business Organisation and History. At Ordinary Level, "failure" rates varied from a low of 2 per cent in Engineering and 3 per cent in Construction Studies to a high of 19 per cent in Agricultural Economics, 12 per cent in Physics and Chemistry, 9 per cent in Physics and 8 per cent in Chemistry. Such variations emphasise the need for greater overall co-ordination of performance standards and marking schemes to supplement the heavy concentration on individual subjects by subject specialists.

Implementation, review and adjustment

Information on standards is given to schools in the forms of individual pupil results. Marking schemes are the main basis which set out information on performance levels and award criteria. However, these are confidential to examiners and are not generally available. The inspectorate issues occasional reports on the performance in individual subjects, but these are not systematic or comprehensive. The NCCA has called for much greater ransparency on performance standards and for much more explicit specification of criterion-referenced aspects of pupil assessment. Such public definition of criteria is regarded by the Council as particularly desirable for key threshold points in the grading system. Educational correspondents in the newspapers are very alert in reporting on trends, patterns, upsets and divergences of grade distributions between subjects. Access to the examination data is now available more readily to researchers and since the examination results have been computerised, the results are available more quickly. The Department of Education's annual Statistical Report gives general tables on aggregate performance levels in the different subjects. The NCCA has been publishing Reviews of the Leaving Certificate Examination since the 1991 examination.

The fact that some teachers assist the inspectorate in devising examinations and that many teachers are involved in the correcting process, working to marking schemes, gives those teachers a "feel" for the standards and what is being expected or rewarded. The various subject associations also pass on information on standards to their members. Performance standards are not independent from the process of curricular definition. The inspectorate is closely involved in both processes. An elaborate structure of assistant examiners, advising examiners, chief advising examiners and chief examiner, is set up to conduct the assessment for both the Junior and Leaving Certificate Examinations. At the outset, Examiners' Conferences are held for each subject area and marking schemes are agreed. Assistant examiners submit cross section samples of their marking for approval to senior personnel who monitor trends. Adjustments may be required on the basis of the sample of the corrected scripts, and regular contact is maintained between the network of examiners. They work to time deadlines with senior inspectors taking responsibility for the final collating and appraisal. Both the Junior and Leaving Certificate examinations are taken in June. The results of the Leaving Certificate are available by mid-August and those of the Junior Certificate in late August or early September.

As has been noted above, marking schemes which guide the scoring of pupils' performances are developed but are not published, or publicly available. The schemes are adapted to suit changing examining formats. The guidelines for high scores such as A1 or A call for student responses that transcend the subject matter taught. They reward evidence of quality analysis, originality of thought or creative, divergent thinking.

As described above, a network of examiners exists with processes for cross checking the ratings of an individual examiner. When results are published appeal procedures exist for re-checking individual candidates' results in the Leaving Certificate, and, from 1994, in the Junior Certificate Examinations, on the payment of a fee and with the support of the school principal. The fee is refunded if the appeal is upheld. Only a tiny proportion tend to be upheld.

The Examination Branch of the Department of Education releases the results of individual pupils to the individual school managers, who, in turn, inform students and parents. General aggregate statistical data are made available to newspaper correspondents and are eventually published in the Department's Statistical Report. The Department of Education does not make the results of individual schools, or pupils or different regions available to the public.

In recent years, research bodies conduct analyses of the results; but traditionally, the Department of Education had been loathe to release examination materials and data to researchers, or to publish research studies on the data. The senior inspectorate approve results before release. The Minister for Education retains the final political responsibility for the probity and integrity of the examination process and standards.

No special provision exists with regard to performance standards for pupils from economically under-privileged backgrounds. Some provision is made for children belonging to linguistic minorities, but such minorities are very small in number in Ireland. Special arrangements are made for pupils with sensory disabilities, such as problems of hearing, sight or speech. Special arrangements are also made for those with physical disabilities. The main forms of provision are extra time arrangements, special supervision arrangements, and the use of appropriate technology. Allowing for extra facilitation, all pupils are expected to take the same examinations and achieve on the common standards.

A pilot alternative Senior Certificate Programme has been operated for a number of years by a small number of schools with a more applied emphasis and more varied forms of assessment than the Leaving Certificate. Since 1995 it has been replaced by a new Leaving Certificate Applied Programme (LCAP), which is expected to incorporate more school-based evaluation. In 1993, the NCCA introduced a special programme at junior cycle for educationally or socially disadvantaged pupils, called the Junior Certificate School Programme. Its pilot phase is operating in about forty schools in the greater Dublin area. It is hoped to establish a national standard for the School Programme and to provide a statement of pupil competencies in terms of nationally validated criteria. There will be a heavy emphasis on school-based assessment, with external monitoring.

The inspectorate reviews the patterns of success and failure rates in each subject annually. Before results are finalised adjustments are sometimes made, with general application, if it is seen that failure or success rates deviate significantly from expected patterns. The outcome of such reviews feeds into the planning for the following year by the inspectorate and advising examiners. The computerisation of results and the more comprehensive statistical data now available are likely to lead to more thorough analyses and review of standards for the future.

The inspectorate has been very keen to hold on to its prerogative on public examinations, although recent official policy statements suggest that the examinations should come under the control of a re-structured National Council for Curriculum and Assessment, external to the Department. Nevertheless, while it may lose the standard-setting process as reflected in the public examinations, it is planned that the inspectorate would be the key agency in advising the Minister about quality assurance overall, in devising strategies to monitor national standards and in making investigations of standards, other than by the public examinations. This would be part of a more modernised, sophisticated process in standard setting and monitoring. It is also envisaged that the inspectorate would issue independent reports on patterns and problems emerging in achievement levels in the education system.

At present, findings about standards have little public provenance. Through the accumulated experience of the inspectorate and their assistant examiners, reviews take place on evolving patterns of performance, and bear in mind new curricular initiatives. As the personnel involved are closely in touch with the curricula and teachers' attitudes, insights and perspectives are fed into the on-going processes, through the committees in question. However, it is not a systematic or publicly discussed process. The form of monitoring is more informal than systematic, but it does feed forward into future approaches. The inspectorate is linked to the National Council for Curriculum and Assessment, and also gives the key professional advice to the Minister on the proposals of that Council, which is an advisory, not an executive body. Thus, the influence of those with responsibility for performance standards is very direct to the Minister, who decides on national curriculum policy.

Problems and critical issues

The issue of performance standards is identified as one of major importance in the reform and development of contemporary Irish education. In an overall appraisal of the issue, it is important to acknowledge strengths of the current system, to diagnose problem areas and to point the way forward to remediation of weaknesses. Space permits this to be done only in summary form.

Among the successful features of the public examinations and standard-setting process in Ireland are:
- the confidence and trust of the public, employers, and higher education institutions in the process, in terms of standards, status and currency;
- the commitment and integrity of the personnel involved in the process;
- the impartiality of the system;
- a good level of predictability of successes in the Leaving Certificate Examination with later success levels in higher education;
- some subjects benefit from a good range of assessment techniques through written, practical, coursework, oral and aural, almost entirely, however, in an external mode;
- the efficiency and economy with which the process is conducted;
- an apparent willingness to improve the data flow and make more comprehensive Chief Examiners' reports available.

There are also weaknesses in the system and the following itemisation seeks to identify these:
- the process has not adapted sufficiently to the phenomenon of mass post-primary schooling and incorporates an over-reliance on verbal and logico-mathematical achievement which makes the examinations not suitable for all students;
- a too heavy reliance is placed on the national, external, public, terminal examinations, which, in turn, rely too heavily on written examinations. This tends to narrow teaching methods and encourages undue rote memorisation by students arising from the nature of the assessments used;
- inadequate attention is being given to formative as distinct from summative assessments as essential components of the teaching and learning process;
- there is a lack of congruence between course objectives and assessment techniques, as in the case of the Junior Certificate;
- the negative impact of the examination on the areas of the curriculum which are not examined for state certification, e.g. social and personal development, religious education and physical education;
- the heavy emphasis placed on the Leaving Certificate Examination as a selection mechanism, particularly for higher education, intrudes on its other role as certification of educational achievement of all pupils;

- the absence and/or inaccessibility of adequate statements of the criteria that are applied in assigning marks or grades. The criterion reference aspect of the examinations needs to be made more formal and explicit;
- there is insufficient targeted analysis and publication of research data relevant to the process;
- the inadequacy of research and development dimension within the examination system;
- the preparedness and attitudes of teachers, whereby they are not prepared to accept more professional responsibility for the continuous assessment of their own pupils' work, even at Junior Certificate levels, for certification purposes;
- the need to win teachers' confidence at primary level that the results of national standardised testing would not be used crudely by officialdom as an accountability measure on schools. Such confidence would help in the introduction of varied forms of pupil evaluation in the primary schools.

Many of these weaknesses are shared by systems in other countries and they do not yield to simple solutions. Yet, if significant and sustained improvement is to be made in the whole area of performance standards and assessment reform, it seems necessary to meet a number of preconditions such as the following:

- an understanding by authorities of the significance of the process and of its multifaceted influences on the education system;
- arising from the above, the need for sufficient investment in good standard setting to allow the process to be modernised in line with up-to-date techniques;
- regular monitoring of the assessment process through the conduct of validity and reliability studies;
- providing systematic training for a cohort of specialists in the field of standard setting;
- allowing time and effort to be applied to researching and piloting of performance assessment instruments at various age and ability levels;
- making assessment skills a more targeted feature of pre-service and in-service teacher education;
- fostering a tradition of on-going informed, critical debate on standards' issues with the help of good published analyses of patterns and problems.

It is also desirable that Ireland extends its involvement with international comparative studies of pupil performance. Despite the qualifications and cautions needed in the interpretation of the data from such studies, they are of significance, particularly to a country such as Ireland which relies so much on the quality of its education system.

Ireland has engaged in studies on reading, mathematics and science with the International Association for the Evaluation of Educational Achievement (IEA), and the International Assessment of Educational Progress (IAEP). It has also, of course, engaged with the OECD's *Education at a Glance* (1995). There is scope for further development and more precision on these complex international studies, before they are likely to have a significant impact on setting performance standards for individual countries. Nevertheless, they do act as a valuable stimulus and spur to the local policy formulators, as, for instance, in the case of science in Irish schools. Such studies give useful, if general, benchmarks and alert countries if they are falling badly behind in some areas. They can also be useful in internal government debates, either as providing assurance that money spent on education seems to be providing results in line with international trends, or help to make the case for increased investment, linked to targeted policy, in an area of weakness, as seen in the light of international trends. With greater occupational mobility, it is also desirable that greater equivalence between international qualifications and certification be promoted.

As is the case with other valuable OECD and international material on education, there is a need for improved dissemination of the relevant information to educational bodies and school personnel throughout the country. Good future-oriented policy is best built on the bases of an informed awareness among the interests involved.

Bibliography

COOLAHAN, J. (ed.) (1979), *University Entrance Requirements and Their Effects on Second Level Curricula*, Irish Federation of University Teachers, Dublin.

COOLAHAN, J. (1981), *Irish Education, History and Structure*, Institute of Public Administration, Dublin.

COOLAHAN, J. (ed.) (1994), *Report on the National Education Convention*, Stationery Office, Dublin.

COOLAHAN, J. and McGUINNESS, S. (1994), *Report on the Roundtable Discussions on Regional Education Councils*, Department of Education, Dublin.

DEPARTMENT OF EDUCATION, *Annual Statistical Reports,* esp. 1992/93, Department of Education, Dublin.

DEPARTMENT OF EDUCATION (1992), *Green Paper: Education For a Changing World,* Stationery Office, Dublin.

DEPARTMENT OF EDUCATION (1994), *Position Paper on Regional Education Councils,* Department of Education, Dublin.

HEYWOOD, J., S. McGUINNESS and D. MURPHY (1980), "Public Examination Evaluation Project Final Report", University of Dublin.

HICKEY, B. and M. MARTIN (1993, 1994), *The Leaving Certificate Examination: A Review of Results for 1991, 1992,* National Council for Curriculum and Assessment, Dublin.

MADAUS, G.F. and V. GREANEY (1985), "The Irish Experience in Competency Testing: Implications for American Education", *American Journal of Education,* Vol. 93.

MADAUS, G.F. and J. MacNAMARA (1970), *Public Examinations: A Study of the Irish Leaving Certificate,* Educational Research Centre, Dublin.

NATIONAL COUNCIL FOR CURRICULUM AND ASSESSMENT (1993), *Curriculum and Assessment Policy: Towards the New Century,* NCCA, Dublin.

NATIONAL COUNCIL FOR CURRICULUM AND ASSESSMENT (1994), *Assessment and Certification in the Senior Cycle: Issues and Directions,* NCCA, Dublin.

OECD (1991), *Review of Irish Education,* Paris.

OECD (1993), *Curriculum Reform: Assessment in Question,* Paris.

OECD (1995), *Education at a Glance: OECD Indicators,* Paris.

PRIMARY CURRICULUM REVIEW COMMITTEE (1990), "Report", Stationery Office, Dublin.

PRIMARY EDUCATION REVIEW BODY (1990), "Report", Stationery Office, Dublin.

"Report on the Intermediate Certificate Examination" (ICE) (1975), Stationery Office, Dublin.

"Report of the Working Party on Assessment for the Junior Certificate" (1992), Department of Education, Dublin (limited circulation).

WILLIAMS, K. (1992), *Assessment: A Discussion Paper,* Association of Secondary Teachers, Dublin.

JAPAN

by

Toshikazu Ishino
Prime Secretary for Education, Japanese Delegation to OECD

Summary

In Japan, the most important educational policy objective is the provision of opportunities for everybody to receive school education of a standardised high quality wherever one lives in the country. The Course of Study – the national standards of curricula – is a main policy measure to attain this objective. Therefore, performance standards can be considered in relation to the Course of Study. The Course of Study has been revised roughly every ten years, on the basis of the recommendations presented by the Curriculum Council, an advisory council to the Minister of Education, Science and Culture (Monbusho). A wide range of views is collected through deliberations at the Curriculum Council, and formal and informal information from local boards of education to Monbusho. Moreover, Monbusho implements the Assessment and National Survey of Curriculum to ascertain the extent to which the content of the Course of Study is understood by pupils and students.

The Course of Study defines the general guideline for organising the curriculum and teaching areas such as subjects, moral education and special activities so that each school may organise its own curriculum on the basis of general standards. In implementing performance standards defined in the Course of Study, various measures, such as the dissemination of the objectives and contents of the Course of Study, textbook authorisation, teacher training and so on are carried out. The judgement about whether each pupil or student has attained the standards is made in the classroom by each teacher. At the national level, the Assessment and National Survey is carried out. In Japan, excessive competition to pass the entrance examinations into upper level institutions has prevented the performance standards defined in the Course of Study from being actually attained in the classroom.

Context

The Japanese compulsory school system

Japan adopts a single-track school system (a 6-3-3-4 system), which is shown in Figure 1. Such a system was introduced on the principle of equal educational opportunity after the Second World War. At the compulsory education level, students attend both elementary schools (six years) and lower secondary schools (three years) or attend special education schools for a period of nine years from the age of 6 to 15. The number of elementary schools and lower secondary schools was respectively 24 776 and 11 192 as of May 1, 1993. The majority of them are established and managed by local authorities.

The modern system of school education in Japan was inaugurated in 1872 after the Meiji Revolution (1868). However, it must be pointed out that a wide diffusion of many small private education institutions called "tera-koya" (school at temple) in the previous era built the foundation for the following development of the school education.

Under this school education system, a period of six years in elementary schools became compulsory in 1907 and divergent pathways had been developed at secondary and tertiary levels. Therefore, roughly speaking, this school education system was a multiple-track school system.

In March of 1946, the United States Education Mission to Japan visited Japan and presented recommendations to reform the old school education system to a single-track 6-3-3-4 school system. The current school education system is in principle based on those recommendations.

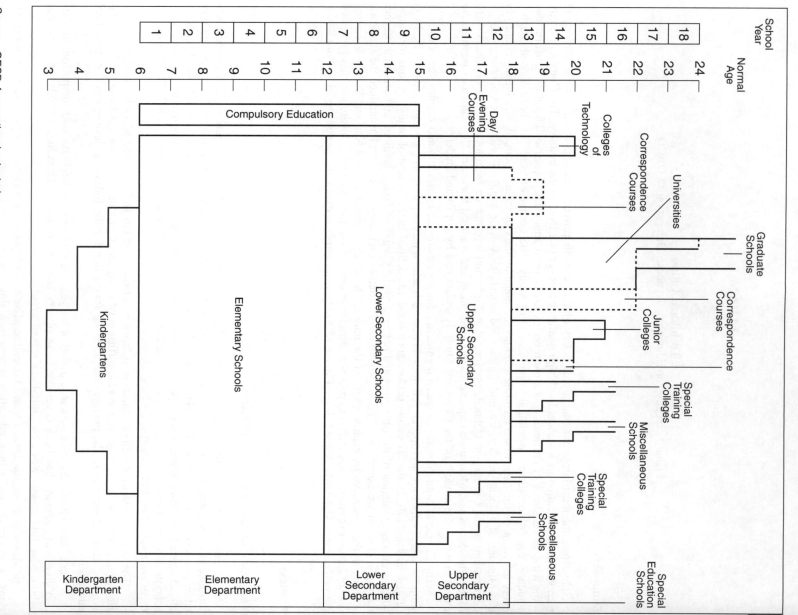

Figure 1. **The Japanese education system**

Source: OECD, from national submission.

150

Since then, the school system at compulsory levels has not been changed, although at the upper secondary and tertiary levels, various new initiatives, such as the introduction of colleges of technology and special training colleges, have been carried out.

The concern about performance standards

In 1947, the Fundamental Law of Education, which defined new educational ideals, such as equality of educational opportunities, compulsory education and co-education, was enacted. In this case, equality of educational opportunities implies not only the guarantee of an opportunity for everybody to receive an education, but also the guarantee of school education of a standardised high quality.

Therefore, the provision of opportunities for everybody to receive school education of a standardised high quality wherever one lives in the country has been the most important educational policy objective. To realise these objectives, various policy measures relating to the curriculum, textbooks, teachers, school facilities, the educational administration and finance, and so on, have been developed.

Even before the inauguration of the modern school education system, the literacy rate among people in Japan was relatively high due to the wide diffusion of ''tera-koya'', as mentioned above. Some persons say the reason is the strong yearning for knowledge among people, who find value in education or learning itself. This phenomenon can also be explained by the fact that a lot of people *are now enjoying lifelong activities as consumption.*

In the Meiji-era, the government adopted the policy of using the school system as an instrument to select highly qualified persons, while in the previous era, personnel selection was mainly based on social classes and families. As a result of this policy, the competition to pass the entrance examinations into upper level institutions, successful entry to which meant success in society, became severe. This trend of excessive competition to pass the entrance examinations into upper level institutions has continued today. However, in this context, people pay attention not to the quality provided in an institution but to the status and popularity of an institution, including the numbers of graduates advancing to famous upper level institutions or entering major enterprises.

In Japan, the importance of the cultivation of persons well balanced in knowledge, virtue and physical strength has been stressed. Therefore, one of the four guidelines for the latest revision of the Course of Study, the national standard for curricula, was ''nurturing well-rounded personalities'', while the other three guidelines were ''nurturing competency for independent learning'', ''emphasising the basics and promoting education for developing individual traits'' and ''appreciating culture and tradition and promoting international understanding''.

In this way, school education is expected not only to improve children's intellectual performance but also to facilitate their mental, moral and physical development. This perspective is reflected in the Course of Study which is considered as a kind of performance standard which can be attained through all school activities. Each time that the Course of Study was revised, the contents of this revision were reported very widely in the mass media and a wide range of discussion was developed not only in the education sector but also at the political level and in society. In that sense, it could be said that there is strong concern for standards in Japan, since Japanese people regard human resources as the most important asset for the development of Japan.

However, it is often said that the trend of excessive competition to pass entrance examinations into upper level institutions prevents schools from attaining the wide range of objectives defined in the Course of Study. In selecting new entrants, not only paper tests but also various measures, such as the utilisation of school records and interviews, are implemented. However, generally speaking, it is thought that the best way to gain admission is to obtain high scores on academic paper tests. Therefore, teachers and students are forced to pay attention exclusively to academic subjects, which are only part of the educational objectives defined in the Course of Study. There is the problem of excessive value placed on the initial educational background of individuals, which is evaluated only by the prestige of the educational institution from which he or she has graduated, with the background of the trend of excessive competition to pass the entrance examinations into upper level institutions. One of the main objectives of the life-long learning policy, which is one of the most important educational policies in Japan, is to change the tendency to place too much importance on the initial educational background of individuals.

The achievement of Japanese students

In Japan, there are no national examinations to judge the achievement of Japanese students. However, the IEA's (the International Association for the Evaluation of Educational Achievement), Mathematics and Science Studies show the relatively high level of achievement of Japanese students, compared with the international average of those countries surveyed, as is shown in Table 1.

151

Table 1.   **Results of the IEA Mathematics Study and Science Study (compulsory level)**

The 2nd Mathematics Study (Preliminary Report)
Highest scoring 3 countries in mathematics by lower secondary grade level
(percentage of correct answers)

	Arithmetic		Algebra		Geometry		Probability, statistics		Measurement	
1st grade	Japan	(60.3)	Japan	(60.3)	Japan	(57.3)	Japan	(70.9)	Japan	(68.6
2nd grade	Netherlands	(59.3)	France	(55.0)	Hungary	(53.4)	Netherlands	(65.9)	Hungary	(62.1
3rd grade	Belgium Canada	(58.0)	Belgium	(52.9)	Netherlands	(52.0)	Canada	(61.3)	Netherlands	(61.9

20 countries participated, such as Japan, the United States, the United Kingdom, and France.
The survey participants: 13-year-old pupils, 20 countries, about 80 000 pupils (in Japan, 1st year of lower secondary school, about 200 schools, 8 000 pupils).
The survey period: 1980-82 (in Japan, fiscal year 1980).

The 2nd Science Study (Preliminary Report)
Highest scoring 3 countries in science by school level and type
(percentage of correct answers)

	Elementary school		Lower secondary school	
1st grade	Republic of Korea	(64.2)	Hungary	(72.3)
2nd grade	Japan	(64.2)	Japan	(67.3)
3rd grade	Finland	(63.8)	Netherlands	(66.0)

22 countries participated, such as Japan, the United States and the United Kingdom.
The survey participants : i) 10-year-old pupils, 15 countries, about 70 000 pupils (in Japan, 5th year of elementary school, about 200 schools, 8 000 pupils); ii) 14-year-old pupils, 17 countries, about 70 000 pupils (in Japan, 3rd year of lower secondary school, about 200 schools, 7 600 pupils).
The survey period: 1983-86 (in Japan, fiscal year 1983).
Source: Monbusho, 1989.

The process of standard setting

The Course of Study as the performance standard

In Japan, as mentioned above, performance standards can be considered in relation to the Course of Study, the national standards of curricula. The Course of study, which is issued by the Ministry of Education, Science and Culture (Monbusho), defines not only the general guideline for school curricula but also the aim and content of each subject and school activity in each grade from kindergarten to upper secondary school, including special schools, and provides the basis for teacher training, textbooks and entrance examinations.

The Course of Study was first set up in 1947, and has been revised roughly every ten years on the basis of experience with earlier versions of the Course of Study. In revising the Course of Study, Monbusho set up the Curriculum Council which is composed of teachers, researchers and other persons of learning and experience, including employers. For example, in the case of the former Curriculum Council which presented recommendations in 1987 and 1988, the total number of members was 64. This groups was comprised of 36 university professors or rectors, 16 school teachers or principals, 4 local education administrators, two employers and 4 other persons. The revision of the Course of Study is conducted on the basis of recommendations presented by the Curriculum Council.

The Council has many sub-groups in order to explore the aim and content of each subject. It took approximately two years for the Council to submit the recommendation when the current Course of Study was revised. While the Council deliberates, it has many occasions to hear the opinions of social partners, such as the association of principals, the parent/teacher association, etc. Moreover, before the Council submits the final recommendation to Monbusho, it publishes the draft recommendation in order to obtain a wide variety of opinions with regard to the future direction of school education from the public.

The standard-setting process

There are about ten school inspectors and forty senior curriculum specialists in Monbusho, who can collect much information concerning the current situation in schools through their networks. At the local level, in local boards of education, there are supervisors for all subjects at each school level, whose assignment is to guide curriculum, teaching, and other professional matters related to school education. They often visit schools to observe classrooms and give guidance and advice to principals and teachers. Their observations and opinions are also transmitted to Monbusho through conferences and workshops.

In addition to this informal way, Monbusho implements several measures in order to prepare the revision of the Course of Study. One is the so-called pilot-school system. Usually, the curriculum is organised in accordance with the Course of Study. However, in order to explore a new type of curriculum or a new type of subject, a different curriculum from the guideline defined by the Course of Study is allowed to be organised in a pilot school which is designated by Monbusho. The results of pilot-schools are deliberated at the Council.

Another measure is the Assessment and National Survey of the Curriculum, which is conducted through nation-wide testing of student achievement in core areas of the Course of Study about every ten years. The objectives of this survey are to determine the scholastic levels achieved by pupils and students in each subject, to ascertain the extent to which the content of the new Course of Study is understood by pupils and students, to clarify the problems involved in teaching pupils and students according to the new curricula and eventually to make use of any findings in improving the curricula and teaching methods in the future.

Two measures are used in undertaking this survey. One is the evaluation by paper test in subjects such as the Japanese language, social studies, science, mathematics and foreign languages. Thirty-two thousand elementary school pupils of the 5th and 6th grades and 48 000 lower secondary school students (16 000 pupils or students for each grade which amounts to about 1 per cent of total pupils or students for each grade) are covered. The other is the evaluation using practical classroom activity techniques in subjects which are difficult to measure through the paper test, such as music, drawing, art, gymnastics and life environment studies. With regard to such subjects as the Japanese language, arithmetic, social studies, science and foreign languages, those aspects not surveyed by the paper test are also evaluated through practical classroom activity techniques. This survey is implemented in five schools for each subject. The outline of the standard-setting process is illustrated in Table 2.

Table 2. The organisation of standard setting

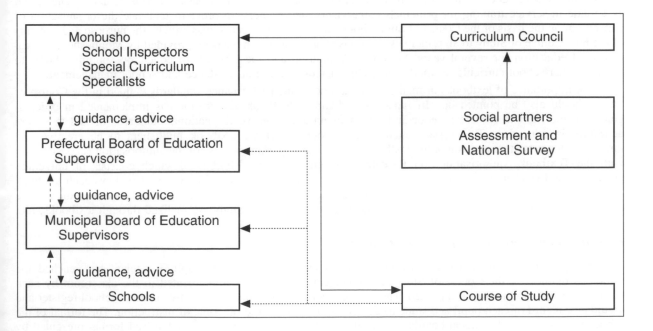

Source: Monbusho.

The standards: content and performance

The Course of Study has been determined on the basis of the following two principles.

- "First is the guarantee of a certain educational level nation-wide, so that all citizens have equal access to an equal quality of education and that all acquire a basic and fundamental body of knowledge which is necessary for every citizen.
- Second is the need for creativity and the initiative of teachers and schools in the development and implementation of curriculum, in the light of the intrinsic importance of conducting education relative to local and school conditions and the age and characteristics of each pupil and also of the need to make educational activities effective at each school (Monbusho, 1989a)."

The Course of Study has a legal status as the standard for curriculum and is mainly divided into two parts, one concerning the general guideline for organising the curriculum and the other related to teaching areas such as subjects, moral education and special activities. The part related to teaching areas may be regarded as having the purpose of directly defining performance standards. This part defines the objective of each teaching area and the objectives and content of teaching at each grade in the descriptions.

The volume of the descriptions is very small, for example, the section on arithmetic in elementary schools is 21 pages, so that each school may organise its own curriculum on the basis of general standards described in the Course of Study, taking into consideration the actual conditions of the community and the school itself, and the developmental level and characteristics of pupils and students. Monbusho and the Prefectural Board of Education publish various guides, manuals and handbooks for teachers in order to assist the school's organisation of curriculum and the teacher's teaching in the classroom. Here, we could illustrate the descriptions of the Course of Study through some examples using the case of arithmetic for elementary schools (see appendix).

Implementation, review and adjustment

The Course of Study is issued by the Minister of Education, Science and Culture by way of notification. Normally, Monbusho sets a preparatory period of several years in order that the purposes and the contents of the new Course of Study can be disseminated to all teachers and the transition from the old Course of Study to the new one can be carried out smoothly. The current Course of Study was issued in 1989 and went into effect in kindergartens in April 1990, in elementary schools in April 1992, in lower secondary schools in April 1993 and in upper secondary schools progressively from April 1994.

Monbusho implements several measures, such as the publication of guides and handbooks for teachers, the conducting of conferences and workshops on a nation-wide scale for principals, supervisors and teachers, and systematic in-service training for principals, supervisors and teachers, in order to facilitate the organisation of curriculum on the basis of the Course of Study. For example, conferences to disseminate the purpose and contents of the new Course of Study to all principals, supervisors and teachers have been provided by Monbusho and local boards of education for several years. Moreover, Monbusho and local boards of education appoint schools to explore better school curricula, methods and techniques of instruction, guidance and school management.

The importance of textbooks in realizing in classrooms the performance standards defined in the Course of Study should also be pointed out. In Japan, the system of textbook authorisation is implemented in order to guarantee the right to receive an education, to maintain and improve the national standards of and to secure neutrality in education. This system attempts to encourage private textbook publishers to be creative and innovative when writing and compiling textbooks. The most important process of the authorisation is consultation with the Textbook Authorisation and Research Council set up by Monbusho, which consists of university professors and teachers of elementary, lower and upper secondary schools. The Council reviews each textbook using Monbusho's guidelines for textbook authorisation, the main point of which is accordance with the Course of Study. Therefore, it can be said that the contents of the Course of Study are realized through textbooks, too.

Evidence of attainment of performance standards

In Japan, there are no national examinations to judge whether each pupil or student has reached the standards defined by the Course of Study. Such judgement is actually implemented in the classroom by each teacher. For that, a school record is used. The school record which is divided into two parts (a school register and a guidance record of each pupil and student) describes the process and outcome of instruction. The format of the school record is issued by local boards of education, taking into account the standardised format presented by Monbusho, which has been revised approximately every ten years in accordance with the revised Course of Study.

In fact, especially in lower and upper secondary schools, paper tests given by each teacher are implemented in each school several times per year in order to judge academic attainment in subjects which can be judged through paper tests. Those outcomes are reflected in the guidance record. The main parts of the school record are usually communicated by teachers to pupils, students and their parents at the end of each semester.

At the national level, the Assessment and National Survey of Curriculum is the only nation-wide test which judges student achievement in core areas. However, the objective of the survey is to obtain information to be used for the improvement of the Course of Study rather than to obtain evidence of each pupil's or student's attainment of performance standards. Therefore, those results are utilised only for deliberation on the improvement of new curricula and teaching methods which may become necessary in the future. Specific results of individuals, schools and regions are not published.

In Japan, national examinations were implemented several times in the 1950s and 1960s. However, such examinations led to severe competition among prefectures in order to obtain good results. In classrooms, teaching was conducted mainly in such a way as to obtain high scores on national examinations, not in a way to realize the educational purpose defined in the Course if Study. The original purpose of the national examination, which was to investigate the effectiveness of schooling and to what extent pupils attained the education purpose, was different from the competition for high ranking. However, the outcome of national examinations was utilised to judge the ranking among prefectures and no other educational activities than the preparation for paper tests of national examinations tended to be developed in schools. Therefore, national examinations were quickly abolished.

It seems to be necessary to refer to the relationship between the entrance examination and the Course of Study. In the case of upper secondary schools, admission of entrants is conducted by the principal of an upper secondary school, based on a selection process that takes into consideration such materials as paper tests, student credentials obtained from the principals of lower secondary schools, and other factors. As for local public upper secondary schools, pupils can apply to any school located in the attendance district where they reside which offers either academic or vocational courses. Nowadays, almost all graduates of lower secondary schools want to advance to upper secondary schools. Paper tests are made by local boards of education (for public upper secondary schools) or private schools (for themselves). One of the most important conditions in giving paper tests is that they comply with the Course of Study, since educational activities in lower secondary schools are strongly influenced by the contents and the levels of paper tests conducted as part of entrance examinations. Occasionally, the contents of paper tests made by some private schools go beyond what is covered in, and the level defined by, the Course of Study. Therefore, Monbusho checks the paper tests of private schools after those tests are implemented, and if necessary, advises the private school to fully take into account the content of the Course of Study in the future. The Course of Study deserves to be recognised as performance standards from this point of view, too.

Example of review and adjustment of performance standards

Next, we could raise one example of review and adjustment of the performance standards, using the case of arithmetic for elementary schools. Table 3 shows an example of results of the Assessment and National Survey of the Curriculum carried out in 1982. According to the results in arithmetic, the score for "mathematical thinking" was lower than that for "knowledge understanding" and "skill". These scores are interpreted in such a way that "Japanese pupils do well on questions that ask for memorised data but they are weak in solving problems that require finding a formula by themselves or applying what has been learned, and thus making judgements based on knowledge" (Monbusho, 1989*b*).

These results were analysed by Monbusho and were used as the basis for deliberations at the Curriculum Council and the revision of the Course of Study. As a result, the current Course of Study, which was revised in 1989, emphasizes the importance of appreciating the advantage of mathematical processing and fostering an attitude to willingly make use of them in life, in the descriptions of the overall objectives of Arithmetic for Elementary Schools, while the former Course of Study described the overall objectives as "to have pupils acquire the fundamental knowledge and skills regarding numbers, quantities and geometrical figures, and to develop their ability and attitude toward dealing with those matters in daily life which demand logical and rigorous thinking". In accordance with the new emphasis, the section of contents was also revised.

Overall process of the 1989 revision of the Course of Study

Finally, we could illustrate the overall process of the 1989 revision of the Course of Study at the national level. Before the Curriculum Council started deliberations in 1985, two councils proposed future orientations

Table 3. **Results of the Assessment and National Survey on pupils' academic attainment**[1]

(average percentage of passing pupils)

Subject	Details	5th grade	6th grade
Arithmetic	Average by area of content	64.6	70.0
	Numbers and calculation	71.4	76.3
	Quantities and measurement	54.2	73.3
	Geometrical figures	69.2	74.2
	Quantitative relations by category of assessment	67.7	66.2
	Knowledge and understanding	70.2	66.6
	Skill	61.2	81.8
	Mathematical thinking	56.0	60.9

1. This survey covered about 17 000 pupils each enrolled in the 5th and 6th grades of elementary school, and was carried out in February, 1982.
Source: Assessment and National Survey of the Curriculum, 1982.

concerning the content and method of education at the elementary and secondary school levels. One was the educational content sub-committee of the Central Council for Education, a main advisory council to the Minister of Education, Science and Culture. In 1983, it presented an interim report that stressed the importance of nurturing competency for independent learning and emphasizing the basics, and pointed out the necessity of reconsidering the composition of subjects in lower grades of elementary schools. The other was the National Council on Educational Reform, an *ad hoc* advisory council to the Prime Minister which was set up in 1984. It submitted four reports which included proposals relating to the basic direction for the improvement of educational content, the content and structure of school subjects and other school activities.

Monbusho carried out the Assessment and National Survey from 1981 to 1984, with regard to the then Course of Study revised in 1977 for elementary and lower secondary schools and in 1978 for upper secondary schools. Thus, Monbusho obtained information about to what extent pupils and students attained the standards defined in the then Course of Study.

Taking into account these situations, the Curriculum Council started to deliberate on how to improve the national standard for curricula in 1985, so that education can keep up with social changes such as the development of an information-oriented society and internationalisation, and the influence of those changes on the consciousness and life style of children. The Curriculum Council presented recommendations in 1987, proposing the four following guidelines:

a) To encourage generous minds and capabilities, through educational activities in order to live an active, productive life, in accordance with the characteristics of the developmental stages of infants, pupils and students, appropriate to each subject matter.

b) To place importance on basic and essential knowledge which is necessary for good citizenship, to enrich education with the goal of encouraging distinctive personalities, and to strive for consistency in the content of each subject matter in all school levels from kindergarten to upper secondary school.

c) To place importance on fostering the ability to act independently in order to cope with the changes in society, and developing a foundation for creativity, and endeavouring to strengthen children's wills to learn independently.

d) To place importance on developing an attitude of respect toward the culture and traditions of Japan, giving children deeper understanding of the culture and history of the world, and thus cultivating qualities as Japanese citizens living in an international society.

In response to the recommendations of the Curriculum Council, Monbusho undertook the revision of the Course of Study and issued the revised Courses of Study for Kindergartens, Elementary Schools, Lower Secondary Schools and Upper Secondary Schools in 1989.

Problems and critical issues

The review of the Japanese system

In reviewing the Japanese system, we could point out the strengths, weaknesses and challenges in the near future.

We suppose that there are two main strengths in the Japanese system. One is a systematised approach in revising the Course of Study. So far, it has been revised about every ten years, taking into account the outcomes of the former Course of Study and various social changes. The structure for revision is also systematised, like the Assessment and National Survey of Curriculum and the Curriculum Council. Moreover, in accordance with the revision of the Course of Study, the contents of teacher training, the standards for textbook authorisation, the standards for equipments to be arranged in schools, and so on are also reconsidered and, if necessary, revised.

The other strength is a dissemination process of the revised Course of Study. After the notification of the revision, a preparatory period is arranged to disseminate the objectives and contents of the revised Course of Study to all teachers through various measures such as the conducting of conferences and workshops and the publication of guides and handbooks. Therefore, each school can define its own teaching principles and organise its own curricula on the basis of a complete understanding about the revised Course of Study.

Next, we could indicate two weaknesses. First, the influence of excessive competition to pass the entrance examinations into upper level institutions should be considered. As already explained, paper tests are required to be in accordance with the Course of Study. However, the priority of teaching in schools is given not to attaining the standards defined in the Course of Study, but rather to obtaining high scores on paper tests. Therefore, not only non-academic teaching areas but also experience and experimental activities related to academic subjects tend to be made light of by pupils, students, parents and even teachers.

Second, it is said that the process of standard-setting in Japan has an *ad hoc* base, and the analytical research concerning the performance standard and the curriculum is not well developed. As mentioned above, in revising the Course of Study the Curriculum Council is set up by Monbusho. The staff of Monbusho, such as inspectors and curriculum specialists, plays the role of its secretariat. However, the Curriculum Council is not a research body but one of deliberation. Even if a lot of research and initiatives in schools are reflected in the deliberations of the Curriculum Council through the provision of information by Monbusho, it seems that a regular body which would investigate performance standards and curriculum matters in a global and deep manner is lacking in Japan. In particular, in radically revising former standards a wide range of research areas needs to be developed. From such a point of view, the current standard-setting system may be examined.

Finally, we would like to discuss some challenges which the Course of Study in Japan is now facing. The first challenge is an assessment issue. The current Course of Study aims at nurturing a well-rounded personality which is able to cope with changes in society and forming the basis for lifelong learning. It is rather easy to assess academic attainment, but to assess a well-rounded personality is a much harder task.

The second challenge is the level and content of the performance standard in a lifelong learning society. One of the main policy issues in Japan, is the promotion of lifelong learning. In order to promote lifelong learning, school education is asked to provide basic knowledge and skills and nurture competency for independent learning. The advancement of an information-oriented society and internationalisation adds new elements to be acquired as basic knowledge and skills. Therefore, how to define the contents of performance standards continues to be an important challenge to educational authorities.

The third challenge is the introduction of a five-day school week. In Japan, a five-day school week on a once-a-month basis has been implemented since the 2nd school term of 1992. As a next step, a five-day school week on a twice-a-month basis will be started next spring. It is also foreseen that a five-day school week will become the norm in the near future. Therefore, how to set performance standards and improve the quality of education in response to the future introduction of a five-day school week is becoming a very important policy issue.

Critical issues

In conclusion, two points can be mentioned. One is that educational objectives widely supported by the public are a precondition for setting performance standards. Moreover, educational objectives, such as the acquisition of cultural heritage, preparation for work and formation of a democratic citizen, are diverse. Therefore, taking into account such important functions of education, the contents of performance standards need to be examined. In the case of the current Course of Study, in particular, the National Council on Educational Reform was given wide and strong attention by the public and very diversified opinions were reflected on the principles for the revision of the Course of Study.

The other point is that performance standards should be linked to the improvement of the quality of teaching and learning at school level. Two aspects are important with regard to this point. First, the objectives of performance standards should aim at, and their contents should contribute to, the improvement of the quality of teaching and learning. Second, various measures, such as teacher training, should be implemented, so that each school and each teacher can improve the quality of teaching in classrooms in order to attain the performance standards.

Appendix

An Excerpt from the Course of Study for Elementary Schools (revised in 1989)

Section 3 Arithmetic

I. Overall objectives

    i) To help pupils acquire the fundamental knowledge and skills regarding numbers, quantities and geometrical figures, develop their ability to consider daily phenomena logically with insight, appreciate the advantage of mathematical processing, and to foster an attitude to willingly make use of them in life.

II. Objectives and contents for each grade

First Grade

1. *Objectives*

    i) To help pupils understand the concept and notation of numbers, and to enable them to use addition and subtraction in simple cases, through such activities as concrete manipulations.
    ii) To help pupils enrich their experiences which are the basis for understanding the concepts of quantity and measurement, through such activities as concrete manipulations.
    iii) To help pupils enrich their experiences which are the basis for understanding the concepts of geometrical figures and space, through such activities as concrete manipulations.

2. *Content*

A. *Numbers and computation*

    i) To enable pupils to express correctly number and orderusing numbers, and through these activities, to help them understand the concept of number.
       a) to compare the numbers of objects by an operation such as correspondence;
       b) to count or express correctly the number and order of objects;
       c) to know the size and order of numbers, to make a sequence of them, and to express them on a number line;
       d) to consider a number in relation to other numbers by taking the sum or difference of them;
       e) to know the meaning of a place value in 2-digit numbers.
    ii) To help pupils to understand addition and subtraction of numbers, and to enable them to use them in computation.
       a) to know the cases in which addition and subtraction are applied, and to express them in formula and interpret them;
       b) to be able to correctly carry out addition of 1-digit numbers, and subtraction as its inverse operation;
       c) to know that addition and subtraction can be applied to 2-digit numbers as well, by dealing with simple cases.
    iii) To enable pupils to classify and express concrete objects by counting them efficiently, dividing them into equal parts, etc.

B. *Quantities and measurement*

    i) To help pupils enrich their experiences which are the basis for understanding the concepts of quantities and their measurement, through such activities as comparing their sizes.

158

ii) To directly compare quantity such as length, area and volume through concrete manipulations.

iii) To compare size in terms of the number of units using a familiar object as a unit.

iv) To enable pupils to tell time.

C. *Geometrical figures*

i) To help pupils enrich their experiences which are the basis for understanding the concepts of geometrical figures and space, through such manipulative activities as observing the shapes of concrete objects and constructing them.

a) to recognise the shapes of objects, and to grasp the features of them;

b) to construct various shapes, and decompose them into more basic shapes;

c) to pay attention gradually to the operations needed for the consideration of geometrical figures;

d) to express the position of an object by correctly using such words concerning directions and positions as "front and rear", "right and left" or "top and bottom".

[Terms and Symbols]

The number of units, the number of tens, +, −, =.

Sixth Grade

1. Objectives

i) To help pupils understand the meaning of multiplication and division of fractions, to enable them to apply them, and to help them deepen their understanding of multiplication and division in general.

ii) To enable pupils to measure the volume of fundamental solid figures. Furthermore, to help pupils know about the system of units of measurement, and to enable them to efficiently measure quantities.

iii) To help pupils consider geometrical figures from the viewpoint of symmetry, etc., and to help them further deepen their understanding of fundamental geometrical figures.

iv) To help pupils deepen their idea of function through the understanding of proportion, etc., and to enable them to make effective use of it for considering quantitative relations. Furthermore, to enable them to consider and represent data statistically, by investigating the distribution of the data, etc.

2. Contents

A. *Numbers and computation*

i) To help pupils understand the meaning of multiplication and division of fractions, develop their abilities to apply such knowledge, and deepen their understanding of mulitiplication and division in general.

a) to summarize the meaning of multiplication and division, including cases in which the multiplier of the divisor is a whole number or fraction;

b) to know how to multiply and divide in fractions;

c) to regard division as multiplication by applying the reciprocal;

d) to integrate multiplication and division of whole numbers and decimals respectively into those of fractions; to represent a number expressed by multiplication and division in fraction form.

B. *Quantities and measurement*

i) To enable pupils to measure the volume of fundamental solid figures through experiments, actual measurement, etc.

a) to know how to measure the volume and surface area of fundamental prisms and circular cylinders;

b) to know how to measure the volume of fundamental pyramids and circular cones; to know how to measure their surface area in simple cases.

ii) To help pupils deepen their understanding of measurement and units of quantities, and further develop their abilities in measurement.

a) to measure efficiently by using proportional relationships, etc.;

b) to understand the metric system and relations existing among its units and to effectively use this understanding in measurement.

C. Geometrical figures

i) To help pupils further deepen their understanding of plain figures.

    a) to understand the meaning of line and point symmetry, and to consider the fundamental figures from the viewpoint of symmetry;

    b) to summarize the understanding of the shape and size of the figures, and to interpret and draw simple reduced or enlarged figures.

ii) To help pupils deepen their understanding of fundamental solid figures through such manipulations as composition and decomposition.

    a) to know about fundamental prisms and circular cylinders;

    b) to know about fundamental pyramids and circular cones.

D. Quantitative relations

i) To help pupils understand the meaning of ratio, and to enable them to use it.

ii) To help pupils further develop their abilities to consider the relation between two quantities which vary in company with each other.

    a) to understand the meaning of direct proportion; to investigate its features bu using algebraic expressions and graphs in simple cases;

    b) to understand the meaning of inverse proportion; to represent it by using algebraic expressions;

    c) to know that there are many cases which are efficiently treated if attention is given to the proportional relation.

iii) To help pupils develop their abilities of statistically considering and representing data, by investigating the distribution of data in simple cases;

    a) to know about table and graphs which represent frequency distibutions;

    b) to know that there are some cases in which the tendency of the population is estimated by the ratio gained from sample data;

    c) to choose suitable tables and graphs in accordance with the purposes and to devise some useful ones.

iv) To enable pupils to gradually arrange in order and investigate the possible cases concerning simple affairs.

Terms and symbols: reciprocal, side face, axis of symmetry, centre of symmetry, value of ratio, more than or equal to, less than.

Note: The section on objectives can be considered as attainment targets for each school level or each grade and that on contents as what should be taught at each grade for pupils or students to attain the targets defined by the objectives.

Bibliography

MONBUSHO (1989*a*), *Japanese Government Policies in Education, Science and Culture 1989, Elementary and Secondary Education in a Changing Society*, Tokyo.

MONBUSHO (1989*b*), *Shogakko Gakushushidoyoryo* (The Course of Study for Elementary Schools), Tokyo.

MONBUSHO (1989*c*), *Chugakko Gakushushidoyoryo* (The Course of Study for Lower Secondary Schools), Tokyo.

MONBUSHO (1994), *Education in Japan, A Graphic Presentation*, Tokyo.

OKAMOTO, K. (1992), *Education of the Rising Sun – An Introduction to Education in Japan,* Sun Printing Ltd., Tokyo.

YAMAGIWA, T. (1994), ''New Trends in the revised curricula in Japan'', *The Curriculum Redefined: Schooling for the 21st Century,* OECD, Paris.

SPAIN

by

Alejandro Tiana-Ferrer
Director, National Institute of Quality and Evaluation (INCE)
Ministry of Education and Science, Madrid

Summary

Performance standards are nowadays a matter of concern and debate in almost every country. Nevertheless, these concern and debate are found in different forms and under variable circumstances. Spain has a very specific situation in respect of performance standards.

The report starts by presenting the context in which performance standards are set. This context is characterised by a wide and far-reaching effort of educational reform, the main lines of which (decentralisation, curriculum change, improvement of the quality of teaching) are described.

Central sections deal with the process of standard setting and the standards themselves. The first one begins by presenting the new model for curriculum design and development, which is crucial to correctly understand the Spanish approach for standard setting. In parallel, it describes the responsibility of the different actors involved in the process. The second section offers a detailed view of what should be considered as standards in the Spanish case, going through the elements of the curriculum and the different levels of specification.

In its final part, the paper presents the mechanism established for the implementation, review and adjustment of the standards, dealing specifically with the support to schools and teachers and the control procedures in the field of curriculum development and student assessment. After that, it reflects upon the main problems and critical issues identified in the process, trying to draw a clear picture of the current situation.

Context

Although concern for educational performance is widespread in our societies, it has to be said that it is not found in every country in identical form. Thus, whilst some countries are involved in a broad debate on the academic standards which can be demanded of pupils and schools and which have led to define these standards in a workable way and to measure them, others have discussed education quality and results in more generic form. Spain belongs to the second of these two groups. Spanish educational and cultural tradition, the particular circumstances of the current education reform process and social awareness on the subject has directed attention towards a wide-ranging series of questions related to improving the quality of education in which defining and measuring standards is not the focal point.

Concern about performance standards in Spain

Performance standards are obviously also a matter of concern in Spain, but in a context characterised by specific circumstances. Firstly, we should point out that the subject does not usually appear in an isolated form, but rather in the context of a broader discussion on the quality of education in general. Secondly, it is usually linked to the performance of the education system, although usually without considering the need to have an operative definition of such standards. Thirdly, Spanish society tends to regard the aims of school as going beyond the mere imparting of knowledge, so that any assessment of performance, must cover all its aspects. Fourthly in the current period of educational reform, the question of levels of performance is necessarily bound up with the transformation process taking place in the organisation and running of schools.

Having said this, it must also be pointed out that a strong ideological undercurrent is revealed in many of the debates on levels of academic performance. This is not exclusive to Spain, but has been shown by authors such as Baudelot and Establet (1989) in a different national context. Other pieces of work have made even greater steps forward, using data to show the inaccuracy of the widespread view that educational standards in our societies are declining (Thélot, 1993).

Whilst these discussions are taking place, empirical data remind us that Spain continues to suffer from inequalities in education. An official report proved this to be the case, in its attempt to study the scope and size of these inequalities (CIDE, 1992). Although these basically revolve around inequalities in access to education, something which has received special attention in Spain in recent years, the report also revealed data on inequalities in performance. It was shown that the length of time spent in the classroom was notably shorter and the qualifications achieved were lower in the case of pupils from more disadvantaged social backgrounds; the same differences, although to a lesser extent, were also shown to depend on pupils' habitats (clearly better in urban areas) and sex (slightly better for women). The report, however, does not enable us to draw conclusions of more detail than this, since precise data is lacking. The absence of national examinations, for example, makes it difficult to compare different regions, sexes and social classes.

In spite of this limitation, the results obtained from international studies undertaken with the co-operation of the IEA and the IAEP show that academic performance does vary from one region to another, and that this cannot be explained purely in terms of economic development. The forthcoming implementation of nation-wide evaluation plans will permit more detailed and deeper analysis of existing inequalities and the design of policies aimed at reducing these.

A process of educational decentralisation

For a correct understanding of the concern for quality and performance in education, account must be taken of the fact that the Spanish education system has been undergoing a process of reform for several years now. The basic characteristics, structure and organisation of the system currently being changed, date from 1970, when the General Law on Education (Ley General de Educación or LGE) was passed within the context of a more wide-ranging process of modernisation in Spanish politics and society (Casanova, 1982; Tiana, 1992). Subsequently, the end of the Franco regime, the transition to democracy and the passing of the Constitution of 1978 changed the basic points of reference according to which the educational system was governed, forcing it to step into line with the new political and social circumstances.

Changes in education had already got underway during the first democratic governments, with the twofold aim of developing the Constitution and adapting the education system to the new social and economic needs. But it was after the socialist victory of 1982 when transformation of the whole system was embarked upon. The general framework for the Spanish education system began to change, and the principles of participation, university autonomy, the right to education and the distribution of educational responsibilities began to be applied.

This final aspect is particularly important to understand the current organisation of the Spanish education system. Indeed, whereas the historical tradition had been based on centralism, from the passing of the Constitution in 1978 onwards, a definite process of transfer of responsibility to the so-called *Comunidades Autónomas* (Autonomous Regions) started. Whilst Spain was not proclaimed to be a federal state, it is nonetheless true that the State comprising Autonomous Regions is quite similar to that model. To a certain extent, its organisation is based on subsidiarity, according to which the State forgoes management of those matters which can be taken on by the regions themselves. This is the feature which best characterises the current process of decentralisation in Spanish education when compared to developments in other countries (De Puelles, 1992).

The educational responsibilities established by the Constitution as exclusive to the State are very limited, basically being confined to the general regulation of the system, the determination of minimum requirements for a school, the conditions for obtaining and issuing qualifications, the regulation of the core curriculum, general planning on education investment, policy on study assistance, ownership and management of Spanish schools abroad, as well as international co-operation on educational matters. The Autonomous Regions, for their part, assume full responsibility for the regulation and administration of all aspects, levels and forms of education, with the only exception being those responsibilities attributed exclusively to the State. This means that the Spanish education system has a common structure and core curriculum for the whole State, but that this is managed in a decentralised way by the Autonomous Regions. We will consider the implications of this for curricular development and assessment at a later stage.

This decentralisation process which was initiated in 1978 has still not reached its completion. At the current time, only seven of the 17 Autonomous Regions (Catalonia, the Basque Country, Galicia, Valencia, Andalusia, Navarre and the Canaries) have assumed full responsibility for education. The other ten will do so gradually over the next few years. The Ministry of Education and Science currently has a dual role to play: on the one hand it has to exercise the functions of the State in education nation-wide, on the other hand, it also has to assume some of the responsibilities which belong to the Autonomous Regions in ten of these regions. It is important to bear this duality in mind to understand some of the issues which will be dealt with below.

Reforming the education system

Together with the transfer of educational responsibility to the Autonomous Regions, the early eighties saw the beginning of the reform of primary and secondary education in a limited and experimental way. Between 1985 and 1986, education policy in Spain was reviewed by the OECD (Ministerio de Educación y Ciencia, 1986) which slightly deflected the experimentation process. From then on, the appropriateness of starting an overall reform of the education system began to be considered, bringing the former experimental period gradually to a close. Thus, in 1987 the Ministry of Education and Science presented a Project for Educational Reform (Ministerio de Educación y Ciencia, 1987) which was widely distributed and debated. As a result of the public debate, which was synthesised into five volumes (Ministerio de Educación y Ciencia, 1988), the so-called White Paper for the Reform of the Education System was published (Ministerio de Educación y Ciencia, 1989). It served as the basis for the subsequent drafting of the new Law on the General Ruling of the Education System (LOGSE), passed in 1990. This was the start of a far-reaching reform of the education system, with a view to responding to social, cultural and economic needs.

The process of educational reform encouraged by the LOGSE is moving in three complementary directions: structural transformation, curricular renovation and improvement of the quality of education. In the first place, the Law transforms the structure of the Spanish education system. With a view to bringing it closer to the models which have found most widespread acceptance internationally, it establishes Primary Education, lasting six years, followed by Compulsory Secondary Education for four years and a two-year Baccalaureate (see appendix). In this division, the Primary level corresponds to the period where knowledge and instrumental skills are acquired, whilst the Secondary involves tackling the different areas and subjects in greater depth. On the other hand, both levels are conceived on a cyclical basis, divided into two-year cycles. Each one of these is conceived to be a single unit, with the final decision as to whether the pupils move on to the next cycle being taken at the end of each. Nonetheless, the second cycle of Secondary Education is organised in a different way from the rest, given the specific characteristics of this level and of the pupils.

As well as restructuring the system, the LOGSE extends compulsory schooling up to the age of 16, thus bringing Spain into line with most of its neighbouring countries. The main novelty, however, is not so much in this extension, but rather in the fact that the model being followed is a comprehensive one, and in accordance with this, all pupils follow the same route through school until the age of 16. Although pupil diversity is adequately dealt with, this does not mean that they are divided into different streams.

The diagram in the appendix shows the new structure of the Spanish educational structure, implementation of which will be completed in 1999. As can be seen, the critical points involve the transition from one level to another, the moments at which decisions on moving pupils up and awarding grades are taken. It is worth pointing out that these decisions are taken by the school itself, with no external examinations. The only examination of this type which exists in Spain follows completion of the Baccalaureate and only affects those pupils who wish to enter university. We should also highlight the fact that, in addition to the vertical progress shown, there are sideways arrows which indicate the way in which pupils can connect between one type of educational or training form and another. Since the LOGSE is being implemented in a gradual way, there is currently an intermediate situation between the old system and the new, which may make it more difficult for the reader to follow. But given that this new system has already been implemented to a great extent, it is generally to this that the report refers, except where the contrary is expressly stated.

Improving the quality of education

The second direction which the reform process is taking refers to the introduction of a new model of curriculum development, which will be dealt with in greater detail below. The third direction is aimed to improve the quality of education, which is considered to be one of the central purposes of the reform carried out.

In fact, whilst recognising that there are other elements which affect the quality of education, the LOGSE devotes a full chapter to the strictly educational factors which contribute to improving it. Specific attention is paid, among others, to in-service teacher training, which has constituted a political priority during this period of reform; autonomy of schools, allowing them to develop their own curricular project; the promotion of research and innovation in curricular, methodological, technological and organisational matters; provision of academic, psycho-pedagogical and vocational guidance; the redefinition of the role of the inspectorate; establishing a new mechanism for the evaluation of the educational system by means of creating the National Institute for Quality and Assessment (INCE).

In the belief that improvement in the quality of education should be an on-going concern of Educational Administration, the Spanish Ministry of Education and Science recently presented a programme comprising 77 measures geared towards this objective (Ministerio de Educación y Ciencia, 1994a). These measures can be divided into six different categories: values in education, equal opportunities for all, autonomy of schools, management and government of schools, teaching staff, and evaluation and inspection. After the current public debate, the measures which are finally approved will be implemented, thus continuing the reform process in the direction indicated.

The process of standard setting

As well as restructuring the education system and adopting a series of measures aimed at improving quality, the LOGSE has introduced a new model of curricular design and development, which is narrowly connected with the process of standard setting. There are two complementary factors which have motivated the introduction of this model:

- Firstly, the need to reformulate the curriculum established in 1970, to make it more coherent and adapt it to new requirements, became evident at the end of the eighties. The highly prescriptive curriculum established had to give way to a more flexible one, in the development of which, the teaching staff were to take a more active role. Schools were to enjoy greater freedom in curricular development than under the previous system. The basis for this was to be found in a constructivist view of learning (Coll, 1987).
- Secondly, the new distribution of responsibilities and the start of the decentralisation process towards the Autonomous Regions referred to in the previous section, demanded the design of a new curricular model in which the core curriculum established by the State would be completed by the Regions themselves.

The LOGSE has tried to respond to the new situation and the needs expressed, developing a curricular model with the following basic features:

- It is an open and flexible model, in the development of which Autonomous Regions, schools and teachers had to take an active part. The purpose of this conception is to allow a wider range of specific aspects to be added to curricula.
- It aims to respond to four fundamental questions which allow the planning and development of educational practice: what to teach, when to teach, how to teach, how and when to assess.
- It is a broad model and is not simply limited to the acquisition of concepts and knowledge, but also includes practical skills, attitudes and values.
- It has two different functions: that of making the intentions of the educational system explicit and that of serving as a guide to teaching.

The curriculum takes on more specific form through three different levels. The first one is the so-called Basic Curricular Design or official curriculum, comprising the compulsory nation-wide core curriculum and the curriculum established by the Autonomous Regions. At the second level there are Curricular Projects corresponding to specific levels and schools, drawn up by the teachers of each individual school. At the third level are the Class Programmes, in which a school's Curricular Project for a particular set of pupils is specified. Each one of them represents one more step in the process of standard setting.

First step: Setting the Basic Curricular Design or official curriculum

The first level of specification of the curriculum is the so-called Basic Curricular Design or official curriculum. This is defined by each Autonomous Region with full educational responsibilities (at the moment the seven mentioned), and must incorporate the core curriculum established across the State. According to the LOGSE, the basic contents of the latter need in no case occupy more than 55 per cent of the school timetable for those Regions which have an official language other than Castilian Spanish and 65 per cent for the other regions.

This core curriculum is intended to be a guide on the one hand and to be prescriptive on the other. This means it serves as a basis for the subsequent curricula developed by the Autonomous Regions, schools and teachers, and which is also compulsory. However, it should be considered as minimum goals for a pupil to reach, and education should not be exclusively limited to them.

With this core curriculum as their basis, the Autonomous Regions establish their respective curricula. Analysing the official curricula of the Autonomous Regions reveals a certain homogeneity between the various area objectives and the attainment targets. The slight variations noted consist of extending some of the goals, objectives or targets, almost always with the intention of including specific features of the Region itself. More differences are visible in terms of contents, given the considerable room for manoeuvre which the various Regions have to complete their curriculum.

Both the Ministry and the Regions have their own institutional arrangements for setting the prescriptive curriculum. The Ministry has a Centre for Curriculum Development, in which around 40 curriculum specialists from different areas and levels are working in the fields of curriculum design and development. The Centre is responsible for proposing the setting of the state-wide core curriculum and the introduction of the necessary changes in it. Autonomous Regions have their own centres, units or services to do similar work in their own territories.

As the core curriculum, whether national or regional, has to be formally approved and passed in the form of a Decree, it is a matter of discussion in the State (or Region) School Council, a body of participation in which teachers, parents, students and administrators are represented. So, the proposals made by the different Administrations have to be subjected to public scrutiny in these bodies. It allows to balance the different views present in the Spanish society about educational objectives and contents.

Second step: Drawing up the school Curricular Project

Once the official curriculum has been established by each Autonomous Region, schools have to adapt it to their particular requirements. This adaptation takes the form of a document called the Curricular Project (in the event that a school offers more than a single level, it must draw up a project for each of them). This document represents a second step in the process of standard setting, now at school level. In fact, when writing it, teachers have to discuss and agree about area objectives, contents, attainment targets and assessment criteria and procedures. Although it is true that certain teams of teachers were already doing this previously, the novelty of the current reform is in making this general practice.

The Curricular Project is a central feature of the Spanish model of curricular development. It constitutes an intermediate link between the official curriculum and the teaching activities which take place in schools and classrooms. Its aim is to ensure the continuity and coherence between the two poles, promoting a specific identity alongside a "school spirit". At the same time, it constitutes an element of reflection on school practice and a stimulus for team work on the part of the teachers (Coll and Martín, 1994).

When a school tackles the task of drawing up its Curricular Project, it has to bear a number of factors in mind. Firstly, it has to relate this to the so-called Educational Project of the school, a document which defines its marks of identification and major aims, in line with the feelings expressed by the members of the school community. Secondly, it has to analyse the context of the school itself, keeping in mind the psychological and social characteristics of the pupils of each level. Thirdly, it must link the project to previous experience of the school. Fourthly, it must take the official curriculum of the corresponding Autonomous Region as a reference point.

Responsibility for drawing up the Curricular Project lies with the team of teachers for the particular level at each school. Co-ordination of the process is assured by the so-called *Comisión de Coordinación Pedagógica* (Commission for Teaching Co-ordination) of the school. Once it has been drawn up, the project is discussed and approved by the Teachers Senate, which takes it to the School Council (comprising representatives of parents, teachers and pupils from the school) to issue their report. Finally, the project is supervised by the Inspectorate, who can suggest further elaboration of specific points.

The drawing up of the Curricular Projects has taken place in parallel with the implementation of the new educational levels. As schools have incorporated the new rulings, they have had to draw up their own projects. The specific process followed has varied from one Autonomous Region to another, but without any extreme differences. It can generally be said that the first version of the project is developed over a period of one or two years. Nonetheless, the Ministry of Education and Science has tried to avoid making the process too bureaucratic, insisting on the need to consider it as something unfinished and to review it from time to time. In accordance with this conception, schools have to draw up an initial proposal at the beginning of the school year, applying it during the year, assessing its repercussions, and where necessary revising it. In reality, the drawing up of the Curricular Project should be conceived of as a lengthy, almost permanent activity, and as a basic ingredient in exercising the profession of teacher. It implies giving as much emphasis to the process as to the product (Coll and Martín, 1994).

Third step: Drawing up the Classroom Programme

The third level of specification of the curriculum is composed of what are known as Classroom Programmes. These consist of specifying the decisions taken in the level or school Curricular Project for each specific group of pupils. The programmes are drawn up by each teacher for his/her particular set of pupils and for each year, including the sequence of contents, the teaching units to be developed and the assessment procedures to be applied. In fact, Programmes set standards for each group of students and year. In a sense, every single teacher has some room for setting concrete standards for their students.

The standards: content and performance

It can be inferred from this presentation that the Spanish education system does not set universal standards for areas and levels as a whole which can be ubiquitously applied in every school, but rather sets certain minimum attainment targets which have to be completed, specified and adapted by each school for its own particular pupils. At national level, the State and the Autonomous Regions set the general attainment targets for area and level in the official curriculum. At school level, the Curricular Project presents the attainment targets for level, area and cycle. At classroom level, the teacher sets the specific targets for his/her subject and group of pupils, on the basis of which the assessment procedures and instruments to be applied throughout the year will be decided. In this section, all these elements will be presented in a detailed form, according with the different levels of responsibility and actors involved in the process.

The Basic Curricular Design or official curriculum

This core curriculum includes various components. Firstly, it states the general goals of the level. There are ten or twelve of these goals, establishing the general abilities which the pupil should have developed or learned by the end of the corresponding level (Infant, Primary, Compulsory Secondary, Baccalaureate). These goals are defined "as a series of different abilities (locomotive, cognitive, affective or emotional balance, interpersonal relationships, and social action and integration) which pupils have to develop and/or learn in the course of their schooling as a consequence of their education, that is, as a consequence of the educational influence which teachers exercise over them" (Coll and Martín, 1993). They are therefore very general goals which have to be specified through the different areas covered.

Secondly, the core curriculum includes curricular areas. In contrast to the system where school work is organised into different disciplines, the Spanish curriculum for compulsory education organises it into broader areas. The areas defined for Primary and Compulsory Secondary Education are those set out in Table 1.

Table 1. **Curricular areas for primary and compulsory secondary education**

Primary Education	Compulsory Secondary Education
Knowledge of the natural, social and cultural environment	Natural sciences, social sciences, geography and history
Artistic education	Physical education
Physical education	Visual and plastic education
Language, official regional language and literature	Language, official regional language and literature
Foreign languages	Foreign languages
Mathematics	Mathematics
	Music
	Technology
	Cross-curricular subjects:
	– civic and moral education
	– education for peace
	– education for health
	– education for gender equality
	– environmental education
	– sexual education
	– education of the consumer
	– road safety

Source: OECD based on national submissions.

168

In each of these areas, the curriculum includes various components:

a) An *overarching statement* or explanation of the sense, approach and the general principles of the area. This constitutes a justification of the area, accompanied by guidelines for its teaching. This extends over several pages (generally six to ten).

b) *General objectives* which the pupil is to have attained by the end of the level. There is also a small number of these (between ten and twelve objectives per area) and they are expressed in terms of abilities. Unlike the level goals, these add an explicit reference to contents. Tables 2, 3 and 4 show a number of general objectives established for different areas of Primary and Compulsory Secondary Education.

c) The most suitable *contents* to develop the abilities included in the level goals and area objectives. This is not a list of subjects to be dealt with, but is rather a catalogue of blocks to be worked on at different cycles in the level. The area contents do not refer solely to those more traditional, conceptually based contents, but also incorporate contents relating to procedures, values and attitudes. The core curriculum distinguishes between those three types of contents.

d) *Attainment targets* or criteria to design activities to enable assessment which are coherent with the general goals of the level and the area objectives. The number of these targets is rather larger than that for the goals and objectives, ranging between about twelve and thirty. Tables 5 and 6 show a few specific examples of attainment targets for some of the areas which come under Primary Education and Compulsory Secondary Education.

Table 2. **Examples of curricular development: mathematics**
Primary education

Goals	b) To communicate by means of verbal, corporal, visual, plastic, musical and mathematical expression, developing logical, verbal and mathematical reasoning as well as the aesthetic sensitivity, the creativity and the capacity to enjoy artistic works and expressions.
	c) To use the adequate procedures to obtain the relevant information in simple problem-solving, and to represent it through codes, taking into account the conditions necessary for its solution.
Overarching statement	[...] in the development of mathematical learning for child and adolescent, experience and induction perform a major role. [...] Mathematics have to contribute in the achievement of general educational objectives linked to the development of cognitive capacities [...though...] its functional value as a series of problem-solving procedures for application in very different fields also has to be emphasized [...]. In society today, it is essential to be able to deal with mathematical concepts related to daily life [...]. Without needing to know the mathematical bases according to which they operate, it is important that pupils dominate functionally basic arithmetic, mental arithmetic, estimating results and measuring strategies [...].
General objectives	3. To use simple calculation and measure instruments deciding, in each case, on the possible relevance and advantages that their use implies and submit the results to systematic review.
	6. To use elementary techniques of data collection in order to obtain information on phenomena and situations in their environment; to represent it graphically and numerically and form a judgement on it.
Contents	THEMATIC BLOCK: MEASUREMENTS
	Concepts: 1) Need and functions of measurement; 2) Reference unit. Unconventional units; 3) The measuring units of the decimal metric system; 4) The measuring units of local use; 5) The measuring units of time; 6) The measuring unit of angles: the degree; 7) Monetary units.
	Procedures: 1) Measurements with conventional and unconventional units; 2) Use of conventional measuring instruments and construction of simple instruments to effect measurements; 3) Elaboration and use of personal strategies to carry out measuring estimates in daily situations; 4) Decision-making on the most adequate measuring units in each case depending on the aim of the measurement; 5) Transformation of measuring units of the same magnitude; 6) Verbal explanation of the process followed and of the strategy used in measurement; 7) Use of the monetary system applying the equivalences and corresponding operations.
	Attitudes: 1) Assessment of the importance of the measurements and estimates in daily life; 2) Interest in careful use of different measuring instruments and employment of adequate units; 3) Enjoyment in measuring with the appropriate accuracy; 4) Curiosity and interest in verifying the measurements of some familiar objects and times; 5) Assessment of the decimal metric system as an internationally accepted measuring system; 6) Tendency to express the numerical results of measurements expressing the units of measure used.
Attainment targets	5. To accomplish estimates and measurements choosing from among the most usual measuring units and instruments, those which are best suited to the size and nature of the object to be measured.
	6. To express the measurements of length, surface, mass, capacity and time accurately, using the usual multiples and sub-multiple and converting units into other units whenever necessary.

Source: OECD based on national submissions.

Table 3. **Examples of curricular development: social sciences, geography and history**
Compulsory secondary education

Goals	*i)* To analyse the basic mechanisms that govern the operation of the physical environment, to evaluate the repercussions that human activities have on it and to contribute actively to its defence, conservation and improvement as a decisive factor for the quality of life.
	j) To know about and evaluate technological and scientific development, its applications and effects on its physical and social environment.
Overarching statement	[...] Teaching in this area aims for pupils to acquire the concepts, procedures and attitudes that are necessary to understand the social and human reality of the world in which they live, to provide them with the possibility [...] of understanding the phenomena and processes that take place around them as a consequence of the complex interaction between human agents and nature; to analyse their location and distribution; to understand the differences and contrasts between societies and groups according to natural and human, particularly economic factors, [...] and, in short, to understand the life of human groups on earth and the principal factors conditioning them [...].
General objectives	4. To identify and analyse the different scales of interactions which human societies establish with their territories in terms of use of space and natural resources, evaluating the economic, social, political and environmental consequences.
Contents	THEMATIC BLOCK: POPULATION AND URBAN AREA

Concepts: 1) Population and resources: demographic models, dynamism and structure of the population; unequal distribution of the population in Spain and in the world; imbalances in population growth and unequal distribution of resources; demographic trends and problems in Spain, Europe and the less developed world. 2) The urban area: the urban fact: evolution and changes; urban space and socio-economic structure; principal urban conglomerations in the world; the cities in the developing and developed world: differences and problems; road networks and traffic problems; traffic procedures; the relationship between country–city; urban society and rural society: ways of life and problems.

Procedures:
A. INFORMATION PROCESSING: 1) Reading and interpretation of aerial photographs, plans and maps of different characteristics and scales; plan and map drawing on the basis of information obtained by various means. 2) Reading and interpretation of tables and graphics of different types and creation of these on the basis of different tables and statistical representations. 3) Establishment of simple correspondences between different types of plans, aerial photographs and maps, and between these and reality. 4) Assessment of the accuracy and objectivity of the expressive resources used in graphics, diagrams, maps and visual documents in general.

B. MULTI-CAUSAL EXPLANATION: 5) Preparing and holding discussions, simulated negotiations, etc., in connection with fictitious or real spatial problems considering the circumstances, the positions and existing alternatives and evaluating their consequences. 6) Comparative analysis of the similarities and differences presented by different territories and countries in relation to the same geographical phenomenon.

Attitudes :
A. CRITICAL RIGOUR AND SCIENTIFIC CURIOSITY: 1) Becoming aware of the serious problems related to the demographic imbalance and the major economic inequalities between the different countries in the world.

B. ASSESSMENT AND CONSERVATION OF HERITAGE: 2) Assessment of the diversity of rural and urban natural landscapes, in Spain, as a natural and cultural treasure that has to be taken care of and preserved. 3) Responsibility and prudence in the use of the public road network as a pedestrian, traveller, etc.

C. TOLERANCE AND SOLIDARITY: 4) Rejection of unequal distribution among the peoples of the Planet and solidarity with those who suffer from lack of resources and food. 5) Rejection of the social inequalities arising as a result of place of birth or residence.

Attainment targets	6. To identify the different uses of land in a given city and its area of influence, analysing them as manifestation of the functional differentiation and social hierarchisation of space.
	7. To locate the urban hierarchy and the major communication and transportation axes in Spain, characterising them as decisive factors in the political and economic organisation of space and as an important manifestation of regional contrasts in Spain.

Source: OECD based on national submissions.

Table 4. **General objectives by area**
Primary education

General objective	First Cycle	Second Cycle	Third Cycle
		Mathematics	
To use simple calculation and measuring instruments deciding, in each case, on the possible relevance and advantages that their use implies and submitting the results to a systematic review.	To use simple calculating and measuring instruments, that could help him/her in his/her task.	To use simple calculating and measuring instruments, evaluating the advantages that their use implies and to contrast the results.	To use simple calculating and measuring instruments deciding, in each case, on the possible relevance and advantages that their use implies and submitting results to a systematic review.
		Knowledge of the natural, social and cultural environment	
		Example A	
To recognise in the elements of the social environment changes and transformations related to the passage of time, to investigate relationships of simultaneity and succession of those changes and to apply these concepts to the knowledge of other historical moments.	To perceive the passage of time through personal rhythms and own activity, acquiring basic notions of time and elementary aspects of historical time (duration, succession and simultaneity) when referred to the present.	To continue to make progress in notions 'past, present, future' bound up with personal and family history, relating it to certain relevant events detached from it and observing relationships of simultaneity and succession.	To recognise in the elements of the social environment, changes and transformations related to the passage of time, to investigate relationships of simultaneity and succession of these changes and to apply these concepts to the knowledge of other historical moments.
		Example B	
	To develop the basic aspects of historical time related to lived experiences.	To develop notions of time that refer to familiar history and, by extension, to the century.	To develop the notions of time which refer to our century and to the time-line of humanity, to emphasize the causal relationships within the concept of historical time and to build chronological axes in which to locate societies, personalities and historical facts.
		Spanish language and literature	
		Example A	
To find in reading a source of pleasure, of information and of learning, as well as a means of further training and linguistic and personal enrichment.	To discover progressively the interest of reading as a source of enjoyment and as a source of information.	To use reading, in addition, to analyse and reflect, appreciating it as a source of information and of learning and as a means of personal enrichment.	To use reading as a source of pleasure, of information and of learning, and as a means of further training and linguistic and personal enrichment.
		Example B	
	To reveal the possibilities of reading as a source of entertainment and pleasure, encouraging in the pupil an active attitude in this learning process, as well as the beginnings of realisation of the need to read as source of information.	To use reading as an instrument of learning and to discover that it is a means to obtain information; to develop the capacity to locate that information; to familiarise with the use of libraries.	

Source: OECD based on national submissions.

Table 5. **Attainment targets by area**
Primary education

Attainment target	First Cycle	Second Cycle	Third Cycle
Mathematics			
To read, write and order natural numbers, interpreting the value of each one of its figures (up to the hundreds), and to accomplish simple operations with these numbers.	To count, read and write numbers up to 100 using the knowledge about the value that indicates the position of the figure.	To read and to write correctly natural numbers of up to five figures, interpreting the positional value of each one of them.	To read, to write and to order decimal numbers, interpreting the value of each one of their figures (until the hundredth), and to accomplish simple operations with these numbers.
To classify forms and geometric figures and justifying classification method.	To recognise objects and spaces with rectangular, triangular, circular, cubic and spherical forms in the environment.	To recognise and to describe forms and geometric figures in the space in which they move (polygons, circles, cubes, prisms, pyramids, cylinders and spheres).	To classify forms and geometric figures, justifying the classification method.
Spanish language and literature			
To read texts of various types with fluency (without hesitations, repetitions or skipping words) using pronunciation, intonation and pace to fit the context.	To use elementary knowledge of the written language (direct correspondence phonemographics and punctuation marks: full stop, question and exclamation marks) to interpret written texts on daily life.	To use the knowledge of the written language (phonemo-graphics correspondences, and punctuation marks) to interpret written texts in common use and to give an intonation which fits the reading of texts.	To read texts of various types with fluency (without hesitations, repetitions or skipping words) using the pronunciation, intonation and pace which fits the context.
To get the gist of written texts in common use, to summarise the main ideas expressed and the relationships that are established between them, and to analyse some simple characteristic aspects of different types of text.	To get the gist of written texts in common use (posters, notes, labels, instructions, stories, etc.) and to identify specific information.	To identify and to summarise essential elements in written texts which are commonly used (simple literary texts, informative texts, etc.).	To get the gist of commonly found texts, to summarise the main ideas expressed and the relationships that are established between them, and to analyse some simple characteristic aspects of different types of text.

Source: OECD based on national submissions.

Table 6. **Attainment targets by area**
Compulsory secondary education

Attainment target	First Cycle	Second Cycle
	Mathematics	
To use integers, decimals and fractions, and percentages to exchange information and to solve problems and situations in daily life.	To use simple integers, decimals and fractions and percentages to exchange information and to solve problems and situations in daily life.	To use negative numbers and powers and square roots, with the conventional notation, in written calculation and in resolution of problems.
To estimate the measurements of surfaces and the volumes of spaces and objects with accuracy, according to the regularity of their forms, as well as their size, and to calculate surfaces of flat forms limited by segments and circumferences, and the volume of bodies composed of orthohedra.	To estimate the measurements of surfaces of spaces and objects, and to calculate it when these are flat forms limited by segments and circumferences, expressing the result in the most suitable measuring unit.	To estimate the volume of the bodies and spaces with a precision according to the regularity of their forms and their size, and to calculate it when these are composed of orthohedra.
	Spanish language and literature	
To use his/her own ideas and experiences for the production of texts intended as literature, consciously using structures of genre and rhetorical procedures and using models of literary tradition.	To identify the gender to which a literary text belongs after reading it completely, to recognise the elements of personal rhetorical procedures used and to give a personal opinion on the most and least appreciated aspects.	To use his/her ideas and experiences for the production of texts intended as literature, consciously using structures of the genre and rhetorical procedures and referring to models of literary tradition.
	Social sciences, geography and history	
To identify the principal economic agents and institutions, as well as the functions they perform in the framework of an increasingly interdependent national economy, and to apply this knowledge to the analysis and assessment of problems and the economic realities of contemporary society.	To recognise the existence of a major technical and social division of labour in our society, and to apply this knowledge to the analysis and assessment of contemporary socio-economic issues or conflicts.	To identify the principal economic agents and institutions, as well as the functions they perform in the framework of an increasingly interdependent national economy, and to apply this knowledge to the analysis and assessment of problems and economic realities of contemporary society.
To indicate in a given pre-industrial, historical or contemporary society or culture, examples of the links that exist between aspects of its social organisation, system of relationship, level of technical development and beliefs, recognising the value of its achievements.		To identify the main characteristics of the industrial revolution and of the postindustrial period and to give examples of the major societal changes during the last 200 years.

Source: OECD based on national submissions.

Tables 2 and 3 provide two concrete examples in which the connection between the different curricular components can be seen. The first row covers some of the general goals of the level, which must be developed (exclusively or, more generally, in a complementary way) through the area selected. It should be emphasised that the goals and the contents do not always coincide exactly, given the general character of the first. The second row covers the part of the overarching statement which has a more direct relation to the teaching and learning of a specific block. In general, conceptual, methodological and didactic references applicable to the teaching of a particular block can be found throughout the statement. Here, however, only a few small components have been chosen. The third row covers the general area objective(s). The abilities to develop through it (them) are related to the block of contents. The latter appears in the fourth row, where a distinction is made between the contents which refer to concepts, procedures and attitudes. In the fifth row are included the attainment target(s) through which the acquisition of the abilities related to this part of the curriculum can be evaluated. It should be indicated once again, however, that in many cases, these targets are not aimed solely at evaluating these specific thematic blocks, but also several others.

Curricular projects and classroom programmes

As it was justified in the previous section, the Curricular Project is of fundamental significance in the organisation of school work. It should reflect the relevant decisions adopted on the following elements of the curriculum (Del Carmen and Zabala, 1991):

a) *General goals of the level*: These are set in the core curriculum, as indicated above. The school must adapt these goals to its specific characteristics, modifying, establishing priorities, adding some new items, developing the existing ones or using similar procedures.
   Furthermore, the cross-curricular subjects must be incorporated into the curriculum.

As an example of how the goals might be adapted, we can quote those modifications carried out by a State school with a large number of pupils included in the Integration Programme for pupils with special educational needs (the adaptation made by the school is written in italics): "To act with autonomy, *where psycho-locomotive possibilities permit,* in routine activities and in group relationships, developing the possibilities to take initiatives with freedom and responsibility, and establishing emotional relationships *based on self-esteem and the acceptance of others*" (Vicente, 1994).

b) *Sequence of objectives and contents of each cycle*: The official curriculum sets out the general objectives for each area, their contents and attainment targets for each level. It does not, however, distribute these objectives, contents and targets in cycles, since this has to be done with reference to the characteristics of each school and its pupils. This represents one of the key decisions which teachers have to make when drawing up the Curricular Project. It should set out the abilities and contents which have to be worked on in each cycle. The document must also include the internal sequence of each cycle, although it does not need to establish specific teaching units, since this is the task of each teacher, forming a part of his/her Classroom Programme. Table 4 presents a number of example of how a sequence of certain general objectives from various areas of Primary Education can be established according to cycles.

c) *Methodological strategies*: The Curricular Project must also include references to methodological strategies to be used by the teaching staff in the school. These strategies have to include elements such as general methodological principles, methodological options for each curricular area, the criteria adopted to put pupils into groups, organisation of space and time at school or selection and criteria for the use of the materials and teaching resources.

d) *Assessment strategies and procedures*: A fundamental element of the Curricular Project refers to what, how and when to evaluate and the effects of this in terms of marking, moving up a grade and information. As regards decisions on assessment, the Curricular Project must first tackle the question of what to assess. The basic decision for this is included in the official curriculum in the form of attainment targets. These targets, as indicated above, do not cover everything that a pupil should learn, but only the especially relevant items learned. On the basis of these, the school should: a) review general targets according to their own characteristics, adapting these where necessary; and b) draw up attainment targets for each cycle, according to the sequence of objectives and contents carried out in the project itself. It should be borne in mind that the main purpose of these targets should be formative although they may also serve as summative. Secondly, the question of how to assess should be tackled, with reference to situations, strategies and procedures. The procedures to be applied have to meet a number of requirements: to be varied; to give specific information about what it is intended to assess; to use different codes; to be applicable in more or less structured school activities; to enable the assessment of transfer of learning; to include self or co-assessment. Thirdly, the Curricular Project must decide when to assess, considering at least three basic times which in turn correspond to other equivalent functions of the assessment: initial, formative, summative. Fourthly, the document must decide on the type of assessment report which is to be used at the school and to whom the information regarding the results of the assessment is to be given. Fifth, the Curricular Project must establish criteria for: *a)* deciding whether or not to move the pupil up to the next cycle or grade; *b)* supporting the pupils who receive negative assessment; and *c)* deciding if a pupil will or will not attain the final qualification.

  e) Measures to ensure diversity: The Curricular Project must, finally, establish the contents and structure of the guidance programmes which are to be developed in the school, the optional subjects to be offered (in the case of secondary schools), the way in which curricular diversification will be organised, as well as the organisation of resources for pupils with special educational needs.

A flexible school-based system of assessment

In line with the Spanish model for designing and developing the curriculum, the mechanism established for the assessment of students has three basic characteristics:

  a) It is a flexible system, since the specific attainment targets and criteria of assessment, accreditation and promotion to the next level are established by each school, through its Curricular Project. This means that the school can adapt the general criteria to its particular circumstances, depending on the particular features of its milieu and its pupils.

  b) It is a school-based system, since the assessment takes place entirely within the school itself. In contrast to other countries, Spain has no national or external examinations, either at the end of the Primary or Secondary Education. Pupils are assessed by their own teachers throughout their period of compulsory schooling. The only external examination takes place after the Baccalaureate for those pupils who wish to enter university. Whilst this is a prerequisite of studying at university, it is not necessary when it comes to obtaining the diploma of Secondary Education Graduate or the Baccalaureate.

  c) It is a system which emphasises the need to assess not only the results the pupil obtains, but also the process of education in the school, the classroom and the teaching carried out by teachers.

According to that model, students are assessed within the school itself. The first consequence of this decision is that schools should fix attainment targets which will be applied to each level, cycle and area in their Curricular Project. These targets should be based on those set out in the official curriculum, but have to be adapted to the school's circumstances and those of its pupils, establishing its sequence in different cycles. The examples in Tables 5 and 6 show how an area attainment target evolves throughout the period of schooling until it is finally achieved at the end of the level. In certain cases, the target is assigned exclusively to a single cycle, whilst in others it is distributed over successive grades and cycles (see Table 5).

On the basis of this sequence of attainment targets, which is associated to a further contents sequence, teachers determine their own assessment mechanisms in their respective Classroom Programmes. Table 7 shows a number of examples of such targets established by teachers in a primary school to assess the abilities acquired by their pupils in a specific cycle and area.

This approach to assessment is based on a constructivist conception of learning, which has inspired the Spanish model of curricular development. From the need for coherence between the curriculum and the assessment of pupils are derived requirements such as the continuous, global and integrated nature of the latter and insistence on the formative, regulatory, guiding and self-correcting nature of the assessment which must be geared to improving processes and results. In daily classroom activities, teaching, learning and assessment are very closely linked, forming part of a teaching and learning continuum.

In line with these general principles, the ministerial regulations establish that assessment should be carried out collectively by the teachers of a group of students under the co-ordination of their corresponding tutor. This group of teachers meets at least three times a year to analyse the learning situation of each pupil, giving him/her a grade. In the event that this assessment is negative, the teachers have to take the necessary reinforcement measures and where necessary adapt the curriculum. The results of these assessments are given to pupils and their families, in accordance with the criteria set out in the Curricular Project.

Approaches to assessment must constitute the basis for moving up a grade, for the accreditations and qualifications attained by pupils. Therefore, at the end of each cycle, the teachers decide on whether or not pupils will go up to the next cycle or level. In the case of pupils with learning difficulties, it is possible to choose between continuing, together with the necessary proposals for remedial activities, or repetition. The last of these two options can only be chosen once during Primary Education and once again in Secondary. The information provided from these assessments is reflected in each pupil's school file and book of school reports. At the end of

Table 7. **Examples of attainment targets at classroom level**

Mathematics. First Cycle. Primary Education

In total, there are 22 targets involved in Classroom Programming. These include the following:

- Counts, reads, writes and uses digits, knowing their value.
- Differentiates between single units, tens and hundreds by their positional value in the number.
- Accomplishes sums.
- Accomplishes subtractions.
- Accomplishes with fluency the mental arithmetic of addition and subtraction resulting in numbers of no more than two figures.
- Compares small quantities (estimating, counting).
- Interprets the results of the effected comparisons.
- Solves simple problems of daily life, to which he/she has to apply operations of addition and subtraction.

Spanish language and literature. First Cycle. Primary Education

---

In total, there are 18 criteria involved in Classroom Programming. These include the following:

- Participates in communicative situations in daily life.
- Observes the procedures of verbal communication.
- Takes an interest and pleasure in participating in these situations.
- Understands simple verbal messages.
- Understands the gist of a text and its explicit elements.

Mathematics. Third Cycle. Primary Education

In total, the Classroom Programming has 8 objectives and a total of 39 criteria, including the following:

Objective of cycle 4: to know and to express precisely the most usual measuring units and to use the appropriate instruments.

Attainment targets:
- Knows the principal units of the Decimal Metric System as well as multiples and sub-multiples.
- Knows the second as a unit for measuring time.
- Transforms units of the same magnitude.
- Uses measuring instruments such as metric tape, stop watch and scale of weights, appropriately.
- Expresses the result of the measurements correctly.

Compulsory Secondary Education, pupils receive an accreditation which shows the school years covered and the marks obtained. In the event of an overall favourable result, they also receive the diploma of Secondary School Graduate.

Implementation, review and adjustment

The model of curricular development, standard setting and performance assessment presented in the foregoing sections is a recent innovation in the Spanish education system. As stated at the outset, this is one of the central pillars of the current education reform process. However, its introduction will logically be a gradual one, and it is hoped that it will be completed within a few years. This is why it is worth analysing what practical form this process is taking.

School performance standards and assessment in practice

In accordance with the curricular model established, in the Spanish case, performance standards could be deemed the equivalents of level goals and area objectives, expressed in terms of abilities to be developed or learned by pupils, specified through area or cycle attainment targets and interpreted by the teachers of a school in their Curricular Project. As a result, in the process of setting standards, the teams of teachers of a school who have to specify the objectives and the attainment targets on the basis of the official curriculum, have a fundamental role to play. And in the formalisation of this process, the Curricular Project has a central place.

It is on these grounds that analysis of the Curricular Projects is essential to ascertain educational practice in schools. In the last two years, the Ministry of Education and Science has developed an ambitious Monitoring Plan for the process of LOGSE implementation, collecting information from teachers, families, head teachers, inspectors and school support services. The study, based on using opinion questionnaires, completed by a qualitative analysis of cases and a detailed examination of a sample of Curricular Projects, has furnished very complete nformation to enable the assessment of the point reached in the process embarked upon (Ministerio de Educación y Ciencia, 1994b). Other analyses have also been based on this data, some of them by those responsible for the overall steering of the process (Coll and Martín, 1994).

An initial set of conclusions which it is worth presenting here are those regarding the preparation of the Curricular Projects, as this will help to place the conclusions dealt with subsequently in context:

a) The first observation is that teachers are experiencing difficulties in drawing up Curricular Projects for their respective schools. In spite of the responsibility and leadership taken on by head teams, the process is not always an easy one, especially for secondary schools.

b) A second general observation is the positive evaluation the process receives in spite of its difficulty. Curricular Projects are seen as useful, as they encourage team work, adapt teaching to suit pupils' characteristics and those of the school, and improve the art of teaching. This overall positive assessment is greater among primary school teachers, who are further into the preparation process.

c) A third observation is that the deadlines set for preparing the projects have been too tight, which has caused more emphasis to be placed on the product itself than on the process, contrary to the intentions of the education authorities.

d) A fourth observation is that quite a few schools consider they have received less than the necessary amount of help to prepare the project. Irrespective of the efforts made by education authorities, there can be no doubt that, in teachers' views, a limited amount of support has been forthcoming. This has led the authorities to offer additional activities in this respect.

When specifically analysing those aspects related to setting standards and establishing assessment mechanisms, a number of other conclusions should be mentioned:

a) In general, the most innovative aspects of the Curricular Project have presented most difficulties. Therefore, aspects such as adapting the goals to the specific characteristics of the school, the sequence of objectives and area contents, decisions on teaching methodology and the selection of curricular material have not presented great difficulty. On the other hand, decisions and procedures for assessment, accreditation and moving pupils up to higher levels have proved far more complex, especially in the eyes of secondary school teachers.

b) The adaptation of the area objectives and level goals to the characteristics of the school and their distribution in cycles have not been especially difficult. Goals and objectives have been adapted in various ways (not necessarily exclusive): i) breaking certain goals and/or objectives down into two or more; ii) establishing priorities in the goals and/or objectives; iii) redrafting certain goals and/or objectives; iv) introducing a certain degree of specification which enables a concrete goal or objective to be better adapted to the characteristics of school and students.

c) The sequence of contents according to cycles is the aspect which has caused least difficulties, perhaps as a result of its greater similarity to traditional teaching practice. Nonetheless, this similarity has meant that certain schools have based their activities on the distribution of contents, without carrying out a detailed analysis of the more complex mechanisms for developing abilities. Although there are many schools which recognise that the new curricular approach has its value, they have little confidence when it comes to implementing it and prefer to adopt more conservative stances, even when they believe it to be necessary to review these at a later stage. Implicitly, they are adopting a gradual approach, which is fairly realistic.

d) In contrast to the preceding case, the decisions pertaining to assessment and moving pupils up and dealing with diversity have been a much more difficult matter for schools. These difficulties have been manifest both in the aforementioned Monitoring Plan (Ministerio de Educación y Ciencia, 1994b), and in the different work done by specialists (Vicente, 1994). On analysing the Curricular Projects and the Area and Classroom Programmes, it can be seen that, usually, decisions on assessment tend to be limited to very general references on continuous and integrative assessment, without specifying the exact measures (procedures, instruments, times) when these will be used in the classroom. Although teachers are aware of the importance of determining a correct sequence of goals, objectives and contents and having a good definition of attainment targets and mechanisms for assessment, they clearly express the difficulty they experience when it comes to carrying this out and to their lack of training. In specific terms, they feel an integrative assessment as set down in the LOGSE to be complicated to achieve.

e) Determining targets according to area and cycle, a central component in the Spanish standard-setting model, is revealed to be one of the aspects with which teachers have most difficulties. Nor do the Area and Classroom Programmes always contain the necessary degree of specification, often being little more than declarations of a far more general nature than is really required. On occasions, attainment targets have been understood as end goals for each subject and level, as in the old-style curriculum.

f) Schools have generally dealt with decisions on moving pupils up in certain detail. Given the scrutiny to which they are subjected by families and students, it is hardly surprising that schools should have been prudent in this respect. It is perhaps this prudence which has led to a more copious and detailed result than might have been expected. In the guidelines provided to schools to develop this aspect of the Curricular Project, an attempt has been made to prompt them to adopt a qualitative and global approach, which, nevertheless, has not always taken place in practice. These criteria for moving pupils up have sometimes been understood to be "the minimum of the minimum". On the other hand, assessment reports are not always consistent with them. All of this goes to show the difficulties which exist when a really integrative assessment has to be undertaken, although prospects for progress in this respect are positive.

Support and control mechanisms

The model for pupil assessment which is currently being implemented in Spain is, as has been stated, flexible and school-based. As assessment is understood to be a constituent part of teaching and learning processes, this flexibility is very advantageous, since it enables an adequate response to the needs of the different schools, teachers and pupils. A second advantage this model offers is that of involving teachers in decision making processes. As has been said, teachers have to draw up a school Curricular Project which must expressly include the attainment targets for the different areas of each level. The requirement that specific decisions be made to assess what pupils are learning, automatically entails teachers taking an active part, considering the teaching to be given and the criteria on which the results are to be assessed. This implies a stimulus for teachers as professionals, although it can present problems in practice.

Together with these advantages, the model presupposes certain risks. The first of these is the possibility of the system splintering and of allowing a loss of control in results. Since schools themselves make the decisions on assessment, promotion and accreditation of students, criteria applied could be too heterogeneous. In an education system like the Spanish one, in which respect for the right to education on conditions of fairness is a fundamental principle, the aggravation of this situation could mean it did not fulfil one of its main aims. A second problem is that of comparing the results of different regions, schools and/or pupils. This is not serious unless it affects the basic rights of the citizen, although, even without doing so, it may make it difficult to steer the education system as a whole.

With the intention of taking the utmost advantage of the benefits of this model and circumventing its difficulties, avoiding the risks and disadvantages set out, education administrative bodies have set a number of different mechanisms in motion. Some of these are geared to controlling the system and providing with information, whilst others are targeted at supporting school development.

Amongst the control and monitoring mechanisms which should be mentioned, are firstly the Inspectorate services. Each regional administration has its own inspectorate the role of which is the control, supervision and evaluation of the education system within its sphere of competence. Its methods of action cover a relatively broad spectrum of areas. On the one hand, the inspectorate monitors the drawing up of Curricular Projects on a regular basis, helping the schools in this process and checking that the result corresponds to what has been established. In this way, it supervises the decisions adopted in assessment (among other aspects), drawing attention to those which are not justified or clash with legal provisions. This makes for a first and elementary level of control. Secondly, schools send a copy of their assessment documents to the inspectorate each year, which can thus ensure that the criteria adopted are being applied, and can then act in cases of incoherences or irregular practice. Finally, examination of the assessment mechanisms applied in a particular school is explicitly included in the Schools Evaluation Programme which the inspectorate has been developing over the last few years (the so-called Plan EVA). Until now, more than 500 schools have been assessed by the inspectorate, which has allowed a specific idea to gel as regards the real application of regulations on this and other aspects of curricular development (Luján and Puente, 1993). It goes into greater detail and depth than the two preceding types of assessment and constitutes a third level to control the system's operation.

A second mechanism to monitor the assessment system comprises the analysis of the results of what are known as "Aptitude tests for university entry". Spanish pupils who have completed their Baccalaureate and wish to gain access to university have to pass these tests, which are held every year and the marks for which, once combined to form an average with those from upper secondary, enable university courses to be chosen. There are a total of eight tests and they are held over two or three days. Some of these are common to all pupils (Language and Literature, Foreign Language, Text Commentary, Philosophy) and others depend on the subjects which have been studied at school. Each university designs its own tests, although the structure and characteristics of these are the same. Furthermore, these are nation-wide examinations, since they permit entry to any Spanish university,

178

once they have been passed. Although that is not the main objective, they help to mitigate the worst excesses of heterogeneity in the assessment criteria adopted by schools in preparing Baccalaureate pupils for tests which are not identical but are comparable.

The results of these tests have come under close scrutiny in the last few years. Social demand for their rigour, reliability, fairness and comparability have led to the writing of a large number of works which allow interesting conclusions on roles and effects to be deduced (Muñoz-Repiso et al., 1991; Muñoz Vitoria, 1993). In fact, these tests have made it possible to obtain a better idea of education results at the end of the Baccalaureate, and at the same time have reduced the risks of fragmenting the assessment system.

A third mechanism takes the form of the new National Institute for Quality and Evaluation (INCE) which started work in 1993. Its basic task is no other than the overall evaluation of the education system. This new body has begun to develop studies which are aimed at getting to know education system results in greater depth by collecting information in schools. Although its action is not limited to a simple examination of students to assess their performance, the information they are able to provide on this is necessarily vital for carrying out synchronic and diachronic comparisons. Thus, the studies currently underway have permitted a better acquaintance with possible inequalities which may exist between regions and types of school, as well as the development of results over a period of time. These studies, which are diagnostic in nature and are carried out on samples of schools and students, must provide the basis for more sustained analysis of the efficacy and efficiency of the education system, supporting decision making. In addition to this, the Institute's actions constitute an essential component in steering the education system.

In the specific field of assessment, it is hoped that the Institute will have a valuable contribution to make: i) that it will enable assessment procedures which are in keeping with the general model of curricular development to be tried out, prompting the spread of new practices; ii) that it will provide teachers, families, administrators and society as a whole with relevant information on levels of achievement in schools and pupils, thus providing feedback to the process of setting standards in schools; iii) that it should provide information on the implementation of the new education arrangements, allowing decisions to be made which will better guide the process.

It is important to point out that the mission of the National Institute for Quality and Evaluation is not to define standards. The Spanish model of curricular development assigns this role to schools. Nonetheless, the information contributed by the studies carried out, must enable schools, teachers, families and society as a whole to reflect on the levels of achievement in the education system and on a possible review of its aims and assessment criteria. From this point of view, it is a crucial mechanism for quality improvement in education.

But the educational authorities are not only limited to establishing mechanisms for controlling the assessment system. Equally or even more importantly than these tasks is that of setting up school and teacher support mechanisms to develop and apply the new curriculum. Among these, the role of the inspectorate should once again be mentioned in its capacity as an instrument of guidance for schools. Far from being limited to controlling the actions of schools, the inspectors work with them in the process of developing the curriculum, offering guidelines and models which they can apply.

Together with the inspectorate, the Teachers' Centres should also be mentioned, which have been offering a wide range of training activities for several years now. It is not difficult to see that the quality of the Spanish model of curricular development is due, in large part, to what is done by teachers. It is for this reason that teacher training has been a key strategy within the Spanish education reform process. Some of the activities concerned have been geared to facilitating the process of introducing the new curricular model, especially those which have been held in schools for their own teachers. Other bodies dependent on the Administration, such as educational Programme Units or psycho-pedagogical support teams, have also co-operated in this task, although they have had different levels of responsibility.

Overall, it can be said that education authorities have created a wide range of instruments to ensure the smooth running of the mechanism set-up. Some of these have been aimed at controlling it, whilst others have tried to give support to those who are responsible for, or participate in, its application. But all of these should be seen as complementary facets of the same strategy.

Problems and critical issues

As it has been pointed out in previous sections, one of the most relevant aspects of the current process of educational reform in Spain is that of extending compulsory secondary education to the age of 16, following a comprehensive school model. This means an increase in the proportion of young people aged between 14 and 16 who will be studying in the general stream of the education system in the next few school years. This situation has given rise to fears, which have on occasions been voiced publicly by people involved in the educational field. Some of these opinions are extremely critical: "the LOGSE and the education reform is leading to a severe deterioration in the contents and standards of what we call secondary education and in the years to come will bring about surprising achievements in what is known as functional illiteracy, lack of the most elementary knowledge, as well as social classism" (Rosúa, 1993). Some teachers put what they see as a drop in standards down to the comprehensive nature of the new style of Secondary Education (Benedito, 1993), emphasising the background to this debate. Such opinions have even caused certain schools to oppose the early implementation of this new secondary system (Pérez de Pablos, 1993).

In spite of the forcefulness of declarations such as the above, opinions are divided. There are a number of people who believe the process embarked upon to be part of a democratic process. Nor is there a lack of schools which view bringing forward the new system of Secondary Education in a positive light, in spite of the difficulties of adaptation which this implies (Cardoso, 1993; Mederos, 1993). And there are more than a few educational experts who consider that the debate is going ahead without the necessary data being provided, and is based solely on personal memories and subjective impressions (Delval, 1990). The complexity of assessing progress or regression, and the need to obtain and to interpret data which will build the debate on strong and objective foundation, has led Spanish education authorities to adopt the decisions which are described in this paper.

Besides this general debate and occasional criticism, mainly centred in the possible connection between comprehensiveness and standards, there are some other difficulties derived from the own characteristics of the model for curriculum development, standard setting and student assessment. First of all, we should refer to the difficulties experienced by teachers in the process of developing the curriculum and drawing up Curricular Projects and Area and Classroom Programmes. Among these, we should cite the marked individualism of a number of teachers, the centralist tradition of the Spanish education system, a certain tendency towards bureaucratisation and an evident distrust of pedagogical leadership. In spite of these difficulties, considerable momentum has been gained in drawing up Curricular Projects in recent years. Many school support services (Inspectorate, Programme Units, Teachers Centres) have focused on the task. Professional media have reflected this process with their difficulties and ups and downs.

Another source of problems could be found in the model established for student assessment. Generally speaking, it could be said that assessing in the classroom has not undergone a marked change. There are two facts which are particularly striking. The first is the diverse nature of practice in schools, where there are still only few teachers who have changed from assessing contents to assessing abilities. The second is the need to think of the development of new assessment procedures as a process, in which teachers must acquire new skills and, in the last resort, undergo a real learning process. Current practice in assessment cannot be termed completely traditional, since there are schools which are developing innovative approaches and techniques in this respect (Murillo and Monge, 1994). But such innovation is still far from being common practice. Hence the importance which the Ministry of Education and Science is giving to the process of implementing the new curricular model, in-service teacher training and the effective support which must be given to schools to carry out these tasks.

Moreover, it can be said that the coherence between the new model of design and curricular development introduced in Spain has still not been taken up in an unequivocal way in the classroom. Given the newness of the situation, this should not seem surprising nor give cause for concern. There is, however, no doubt that it will demand constant effort on the part of the Administrations (national and regional) to ensure that the general principles of the new curricular model are put into practice. It is true that, until now, educational practice has not covered the innovations introduced in the Reform and that still only limited change is visible, but it can be expected that in the next few years the effects of the implementation and dissemination of the new model, will begin to be noticeable. As has been emphasised on various occasions throughout the paper, this requires continued insistence on teacher training strategies and support for schools.

Before concluding, it may be worth filling this final section with a few general and personal reflections on the subject in hand. Firstly, it should be stressed that all societies show a more or less pronounced interest in the achievements of their education system, although not all express this interest in an identical way. Every education system has its own context, its own history, traditions and characteristics which define the shape taken by the debate on standards and the decisions that have to be adopted in this respect.

Secondly, it would seem clear that any approach to establishing standards and taking decisions on assessment procedures should be couched in a coherent model of curricular design and development, respecting its peculiarities. Otherwise, we run the risk of setting up separate or even divergent mechanisms which threaten the necessary coherence of the system.

Thirdly, the Spanish experience would seem to vouch for an understanding of standard setting as not simply a form of controlling and monitoring the results of the education system, but also as a means or renewing school practice. Social expectations generated by this issue constitute a powerful driving force within education systems.

Fourthly, it should be pointed out that in the specific case of Spain, assessment should not be understood as a simple means of marking students, but as part of the core of the teaching and learning process, all of the components of which are affected. For this reason, the design and implementation of the assessment mechanisms must be consistent with the curricular model adopted, so as to avoid the curriculum being indirectly affected by the assessment.

Finally, the above remarks impose certain requirements when education systems are comparatively analysed. As comparison is both possible and desirable, it should be carried out in a way that respects the characteristics and aims of each education system, without distorting the interpretation of the results.

New structure of the Spanish education system

LGE (1970)

LOGSE (1990)
LRU (1983)

SPECIALIZED STUDIES

COMPULSORY
EDUCATION

| PRE-SCHOOL EDUCATION | BASIC GENERAL EDUCATION (EGB) | MEDIUM LEVEL EDUCATION |

UNIVERSITY

Diploma of Basic Engineer

Graduate or Advanced Engineer

Doctorate

FP I — 1 2
FP II — 1 2 3

Kindergarten
Pre-School

Initial Cycle
Middle Cycle
Higher Cycle

BUP — 1 2 3

COU

Cursus — 1 2 3 4 5 6
1 2

Age — 0 1 2 3 4 5 6 7 8 9 10 11 12 13 14 15 16 17 18

1 2 3 4 5 6 1 2 3 4 5 6 1 2 3 4

BACHILLERATO — 1 2

Higher Level FP

Medium Level FP

UNIVERSITY

Advanced Engineer

Graduate

Doctorate

Diploma of Basic Engineer

First Cycle
Second Cycle

First Cycle
Second Cycle
Third Cycle

First Cycle
Second Cycle

INFANT EDUCATION

PRIMARY EDUCATION

ESO

SECONDARY EDUCATION

COMPULSORY EDUCATION

University Entrance Examinations

SPECIAL EDUCATIONAL SYSTEM:
Arts and Languages

Non-Univ.
Higher Ed.

FP: Vocational education.
Source: OECD, based on national submission.

182

Bibliography

BAUDELOT, C. and ESTABLET, R. (1989), *Le niveau monte,* Ed. du Seuil, Paris.

BENEDITO, J. (1993), "La otra cara de la LOGSE", *El País,* 9 November.

CARDOSO, H. (1993), "Reforma y nueva identidad profesional", *El País,* 8 June.

CASANOVA, J.V. (1982), "The Opus Dei ethics and the modernization of Spain", Unpublished PhD thesis, New School for Social Research.

CIDE (1991), *Estudio experimental de pruebas objetivas para el acceso a la universidad. Informe final,* Ministerio de Educación y Ciencia-CIDE, Madrid, mimeo.

CIDE (1992), *Las desigualdades de la educación en España,* Ministerio de Educación y Ciencia-CIDE, Madrid.

COLL, C. (1987), *Psicología y currículum,* Ed. Laia, Barcelona.

COLL, C. and MARTIN, E. (1993), "La evaluación del aprendizaje en el currículum escolar: una perspectiva constructivista", in Coll, C. *et al., El constructivismo en el aula,* Ed. Graó, Barcelona, pp. 163-183.

COLL, C. and MARTIN, E. (1994), "Aprendiendo de la experiencia", *Cuadernos de Pedagogía,* No. 224, pp. 8-15.

DE PUELLES, M. (1992), "Informe sobre las experiencias de descentralización educativa en el mundo occidental", *Revista de Educación,* No. 299, pp. 353-376.

DEL CARMEN, L. and ZABALA, A. (1991), "Guía para la elaboración, seguimiento y valoración de proyectos curriculares de centro", Ministerio de Educación y Ciencia-CIDE, Madrid.

DELVAL, J. (1990), *Los fines de la educación, Siglo XXI,* Madrid.

LUJAN, J. and PUENTE, J. (1993), "El Plan de Evaluación de Centros Docentes (Plan EVA)", *Bordón,* Vol. 45, No. 3, pp. 307-320.

MEDEROS, A. (1993), "Un año de intuiciones", *El País,* 4 May.

MINISTERIO DE EDUCACION Y CIENCIA (1986), "Examen de la política educativa española por la OCDE", Ministerio de Educación y Ciencia-CIDE, Madrid.

MINISTERIO DE EDUCACION Y CIENCIA (1987), "Proyecto para la Reforma de la Enseñanza", Ministerio de Educación y Ciencia, Madrid.

MINISTERIO DE EDUCACION Y CIENCIA (1988), "Papeles para el debate", Ministerio de Educación y Ciencia, Madrid, 5 vols.

MINISTERIO DE EDUCACION Y CIENCIA (1989), "Libro Blanco para la Reforma del Sistema Educativo", Ministerio de Educación y Ciencia, Madrid.

MINISTERIO DE EDUCACION Y CIENCIA (1994*a*), "Centros Educativos y Calidad de la Enseñanza. Propuesta de actuación", Ministerio de Educación y Ciencia, Madrid.

MINISTERIO DE EDUCACION Y CIENCIA (1994*b*), "Plan de Seguimiento de la Implantación de la LOGSE. Informe de Síntesis", Ministerio de Educación y Ciencia, Madrid, mimeo.

MUÑOZ-REPISO, M. *et al.* (1991), "Las calificaciones en las pruebas de aptitud para el acceso a la universidad", Ministerio de Educación y Ciencia-CIDE, Madrid.

MUÑOZ VITORIA, F. (1993), "El sistema de acceso a la universidad en España, 1940-1990", Ministerio de Educación y Ciencia-CIDE, Madrid.

MURILLO, F.J. and MONGE, C. (1994), "Análisis del modelo de evaluación de los aprendizajes en Educación Secundaria Obligatoria", unpublished paper, mimeo.

OECD (1994), *Making Education Count. Developing and Using International Indicators,* CERI, Paris.

PEREZ DE PABLOS, S. (1993), "Reforma sí, reforma no", *El País,* 11 May.

ROSUA, M. (1993), "Enseñanza media: de la guardería a la jungla", *El País,* 2 March.

THELOT, C. (1993), *L'évaluation du système éducatif,* Nathan-Université, Paris.

TIANA, A. (ed.) (1992), "La Ley General de Educación, veinte años después", *Revista de Educación,* Special Issue.

TIANA, A. (1993), "Perspectivas españolas actuales para la evaluación del sistema educativo: El Instituto Nacional de Calidad y Evaluación", unpublished paper, mimeo.

VICENTE, M.L. (1994), "Una perspectiva desde el asesoramiento externo", *Cuadernos de Pedagogía,* No. 223, pp. 63-67.

SWEDEN

by

Ulf Lundgren
Director General, National Agency for Education

Summary

Under the 1991 reform of the education system control of schools shifted from the national to the municipal level. This decentralisation was linked to a move from control of educational processes to "steering by goals" or a focus on educational outcomes. A National Agency for Education was created which will report to Parliament every three years on students' performance standards. The national curriculum (*läroplan*) has been slimmed down so that it focuses on national educational goals, leaving more space for professional judgement and responsibility to be exercised by municipalities, schools and teachers. National assessment procedures are being developed.

Context

The educational debate in Sweden over time has swung back and forth on the question of standards and performances. The debate seems to reflect the state of the economy rather than results of actual evaluations of school performance. In the mid-eighties there was heavy criticism of standards, launched by a study on "functional illiteracy". In this study it was claimed that a large proportion of leavers from the nine-year compulsory school had not mastered basic skills in reading and writing. The conclusions from this study can be criticized on grounds of the criteria used. "Back to basics" demands were heard following this study, however, and a union was even founded named "Knowledge in Schools". Results from the IEA study on mathematics nourished the debate. One consequence of this debate, it seems, was an increase in performance test use in schools. In the past few years the issue of standards has appeared in both the debate on efficiency and the costs of schooling, and the discussion of the political governing of the school system.

The term "standard" is difficult to translate in an idiomatic way. The word is sometimes used, but since curricula, syllabi and criteria for marks together form the actual demands or standards in Sweden, the term "standard" is used here to mean the interrelation between curricula, syllabi and criteria for marks, or the goals in curricula and syllabi, or criteria for marks. In this paper "standards" is used to be synonymous with the interrelation between curricula, syllabi and criteria for marks – not in the sense of a paragon, but rather a set of just goals and criteria to which educational outcomes are to be related.

Since 1991 the school system has experienced rather pervasive changes. From a centralised school system steered with state subsidies accompanied by detailed regulations, the system has evolved towards decentralisation and deregulation.

On 1 January 1991 the municipalities assumed undivided responsibility for the schools. No rules exist concerning organisation. It is up to each municipality to organize the school in order to fullfill the demands given in the Education Act, the National Curriculum and in National Syllabi. Through national goals and demands on results, the government and the Parliament exercise influence and control.

The reform of 1991 concerned responsibility and governing (steering) of the education system. It meant a new system for state subsidies. Rules underwent transformation. There was both deregulation and sharpening of rules. The Education Act was partly changed. The reform presumed a change in the structure and content of the National Curriculum. As a consequence a Committee was given the task of preparing a new curriculum in accordance with the new system for responsibility and steering. A new curriculum for both the compulsory school and the upper secondary systems is now in a process of implementation. The upper secondary school system has been reformed and all study lines are now three years long, which means that for almost all students the school system comprises twelve years of schooling. In process is a further development of upper secondary school aiming at a broader choice of courses for students within the main 16 national programmes. The municipalities can also define local courses.

The tertiary education system has been reformed, giving more freedom for the individual university or college to decide on entry, study programmes and examinations. State economic support will gradually be linked to results and outcomes.

Schools currently start for children at the age of seven. A child can start at the age of six. Pre-school is not compulsory, but most children do attend at the age of six. Before 1997 all children will attend school at the age of six. A committee (SOU, 1994) has presented various models for integrating preschool in the compulsory school system. To prolong the nine-year compulsory school to ten years is one model.

The possibility to start private or independent schools has been opened up. An independent school, if it is approved by the National Agency for Education, will obtain economic support corresponding to 85 per cent of the average student cost to the municipality in which the independent school is located.

In relation to changed curricula a new marking system has been introduced. To support the teachers a national testing system is under development.

Responsibility for schools has thus been decentralized. Their government is now effected less through subsidy and regulation, but is centered on goals and results. The central administrative structure has evolved as well. The National Board of Education and the Regional Boards were replaced by the National Agency for Education on July 1, 1991. The role of the former national agencies was related to the economic and juridical governing of education. Thus the Regional Boards, for example, controlled the organisation of schools in each municipality and aimed primarily at optimizing fit with the rules for obtaining state subsidies.

The new National Agency for Education is responsible for national evaluation, inspection and supervision and the national development of the educational system.

The education system

The public school system in Sweden comprises compulsory schooling for nine years and various types of voluntary schooling. More than 90 per cent of the students go on to attend upper secondary schools. Compulsory schooling institutions comprise compulsory basic school, Lapp nomad school, special school (for children with impaired vision, hearing or speech) and compulsory school for intellectually handicapped adults.

The Education Act stipulates equal access to equivalent education for all children and young persons, regardless of sex, geographical location and social and economic circumstances. The Act lays down that education must "give the pupils knowledge and skills and, in partnership with homes, promote their balanced development into responsible individuals and members of society". Allowance must be made for pupils with special needs. Adults are entitled to education under the Education Act. This can take the form of municipal adult education *(komvux)* or adult education for intellectually handicapped adults *(särvux)*.

The structural features of the school system

Curricula, national goals and objectives as well as guidelines are decided upon by the Parliament *(Riksdag)* and the government. Education funds are provided to municipalities as part of lump sum state subsidies.

Within the goals and frames defined by the *Riksdag* and the government, each individual municipality is free to decide how the the schools are to be run. A *municipal school plan* must be adopted, describing how school activities are to be funded, organised and evaluated.

The principal *(rektor)* of each school unit is responsible for drawing up, implementing and evaluating a *local school plan* based on the national curricula and the municipal school plan. This responsibility must be carried out with the colloboration of the teachers.

The National Agency for Education is the central administrative body and thus responsible for follow-up (national statistics), school evaluation and development in the public sector. Permission to start independent schools on the primary and lower secondary level (grades 1 to 9) is given by the Agency, while permission for the upper secondary level is given by the government.

The Agency is required to furnish the *Riksdag* and government with a comprehensive report on the state of Swedish schooling at three-yearly intervals. These reports form the basis of a *national development plan* for schools. The Agency also regularly furnishes the municipalities with results from various evaluation projects and delivers statistics in order to create a baseline for evaluation on the local level, within which comparisons between municipalities and individual schools can be performed. It is also the duty of the Agency to supervise or inspect schools so as to ensure that the provisions of the Education Act are complied with and the rights of individual pupils respected.

The governing of the educational system is outlined in Figure 1.

Figure 1. **Governing of the education system**

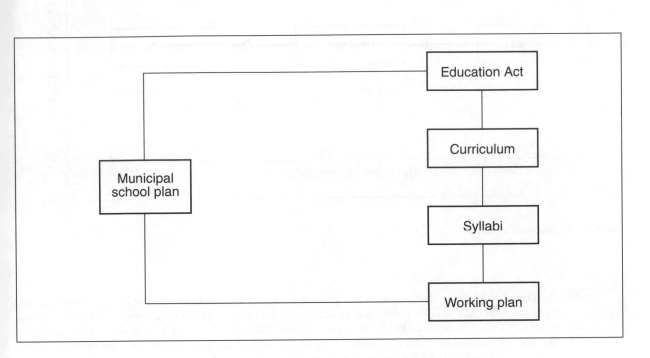

Source: U. Lundgren for OECD.

The *Riksdag* and the government define the National Curriculum for the entire school system and decide on the syllabi for the various school subjects and courses in the compulsory schools.

For the upper secondary school system the responsibility of defining syllabi for the various courses is delegated to the National Agency for Education.

The municipal governing board or the school board defines the municipal school plan. Within each school unit the principal is responsible for defining the local working plan, *i.e.* a form of school-based curriculum. On each level – state, municipality and school unit – there is identified responsibility for the follow-up of decisions taken and results evaluations.

Thus there is a clear division of responsibility and hence accountability between on one hand the administrative bodies and the professionals (*i.e.* the principals and the teachers) and on the other hand the various levels (*i.e.* state, municipality and the individual school, see Figure 2).

National responsibility for setting goals (standards) and controlling results is executed by the *Riksdag* and the government and partly delegated to the National Agency for Education. The municipalities are responsible for distributing resources and for using state subsidies in such a way that organisation and operating conditions are optimal for achieving the national goals. The professionals, *i.e.* the school leaders and the teachers, are responsible for designing teaching (choice of material, methods, etc.) such that students can achieve the national goals.

Figure 2. **Different levels of responsibility**

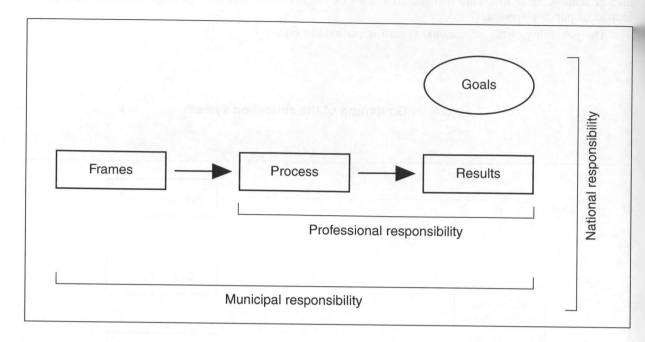

Source: U. Lundgren for OECD.

In this governing model, the manner in which goals are formed and decided upon is crucial. The National Agency is responsible for national evaluation and inspection of the system. The municipality in turn is responsible for the inspection and evaluation of the local school system. The school unit (school leaders and teachers) is responsible for the evaluation of teaching results. Part of the inspection and supervision programme of the National Agency for Education is to determine that these game rules are respected.

The earlier system for governing built extensively on the control of inputs. Thus the state gave subsidies to the municipalities. These funds covered about 50 per cent of the total running costs and were linked to teacher salaries. There was a regulated time scheme stating how many lessons were to be given for each school subject. Different categories of teachers had different regulated teaching times fixed by central negotiations and agreements. In this way, economic steering was built on a chain composed of three links: the number of lessons to be taught, teachers' teaching time and teacher salaries. Beside state funds for teacher salaries there were funds earmarked for special needs or groups, such as economic support for special education, etc. With the decentralisation of 1991 the state subsidies changed to undifferentiated support. The municpalities could use the subsidies in what they defined to be the most effective way, as long as the resources were given to education. In 1992 the money for education was amalgamated with all state money to the municipalities. All state subsidies are paid in a lump sum.

Along with economic support to the municipalities there were delivered rules for how the resources were to be used: rules concerning school organisation, the number of pupils per class, etc. One important task for the former Regional Boards of Education was to control the school organisation in each municipality. When the composition of state subsidies changed, the mass of rules was reduced, producing a new regulation or (perhaps better phrased deregulation). As a consequence the central administrative direction and tasks had to change. Thus the former central bodies were terminated and the National Agency for Education was funded.

Curriculum, goals and standards

The term "curriculum" is, like the term "standard", difficult to translate into Swedish. The term *Läroplan* means literally a "plan for learning or teaching". The *Läroplan* or National Curriculum has traditionally been a rather extensive document. It formerly gave the overarching national goals and guidelines. It prescribed the specific content units to be taught in each grade and included the time scheme giving the number of lessons for each grade in each subject.

From 1962 to 1980 there was a change in the content of the curriculum substituting goal orientation for content orientation. The time schedule was revised to give the number of lessons per stage (three year periods). Still the *Läroplan* was a rather extensive document including guidelines even for teaching methods. Abolishing this regulated steering system for a more goal-oriented system has implied a change of the very concept of curriculum.

In 1991 a committee was formed to develop a new curriculum system for the entire school system. The main task for the Committee on Curriculum was to draw up proposals for a goal-based curriculum (representing as such an extension of the Education act) for the compulsory schools, the upper secondary schools, and municipal adult education, as well as to propose time tables and syllabi for compulsory schooling. In addition it had the task of working out proposals to prepare children for future school activity and strengthening teaching in Swedish and foreign languages in different types of schools. The Committee had also a number of other tasks concerning upper secondary education.

The Committee was chaired by the Director General for the National Agency for Education (a former professor of education and vice chancellor of Stockholm Institute of Education). The members of the Committee included a professor of physics and head of an institute for environment studies; representatives of the Ministry of Social Affairs; a department head at National Agency for Education; an education department head at Volvo; a former head of the department of Guidence at Stockholm Institute of Education; the Director-General of the Agency for the Handicapped in Schools (former head of department at the National Board of Education).

In fall 1991 the government changed. In December, the Committee was given new directives and new members. The chairman was the same but the number of members was reduced.

In 1992 the Committee delivered its main report (SOU, 1992). The proposal was sent out for public debate before a bill was presented to the *Riksdag*. In 1993, the *Riksdag* decided on the main guidelines for the new curriculum and the government took the decision on the new National Curricula. The reactions to the proposal were on the whole positive. Teachers' unions agreed on the main lines, but had constructive criticism concerning details.

The term curriculum *(läroplan)* conveys now a relatively small document. It first defines what each school shall strive to ensure that each pupil acquire, then, what each pupil leaving the school should have achieved. The curriculum also tells what each teacher shall do and what is the responsibility of the principal. For each subject in the compulsory school there is a syllabus.

The new *Läroplan* states goals for compulsory schooling.

The school shall strive to ensure that each child:

- develops curiosity and desire to learn;
- develops his or her own way to learn;
- develops as a habit to independently formulate standpoints based on knowledge as well as reason and ethical considerations;
- achieves good knowledege within school subjects and subject areas;
- develops rich and elaborated language and understands the importance of cultivating one's language;
- learns to work both independently and with others;
- learns to communicate in a foreign language;
- acquires necessary knowledge and experiences in order to be able to make well grounded choices concerning further education and vocation; and
- learns to use knowledge as a tool to:
  • formulate and test assumptions and solve problems;
  • reflect on experiences; and
  • critically scrutinize and evaluate propositions and conditions.

Pupils' achievement goals can be seen as a form of standards.

The school's responsibility is to ensure that every child leaving school:

- masters the Swedish language and can listen and read in an active way and can express ideas and thoughts in speech and in writing;
- masters basic mathematical thinking and can apply it in everyday life;
- knows and understands basic concepts and contexts within natural scientific, technical, social scientific and humanist areas of knowledge;

- has developed creative ability and increased interest in taking part in the cultural life;
- has insight into central parts of our Swedish and Nordic, including Samic, and Occidental cultural heritage;
- has developed an understanding of other cultures;
- can communicate in speech and writing in English;
- have knowledge of the rationale behind laws and norms in society and know rights and responsibilities in school and in society;
- have knowledge of the interrelation between nations and geographical areas;
- have knowledge of the conditions for a good environment and understand basic ecological relations;
- have basic knowledge of the conditions for good health and understanding of health consequences of the personal lifestyles;
- have knowledge about media and their role; and
- have deepened knowledge within some school subjects chosen.

For each school subject there is a courseplan – a syllabus. In this syllabus there are goals to strive for and goals to have achieved by grade 5 and by the end of compulsory schooling at grade 9.

For the upper secondary school system there is a curriculum of similar construction, *i.e.* with goals to strive for and goals to achieve by the end of the upper secondary school. The upper secondary school system contains 16 national programmes. For each programme there are programme-specific goals and for each course within the programmes there is a syllabus.

The upper secondary school system is thus course-based. To give a structure for the courses there are programmes. Every subject consists of one or more parallel or supplementary courses. Each course comprises at least 30 hours' study time and can be studied intensively. Grades are awarded at the end of each course.

The upper secondary school offers at most sixteen national programmes. Two of the programmes – Natural Science and Social Science – focus more on university entry. About 10 weeks of the other, more vocational programmes have to be spent at a workplace out of school. Most of the programmes are divided into various branches for students to choose among from the second year. Some schools, however, do not offer all programmes and branches. Schools can also create local branch programmes. For the upper secondary schools there are more than eight hundred course syllabi.

The curriculum is then the basic steering document. The syllabi it supplies will be adjusted continuously based for example on results from evaluations, but the curriculum will have, if not an eternal character, a longer lasting life. Timetables are produced in a special act directed towards the municipalities, regulating the teacher-led time each student is guaranteed. For compulsory school this is 6 665 hours divided into various subjects. For the upper secondary school it is for academically oriented programmes 2 180 hours and for the other programmes 2 400 hours. A municipality can of course offer more teaching time.

The whole construction of the curriculum governing system entails a space for professional decisions. In the individual school the curriculum will be concretized in a local working plan. This means that teachers much more than before will have the freedom to choose content and above all methods. On the other hand they are accountable for delivery of what is demanded in the curriculum. To support principals and teachers in their work, the National Agency for Education will publish reference material (*i.e.* evaluation reports, reports from schools, etc.) and in various ways help schools to create networks and to share experiences.

This curriculum system can be labelled a system for governing by goals and results built on the assumption that there must be a space for influence on each level and a partnership between levels.

State governing of education has thus changed from control of input to control of output. The Education Act is sharper than before and inspection and supervision of how the Act is maintained has sharpened. The same is true for demands on evaluations on all levels. At the same time the governing system is not "clean" in the sense of being a pure goal-governed system. There is still a timetable, even though it gives much more space for local as well as individual choice.

The relationship between the various goals expressed in curricula and syllabi can be represented graphically in the following way (Figure 3).

Assessment and evaluation

Assessments and evaluations have to be understood on two different levels.

On the system level, evaluations are carried out as a part of the governing system. The idea here is to develop new knowledge, improve the bases for decisions and create an intellectual context for development by having evaluations as an integrated part of the educational work. On the state level the National Agency for

Figure 3. **Relationship between the various goals**

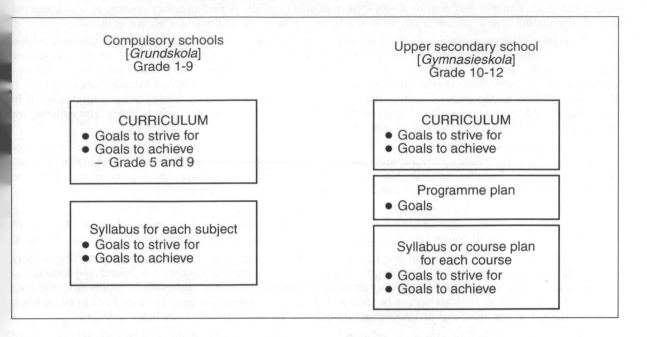

Source: U. Lundgren for OECD.

Education will every third year deliver to the *Riksdag* and the government a comprehensive report on the state of Swedish education. This report gives at the same time to the municipalities a basis for national comparisons. The government will, from this report, make an evaluation and present a plan for development over the next three years. The evaluations carried out by the National Agency serve also to give signals for inspections, supervisions and for recommendations to the government and the *Riksdag*. The municipalities are responsible for the quality of their school system and must follow and evaluate processes and results. The individual school must evaluate its work. These evaluations will include various and different aspects and they will use various tools. Assessments in terms of tests will for example be one tool for evaluations.

System-level assessments and evaluations are relatively new to Sweden. Sweden on the other hand has a long tradition of evaluating and assessing individual students and individual results; this is in particular linked to the marking system.

As early as the Education Act of 1820 there was a regulation concerning marking and scales for marking. Up to the educational reforms in the sixties the marking of the individual student was supposed to be based on absolute criteria. The teacher was the one to make the marks and there was no legal possibility to change the marks given. To support the teachers and give norms for marking, central test were sucessively built up. For the students leaving the upper secondary school system *(gymnasium)* there were entrance examinations at the university. In the 20th century the examinations were moved out to the schools. University teachers conducted oral examination of students at the the end of the last semester. Before these oral examination the students had to go through written tests developed and distributed by the National Board of Education.

With the expansion of the educational system and accompanying limitation on university entrance the marking system came under debate. During the extensive educational reform period in the sixties and seventies the rule of marks for entrance to higher education came in focus. With the comprehensive school and the integrated upper secondary school (integration of academic and vocational study schools) the marking system changed from an absolute system to a relative system. The marks were distributed in five categories along a Gauss curve (7, 24, 38, 24 and 7 per cent). Standardised tests were distributed to the schools to supply a standard for marking. These tests cover Swedish, Mathematics and English.

The new marking system came immediately under criticism and the seventies and eighties saw a round of investigations and commissions. During the seventies voices were heard arguing for abolishing the marking system and introducing an non-marking school system. In 1990 a working group presented a report proposing to replace the relative marking system by a new system related to goals. A parliamentary committee was given the task of formulating a new system. This work was linked to the work of the Curriculum Committee.

The results from the commission were heavily criticised and in the Bill authored by the government the proposal was changed. The system decided upon by the *Riksdag* builds on marks from grade 7 for the compulsory school. The marks are in six steps from A (Excellent) to F (Failed). To support the teachers the National Agency for Education has been given the directives to develop tests in English, Swedish and Mathematics for grade 9. Thus these subjects are the same as in the earlier standardised test system and are treated as the central subjects in the curriculum (despite representing little more than 40 per cent of guaranteed teaching time). The syllabus for each subject will be supplemented with criteria for marking.

For the upper secondary schools there will be four grades and for each course there will be criteria for marking. The National Agency for Education has been given the directives for developing tests not only in the same three subjects (Swedish, English, Mathematics) but in French and German, as well as to investigate the possibility of testing within other subject and areas (such as vocational competence).

The National Agency for Education is also developing diagnostic tests for grade 5 and 7. In grade 5 the curriculum defines specific achievement goals, creating a ''control station'' in the sense of checking the level of basic skills of the pupils. It forms, hence, a basis on which decisions on extra support to students can be taken.

It is thus an elaborated assessment program that is now in a stage of development and which will gradually replace the standardised tests. The feasibility of national test banks, where teachers can deliver and take items, will be studied. Systemic evaluations are also under development. Of course aggregates of results from the tests produced for diagnosing and marking can be used as indicators of system outcome, but they have to be supplied by tests oriented to specific areas of interest and designed to measure specific knowledge and skills.

The marking and testing system in relation to curriculum demands in the compulsory school can be illustrated as indicated on Figure 4.

Figure 4. **An illustration of the marking and testing system in relation to curriculum demands**

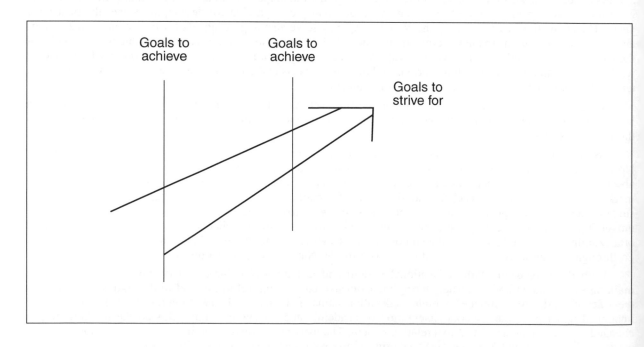

Source: U. Lundgren for OECD.

The National Board of Education started a program called the National Evaluation (NE) directed towards the results from the last grade in the compulsory school. This program was taken over and finalised by the National Agency for Education. All subjects were tested extensively within a sample of 100 schools and 10 000 pupils. The tests were developed to cover not only the content of the courses but also the cognitive level. In addition to these subject oriented tests an extensive integrated problem solving test was used. A study of each school concerning culture, climate, management, etc., was carried out. The results of this evaluation formed the basis for the report from the National Agency for Education on the State of Education in Sweden delivered in 1993. The next report on the state of education will be delivered in 1996. To this end a new study on the compulsory schools is underway together with a parallel study of the upper secondary school. In this latter study the students from the first NE study will be followed into the upper secondary school.

Aside from this NE study, Sweden has participated in the IEA reading study and in earlier IEA mathematics studies. Sweden is also participating in the IEA Third International Mathematics Study project. The achievement results from these studies supplemented with studies of results from the central standardised tests and results from various specific research and evalauation studies are presented in the 1993 report on the state of education *(Bilden av Skolan,* 1993).

The results show:

– very good average achievements in reading. However there is a "tail" group of students showing an unacceptable level;
– acceptable results in most subjects;
– the pupils have problems with concepts within natural science and to a lessert extent in social science;
– the pupils have problems in combining knowledge from different fields and integrating them in problem solving.

Some of these results can be explained as problems coordinating teachers which ideally would include working in partnership over subjects and grades. The teaching is in general traditional classroom teaching, giving students not enough influence or possibilities to develop individually.

The statement that acceptable results were found is said on a rather abstract level. Going deeply into the results from this evaluation the picture is of course much more detailed and complicated. The results have been published in a series of reports which have been analysed by schools and used in in-service training. The NE study is in that respect not only a study giving indications on results but also a source and an instrument for school and professional development. The results have also been used in reworking syllabi and teaching material.

The results of these evaluations have launched series of studies to identify explanations and measures for change. For the next three-year period the National Agency for Education has set priorities on the teaching of mathematics and natural science and student participation and influence.

The outcome is of course related to various background factors. In the NE studies there are covariations with the schools. A positive school culture, meaning a visible and clear management, teacher cooperation and better allocation of resources, is accompanied by higher outcomes. Studies on student background mirror the well-known patterns.

The process of standard setting

In this paper we have used "standards" to be synonymous with the interrelation between curricula, syllabi and criteria for marks, *i.e.* as a set of goals and criteria to which educational outcomes are to be related.

Figure 5 can illustrate this interrelationship.

The National Curriculum is decided upon by the government from guidelines given by the *Riksdag.* The syllabi for the compulsory school are defined by the government and the syllabi for the upper secondary school by the National Agency for Education. Criteria for marking is defined by the National Agency for Education.

Establishing goals and criteria is a process in which various expert groups (schoolteachers, university teachers, subject experts) are engaged. When the goals are established implementation starts, followed by an evaluation. In the governmental development plan the continous development of syllabi will build on a process starting with a goals proposal by subject experts. Their proposal will take into consideration the results from evaluations. This will lead to a form of pre-product that will be tested by teachers. The revised outcome will once again be tested before finalisation of syllabi.

Figure 5. **Interrelationship between curricula and criteria for marks**

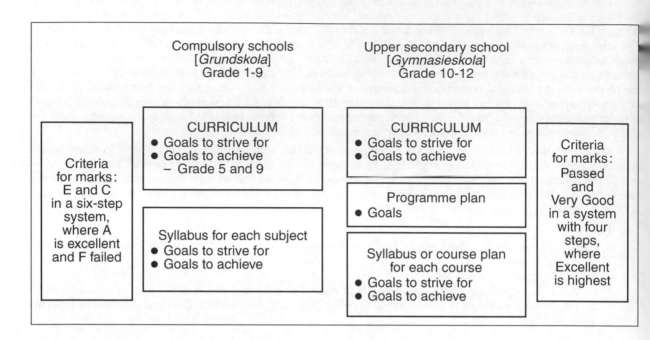

Source: U. Lundgren for OECD.

The National Agency for Education

The role and tasks of the National Agency for Education have been briefly described above. However its structure in relation to the setting of standards and in relation to assessment system is worth examining.

Its tasks can be described as:

- To follow, by collecting national data, how the educational system develops and changes. This includes producing a national statistic and indicator system, of which the national assessment system is a part.
- To evaluate the education system, *i.e.* to carry out studies in order to evaluate how goals are achieved. A national system can never be evaluated in all its parts. Priorities on evaluation studies build then on directives from the government and the *Riksdag,* signals from the follow-up programme and results from evaluation studies. To evaluate outcome requires access to standardized tests, used for marking or developed specifically for systemic evaluation purposes.
- To inspect and ensure that the Education Act and the Curriculum are followed, that the rules are followed and the rights of the individual pupil are protected.
- To be responsible for the national development of the school system. This role has two sides. One is to administer and refine the goal and result oriented governing system by developing syllabi and tools for evaluation. The other is to develop information and knowledge as a steering device, *i.e.* to furnish the *Riksdag,* the government, the municipalities, teachers and the public with knowledge and information about the results of the educational system.

The work within the National Agency of Education is organised in two unit: a central unit in Stockholm and one field organisation. These two units count a little more than 100 persons each. The field organisation is under change from an organisation spread all over the country to a more concentrated organisation. It will include 12 working groups with minimum 5 persons in each. Each group is responsible for a group of municipalities. They will each year produce a report on the state of education in each municipality and they will be responsible for giving the municipalities information about the national state of education. They will also participate in various projects.

Besides ongoing administrative duties the work within the Agency is built on projects. Resources corresponding to 100 man-years are allocated to experts. The projects are organised within five programmes:

- follow-up statistics, indicators and tests;
- evaluation;
- national development;
- inspection and supervision;
- research.

These programmes are in their turn coordinated in a policy programme. The follow-up programme describes the educational system in terms of student flow, costs, results from tests. This forms a basis for project priorities within the evaluation programme and the results from these programmes will influence the programme on research, the programme for national development and the programme for inspection and supervision. The production of the report on the state of education that will be produced every three years functions also as a link within and between programmes and projects. The government and the *Riksdag* will also launch projects. Every year the government gives specific orientations for the work.

Preconditions and problems

The reforms during the last five years introduce a new way of governing education and new ways for professional development. There are two reasons for these changes. One is economic. Moving decisions as close to production as possible may develop more efficient and optimal ways of using resources. The other is to prepare the school system for the future. The Swedish society is going through rapid changes of an economic as well as of a cultural nature. On the horizon is a society in which the access and use of knowledge will be the "hub of the wheel". These changes demand new definitions of the role of schooling. To redefine and develop the schools, teachers as professionals must be supported and given possibilities to develop their work.

The former school system created teachers who followed rules and were given little creative license. The ongoing changes recognize professional skills but at the same time make the teacher more visible and thus accountable for outcomes. The implementation of these reforms comes during a period when the municipalities have been forced to cut back on resources to schools.

These changes can be described as partly slow and partly fast. Teachers are opposed to the municipality being their employer rather than the state. There are municipalities that do not have the ability to live up to the role of a good employer. But there are also municipalities that have seized the initiative to develop the school system in new ways.

Policy formulation and decision making

The changes of the Swedish education system can be described as a change of control from "input" to "output". This means that educational policy is more than before directed towards the determining of goals and outcomes. With this change standards are coming into focus, and the problems of measuring outcomes emerge. The decision process concerning goals and responsibilities for control and evaluation of outcomes has been described. It is however a new endeavour, a new undertaking which is not tightly modelled. Basic for evaluation and assessment is that no one method shall be used and no one actor held as responsible. Thus there is shared responsibility between the state, the municipalities and the schools, where various methods and means can be used. Basic too is that the various results of evaluations and assessments form grounds for continous developments and tests of goals or standards. The main problem to be handled in the future will be how to handle knowledge about and information from the system in a democratic way, with public insight and balancing the demands of tradition with demands for change.

Bibliography

SOU (1992), *Skola för bildning* (A School for Life), Utbildningsdepartementet, Stockholm.

SOU (1994), *Grunden för livslångt lärande* (The basis for life-long learning), Utbildningsdepartementet, Stockholm.

Bilden av skolan (1993) (The school portrayed), Skolverket, Stockholm.

UNITED STATES

by

Eva L. Baker
UCLA National Center for Research on Evaluation, Standards, and Student Testing (CRESST)
and
Robert L. Linn
University of Colorado at Boulder
National Center for Research on Evaluation, Standards and Student Testing

Summary

This paper will describe the role of standards and assessments in the present cycle of educational reform of the United States. Its major sections include a brief description of the American educational system and a reprise of the key elements of the educational reform undertaken in the last decade, including the ascendant role of standards and new forms of assessment, particularly their evolving defining and articulated purposes. We will conclude with the ways in which performance standards, as variously defined, are practically implemented. Illustrating with particular case studies of high profile performance standards activities, we will project a set of problems that need sustained technical and policy attention for their solution.

The U.S. educational system

It is incontestable that the U.S. educational system is complex and defies neat summary. It is a mixture of independent and hierarchical policy and operational organizations. Paradoxically, its national character resides in its historical investment in decentralization. The U.S. Constitution assigns educational responsibility principally to the states, and each of the fifty states has developed its own particular flavor. Without exception, each state has a chief education officer, either elected at large or appointed to serve. Although often a non-partisan office, candidates for the position of chief state school officer may be supported openly or in thinly disguised ways by one or another of the two major political parties. The portfolio of the chief education officer may focus exclusively on the public schools from kindergarten through secondary school. In some states, responsibility also may include postsecondary education, libraries, museums, or other less formal educational venues. The policy-making group in each state guiding the commissioner or superintendent (as the chief officer is usually termed) is the state board of education. This group, usually a combination of public representatives with educational, business, academic, or professional credentials, may be elected or appointed. In either case, they may be chosen from the entire state or to represent particular jurisdictions. Clearly the choice of election or appointment influences the chief officers' and the state boards' perception, timing, and locus of accountability. Boards may be augmented with ex officio members.

The chief state officer serves as the head administrator of a department of education, staffed by professionals with responsibilities to implement policies approved by their state board of education and their state legislatures. State boards and departments of education provide for additional public participation by the appointment of standing commissions to deal with issues of curriculum, teacher certification, or higher education policies. These commissions generally include strong representation from educators and academics as well as from the public sector. State legislatures have also created special-purpose commissions and *ad hoc* review groups to deal with particular proposals for reform. There is considerable variation in the degree to which individual state depart-ments of education balance their agenda between initiation of reform and compliance. The policies of each of the state education agencies reflect traditions in the roles of state and local educational authorities and are influenced by factors such as the vast differences in size and composition of the school population, from tens of thousands to many millions of children, or from culturally homogeneous to enormously diverse in language and economic backgrounds.

In every state, save Hawaii, the state educational system, its board of education, and chief officer, and bureaucracy both oversee and operate interactively with local school districts. In Hawaii, the state and local educational agencies are conterminous. In the United States, there are more than 15 000 local school districts, a factor of 300 over the number of state authorities. Local school districts have jurisdiction over elementary and secondary schools, although some may also include preschools and two-year postsecondary institutions. As do the states, local school districts dramatically differ in size, from one or two schools to mega-districts like Los Angeles or New York City, serving 700 000 to one million students, thousands of teachers, and hundreds of schools. Local school districts mirror state organizational structures. Policy is set for them by school boards made up of public representatives. Most of these school boards are elected by the public every two or four years, with staggered terms for continuity. School board elections are often hotly contested; recall elections to depose a board member who has offended a large constituency are not uncommon; and many board members, although receiving nominal compensation, devote considerable energy to their tasks.

These boards have the responsibility for budget, curriculum, operations, and accountability policy. Local school districts must operate within the guidelines and legislatively enacted codes of their states. In the last twenty years, assessing the comparative influence of local versus state school authority, a shift has occurred between the relative influence of state and local school agencies. Although responsibilities for day-to-day educational services remain local, the increasing share of local educational costs borne by states has resulted in centralization of curriculum and assessments. The power first shifted from local school boards to the state departments of education. Yet, as education has become for many states the largest single budget item, educational policy has been seized as a principal issue by the elected state legislatures and the states' overall executives, the governors. Large local school districts represent exceptions to the trend of centralization of power to states. Because they may have strong and direct lines of communication with state legislatures and governors, they may negotiate particular issues or dispensations from certain statewide mandates.

The federal government has limited authority in education matters in the United States; nonetheless, it has had significant influence on educational practices in the states, districts, and schools. There is a current debate about whether this influence is positive or intrusive. The federal government implements special programs authorized by Congress to contribute to the educational opportunities of disadvantaged children and special populations, including those with limited English proficiency, those with physical and mental disabilities, and children with other identified needs. These programs contribute significant resources to participating states. In crafting the laws, in implementing guidelines for local operation of these programs, and in determining the means to evaluate the success of these efforts, the legislative and executive arms of the federal government have a means to set expectations for the groups targeted by the legislation. In fact, their efforts have had impact on the rest of American students as well. One particular example was the requirement that a special federal program needed to be evaluated by using standardized tests, administered on a pre- and post-basis, and reported in terms of national norms. As a result, many school districts adopted a single standardized test for all their students and created public expectations of annual reporting of growth through these measures.

A second, much less expansive way in which the U.S. government influences local public education, is in its support of research and dissemination functions. Periodically, agencies of the federal government have supported the design of new teaching materials, teacher training opportunities, and technical assistance. They also support research on fundamental educational processes, such as learning, teaching, assessment, and organization. For example, in the last 30 years or so, the U.S. government has supported a network of educational research and development activities, supplemented by technical assistance service agencies. Organizations participating in research and development do not promote a particular version of the educational reform agenda, but rather provide information and options intended to improve the conceptualization and support of learning, the practice of teaching, and the design of evaluation and governance models. These research organizations function in universities, or as independent non-profit or profit-making entities.

U.S. political realities have made national coherent programmatic action in support of education very difficult. For the most part, federal financial support has been given to the states with very few guidelines or conditions. Governors, state boards, local educational authorities, and politicians on the right and on the left seek to guard against the danger they perceive in the control of local education agendas from a distal, central source. Through the availability of marginal but discretionary resources, federal programs have reached more than 70 per cent of the schools in the country. But in general, the federal role of education is to identify important priorities and to provide resources to states and localities for implementation. All federal programs must operate in a tradition that preserves the prerogatives of states and local school districts. Naturally, there are contentions about the location of boundaries among prerogatives.

Although the U.S. government does not control formally the processes of American schools, that is not to say that other national agents have little influence. In fact, because most of the instructional materials, such as textbooks, are commercially developed, there is in fact a *de facto* menu of curriculum embodied in the books and materials that are sold by commercial firms. In general, the process for curriculum marketing involves the presentation of options by commercial textbook publishers to the state board of education or to its delegated body for review at particular grade levels, for example, elementary school, and for particular subject matters, for instance, mathematics or history. Usually states will make primary and alternate choices. Local school districts generally make their selections within these approved choices, for which they typically receive financial incentives for compliance. Because economic considerations preclude creating separate sets of text materials for each state, in practice, the decisions of a very few large states with centralized curriculum selection processes set the boundaries for what is available for other states. A similar situation exists in the area of student achievement testing. A handful of test publishers have a limited number of achievement measures in their inventories. Although these are more frequently modified under contract to meet a particular state need, in fact the majority of achievement tests used in U.S. schools as measures of general system monitoring are commercial products. These commercial tests and textbooks serve as centralizing agents and an important, although indirect, nationalization force in U.S. educational enterprise.

A final background note important to understanding the character of American education is the precept of equal educational opportunity. Although in practice never yet fully realized at rhetorical, political, and value levels, Americans have long believed their schools should provide educational opportunities for students of all economic, linguistic, and cultural backgrounds. Although approximately 25 per cent of American students advance to a four-year postsecondary educational experience, U.S. policy has been directed to assuring that ethnic and economic backgrounds are reasonably well represented in secondary school graduation and in admission to postsecondary schools. To that end, both sanctions and incentives have been employed. For example, when pass rates on tests required for secondary school diplomas discriminated against students of African-American background, legal challenges were posed to the state. The Office of Civil Rights, for example, has made formal inquiries into the acceptance-denial rates of Asian students at the university level, raising the question of overrepresentation. Obviously, these contradictory legal challenges could not result in simultaneous rational policies; instead, they indicate the tension and concern for fairness and equality in U.S. educational matters.

This commitment to equality, in the light of these conflicts, has in part led the U.S. to avoid *de jure* approaches to early decisions for students about their likelihood to succeed at academic postsecondary institutions. Therefore, most students complete a general academic program in secondary school, one which has been strengthened in the numbers of required courses in mathematics and English language. The equal opportunity commitment is also responsible for policies that encourage children in all educational authorities to complete a full 12- or 13-year educational program, culminating with the high school diploma. This orientation has been informally supported by the lack, until very recently, of secondary education options leading to early careers in the work force rather than college admission.

Yet, the realities of the schools change as conflicts in U.S. society surface. Increasing opportunities for women and the present U.S. economic environment have led to their greater participation in the work force. As a result, schools and other institutions are expected to expand their participation in the overall education of children. Greater career opportunities for women have also reduced the proportion of highly educated women entering the teaching field and have led to a need to improve approaches to teacher recruitment, training, professional development, and sustenance. As a result, program changes for teacher education have been made in higher education institutions and in the credentialling standards of states. Teachers' salaries have been raised, and efforts have been made to improve their work environments. But to date, weak economic growth has left some of these goals unmet, and even others likely to be undone. States differ greatly in their level of teacher compensation, their career advancement patterns, in work environments, such as class size (ranging, for instance, from 22 to 40 students). Teacher unions differ by locality in the extent to which they initiate support or resist various proposed educational changes.

As in past epochs of high immigration and low economic growth, segments of the public have developed some resistance to compensatory or equal opportunity approaches. The public schools, in some states with high proportions of minority students, are under increasing scrutiny. Significant political movements have been mounted to provide public support for private schools using voucher or similar programs. At the heart of this challenge are two related concerns: *a)* that educational programs are being simplified to meet the needs of students of different cultural, linguistic, or economic background than the majority student; *b)* that the schools themselves are organized in such a way to protect and sustain their own bureaucracies as opposed to educating children. These issues have driven the educational establishment to seek substantial reform, undertaken at a time when financial resources are scarce. Furthermore, reviews of existing policies of equal opportunity are underway more broadly in the society. For instance, affirmative action policies are being reconsidered at all levels of government, with concern by critics that goals to increase the participation of segments of the population in the work force have created a new kind of unfairness that should be remedied. Similar proposals to revisit the types and kinds of social services available to immigrants attempt to redefine what equal opportunity means.

U.S. educational reform and the development of content standards

Almost since its inception, the U.S. public education system has been subjected to scrutiny and repeated calls for improvement and change. Yet, the system has been remarkably adaptable to the changes in geography, demography, and ideology that have characterized the development of its goals. Two distinguishing features of the U.S. setting may provide an important context to understanding educational reform efforts and prospects. First, the area of education is less likely to be considered the province of expertise, when compared with other public endeavors, for instance, the delivery of health care or the criminal justice system. On an absolute level, respect for U.S. precollegiate educational institutions is not high, and, in fact, colleges and universities are also treated with increasing scepticism. Teachers' knowledge and competence are often publicly challenged, although there are some visible efforts to identify and acknowledge excellent teaching in both public and private recognition ceremonies. Lay opinion, expressed through local media and governance structures, and correspondingly held public values, has frequently had greater impact in influencing the course of educational reform than has the expert judgement or experience of teachers or scholars.

Second, public interest plays out in the importance of law and litigation as means to direct the education system. Legislation developed from special interests at state levels has resulted in a bewildering number of rules and regulations. These rules cover topics from the number of minutes of instruction in particular subject matters, to insurance provisions, to procedures to deal with armed students. Some regulations address topics to be taught in schools, topics that have been introduced by particular advocacy groups. These requirements generate controversy because they often include areas outside of typical academic pursuits, such as AIDS prevention or personal health. Schools or systems must document compliance with certain regulations, generating microbureaucracies and administrative costs beyond those needed for actually teaching students. Moreover, litigation has been used as a major form of redress to resolve issues of authority as they intrude on privacy and equal opportunity in the schools. These issues are subject to suit because they are guaranteed by the U.S. Constitution and its amendments. Challenges are raised on behalf of individual parents, students, teachers, and or other school personnel, or by professional or advocacy organizations, and are initiated by members of every political stripe. Because of the frequency and activism of the legal process, many school districts and state education agencies maintain defensive postures. Potential legal recourse is always a consideration before the initiation of new policies and programs. Both legislatively imposed constraints and the threat of legal action serve to limit the flexibility of educational planning and operations.

It is against this backdrop that the current prospects for U.S. educational reform must be analyzed. In the 1980s, following the release of the study *A Nation At Risk* (1983), a series of parallel reforms began to be enacted. One set focused on strengthening the content requirements in schools, resulting in raising the number of courses required for graduation in particular subject areas. A second wave of reform focused on the teaching profession, particularly on the areas of recruitment, development, and training. A third major change involved the "restructuring" movement, essentially approaches to the devolution of authority and responsibility for school programs and operations to the individual school site level. Devolution worked paradoxically to reduce the impact of local school districts, while simultaneously strengthening the impact of state-level mandates. In the late 1980s, some states embarked on a more systematic course of educational reform. For example, in California and Connecticut, reform focused first on the topic of clarifying content to be learned in schools and resulted in statements called frameworks in particular subjects or common "cores" of learning. These frameworks were to specify broadly the content and knowledge expectations for students and to serve as guidance for related educational functions, including text book and materials selection, teacher professional development, and evaluation of students.

Some of these reforms, in Texas, Arkansas, and Kentucky, were the products of leadership somewhat outside the normal educational channels of superintendents, school boards, and local school districts. The leadership of governors or of the legislatures promoted educational change, articulating a trade-off of greater flexibility, and more resources for higher accountability. The new focus on student competency differed from past reforms that emphasized minimums or the least common denominator of achievement for all students. Instead, the new reforms emphasize high standards of expectation for all students.

In deeper background, private and quasi-governmental reform initiatives were also developing. The National Board for Professional Teaching Standards was created to establish performance standards and assessments for excellent teachers. Researchers were promoting models of teaching, learning, and school change that emphasized a more interactive and constructivist approach to instruction, less homogeneous grouping of students, and more focus on support mechanisms for individual students, including processes for extending the school day, providing homework centers, and other after-school enrichment options.

Major actors in the reform discussion were members of the business community, in their local, state, and national roles, who promoted reform as the means to restore U.S. economic strength.

In 1989, at an historic meeting on education attended by the governors and the federal administration, a set of National Education Goals was articulated, later endorsed by President Bush in 1990, and proposed as legislation in 1991. One element of this legislation created a council jointly appointed by the governors, the administration, and by Congress, to consider whether national standards and national assessments were desirable and feasible. The deliberations of this council resulted in recommendations supporting the development of state-by-state standards and assessments on a voluntary basis. Of particular concern during this deliberation were two issues: *a)* how to assure that high standards and challenging assessments improved the performance of disadvantaged students; and *b)* the preservation of state and local authority for educational matters.

In support of goals of the *Raising Standards for American Education* document, the federal government supported the development of content standards (a variation on curriculum frameworks) starting in a number of subject matter areas: history-social studies, science, English language arts, geography, and civics. Following on the widely praised model developed in mathematics by the National Council of Teachers of Mathematics, subject matter specialists and teachers were encouraged to delineate the content standards expected of students. Additional groups lobbied to have national standards developed in their fields, since such standards would be required for inclusion in school programs. This inclusion decision would clearly have impact on undergraduate and graduate programs in the subject matters at the college and university level in terms of areas in which teachers would need strong undergraduate preparation. The first group of subject matter standards are now beginning to be delivered and scrutinized. For example, the standards produced in history were widely criticized for under-representing the roots of Western civilization in the American democracy and were repudiated by a vote in the U.S. Senate. Attacks have appeared on the idea of standards themselves with disengagement from the politically bipartisan agreement in Charlottesville, Virginia.

In many states, reform that centers on standards and new kinds of assessments is underway. It is clear that many states are struggling with the problem of making coherent choices among competing standards within and between subject matters. Because of their scope, any one set of subject matter standards, if taken seriously, could easily consume all available student time. Secondly, the subject matter focus of these standards conflicts with another stream of reform: efforts to make school learning more interdisciplinary and more applicable to tasks in real, out-of-school settings, where knowledge from a variety of venues is integrated. Third, in part stimulated by the business community and national panels on problems of the work force, the emphasis on subject matters by standards may not directly serve the needs of the majority of American students not focused on full-time college or university studies. Comparable standards have been set for the development of work force skills, although the procedure for their integration in school curricula have not been thoroughly worked out.

Nonetheless, led by their governors and state education executives, virtually every state is engaged in a systematic rethinking of its educational offerings, of its means of supporting teachers to reach new goals for students, and of its processes for assessing student accomplishments.

Assessments

The U.S. has had a highly developed system for measuring student achievement, and this system has been used extensively in school systems, at state levels and at the national level for a variety of purposes. The purposes include general system monitoring, program or policy evaluation, individual placement and certification, and diagnosis and remediation. For the most part, testing and assessment needs have been met by a set of commercial companies who develop, sometimes administer, score, and report results to clients. For the most part, many of these measures have been developed to assure that these processes can occur economically. In addition, the history of test development in the United States has created expectations for high technical standards of validity and reliability. These are usually achieved through the application of statistical models dependent upon wide sampling of content and normative comparisons of students and schools. For the most part, these requirements have been met by standardized multiple-choice tests. The U.S. penchant for educational litigation earlier noted has reinforced the need for tests that are technical defensible, particularly in their fairness to members of disparate populations.

Test design options

Technical defensibility is one reason for which U.S. educators have used multiple-choice tests as their preferred measures almost without regard to the purpose of the test. Multiple-choice designs also were cost sensitive, for they were cheap to prepare and score. Although examinations requiring students to write essays or prepare projects were sometimes used by teachers to give students marks, open-ended assessments were not often used for publicized accountability purposes. Constructed, open-ended assessments had been a part of the early National Assessment of Educational Progress (NAEP) in the 1970s. NAEP was originally conceived both to be a reporting mechanism to monitor national educational attainment and to exemplify and lead the nation's schools in new approaches to assessment. Yet, over the years, needs for efficient information about attainment drove out the assessment leadership role of NAEP. Only recently has it moved from substantially a multiple-choice or constrained test to an open-ended set of measures.

The movement to use more open-ended assessments grew in the 1980s, particularly in the area of student writing. Many states developed or contracted the development of writing assessments, which asked students to prepare essays rather than to edit or evaluate given pieces of work. Although vocally opposed by some members of the testing establishment, the argument for validity (measure writing if that is the goal) overcame objections. Considerable efforts in research and practice have created technical standards for the design of writing tasks and of scoring rubrics. The experience in writing set the stage for considering an expansion of open-ended assessments in other subject matters for use in large-scale or accountability situations. Widespread dissemination of the British experiments in the late 1980s and early 1990s also influenced a broadening of testing approach in the U.S. Examples of European school-leaving examination questions were circulated and encouraged U.S. educators to adopt more open-ended testing approaches. The history of performance assessment in the U.S. military, typically used to assess procedural knowledge or strategy in simulated or on-the-job environments, also contributed to the growing credibility of measures of performance. Furthermore, some educational researchers in the U.S. charged that the low standards of the curriculum were in part caused by the lack of challenge in multiple-choice measures.

In sum, the reforms focusing on higher educational expectations, on new approaches to teaching and learning, and information on assessment from outside sources converged and stimulated an unprecedented degree of agreement among constituencies for educational change: Business leaders, policy makers, teachers and administrators, and researchers have all been vocal in support of assessment reform, even if some may have only vague ideas of what they are actually supporting. Now, at least 16 states have some form of performance-based assessment on a statewide basis. Others have joined in consortia to develop new assessments and 90 per cent of the states have plans to change their assessment systems. There remains some strong suspicion in segments of the public that open-ended assessments are a way to relax rather than raise expectations. Parents worry that these newer (for the U.S.) forms of assessment are subjective and that any answer will do, a fear that connects to the scepticism about teacher quality. Establishing credibility for these assessments will minimally depend upon the creation and publication of obviously challenging measures and providing unassailable evidence of their technical quality.

Despite the need for credibility, a number of technical concerns about performance assessment remain, particularly where results of their use will have dramatic consequences for individual students and schools. One troublesome dilemma is the trade-off between adequate sampling of subject matter and the constrained time and resources available for testing. Subject matter sampling decisions interact with the inferences derived from the measures, because different schools may very well teach different aspects of subject matter, and restrictive subject matter representation could result in mismatches between test and instructional content. That these assessments will actually be sensitive to educational interventions is a matter of faith. When assessments have broad boundaries and very general scoring criteria, for example, elaborated versus basic, it is just as possible that individual talent is the major source of variation as the effects of schooling. Because of the striking diversity of student backgrounds in some states and cities, an additional set of problems exists. For example, is it possible that such assessments can be customized for use with students of non-English backgrounds and simultaneously maintain the quality of measurement? How will accommodations or adaptations affect the ability to compare the results of different groups?

Assessment, however it occurs, clearly operationalizes the meaning of content standards or curriculum frameworks. It is a key element in understanding the intentions of educational reforms and sends a signal to school practitioners about what is valued. How performance standards fit into the relationship between content standards and assessment is not yet clear.

We have described the American educational system so far in order to give some understanding of why current practices in the identification of performance standards are as they are and the options and choices the nation faces in the future.

An essential attribute of any accountability-focused educational system is the way in which one determines success or infers the need to invest differently in educational services. Performance standards serve as a system to divide performers into those who have attained or have yet to attain desired outcomes. These performance standards may also serve as the framework for the public reporting system for educational accomplishment. Reports are promulgated about the average performance of students in a particular subject, or the numbers who have met prespecified levels of accomplishment. If content standards or curriculum goals and targets tell us what is to be learned, and assessments allow us to measure learning, performance standards are to provide guidance about how much or how well students have learned. They are the operational statement of expectations.

Looking at performance standards from a narrow, operational perspective, three major technical approaches have been taken in their formulation. The first two of these take a linear approach starting from the articulation of goals or content standards. Defining performance standards follows the statement of content standards; performance standards may be verbal descriptions of attributes of desired skills at a particular age or proficiency level. For example, the statement that proficient writing is elaborated with detail and uses a clear line of argument or progression would be an example of descriptive performance standards. The descriptive performance standards are intended to influence the design of the assessment tasks and the approaches used for their scoring. They also may directly imply reporting categories as well.

A second approach to performance standards begins as well with goals or content standards but, forgoing verbal description, operationalizes their meaning in a set of assessment tasks. Variation in the challenge of the tasks themselves serves to illustrate expectations for students, as do model performances that exceed, satisfy, or fail to meet standards. A third form of performance standard involves a pre-existing item pool intended to measure the general articulated goals. With this approach, performance standards may take the form of identifying quantitative "cut-scores" or levels of attainment. This approach assumes that the test items measure the same general dimension so that more accurate, right answers connote greater competence. In the U.S. considerable research has been undertaken to develop approaches to this sort of performance standard-setting. Tests using extensive, open-ended tasks, measuring very different dimensions of content may be ill-served by this cut-score approach to performance standard-setting. In these cases, performance may need to be set in terms of qualitative characteristics, categories of calling for similar and dissimilar knowledge and skills. Reports of performance in these categories may provide more useful information than the assumption of a linear scale and different quantitative standards of performance.

Some performance levels have focused on different types of quantitative goals, specifying proportions of the group intended to meet particular standards. "Eighty per cent of students should master 75 per cent of the items tested" and "failure on no more than one aspect of a multistep task is acceptable for 90 per cent of the students" represent the sort of performance standards often used for the design and evaluation of U.S. training programs in the business and military sectors.

Nonetheless, these technical definitions are far beyond the thoughts of many charged with setting performance standards. In many states, at the present time, special commissions on performance standards have been appointed by legislatures and governors. These consist of broad representation of the public, parents, policymakers, school leaders, the business community, and teachers. Most of these groups are struggling with the rudiments of selecting general goals or content standards rather than any precise notion of real standards of performance. Most are using descriptive approaches that generally sketch the characteristics or type of content they expect students to have learned by particular points in their schooling, for example, by the end of elementary education. In practice, then, the term performance standard has a loose definition, perhaps assigning different content standards to age ranges, but stopping well before qualitative or quantitative standards of performance have been articulated.

In the next section, we are going to describe experiences with the setting of performance standards drawn from three very different contexts. The first will describe the practices used in setting cut-scores for the Advanced Placement Examinations, voluntary examinations for college-bound students, offered on a national basis annually. These examinations are drawn from a fairly explicit set of curricular expectations, and students take courses to prepare for them specially. A second example comes from the experience of setting performance standards for National Assessment of Educational Progress (NAEP). The third describes the standard-setting processes of states committed to using performance-based assessments.

The Advanced Placement (AP) Program provides a mechanism for secondary school students to take college-level courses and receive college credit from a large number of colleges and universities in the United States based on their performance on AP examinations. The program is sponsored by the College Board and is open to any secondary school that chooses to participate. Each course offered by the program includes a course description that provides recommendations regarding the content and skills to be taught and an examination that is tied to the description. AP Examination results are scored under the auspices of the College Board and reported directly to colleges at the student's request.

Most AP Examinations consist of a multiple-choice section and a free-response section. Although the weights differ from one subject matter examination to another, a composite score is obtained as a weighted combination of the two section scores. The weights for the two sections are reported for the 1986 subject matter examinations in the AP technical manual [College Entrance Examination Board (CEEB), 1988, Table 4.12]. With the exception of Studio Art, which was 100 per cent free response, the relative weights range from 30 per cent multiple choice and 70 per cent free response for History of Art to 75 per cent multiple choice and 25 per cent free response for Music: Listening and Literature. In most cases, the weights are proportional to the time allowed for each section, and the most common weights are 50:50.

Composite scores have ranges that vary from one subject matter examination to another and from one year to another for the same subject. The composite scores are not reported directly, but are used to determine AP grades. The reported AP grades are the scores that are used in college decisions to award college credit and are the scores that are intended to be comparable from year to year.

The AP grades are reported on a five-point scale. The "grades are: 5, very well qualified; 4, well qualified; 3, qualified; 2, possibly qualified; and 1, no recommendation" (CEEB, 1988, pp. 31-32). Performance standards on an AP examination are established through a judgmental process that determines the four grade boundaries (*i.e.*, the performance standards) on the composite score scale. The AP technical manual provides the following description of this judgmental process:

> "Specifying the four grade boundaries is not a simple mechanical process. It can neither be assumed that a given AP Examination is just as difficult as the corresponding examination in a previous year nor that the candidate group is equally strong. Therefore, the Chief Readers select the grade boundaries anew each year for their respective AP Examinations. The choice of each boundary is a judgement base on evidence (CEEB, 1988, pp. 32-33)."

Educational Testing Service staff provide statistical evidence, assistance, and advice, but the Chief Reader is responsible for setting the boundaries. Four types of evidence are presented for use by the Chief Readers: *a)* distributions of grades from previous years; *b)* statistical summaries of candidate performance on multiple-choice items that are repeated from a previous edition of the examination; *c)* a "listing or roster of scores on each section, subsection, and individual free-response question for a sample of candidates at each composite score level"(p. 33); and *d)* results of studies of the comparability of AP and college grades. Chief Readers may also rely on their own experience from review of candidates' free-response answers.

Personal experience in grading and profiles of performance on parts of an examination for various composite scores (the third type of evidence) could be used for most any effort to establish performance standards for a given assessment. The first two types of evidence (previous grade distributions and statistics based on repeated multiple-choice items) are potentially relevant to continuing assessment programs but do not help in the establishment of initial performance standards. Even for a continuing assessment program, the amount of weight given to these first two types of evidence in determining the standards depends upon judgement about the likelihood that the current assessment is more or less demanding than previous assessments and the likelihood that the achievement of the examinees taking the current assessment is better or worse than that of examinees from previous years.

The fourth type of evidence (results of comparability studies of AP and college grades) is perhaps the most unusual and is the only source of evidence that attempts to use an external criterion to inform the standard-setting judgement. Studies of the comparability of AP and college grades are done for all new AP Examinations and are repeated periodically for established AP Examinations (CEEB, 1988). In a typical study of the comparability of AP and college grades, a portion of an AP Examination is administered to college students who are enrolled in courses for which a college would normally award credit based on AP Examination results. Statistical analyses of the results provide a comparison between existing AP grading boundaries and the grades assigned independently by college professors.

The National Assessment of Educational Progress (NAEP) was initially designed in the mid 1960s to provide dependable measures of the progress in student achievement in the United States on a periodic basis. Although the fundamental objective of measuring educational progress for the nation has not changed, NAEP has undergone a variety of modifications during the quarter century since the first National Assessment was administered in 1969. Of particular relevance to the focus of this paper are changes in the ways in which NAEP results are reported.

The early assessments reported results at the individual item level. Released items (referred to as exercises) were presented along with the percentage of students who answered the item correctly or performed the task successfully. Average percent-correct statistics were used to summarize the results, but those statistics have a number of limitations, including the requirement that identical sets of items be used when comparisons are made from one assessment to the next or among results for different grades (see Phillips *et al.,* 1993, for a more complete discussion).

Starting in 1984 the NAEP results were reported in terms of scale scores for each content area. With the exception of the Writing Assessment, the scales were developed using item response theory. Results were summarized using means and selected percentile points. ''Anchor Points,'' which correspond to selected scores on the scale corresponding to the combined age group mean and one or two standard deviations from the mean, were also used. The anchor points were accompanied by descriptions of what students scoring at or near those points were able to do on the assessment (see Phillips *et al.,* 1993).

The first use of performance standards-based reporting of NAEP results was with the 1990 mathematics assessment when the National Assessment Governing Board (NAGB) developed its first set of ''achievement levels.'' Among other responsibilities, the 1988 legislation that created NAGB charged the board with the task of ''identifying appropriate achievement goals for each age and grade in each subject area to be tested under the National Assessment'' (Public Law 100-297). NAGB interpreted this part of the legislation as a mandate to set performance standards for NAEP, which were labelled achievement levels. Although other approaches might have been used to fulfil this responsibility (*e.g.,* establishing targets in terms of the percentage of students scoring above existing anchor points), the approach of setting standards that establish what students should be able to do was consistent with several other national efforts that encouraged the establishment of standards of student achievement (*e.g.,* the National Education Goals Panel, 1992; the National Council on Education Standards and Testing, 1992).

NAGB provided policy definitions for three achievement levels labelled Advanced, Proficient, and Basic. Starting with those policy definitions, panels of judges developed operational definitions of the levels and identified cut-scores for the levels based on ratings of the NAEP item pools for each grade. The work of the panels of judges was used by NAGB to establish three cut-scores that divided the NAEP proficiency scale into four regions: Below Basic, Basic, Proficient, and Advanced.

Three separate evaluations of NAGB's initial effort to set achievement levels for the 1990 mathematics assessment all reached negative conclusions regarding both the process and the outcome of the undertaking (Linn *et al.*, 1991; Stufflebeam *et al.*, 1991; U.S. General Accounting Office, 1993). Among the major criticisms were the following: *a)* the achievement level descriptions and associated exemplar items did not adequately coincide with actual performance of students scoring at a given achievement level; *b)* there was a lack of evidence to support the validity of interpretations invited by the achievement level descriptions; *c)* the NAEP item pool was not adequate to measure the advanced levels; *d)* the judgement process was too demanding for raters; and *e)* the standards were overly dependent on the particular sample of judges. It should be noted that NAGB made adjustments in response to some of the early criticisms (*e.g.,* the lack of coherence of levels from grade to grade noted by Linn *et al.,* 1991) which included the assembly of additional panels of judges. Because of technical difficulties, NAGB also re-established achievement levels for mathematics in 1992. In addition, achievement levels for the reading assessment were established for the first time in 1992.

The 1992 achievement levels also proved to be controversial despite efforts by NAGB and its contractor, the American College Testing Program (1993), to improve the standard-setting process. The first evaluation of the 1992 effort (Burstein *et al.,* 1993), which focused exclusively on the adequacy of the descriptions of the 1992 levels in mathematics, concluded that the descriptions and associated exemplar items did not adequately characterize what students scoring at a given level can do. The lack of correspondence between achievement level descriptions and exemplar items in mathematics, on the one hand, and actual student performance on the assessment, on the other, led to changes in the selection of exemplar items and the descriptions used for the 1992 reading achievement levels. Nonetheless, both the 1992 mathematics and reading achievement levels were judged to be unacceptable in two other evaluations (National Academy of Education, 1993; U.S. General Accounting Office, 1993).

The National Academy of Education (NAE), while strongly affirming "the potential value of voluntary national standards that exemplify challenging curricular and performance expectations" (1993, p. xxiv), was critical of many aspects of process used to set the achievement levels and of the resulting levels and descriptions. The NAE evaluation concluded that the method used as well as "other item judgement methods are fundamentally flawed" (p. 132) and therefore recommended that NAGB and the National Center for Education Statistics "discontinue reporting by achievement levels as used in 1992" (p. 132). As is obvious from the title of its report, *Educational Achievement Standards: NAGB's Approach Yields Misleading Interpretations,* the GAO evaluation was also highly critical (U.S. General Accounting Office, 1993).

The NAE recommended that achievement level results be published separately from the main NAEP results in research and development reports while a longer-range effort is undertaken to establish performance standards on NAEP. NAGB and its consultants (Cizek, 1993; Kane, 1993) have attempted to rebut many of the criticisms of the achievement levels, and the board remains firmly committed to reporting achievement level results.

In an effort to resolve conflicts regarding achievement levels, NAGB and the National Center for Education Statistics sponsored a conference on standard-setting in October 1994. A variety of perspectives were represented at the conference. There was considerable agreement on the desirability of establishing standards, the need to make them understandable to a wide variety of audiences, and the importance of broad representation in the formation of panels of judges. There was also strong support for the creation of descriptions that are valid reflections of what students who meet a given standard of performance know and can do. There was less agreement, however, about the best way to accomplish that end and about the criteria that should be used in evaluating the degree to which the goal was achieved. For example, should students who meet a given standard be able to do all, two-thirds, or a majority of the tasks that are implied by the description?

The other large issue that remained unresolved concerns the judgements that panels of judges are asked to make. The traditional approach, which involves judgements regarding expected performance of students who meet a given standard separately for each individual item or task on an assessment, remains the preferred approach of one group of experts, but continues to be rejected by another group that argues that judgements need to be based on a consideration of a complete record of performance (*e.g.,* the pattern of responses to all assessment items and tasks) for actual students. The latter position is reflected in the report of the National Academy of Education (1993), while the former position continues to be adhered to by NAGB and its consultants.

State assessments

A number of states have adopted or are in the process of developing standards-based reporting procedures for their statewide assessments. This introduction of standards-based reporting coincides with the movement toward a greater reliance on performance assessments and is consistent with the national press for the development of student performance standards (see, for example, National Education Goals Panel, Goals 3 and 4 Technical Planning Group on the Review of Education Standards, 1993).

Performance standards divide the continuum of student attainment on an assessment into two or more levels of achievement. The number of levels varies from state to state. In the 1970s and 1980s many states introduced minimum-competency testing programs that required the establishment of a minimum standard of performance for the award of a high school diploma. Some states still have minimum competency or certification testing programs where the emphasis is on a single, pass-fail standard. The recent emphasis on standard-based reporting, however, usually has more than two levels.

Kentucky, for example, has set three performance standards in each content area resulting in four levels of achievement that are labelled Distinguished, Proficient, Apprentice, and Novice (Trimble, 1994). Each labelled performance level on the Kentucky Information and Reporting System (KIRS) is accompanied by a definition that is intended to communicate what students achieving at that level are able to do. The levels were defined in response to the Kentucky Education Reform Act (KERA) of 1990 requirement that schools be held accountable for increasing the proportion of "successful" students. Hence, the system began by defining the Proficient standard to correspond to a level of performance where a student would be considered successful, which, among other things, is intended to indicate that a student has the "skills necessary to function in a complex and changing civilization" (KERA, 1990). Students who perform at the Novice level demonstrate little, if any, of the skills and understandings defined by the Proficient standard. The Apprentice level is intermediate between Novice and Proficient and students at that level need to provide "tangible evidence of 'making progress' toward the Proficient standard" (Trimble, 1994, p. 47). Distinguished, the highest level, "was established to recognize the accomplishments of a small percentage of students who exceed even the Proficient standard"*(ibid.).*

Maryland has set four standards that yield five levels of achievement for the Maryland School Performance Assessment Program (MSPAP). The numbered levels, where 1 is the highest and 5 is the lowest, are each described by a list of activities that students scoring at that level on the assessment are able to do (e.g., at level 1 in mathematics students are, among other things, able to "make predictions using basic concepts of probability in abstract settings" while students scoring at level 4 are able to "describe relationships among data in a chart/table", Westat, 1993, pp. 16-17).

Results on the California Learning Assessment System (CLAS) are reported in terms of six performance levels, with 6 denoting the highest level of performance and 1 the lowest (CTB/McGraw-Hill, 1994). As is true for the MSPAP, the CLAS levels are not labelled, but each is defined by a description of what students who score at that level can do.

The procedures used by states to establish performance standards vary in their details but share a number of common features. Usually, the process has two key components: a) the definition of performance levels; and b) the mapping of scores on the assessment into the performance levels. Both components rely on judgements of one or more panels that are assembled specifically for that purpose. Although described separately here, the tasks of developing definitions and mapping assessment results into performance levels are sometimes done iteratively through three or more steps (e.g., define levels, map assessment scores into levels, revise level definitions).

Definitions of performance levels typically start with a predetermined number of levels. Panellists may be asked to review a state curriculum framework or content standards as well as actual assessment tasks. They may begin with policy statements regarding the standards that are provided by the state legislature or the state school board. As was implied above, the legislative requirement of defining "successful" students led to an initial focus on the Proficient standard in Kentucky, for example. A higher standard, Distinguished, was added to provide recognition for exceptional achievement and lower standard. Apprentice, was added to acknowledge students who were making progress but had not yet achieved the Proficient level, and with three standards, the fourth performance level, Novice, was defined by default.

Starting with a broad framework and possibly general policy-level description of standards, panels of judges typically are asked to develop and refine definitions of performance levels. The emphasis is usually on defining performance that students "should" achieve and hence is forward looking rather than purely normative in nature. States vary in how closely tied the definitions of levels are to the actual assessments. In Maryland, for example, panellists were instructed to include in the description of a given proficiency level only student outcomes or aspects of performance that were actually assessed (Westat, 1993, p. 14). This procedure is intended to avoid problems that have been encountered in other assessments where the descriptions included aspects of performance that are not assessed and therefore may not validly describe what students who achieve a given level actually know or are able to do.

In some assessments, the levels correspond naturally to the score categories defined by scoring rubrics used for open-ended student responses. This direct correspondence between a scoring rubric and the performance levels used for reporting is, perhaps, most common for writing exercises. In some states writing assessments, a single prompt may be used at each grade where students are assessed. Student essays are scored according to state scoring rubrics, which typically have 4, 5, or 6 score levels. With results from a single performance task scored on 4- to 6-point scale it is natural to simply use those scores to correspond to performance levels.

Scoring rubrics are also sometimes translated directly into performance levels where multiple tasks are included in the state assessment. For example, although each student responded to only one prompt, several different prompts were administered to different samples of students in the 1993 CLAS reading assessment. Student responses were all scored on a 6-point scale and those six score points were judged to correspond directly to the six CLAS performance levels by the committees assembled to develop descriptions of performance levels and map student performance on the assessment into those levels (CTB/McGraw-Hill, 1994).

Where assessment scores have more possible values than performance levels, some process is needed to map scores into levels for purposes of reporting. Most often the mapping consists of setting a series of cut-scores that divide the scores into as many ranges as there are performance levels. Scales based on item response theory models such as the ones used in each grade and content area for the MSPAP provide a direct way of arranging student performance and assessment tasks on the same scale. As was done for MSPAP, judges can be asked to identify regions of the scale where the associated items correspond most closely to the definitions of student performance for a given level. By a process of averaging, those judgements are readily converted to cut points on the scale which then map the scale scores for students into the proficiency levels.

With a small number of open-ended assessment tasks the judgement process may involve a review of exemplar student performances corresponding to each possible score. Such a process was followed in Kentucky where content committees reviewed sets of student responses to three tasks per student. The sets of student responses corresponded to each of 10 possible score points (3 to 12 for the sum of scores of 1-4 on three tasks per student), and judges were asked to convert each of the scores on the 10-point scale into one of the four Kentucky proficiency levels (National Academy of Education, 1993).

A slightly more complicated mapping procedure is illustrated by the conversion of student assessment results in mathematics to performance levels on the 1993 CLAS. As part of the matrix sampling design, each student responded to one open-ended mathematics problem and seven multiple-choice items on the 1993 CLAS. Rather than trying to place both open-ended tasks and multiple-choice items on a single scale, judges were asked to review the 32 cells of a 4 by 8 matrix of possible student outcomes (4 possible score levels on the open-ended task by the 8 possible scores of 0 to 7 for the number correct score on the multiple-choice items). For each of the 16 possible combinations of open-ended tasks with sets of multiple-choice items used in the 1993 CLAS matrix sampling design, judges were asked to map each of the 32 cells into the six performance levels used by California.

Standard-based reporting of results by states is a relatively recent phenomenon. Thus, it is too early for any comprehensive evaluation of the approach. Certainly, none of the state standard-setting efforts has undergone the kind of stringent evaluation to which the NAGB standard-setting effort for NAEP was subjected. Two things are clear at this stage, however. First, the standards-based reporting of results is popular among state policy-makers and directors of assessment programs. Second, there is strong encouragement for increased use of performance standards in both federal and state legislation. States are encouraged to develop performance standards by the Goals 2000: Educate America Act that was signed into law by President Clinton in the spring of 1994. That encouragement is reinforced by requirements in the subsequently enacted Improving America's Schools Act that authorizes $7.4 billion for the Title 1 compensatory-education program targeted at schools serving children from low-income families. Schools receiving Title 1 funds will be required to report progress in terms of the percentage of students who are meeting advanced, proficient, or partially proficient levels of performance. Hence, an increased emphasis on the use of performance standards by states can be anticipated.

Performance standards and inferences from assessment

The key issue in the design of performance standards is the degree to which the standards are set with an eye to the purpose for which the assessment is designed. If the purpose of the assessment is to operationalize a quota in which limited spaces are allocated to the best students, then the details of performance assessments may not be of much interest, save the estimation of the likelihood of misclassifying individuals. If the performance standards are set to provide targets for educational systems to reach, then it is important that the attributes used to define the highest levels of performance are those which the system can address. Very little research has been conducted to validate performance standards, particularly those that include specification of student response attributes. The validation of standards raises deeper questions of assessment purposes. Are the purposes of assessments fundamentally to make predictions about students' success in the workplace, or in higher or further education? When educational systems serve increasingly diverse students, questions of the postmodern type abound. Should all students reach the same standards? Are there comparable but different standards students of different backgrounds or different aspirations might meet? How is comparability established to assure that systems of multi-tiered quality do not develop? How does one push for national educational improvement in a federal system, with strong local and site control of goals, curriculum, and testing programs? How do we manage the tension between homogeneity and adaptation when we have different approaches, strategies, and belief systems in the public?

Finally, the United States know little about how to set up procedures to yield quality and valid performance standards. Who should participate? What content, school or technical background should participants have, if any? At the present, approaches to setting performance standards vary considerably, from those that simply attempt to arrive at consensus to those that systematically provide various kinds of information about students, normative performance, and model answers to the standard-setting group. As noted above, the relationship is yet unclear between the design of scoring rubrics, created in part to achieve high technical standards, and the development of reporting categories, which need to have public credibility. Should rubrics and standards be simultaneously developed? Does it matter which comes first?

Last, there is a set of issues around the use of performance standards to make judgements about institutions as well as individuals. Although different viewpoints clearly exist, there is some sentiment to provide contextual information to aid in the understanding of levels of attained performance. Context can be introduced by statistical adjustments of scores, to show how students would have performed had they had similar backgrounds, school or classroom sizes, etc. The statistical adjustment approach is criticized because it masks, and usually overestimates the measured performance of the least well performing students in the system. Other strategies for contextualizing performance include the concurrent reporting of collateral data regarding school resources, student backgrounds, and information about students' opportunity to learn assessed material. This set of information may be useful not only to help the target audiences to understand why different institutions outperform others, but to guide improvement of performance.

Without doubt, the U.S., with its decentralized approach to education, has a complex path to negotiate if it is to emerge with high quality performance standards that meet educational and public criteria for effectiveness, utility, and credibility.

Bibliography

Advanced Systems in Measurement and Evaluation Inc. (1992), *Kentucky Instructional Results Information System 1991-1992,* technical report, Dover, NH.

American College Testing Program (1993), *Setting Achievement Levels on the 1992 National Assessment of Educational Progress in Mathematics, Reading and Writing: A Technical Report on Reliability and Validity,* Iowa City, IA.

BURSTEIN, L., KORETZ, D. M., LINN, R. L., SUGRUE, B., NOVAK, J., LEWIS, E., and BAKER, E. L. (1993), *The Validity of Interpretations of the 1992 NAEP Achievement Levels in Mathematics* (Technical Report), University of California, National Center for Research on Evaluation, Standards, and Student Testing, Los Angeles.

CIZEK, G. (1993), "Reactions to National Academy of Education Report, Setting performance standards for student achievement", Unpublished manuscript, University of Toledo, Toledo, OH.

College Entrance Examination Board (1988), *The College Board Technical Manual for the Advanced Placement Program,* New York.

CTB/McGraw-Hill (1994), *California Learning Assessment System, 1993,* Preliminary technical report, Monterey, CA.

KANE, M. (1993), "Comments on the NAE Evaluation of the NAGB Achievement Levels", Unpublished manuscript, University of Wisconsin, Madison, WI.

Kentucky Education Reform Act of 1990, 158.645.

LINN, R. L., KORETZ, D. M., BAKER, E. L., and BURSTEIN, L. (1991), *The Validity and Credibility of the Achievement Levels for the 1990 National Assessment of Educational Progress in mathematics,* University of California, National Center for Research on Evaluation, Standards, and Student Testing, Los Angeles.

National Academy of Education (1993), *Setting Performance Standards for Student Achievement. A Report of the National Academy of Education Panel on the Evaluation of the NAEP Trial State Assessment: An Evaluation of the 1992 Achievement Levels,* Stanford, CA.

National Council on Education Standards and Testing (1992), *Raising Standards for American Education: A Report to Congress, the Secretary of Education, the National Education Goals Panel, and the American People,* U.S. Government Printing Office, Washington DC.

National Education Goals Panel (1992), *The National Education Goals Report, 1992: Building a nation of leaders,* U.S. Government Printing Office, Washington DC.

National Education Goals Panel, Goals 3 and 4 Technical Planning Group on the Review of Education Standards (1993), *Promises to Keep: Creating High Standards for American Students,* Washington, DC.

PHILLIPS, G. W., MULLIS, I. V. S., BOURQUE, M. L., WILLIAMS, P. L., HAMBLETON, R. K., OWEN, E. H., and BARTON, P. E. (1993), *Interpreting NAEP scales,* National Center for Education Statistics, Washington DC.

Public Law 100-297 (1988), *National Assessment of Educational Progress Improvement Act (Article No. USC 1221),* Washington, DC.

STUFFLEBEAM, D. L., JAEGER, R. M. and SCRIVEN, M. (1991), *Summative Evaluation of the National Assessment Governing Board's Inaugural Effort to Set Achievement Levels on the National Assessment of Educational Progress,* National Assessment Governing Board, Washington DC.

TRIMBLE, C. S. (1994), "Ensuring educational Accountability", in T. Guskey (ed.), *High Stakes Performance Assessment: Perspectives on Kentucky's Education Reform,* Corwin Press, Thousand Oaks, CA, pp. 37-54.

U.S. General Accounting Office (1993), *Educational Achievement Standards: NAGB's Approach Yields Misleading Interpretations,* Report No. GAO/PEMD-93-12, U.S. Government Printing Office, Washington DC.

Westat, Inc. (1993), *Establishing Proficiency Levels and Descriptions for the 1992 Maryland School Performance Assessment Program (MSPAP),* Rockville, MD.

SYNTHESIS

by

Eva L. Baker

The purpose of this synthesis is to explore the implications for educational reform in the United States of the OECD comparative study of performance standards. To provide some context for the reader, the synthesis briefly reprises major shifts in the intellectual underpinnings of U.S. educational reform and reports on its present prospects. The major analytical section, however, posits a functional model of reform that includes key elements thought to be necessary for successful operation of a dynamic educational system. As a special case, performance standards will be characterized as they support different elements and functions of reform as described in the country case studies provided by OECD scholars, with particular emphasis on the U.S. setting. Finally, a discussion will consider the ways the U.S. and other governments could profit from the OECD case studies of performance standards.

U.S. background

Educational reform, for reasons of constitutional authority, tradition and continuing predisposition, arises from three levels of authority: local, state, and national sources. Unlike the systems of the majority of OECD countries, in the U.S. the national (federal) authority possesses relatively weak responsibility for the design and virtually no responsibility for the actual operation of educational systems. It is clear as well that in the last twenty years, state governments have demonstrated increased leadership in the area of educational policy, particularly on matters of school finance, teacher certification, and the expectations for school programs. Major changes to fiscal policies have resulted in states bearing an increasing share for the support of schools. As a consequence, states have been aggressive in their pursuit of policy revisions. A number of specific policies have been addressed to educational reform including the development or substantial modification of curriculum frameworks to guide desired student attainments, the introduction of goals related to success in the workplace, the development of assessment systems at the state level to monitor or to certify student achievement in academic and work skills areas, and the creation of explicit rules for the adoption of texts and other instructional materials purchased from the commercial sector. While these policy areas are traditional features of many OECD country systems, attention to these areas in the U.S. at the state level has led to an attempt to consolidate at state centers new and stronger educational authority and represents a net shift from local control to more centralized authority over education. Given the size of some states, for instance 30 million or more citizens in California alone, policy reform of this scope is easily analogous to that of some of OECD nations.

Attributes of educational reform

Although thoroughly discussed in the individual country reports, it is worth revisiting at a summative level the model of educational reform that appears to have international currency. First, there is a dual emphasis on improving educational quality and improving access to educational services for increasingly diverse student populations, goals which result in the well-known North American tension between excellence and equity. Second, there is a sense that educational practices and outcomes must be increasingly relevant to the demands of the societies in which they are embedded as well as to expectations to maintain international economic competitiveness. Third, the fitful history of educational reform has induced the view that educational change should be systemic, that is, it must consider in parallel key parts of the endeavor so that changes in one area will support goals and processes of other areas. For example, curriculum change should be supported by concurrent adjustments in teacher preparation. Fourth, education must be a cost-sensitive enterprise, and expenditures must be carefully justified in the light of their impact. Consequently, greater interest has been expressed in the accountability of educational systems, the ways in which they demonstrate their impact, and the ways in which relatively inexpensive sources of information can be used to improve them.

These components of educational reform are not without their critics inside and external to the educational field. Critics from within the field note with some alarm the process of centralization, quantification, and the influence of economic metaphors in educational policy formation. There is concern that the idea of systemic reform somehow equates to Utopian notions of education, notions bound to fail because they emphasize idealized and uniform views. Others, from outside education, are skeptical about systemic educational models, particularly those embodying new views of learning, teaching and assessment. Failure to do a good job using old methods does not automatically build confidence in attempts to meet more complex and ambitious goals. Some worry that the moving target of educational reform is simply a device to avoid real accountability that comes with a stable system.

A functional model of educational reform in multinational use

The following model (see Figure 1) is offered as an overview of educational reform applicable in various countries. The framework is similar to those previously employed to represent descriptive models such as educational indicators. Such models rely on categories of inputs, processes, and outputs and posit a loose, causal relationship. The reform model differs from indicator models in a major way, for input, process, and output categories serve to classify functions served by reform in various countries rather than as a structure to subsume data sources. Each of the categories could be expanded almost exponentially. For example, the contextual inputs could be greatly augmented to provide details about traditions, and expectations. For purposes of this analysis, they are presented at their present high level of abstraction so that international audiences may apply them to the relevant array of societal conditions. This general model will be explicated in the light of the problem of setting useful performance standards for educational attainment. It could be similarly applied to other educational issues, such as governance, teacher development, and curriculum development.

Figure 1. **Applying the reform model to performance standards**

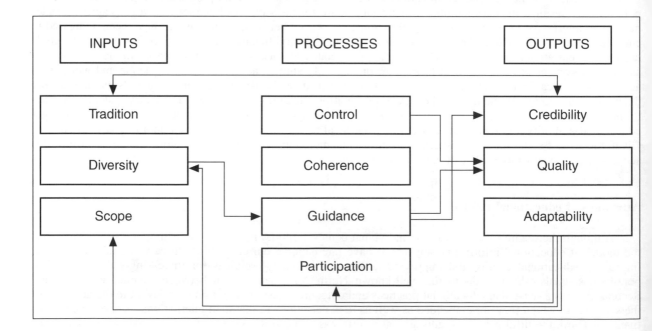

Source: Eva Baker for OECD.

212

Performance standards

In the United States, the use of the term "performance standards" is subject to wide interpretation. In uses in formalized procedures of instructional development and training, for instance, in the military or in business and industry, performance standards signify the level of attainment groups of individuals need to meet. Most commonly these were expressed as percentages of correct scores on a pool of discrete test items, although in some versions they included the goal statement of how many individuals, for instance, 80 per cent, would need to meet the desired percentage of achievement. In other cases, where responses were more qualitative, performance standards were set by specifying attributes that the criterion example would have to meet, such as "no spelling errors" in an essay. In the present iteration of the interpretation of the term, the use of proficiency levels or cut-scores continues for some to refer to criteria used to classify students as very successful, adequate, or unsuccessful. For other users, however, the term performance standards is used to signify the behavior students are expected to exhibit to demonstrate their achievement. Some educators consider performance standards operationalized by examples of assessment tasks students complete, such as solving problems with particular characteristics, or interpreting literature of certain types. In the international community, much broader interpretations of performance standards are made. For some, they are the descriptions of the expectations of the system, not only including what levels of attainment will be reached but related to broad distributions of educational access, for example, 10 per cent of students will matriculate to the highest levels of postsecondary education.

In the United States, definitions of performance standards remain relatively concrete. A key question in the U.S. relates to the validity of these performance standards, however expressed, insofar as they communicate adequately the desired end-states of students at varying curricular points. This question is not surprising in the light of the quantitative and research orientation of U.S. academics.

A variety of approaches are used to establish formal, public performance standards. One common strategy to determine levels of achievement desired involves the application of judgment. Professional judgment of teachers, subject-matter experts, or other academic or school-based constituencies brought together for this particular purpose is perhaps the most frequent approach, varying in details of group composition, the level of abstraction of the task, types of directions or data provided, and guidance by authority. In recent years, these standard-setting groups frequently have been expanded to include various representatives of the public, including those from business and other non-educational sectors, as a tactic to expand the base of judgment and to build constituency support for the resulting product.

There have been other, more technical approaches used to augment judgmental strategies for setting performance standards. One such technique depends upon estimating the number of classifications to which students will be assigned and then predicting the likelihood of misclassifications. False-positive or false-negative probabilities can be estimated, and policy can be set in the light of which kind of error is seen to be more grievous. Another approach is to take various samples of student performance, treat them as replicates, and examine stability of classifications. Classification error obviously depends upon the quality of the measures used to generate scores as well as the levels selected for boundaries between categories.

At the heart of the discussion of performance standards is what they might be used for. Clearly there is global intent that they guide the development of the measurement system and the instruction designed to develop desired student accomplishment. There is also the desire to use them to set standards for individuals (in the case of certification of performance by examination) and institutions (in the case of determining whether schools are making adequate progress in educational reform). Just as analysts have questioned whether a single test or set of measures can be aptly used for a variety of purposes, there remains the question of whether publicly specified performance levels can simultaneously serve multiple purposes with equal validity.

Let's consider elements in the model as they play out in the development and character of performance standards. Notice that the relationships as indicated by directional arrows in Figure 1 are complex and their strength will differ from country to country. In considering the developments in the U.S. with respect to the model, it will be shown that the focus on performance standards is undertaken to strengthen system processes of control, coherence, guidance, and participation, as well as to set clearer boundaries for the measurement quality of educational attainments.

Tradition

Tradition refers to the cultural values and operational expectations for the education system. It includes the extent to which education is perceived as a primary value in the general society and how that value is distributed among sectors in the society. More refined analyses would reveal whether the value held for education is attributed to its contribution to a strong economy, to the development of individual autonomy and flexibility, or to the development of an academic elite, among other options. A second factor influenced by tradition is the perceived effectiveness of the educational system. Such perceptions are influenced by the extent to which various sectors of society assume the competence to criticize the system of education, or at least certain of its components. In the United States, for example, it has been commonplace to criticize the productivity and impact of the precollegiate educational system, but to trumpet the quality and effects of the network of colleges and universities. This tendency is connected to another feature of national educational tradition, that is, the level of trust accorded to classroom teachers. The interaction of teachers' reputations as acknowledged educational experts contributes to and is formed by the value and reputational status of the educational enterprise as a whole. In the recent past, United States teachers have held relatively low professional status. The quality of their training has not been highly regarded, the selectivity of the system has been reputed to be relatively low, and thus dependence upon teacher judgment as a strongly valued indicator of student attainment has dropped precipitously. The category of tradition in this model also subsumes historically important characteristics of governance, structure, and operations in educational systems-in effect, where the balance is struck between centralized and devolved responsibility, how professional and lay responsibilities interact, and how the quality of educational outcomes is typically assessed. Traditions in governance in the U.S., with the assumption of educational control sited at the local level, support the lack of codified or otherwise explicit educational standards. It is only the move to more uniformity, articulated as the need for comparisons, national standards and national tests, that has required the explicit statement of performance standards at the state level.

Diversity

Diversity refers simultaneously to a number of important areas. First, we must consider the range or uniformity of expectations for the schools, both in view of environments for teaching and in the light of the student competencies they intend to develop. Locally controlled systems have promulgated somewhat different educational expectations. It is also clear that systems that predominantly serve identifiable subsets of the student population many times develop different expectations and standards for those students. Systems such as those in the U.S. deal with diversity in every respect: the size of the geographical area served by the educational system; the density of population; the socioeconomic experiences of the students; the average residential period in the service area; the languages spoken in the home; the diversity (or lack thereof) of the teaching staff in terms of cultural and language background, preparation, and age; the level of financial support for the schools; the type and frequency of parental engagement in education.

A correlated issue relative to diversity is the degree to which the education formally acknowledges its existence. Acknowledgment can take the form of the recognition and redress of differential access to educational opportunities and the nature of efforts made to extend educational options to various constituencies. To be considered here are whether accommodations and adaptations for individuals and groups are in place, what the nature is of such extensions, and, importantly, whether these adjustments are perceived as equitable. In the U.S., the public discourse has mushroomed on the topic of accommodations in both education and workplace for groups heretofore designated as disadvantaged. For instance, arguments have been strongly put forth to attenuate the compensatory assistance given to minority groups by educational systems in higher education admission decisions. While the impetus of these accommodations has been to increase fairness in the system, the racial or ethnic bases of them are criticized by sectors of the society arguing that the remedies introduce new forms of inequity. Alternatives proposed include accommodations based on economic disadvantage, an approach likely to be criticized as well. Here questions about diversity intertwine with views about uniformity. Are performance standards intended to be identical for all students, regardless of background, motivation, and capability? Are students permitted flexibility, for instance, in the selection of areas in which they wish to become especially accomplished? Are the minimums or core areas the same for all? Are differential interpretations of performance of individuals or schools permissible? For example, if statistical adjustments are made to account for disadvantage in educational background, prior attainment, resources, or socioeconomic status, are performance standards providing the level of guidance desired? Will they be interpreted appropriately? Do they foster equity? No complete answers exist for these questions, which go to the heart of discussions of fairness.

Scope

A third category of input or contextual issue involves the scope of the education system. Scope embraces the concepts of the range of goals served by the system, its breadth and ambition. This analysis involves the elaboration of the types of educational institutions available, the ambition and extensiveness of their curriculum offerings, the extent to which priorities are evinced in the design and operation of school programs and educational institutions, and the collaboration – either active or de facto – of other public and private entities with the formal educational system in meeting its needs. Scope is closely related with resources and the extent to which educational systems can be said to be well resourced given the range of action they undertake.

The processes of educational reform: performance standards as strategy

Educational reform operates to support systemic functions. The functions identified include how the system operations and performance are controlled, how coherence and focus are supported, how guidance is shared, and the degree to which participation from various constituencies is desirable and productive. In this analysis, it is clear that performance standards may play important roles in these functions, a point illustrated in the U.S. case.

Control

When reviewing the educational systems of many OECD countries, centralized control allows for systematic and relatively rapid change. Control is formulated as the set of procedures, requirements, and sanctions used to manage the direction of systems. When authority is centralized, it is relatively easy to promulgate new regulations (although differences in compliance are bound to exist). Centralized expectations about curriculum goals, about choice of instructional materials, about teacher selection, training, certification, and employment may be made clear. Variations in control include the number of recognized levels of authority and strategies to maintain the focus of their attention and response. A second dimension of control is the locus of initiation for activity. Are there mechanisms for initiation at other than top levels? Is such initiation an expected or unusual event? Control also involves the allocation of rewards and sanctions. Their assignment depends upon the clarity of understanding among system personnel about consequences of action, as well as the distribution between positive and negative sanctions invoked. Other variables related to the perception of control are the intensity, interval of consequences and the degree to which there is explicit linkage of system performance with sanctions and rewards. Control may be located in a number of places: in government through legislation or regulation; in professional societies related to standards of state-of-the-art practice and ethics; or, more informally, in the pressure exerted by peers or community to adhere to particular standards of behavior. One clear approach to control involves the application of identified quality control mechanisms. Countries with exit examinations possess a mechanism to control educational offerings, through the creation of boards of studies and examination councils and reports of results of student examinations.

In countries with decentralized educational authorities, the mechanisms existing for control may also reside in the perceived responsiveness of systems to local needs, for example, through local elections of school governance groups. Control of quality has also been typically exerted through regulation and standards of practice. Regulations may specify how much time students must engage in particular subjects, the number of courses in teacher preparation sequences, requirements to teach health and life skills in addition to standards curriculum, and rules about offering instruction in various languages. Standards of practice shift so that teachers in the 1950s might have been judged on their lecture style, in the 1960s on their ability to deliver up-to-date subject matters and classroom management, in the 1970s on the quality of their behavioral objectives for students, in the 1980s on their ability to group children heterogeneously, and in the 1990s on their ability to teach interdisciplinary topics. In other words, although wise practitioners and academics decry the practice, there remains the search for and temporary fixation on the "best" approach to a particular area – a quest sure to fail within each country given the individual strengths and weakness of teachers and students. As a result, techniques or methods have been promoted as the true solution to educational ills in a particular discipline or for a type of student. This focus on process has not worked because standards of practice are subject to unstable beliefs. These views are derived from a variety of sources, including experimentation, extrapolation, research and development, or novelty. This instability, borne of the relatively fleeting consensus on desirable strategies and the continuing importance of local autonomy in the U.S., has resulted in educational systems that lurch sporadically from solution to solution. As a result, a focus on process control is almost always out of date. Instead, joining most OECD countries, the U.S. has begun to strongly focus on educational attainment. In state after state in the U.S., numbers of regulations specifying classroom requirements are being reduced, with the assumption that increased freedom of action will support the accomplishment of desired goals. Nonetheless, the specter of process control remains embedded in the nature of certain curriculum goals and in the performance standards set for them. For example, in the state of California, the review of language arts goals shows that it is difficult to disentangle the support of a "whole-language curriculum" from the more general desire to have children read with comprehension and write lucidly. The very manner in which performance standards are phrased communicates preferences for educational methods, preferences which may or may not be very well justified. Thus, even the use of performance standards to transfer attention away from specification of educational process to accountable performance becomes corrupted by the infusion in their formulation of the educational methods of the moment

Coherence

A second general and desirable feature of reform is its coherence. Reform efforts should mutually support and relate to one another in a logical way. At the broadest level, for example, teacher preparation programs should connect and support particular curriculum innovations. Indeed, the principle is even true when one looks at the system from the child's point of view. For instance, it could be argued that children should be given instruction in science that is compatible with overall approaches to problem solving to be engendered by the educational system. Otherwise, children may have difficulty in sorting through when to use various approaches. Another formulation of coherence can be drawn from the extent to which students in the educational system share in common experiences that would provide policy-makers and teachers with a clear understanding of the order and nature of their learning. In many OECD countries, national curriculum statements and monitoring present one approach to the creative preservation of coherence in education.

In decentralized systems such as those in the U.S., sources of coherence have been weak, for the most part. Because curriculum statements have not had much functional power, sources of coherence are almost always indirect. One source has been the expected experiences of teachers in preparation in higher education. Institutions of higher education develop their own teacher preparation curricula, and even the same course at the same institution may have vastly different content when taught by a different professor. So it is chimerical to think that coherence would be a product of teachers' postsecondary experience. Another potential source of coherence of experiences for students occurs through their examination processes. But because no common exit examinations exist in the U.S., this is only a potential outcome. University admissions tests, for the most part, emphasize general verbal, quantitative and analytic ability as opposed to the mastery of particular domains of knowledge and do not provide sufficient guidance for curriculum design.

In the U.S., system coherence seems to have come in the past from three major and disjunct sources. First is the promulgation of course requirements for entry into colleges and universities. Although these differ at the margin, they in general emphasize experiences in literature, higher mathematics, laboratory science, and to a lesser extent, foreign language. Their impact might be thought to be limited to only the college bound student, but in fact, the impact of academic standards has at least superficially affected most educational systems, without regard to their principal clients. A second source of coherence relates to the materials used in classrooms. Relatively few commercial publishers provide most of the textbooks and adjunct instructional materials for students. The design of these materials is market-driven and influenced by preferences, specifications, and adoptions of relatively few large states, as publishers are unable to adapt materials profitably for smaller groups of users. Some states and local districts provide a list of options for schools to select among, undermining in the name of adaptation and local autonomy, common experiences derived from common materials. It is also a reasonable speculation that the reliance on technology-delivered instruction will permit adaptation to local requirements not heretofore possible because of cost. A recent and hopeful development is the expectation to evaluate instructional materials, texts or computer-based programs in terms of the extent to which they support explicit statements of goals or standards.

It is obvious that the mere statement of performance standards does nothing in itself to ensure reflexively their coherence, particularly from the viewpoint of an individual child. In the early stages of the development of standards it appears that it is hard to keep raging educational ambition in check, and content and performance standards have proliferated beyond that which any individual child could learn, no matter how gifted or industrious. Too many competitive, discrete educational topics are deemed essential. Worse, no strategy for sorting through and balancing desires with feasibility has emerged. This profusion of options has created another opportunity for incoherence in that, as a practical matter, public policy groups must pick and choose from among desirable outcomes those that they believe the system can foster. Often this selection is more of a political bargain than an intellectual enterprise, with topics and goals traded off in one subject for decision-making prerogative in another. Nonetheless, because it is still the case that performance standards are regarded as public documents, their explanation makes it possible to note gross inconsistencies and gaps, and to create, over time, better formulations of goals and intentions. There is also the persistent, and unanswerable question about the optimal sort of coherence to be desired in any educational system.

Guidance

If control is formulated as the means of managing the direction of a system, and coherence is conceived as the character of desired interrelationships and supportive opportunities, guidance consists of the form and types of information provided that are needed to generate willing compliance by participants. It is a softer, gentler form of control. Guidance provides cues for translating requirements into procedures and actions and usually permits some interpretive latitude. Curriculum handbooks, teacher manuals, and teacher development workshops are all traditional forms of providing guidance to school practitioners about the goals and approaches desirable for educational improvement. In certain countries, the use of inspectorates or quality assurance groups provides guidance relevant either to particular purposes or programs, or in the general direction of improvement. Based on site visits and face-to-face meetings with skilled professionals, inspections may have a technical assistance and collaborative character. On the other hand, they may verge toward the control side of the model when they are seen as accreditation events.

Guidance can be inferred from observing the workings of another educational setting or system. In relatively informal ways, systems can perceive directions, strategies, and solutions to local problems. The opportunity systems for these outward looks, even if the field of vision is relatively restrictive, can provide an index of the extent to which guided innovation is valued.

Performance standards can serve as another source of assistance for teachers and curriculum developers, provided the standards are conceived and conveyed in an appropriate fashion. One major way performance standards can provide help to teachers is to clarify the order and nature of expectations for different-aged learners or for the same-aged students at different attainment levels. If performance standards in a particular area, such as written composition, have both increasing task complexity and increasingly rigorous standards for use to judge the quality of student responses, because of either student age or the achievement level (*e.g.*, proficient compared to advanced), then we can expect the stated progression to have clear instructional implications for students. Secondly, the details of the standards, particularly the enunciation of essential quality criteria, provide particular cues on how instruction itself should be organized. For instance, if students' writing ability is to be judged in part by their reliance on concrete illustrations of general points, then teachers would be guided to provide subtasks in instruction that involve the identification and aptness of such illustrations. One of the problems with performance standards, of course, is that they may be written in too general a form to provide specific instructional cues; on the other hand, they may be equally useless if they are expressed solely in quantitative terms, such as the percentage of children who scored at a particular scale value on a test. One potential point of difficulty is finding a way to assure that the description of the performance standard, the verbal intent, matches well with the actual test or assessment given to students, the ways students' answers were judged, and the analysis and reporting approaches adopted. At any of the points it is possible to move, perhaps only subtly, to results that actually have a very different operational meaning than what was articulated in the performance standards statements.

Participation

A fourth characteristic of educational reform processes that differentiates OECD countries is in the area of participation in educational decision-making. Participation differs in countries in terms of the involvement constituencies, the relative dominance of particular groups, the timing and type of engagement, and lines of communication provided to support the transmission of, and reaction to, ideas.

The degree to which participation is seen to be desirable is influenced strongly by traditions of responsibility and authority, general satisfaction with the system's effectiveness and scope, and the diversity of the publics served by educational programs. Constituency participation in setting performance standards is also influenced by the technical character of the approach taken. For the most part, discussions of performance standards and their development have involved various members of the education constituency: teachers, subject matter experts, administrators, policy-makers, and parents. In most cases, representatives of the public at large and specifically business and industry have been included. Where standards have been developed for workforce expectations, the distribution has been appropriately modified. Other groups involved in these processes have been selected because they typify important classes of student interests, for example, those with various ethnic, language, socioeconomic, gender, and racial backgrounds.

The differential dominance of these groups changes with time and with perceptions of competence and power. Teachers, although usually providing major membership to standard-setting exercises, have in general been less prominent in recent efforts, giving way to members of the public and the business sectors.

Participation ranges from functional to symbolic; both ends of the distribution have utility in moving educational agenda forward. One way to determine the extent to which participation seriously informs outcomes is to study the type of engagement and timing of participatory activity. Some groups initiate, design, review, decide and ratify. Others provide only a few functions, and the differences in types of engagement depend upon the extent to which authority is assigned to the participating groups. Furthermore, the point of entry into the process and the amount of time available similarly cue intent, for instance, in the case where groups are brought late into a process to respond to drafted material. Finally, it is important to determine the degree to which lines of communication are encouraged to enhance participation. Good communication permits the deeper understanding of the issues but also raises control issues related to the extent to which the participation is to be broad based and provide a summary of widespread views, whether the representative speaks as an individual on behalf of an untapped group, and the extent to which more than one constituency is encouraged to caucus and consolidate perceptions. Participation in the statement of U.S. performance standards has shown almost every variation described above.

System outcomes

In these times, educational systems emphasize their improvement in reaching goals by measuring performance. In the previous discussion of performance standards the role of outcome measurement and levels of attainment was described. At this point, it is important to moderate the analysis of outcomes by raising three important dimensions to their development and use: credibility, quality, and adaptability.

Credibility

The historical investment in standardized measures paired with the openness of criticism of the U.S. educational system have raised credibility questions about the measurement of educational goals. The specification of new kinds of performance standards has suggested changes in the types of measures that should be used, away from multiple-choice commercially available tests toward more performance-based assessment. New approaches upset the stability of the system and raise questions about the appropriateness of prior beliefs. It is hard to argue briefly and non technically why existing measures may be no longer sufficient. Skepticism about the difficulty, fairness, and trustworthiness of new examinations has undermined in some locations the entire reform agenda. Beliefs are expressed that new types of assessments have been adopted as means to avoid rather than to strengthen accountability. Experiences in the U.S. suggest that it is essential to conduct a better analysis of important audiences to address about prospective changes in the measurement base. A focus only on the educational community, even augmented by participatory groups, is much too narrow in a society where many educational institutions are viewed with growing suspicion. Each of the identified audiences will need messages and ideas tailored so that they can understand, evaluate, and possibly support change.

One negative factor in the development of credibility has been the tight schedule for educational change. Paradoxically, credibility depends on both having enough time to educate communities and simultaneously moving rapidly enough to be regarded as an active, directed entity. No ready set of mechanisms or approaches has yet been developed to promote credibility, save in those cases where the electorate voted for massive educational change. In those cases where change is incremental and emerges over time, the need to provide clear examples of new measures is a first step. These examples should be supported by evidence of their impact, if any, in other locations, or at least testimonials by reputable experts from across the political spectrum. For example, indicating that performance-based measures have been widely used in the evaluation of business performance and of the combat readiness of military personnel provides a credible source of evidence for some.

Quality

Real credibility grows from high-quality measures. In the U.S., claims for new measures have continued to outstrip their documentation. Some technical issues related to the ability to provide individual scores that meet U.S. legal challenges to fairness and prediction remain. The fact that the scientific base of new assessments is rapidly evolving may help in the future but at the present time leads to equivocation, reliance on future promise, and only occasionally to useful recommendations.

The estimates of quality of assessments, and of the trust we place in the performance standards they are thought to represent, depend upon our concepts of validity. The various purposes for assessments and performance standards and the number of purposes assigned to any particular examination create different technical requirements. Among the many questions are the following: the size of the domain assessed, the boundaries on interdisciplinary domains, the types of cognitive demands, the degree to which performance generalizes, as well as issues of reliability, stability, and fairness to students from various backgrounds. Each of these areas requires programmatic research in order to provide satisfactory guidance for design, use, and reporting of new measures. Will there be time and resources to develop the appropriate scientific base for new assessments before skepticism, overpromising, and retreats to earlier measurement approaches take over? The answer, at least in the U.S., is not at all clear.

Adaptability

The final point in the model related to outcome measurement is the issue of adaptability or the extent to which outcomes are subject to change. Adaptability underlies the system's capacity to expand, contract, or to change direction over time. For in the U.S., the understanding has only recently dawned that many attempts at educational reform were doomed because of the reliance on outcomes measures used to assess progress and accountability which did not support the direction of desired change. Outcomes, of course, will be adapted to public goals. One question is the direction of change, whether it will push toward high levels of expectation and challenge for children and their schools or whether it will regress and constrict to fewer or lower standards. A second question involves the anticipated cycles of change. How long do systems need to be stable? What intervals can be expected for stability? Are cycles estimated by judging the point of full implementation by leading schools and systems, by a majority of educational institutions, or by the lagging institutions? On the point of outcome measurement explicitly, what happens when new forms of assessment are introduced to old trend lines used to gauge system progress over long periods of time? It is clear, for instance, that present techniques for linking disparate assessments are inadequate and new approaches need to be conceived to permit cross-referencing among measurement methods. Is change or adaptation best served by targeting segments for change systematically? For example, if the content area of mathematics is the first to move to full implementation of curriculum and outcome measurement, should it, or a subset, be systematically revisited in a fixed interval to consider refinement, revision, or revamping? In reality, system change is less a feature of macroplanning in the U.S. than the happenstance confluence of resources, politics, and innovative ideas. In the area of measuring performance, however, it is clear that a variety of strategies can be considered for the systematic adaptation of measurement systems. Some states have adopted a substitution approach, out-with-the-old, in-with-the-new, babies and bathwater notwithstanding. Others have employed dual systems of performance-based and standardized tests, risking confusion and conflicting signals about importance. Certainly, in the next few years as expectations for system changes grow, we will learn more about how to phase in new systems and what elements of existing measures can be retained for various intervals suited to particular purposes. One hopes balance will be a guiding principle.

Implications and summary

Common issues face all OECD educational systems. These include the pressures to diversify their services and their clients, the importance of accountability to improve performance, the development or maintenance of credibility of the systems, and the realities of economic pressures, within the educational system itself, in the societies that support the system, and the emerging reality of world economic models. Scope, tradition, and diversity affect the manner in which systems move to meet new needs or to improve their effectiveness in accomplishing existing goals. Furthermore, all systems share common strengths and maladies, although in varying degrees. There is overlap in every system, although sometimes redundancy in goals, delivery, and measurement is desirable. Every system is subject to cycles of development and periods of high and lower public and political support. Issues of technical quality are represented and resolved in every system, as are needs for verification of system operations and outcomes. In the U.S., a concerted reform effort developed in the states and to some degree was ratified and extended by various national bodies. Reform is underway, intended to improve markedly the quality of precollegiate education. The clear goals are to develop greater coherence, stronger controls on output, and increase productivity, while simultaneously addressing student audiences of increasing diversity in background and preparation. There continues to be optimism that these goals can be met, but the outward look at OECD practices provides important grounding for our expectations.

What are the ways in which we can learn from the OECD studies? We have seen that the ways tradition, control, and outcome measure components of the reform model differently function in the participating studies. In the U.S., performance standards are fashioned in part to supply sources of control, guidance, and coherence for the system and to present an opportunity for greater public participation. Our choices in ways to learn from OECD countries are multiple. Because our contexts are so different, direct application and transfer are impossible. One option is to abstract lessons from the functioning of other systems. For example, in Germany, the press for uniformity among the *Länder* is relatively low because the credibility of state systems is high. A second form of learning is emulation, that is, applying the essence rather than the details of particular approaches. For example, as we move in various states toward examination structures, we should learn from our British and Australian colleagues about how to develop examination systems that operate with public credibility, while in the U.S. we strive simultaneously to meet requirements imposed by our quantitative orientation, commitment to fairness, and anticipated challenges in the legal system. We can also study how change is accomplished in countries that are moving in various directions in the areas of common curriculum, examinations, and articulation of priorities. France, Sweden, and others provide cues to assist us in the selection of sectors for incremental change. Taken as a whole, the studies provide an opportunity for the U.S. to accelerate its educational change by sidestepping known difficulties and anticipating and planning for others. We have learned from OECD reports to imagine multiple uses for performance standards. We can see them not only as blueprints for curriculum design and assessments, their present formulation in the U.S., but perhaps as they are used in Spain: as consolidations of important societal values. The symbolic use of these standards and the processes through which they are developed can unify and strengthen belief in, and purpose of, education. The OECD country studies provide invaluable assistance to our reflection and search for strategies to improve our students performance.

MAIN SALES OUTLETS OF OECD PUBLICATIONS
PRINCIPAUX POINTS DE VENTE DES PUBLICATIONS DE L'OCDE

GENTINA – ARGENTINE
os Hirsch S.R.L.
ría Güemes, Florida 165, 4° Piso
Buenos Aires   Tel. (1) 331.1787 y 331.2391
Telefax: (1) 331.1787

STRALIA – AUSTRALIE
. Information Services
Whitehorse Road, P.O.B 163
ham, Victoria 3132   Tel. (03) 9873.4411
Telefax: (03) 9873.5679

STRIA – AUTRICHE
old & Co.
ben 31
n I   Tel. (0222) 533.50.14
Telefax: (0222) 512.47.31.29

LGIUM – BELGIQUE
n De Lannoy
enue du Roi 202 Koningslaan
060 Bruxelles   Tel. (02) 538.51.69/538.08.41
Telefax: (02) 538.08.41

NADA
nouf Publishing Company Ltd.
4 Algoma Road
awa, ON K1B 3W8   Tel. (613) 741.4333
Telefax: (613) 741.5439

res:
Sparks Street
awa, ON K1P 5R1   Tel. (613) 238.8985
Yonge Street
ronto, ON M5B 1M4   Tel. (416) 363.3171
Telefax: (416)363.59.63

s Éditions La Liberté Inc.
20 Chemin Sainte-Foy
inte-Foy, PQ G1X 3V6   Tel. (418) 658.3763
Telefax: (418) 658.3763

deral Publications Inc.
5 University Avenue, Suite 701
ronto, ON M5H 3B8   Tel. (416) 860.1611
Telefax: (416) 860.1608

s Publications Fédérales
85 Université
ontréal, QC H3B 3A7   Tel. (514) 954.1633
Telefax: (514) 954.1635

HINA – CHINE
nina National Publications Import
xport Corporation (CNPIEC)
Gongti E. Road, Chaoyang District
O. Box 88 or 50
ijing 100704 PR   Tel. (01) 506.6688
Telefax: (01) 506.3101

HINESE TAIPEI – TAIPEI CHINOIS
ood Faith Worldwide Int'l. Co. Ltd.
h Floor, No. 118, Sec. 2
hung Hsiao E. Road
aipei   Tel. (02) 391.7396/391.7397
Telefax: (02) 394.9176

**ZECH REPUBLIC – RÉPUBLIQUE
CHÈQUE**
rtia Pegas Press Ltd.
arodni Trida 25
OB 825
11 21 Praha 1   Tel. (2) 2 46 04
Telefax: (2) 2 78 72

ENMARK – DANEMARK
Munksgaard Book and Subscription Service
5, Nørre Søgade, P.O. Box 2148
K-1016 København K   Tel. (33) 12.85.70
Telefax: (33) 12.93.87

EGYPT – ÉGYPTE
Middle East Observer
41 Sherif Street
Cairo   Tel. 392.6919
Telefax: 360-6804

FINLAND – FINLANDE
Akateeminen Kirjakauppa
Keskuskatu 1, P.O. Box 128
00100 Helsinki
Subscription Services/Agence d'abonnements :
P.O. Box 23
00371 Helsinki   Tel. (358 0) 121 4416
Telefax: (358 0) 121.4450

FRANCE
OECD/OCDE
Mail Orders/Commandes par correspondance:
2, rue André-Pascal
75775 Paris Cedex 16   Tel. (33-1) 45.24.82.00
Telefax: (33-1) 49.10.42.76
Telex: 640048 OCDE
Internet: Compte.PUBSINQ @ oecd.org

Orders via Minitel, France only/
Commandes par Minitel, France exclusivement :
36 15 OCDE

OECD Bookshop/Librairie de l'OCDE :
33, rue Octave-Feuillet
75016 Paris   Tel. (33-1) 45.24.81.81
(33-1) 45.24.81.67

Dawson
B.P. 40
91121 Palaiseau Cedex   Tel. 69.10.47.00
Telefax : 64.54.83.26

Documentation Française
29, quai Voltaire
75007 Paris   Tel. 40.15.70.00

Economica
49 rue Héricart
75015 Paris   Tel. 45.78.12.92
Telefax : 40.58.15.70

Gibert Jeune (Droit-Économie)
6, place Saint-Michel
75006 Paris   Tel. 43.25.91.19

Librairie du Commerce International
10, avenue d'Iéna
75016 Paris   Tel. 40.73.34.60

Librairie Dunod
Université Paris-Dauphine
Place du Maréchal de Lattre de Tassigny
75016 Paris   Tel. 44.05.40.13

Librairie Lavoisier
11, rue Lavoisier
75008 Paris   Tel. 42.65.39.95

Librairie des Sciences Politiques
30, rue Saint-Guillaume
75007 Paris   Tel. 45.48.36.02

P.U.F.
49, boulevard Saint-Michel
75005 Paris   Tel. 43.25.83.40

Librairie de l'Université
12a, rue Nazareth
13100 Aix-en-Provence   Tel. (16) 42.26.18.08

Documentation Française
165, rue Garibaldi
69003 Lyon   Tel. (16) 78.63.32.23

Librairie Decitre
29, place Bellecour
69002 Lyon   Tel. (16) 72.40.54.54

Librairie Sauramps
Le Triangle
34967 Montpellier Cedex 2   Tel. (16) 67.58.85.15
Tekefax: (16) 67.58.27.36

A la Sorbonne Actual
23 rue de l'Hôtel des Postes
06000 Nice   Tel. (16) 93.13.77.75
Telefax: (16) 93.80.75.69

GERMANY – ALLEMAGNE
OECD Publications and Information Centre
August-Bebel-Allee 6
D-53175 Bonn   Tel. (0228) 959.120
Telefax: (0228) 959.12.17

GREECE – GRÈCE
Librairie Kauffmann
Mavrokordatou 9
106 78 Athens   Tel. (01) 32.55.321
Telefax: (01) 32.30.320

HONG-KONG
Swindon Book Co. Ltd.
Astoria Bldg. 3F
34 Ashley Road, Tsimshatsui
Kowloon, Hong Kong   Tel. 2376.2062
Telefax: 2376.0685

HUNGARY – HONGRIE
Euro Info Service
Margitsziget, Európa Ház
1138 Budapest   Tel. (1) 111.62.16
Telefax: (1) 111.60.61

ICELAND – ISLANDE
Mál Mog Menning
Laugavegi 18, Pósthólf 392
121 Reykjavik   Tel. (1) 552.4240
Telefax: (1) 562.3523

INDIA – INDE
Oxford Book and Stationery Co.
Scindia House
New Delhi 110001   Tel. (11) 331.5896/5308
Telefax: (11) 332.5993

17 Park Street
Calcutta 700016   Tel. 240832

INDONESIA – INDONÉSIE
Pdii-Lipi
P.O. Box 4298
Jakarta 12042   Tel. (21) 573.34.67
Telefax: (21) 573.34.67

IRELAND – IRLANDE
Government Supplies Agency
Publications Section
4/5 Harcourt Road
Dublin 2   Tel. 661.31.11
Telefax: 475.27.60

ISRAEL
Praedicta
5 Shatner Street
P.O. Box 34030
Jerusalem 91430   Tel. (2) 52.84.90/1/2
Telefax: (2) 52.84.93

R.O.Y. International
P.O. Box 13056
Tel Aviv 61130   Tel. (3) 546 1423
Telefax: (3) 546 1442

Palestinian Authority/Middle East:
INDEX Information Services
P.O.B. 19502
Jerusalem   Tel. (2) 27.12.19
Telefax: (2) 27.16.34

ITALY – ITALIE
Libreria Commissionaria Sansoni
Via Duca di Calabria 1/1
50125 Firenze   Tel. (055) 64.54.15
Telefax: (055) 64.12.57

Via Bartolini 29
20155 Milano   Tel. (02) 36.50.83

Editrice e Libreria Herder
Piazza Montecitorio 120
00186 Roma   Tel. 679.46.28
Telefax: 678.47.51

Libreria Hoepli
Via Hoepli 5
20121 Milano Tel. (02) 86.54.46
Telefax: (02) 805.28.86

Libreria Scientifica
Dott. Lucio de Biasio 'Aeiou'
Via Coronelli, 6
20146 Milano Tel. (02) 48.95.45.52
Telefax: (02) 48.95.45.48

JAPAN – JAPON
OECD Publications and Information Centre
Landic Akasaka Building
2-3-4 Akasaka, Minato-ku
Tokyo 107 Tel. (81.3) 3586.2016
Telefax: (81.3) 3584.7929

KOREA – CORÉE
Kyobo Book Centre Co. Ltd.
P.O. Box 1658, Kwang Hwa Moon
Seoul Tel. 730.78.91
Telefax: 735.00.30

MALAYSIA – MALAISIE
University of Malaya Bookshop
University of Malaya
P.O. Box 1127, Jalan Pantai Baru
59700 Kuala Lumpur
Malaysia Tel. 756.5000/756.5425
Telefax: 756.3246

MEXICO – MEXIQUE
OECD Publications and Information Centre
Edificio INFOTEC
Av. San Fernando no. 37
Col. Toriello Guerra
Tlalpan C.P. 14050
Mexico D.F.
Tel. (525) 606 00 11 Extension 100
Fax : (525) 606 13 07

Revistas y Periodicos Internacionales S.A. de C.V.
Florencia 57 - 1004
Mexico, D.F. 06600 Tel. 207.81.00
Telefax: 208.39.79

NETHERLANDS – PAYS-BAS
SDU Uitgeverij Plantijnstraat
Externe Fondsen
Postbus 20014
2500 EA's-Gravenhage Tel. (070) 37.89.880
Voor bestellingen: Telefax: (070) 34.75.778

NEW ZEALAND
NOUVELLE-ZÉLANDE
GPLegislation Services
P.O. Box 12418
Thorndon, Wellington Tel. (04) 496.5655
Telefax: (04) 496.5698

NORWAY – NORVÈGE
Narvesen Info Center – NIC
Bertrand Narvesens vei 2
P.O. Box 6125 Etterstad
0602 Oslo 6 Tel. (022) 57.33.00
Telefax: (022) 68.19.01

PAKISTAN
Mirza Book Agency
65 Shahrah Quaid-E-Azam
Lahore 54000 Tel. (42) 353.601
Telefax: (42) 231.730

PHILIPPINE – PHILIPPINES
International Booksource Center Inc.
Rm 179/920 Cityland 10 Condo Tower 2
HV dela Costa Ext cor Valero St.
Makati Metro Manila Tel. (632) 817 9676
Telefax : (632) 817 1741

POLAND – POLOGNE
Ars Polona
00-950 Warszawa
Krakowskie Przedmieácie 7 Tel. (22) 264760
Telefax : (22) 268673

PORTUGAL
Livraria Portugal
Rua do Carmo 70-74
Apart. 2681
1200 Lisboa Tel. (01) 347.49.82/5
Telefax: (01) 347.02.64

SINGAPORE – SINGAPOUR
Gower Asia Pacific Pte Ltd.
Golden Wheel Building
41, Kallang Pudding Road, No. 04-03
Singapore 1334 Tel. 741.5166
Telefax: 742.9356

SPAIN – ESPAGNE
Mundi-Prensa Libros S.A.
Castelló 37, Apartado 1223
Madrid 28001 Tel. (91) 431.33.99
Telefax: (91) 575.39.98

Mundi-Prensa Barcelona
Consell de Cent No. 391
08009 – Barcelona Tel. (93) 488.34.92
Telefax: (93) 487.76.59

Llibreria de la Generalitat
Palau Moja
Rambla dels Estudis, 118
08002 – Barcelona
(Subscripcions) Tel. (93) 318.80.12
(Publicacions) Tel. (93) 302.67.23
Telefax: (93) 412.18.54

SRI LANKA
Centre for Policy Research
c/o Colombo Agencies Ltd.
No. 300-304, Galle Road
Colombo 3 Tel. (1) 574240, 573551-2
Telefax: (1) 575394, 510711

SWEDEN – SUÈDE
CE Fritzes AB
S–106 47 Stockholm Tel. (08) 690.90.90
Telefax: (08) 20.50.21

Subscription Agency/Agence d'abonnements :
Wennergren-Williams Info AB
P.O. Box 1305
171 25 Solna Tel. (08) 705.97.50
Telefax: (08) 27.00.71

SWITZERLAND – SUISSE
Maditec S.A. (Books and Periodicals - Livres
et périodiques)
Chemin des Palettes 4
Case postale 266
1020 Renens VD 1 Tel. (021) 635.08.65
Telefax: (021) 635.07.80

Librairie Payot S.A.
4, place Pépinet
CP 3212
1002 Lausanne Tel. (021) 320.25.11
Telefax: (021) 320.25.14

Librairie Unilivres
6, rue de Candolle
1205 Genève Tel. (022) 320.26.23
Telefax: (022) 329.73.18

Subscription Agency/Agence d'abonnements :
Dynapresse Marketing S.A.
38 avenue Vibert
1227 Carouge Tel. (022) 308.0
Telefax: (022) 308.0

See also – Voir aussi :
OECD Publications and Information Centre
August-Bebel-Allee 6
D-53175 Bonn (Germany) Tel. (0228) 959
Telefax: (0228) 959.1

THAILAND – THAÏLANDE
Suksit Siam Co. Ltd.
113, 115 Fuang Nakhon Rd.
Opp. Wat Rajbopith
Bangkok 10200 Tel. (662) 225.95
Telefax: (662) 222.5

TURKEY – TURQUIE
Kültür Yayinlari Is-Türk Ltd. Sti.
Atatürk Bulvari No. 191/Kat 13
Kavaklidere/Ankara Tel. 428.11.40 Ext. 2
Dolmabahce Cad. No. 29
Besiktas/Istanbul Tel. (312) 260 7
Telex: (312) 418 29

UNITED KINGDOM – ROYAUME-UI
HMSO
Gen. enquiries Tel. (171) 873 8
Postal orders only:
P.O. Box 276, London SW8 5DT
Personal Callers HMSO Bookshop
49 High Holborn, London WC1V 6HB
Telefax: (171) 873 84
Branches at: Belfast, Birmingham, Bristol,
Edinburgh, Manchester

UNITED STATES – ÉTATS-UNIS
OECD Publications and Information Center
2001 L Street N.W., Suite 650
Washington, D.C. 20036-4910 Tel. (202) 785.6
Telefax: (202) 785.0

VENEZUELA
Libreria del Este
Avda F. Miranda 52, Aptdo. 60337
Edificio Galipán
Caracas 106 Tel. 951.1705/951.2307/951.12
Telegram: Libreste Carac

Subscriptions to OECD periodicals may also
placed through main subscription agencies.

Les abonnements aux publications périodiques
l'OCDE peuvent être souscrits auprès de
principales agences d'abonnement.

Orders and inquiries from countries where Distrib
tors have not yet been appointed should be sent te
OECD Publications Service, 2 rue André-Pasca
75775 Paris Cedex 16, France.

Les commandes provenant de pays où l'OCDE n'
pas encore désigné de distributeur peuvent êtr
adressées à : OCDE, Service des Publication
2, rue André-Pascal, 75775 Paris Cedex 16, Franc

10-199